Liabilities and Modern Artificial Intelligence

This book addresses how private law liability should be assigned in contexts where modern forms of AI are deployed.

AI as a technology holds the potential to radically improve global society, yet the pace of its advancement far outstrips the pace at which legal systems are responding. This book explores legal approaches to AI, how AI should be legally characterised, and proposes an overarching theoretical liability framework termed the Tri-Phase AI Liability Model. This framework is flexible in nature and considers the type of AI, the context in which it is deployed, who has the most control over the AI system and the capacity of a deployed AI. In response, this book brings greatly needed clarity to the evolving landscape of AI governance, aiding in resolving existing and emerging private law challenges.

This book is a timely response to the urgent need to resolve private law liabilities and will appeal to legal professionals, policy makers, and scholars looking to understand or contribute to the current and future governance of AI within private law.

Estelle Wallingford is a legal academic based in the Department of Business Law and Taxation in the Monash Business School at Monash University, Australia. Her research examines the legal implications arising from the deployment of emerging technologies with a particular interest in artificial intelligence.

Law and Change: Law in Times of Crisis

Artificial Intelligence (AI) is touted as the remedy for many of the economic, social, political and cultural contentions in an epoch where social demographics are unbalanced, economic growth is slowing, labour markets are fragile, and global trade is wracked with protectionism. The arrival of the pandemic has heightened calls for AI and big data to help innovate economies out of the worst. This transition presents significant challenges for the ecosystems of law firms, and the requirements of due process in the exercise of litigation. Against the realisation of seismic shifts brought about by current and impending global watersheds, this series reflects how first the pandemic and then inevitable future crises will change the law, and how law can be understood as a change agent, talking to today in upheaval, and to new tomorrows.

The series provides a space for scholars, educators, practitioners and leaders to share their contributions on the present and future relevance of the law and reflect on law and change and change through law in times of global crises. The contributions will be critical, focusing on contemporary challenges to social ordering and global sustainability where law in context has much to say. In addition, the series will question law's regulatory relevance across a wide range of substantive and procedural fields currently facing transition.

Series Editor
Professor Mark Findlay, Singapore Management University, Singapore

Titles in this series include:

Digital Health Technologies
Law, Ethics, and the Doctor-Patient Relationship
Carolyn Johnston

Regulating Gig Work
Decent Labour Standards in a World of On-Demand Work
Michael Rawling and Joellen Riley Munton

Recreating Creativity, Reinventing Inventiveness
Challenges Facing Intellectual Property Law
Edited by Nikos Koutras and Niloufer Selvadurai

Liabilities and Modern Artificial Intelligence
A Tri-Phase Model
Estelle Wallingford

Liabilities and Modern Artificial Intelligence

A Tri-Phase Model

Estelle Wallingford

Routledge
Taylor & Francis Group
LONDON AND NEW YORK

First published 2026
by Routledge
4 Park Square, Milton Park, Abingdon, Oxon OX14 4RN

and by Routledge
605 Third Avenue, New York, NY 10158

Routledge is an imprint of the Taylor & Francis Group, an informa business

British Library Cataloguing-in-Publication Data
A catalogue record for this book is available from the British Library

Library of Congress Cataloging-in-Publication Data
Names: Wallingford, Estelle author
Title: Liabilities and modern artificial intelligence : a tri-phase model / Estelle Wallingford.
Description: Abingdon, Oxon [UK]; New York, NY: Routledge, 2025. | Series: Law and change | Includes bibliographical references and index.
Identifiers: LCCN 2025014349 | ISBN 9781041020653 hardback | ISBN 9781041020585 paperback | ISBN 9781003617549 ebook
Subjects: LCSH: Artificial intelligence–Law and legislation | Liability (Law)
Classification: LCC K564.C6 W347 2025 | DDC 343.09/998–dc23/eng/20250331
LC record available at https://lccn.loc.gov/2025014349

ISBN: 9781041020653 (hbk)
ISBN: 9781041020585 (pbk)
ISBN: 9781003617549 (ebk)

DOI: 10.4324/9781003617549

Typeset in Galliard
by Deanta Global Publishing Services, Chennai, India

To my mother, Madaline, and my sister, Amelia,
whose love, support and patience made this endeavour possible.

Contents

List of Figures

List of Tables

Table of Cases

Australia

Australian National Railways Commission v Ranger Uranium Mines Pty Ltd (1989) 51 SASR 475 219
Commissioner of Patents v Rokt Pte Ltd (2020) 379 ALR 86 112, 113
Commissioner of Patents v RPL Central Pty Ltd (2015) 328 ALR 458 113
Commissioner of Patents v Thaler [2022] FCAFC 62 119, 120
Computer Edge Pty Ltd v Apple Computer Inc (1986) 161 CLR 171 113
Encompass Corporation Pty Ltd v InfoTrack Pty Ltd (2019) 372 ALR 646 113
Field v Shoalhaven Transport Pty Ltd [1970] 3 NSWR 96 76
Knapp v Knapp [1944] SASR 257 97
Mahony v J Kruschich (Demolitions) Pty Ltd 59 ALJR 504 172
Mainbridge Industries Pty Ltd v Whitewood (1984) 3 IPR 97 114
Mainbridge Industries Pty Ltd v Whitewood (1985) 6 IPR 239 112
March v Stramare (E & MH) Pty Ltd (1991) 171 CLR 506 158
National Research Development Corp v Commissioner of Patents (1959) 102 CLR 525 112
Oceanic Sun Line Special Shipping Company Inc v Fay (1988) 165 CLR 197 219
Research Affiliates LLC v Commissioner of Patents (2014) 316 ALR 135 113
Ryan v R (1967) 121 CLR 205 67
Star Micronics Pty Ltd v Five Star Computers Pty Ltd (1990) 18 IPR 225 113
Stephen L. Thaler [2021] APO 5 119
Thaler v Commissioner of Patents [2021] FCA 879 118, 120

New Zealand

Ruscoe v Cryptopia Ltd (in liq) [2020] NZHC 728 99, 101

Singapore

B2C2 Ltd v Quoine Pte Ltd [2019] SGHC (I) 03 2, 100, 104, 105
Quoine Pte Ltd v B2C2 Ltd [2020] SGCA(I) 2 105

United Kingdom

United States

Table of Legislation

Australia

European Union

United Kingdom

United States

Table of Statutory Instruments

Acknowledgements

Funding Acknowledgement

This book is an expanded version of my doctoral research, which was supported by an Australian Government Research Training Program (RTP) Scholarship.

AI Use Acknowledgement

I used ResearchRabbit and Scopus AI, literature mapping tools, to efficiently identify and classify relevant literature considered in the monograph. The use of these tools was to enhance the efficiency of the research process.

I also used Claude (version 3.5 Sonnet), a generative AI tool, to brainstorm ideas for the name of the monograph and the names of the two models presented in the monograph. The use of this tool was to stimulate creative naming ideas. These AI-generated ideas were then critically evaluated, adapted and refined by me to ensure they appropriately fit the project's context and requirements.

While using these AI systems for this monograph (and not my doctoral thesis), I maintained rigorous human oversight over the process and ensured all final decisions were made by me.

Personal Acknowledgement

I would like to acknowledge and thank the following people who supported me in the journey of completing this book.

As this book is an expansion of my doctoral research, I would like to first thank my doctoral supervisory team from the Law Faculty at Monash University. For the majority of my candidature, I was extremely fortunate to work with Janice Richardson and Maria O'Sullivan. Their skills complemented each other perfectly, making them the dream supervisory team. I am grateful that they respected I had a clear vision for the project whilst gently guiding me at the same time. I am extremely appreciative of the interest they took not only in my doctoral thesis but also in my development as an academic more broadly. I would like to thank Genevieve Grant and Joanna Kyriakakis for joining the project as associate supervisors shortly before submission. I appreciate how they respected that the project was at an advanced stage whilst still providing meaningful support to enable completion.

I also wish to thank the broader community within the Law Faculty. Special thanks to the two Higher Degree by Research (HDR) Directors during my candidacy: Julie Debeljak and Patrick Emerton. I appreciate how Julie made an effort to know each and every research degree candidate in the faculty. I also wish to acknowledge the support of Patrick Emerton in the first part of my candidacy, in a time of great uncertainty as the global pandemic was unfolding. The Law Research Services team during my candidacy, in particular John Rabling and Bridget Sadler for supporting the wider research student community; Bridget especially, for being a point of contact and genuinely caring about the welfare of students. I would like also to thank our wonderful law librarians for their assistance in locating items, particularly when the library was closed at the height of the pandemic.

I would like to acknowledge the support of the following academics who served as panellists for my various doctoral milestones (alphabetically by last name): Patrick Emerton, David Frydrych, Nadir Hosen, Joanna Kyriakakis, Yee-Fui Ng, Moira Paterson and Normann Witzleb. I appreciate the time each panel member took to provide thoughtful and constructive feedback.

In converting the thesis to a monograph, I am immensely grateful to my doctoral examiners, Phillip Morgan and Simon Chesterman, who kindly provided thoughtful comments on not only the doctoral thesis itself but also for offering insightful suggestions on how to expand the project for publication as a monograph. Many of these suggestions have been incorporated into the expanded version in this book. I appreciate their support of my career beyond my doctoral examination.

To Christopher Marsden and Paul Burgess of the Monash Digital Law Group for their continued interest in my career. For enabling me to present my research at 'work-in-progress' sessions to the Group as I expanded the thesis to a monograph and for the supportive feedback from the Group at these sessions.

This book has also benefited from the feedback and constructive criticism of anonymous reviewers who helped shape the work into its current form, for which I am thankful. I would like to also thank my Routledge editors, Kendrick Loo and series editor Mark Findlay, for seeing the potential in this work for a wider audience and for their support in bringing the project to fruition.

Throughout both my doctoral studies and in the process of expanding the thesis into a monograph, I have been fortunate to also have the support of my colleagues in the Department of Business Law and Taxation in the Monash Business School. I appreciate each person who took the time to check in and ask how I was progressing, supporting me in my journey completing both the thesis and, in turn, this book. Thanks in particular to John Bevacqua, Carolyn Sutherland and Dominique Allen for their guidance and mentorship;

for being so approachable and supportive. A huge thanks to Catrina Denvir for her detailed interest and support in my journey converting the thesis to a monograph. From reading through my book proposal to making the simple, but profound, suggestion that I should give a name to my liability model.

Lastly, with immense gratitude, I wish to acknowledge the family members whose support powered me in this journey. Firstly, without meaning to belittle the support of the humans I have identified here, I do wish to acknowledge the impact of my fur-child (dog), Gracie-Mae. Completing research can be isolating at the best of times, let alone during a global pandemic. I am grateful to Gracie for sitting by my side for nearly every word I wrote and reminding me that sometimes it is not only okay but essential to go 'outside!'.

My younger sister Amelia Wallingford, whose endless positivity never ceases to amaze me, for allowing her positivity to be contagious. I appreciate her unconditional support in all aspects of my life. Finally, my mother, Madaline Wallingford, whose unwavering belief in me is always a source of continued strength. Whilst undertaking a PhD and aspiring to expand it into a monograph has very much been a decision of my own, it is a dream I would not have been able to contemplate had I not had the privilege of her love and support all these years.

Introduction

0.1. Artificial Intelligence: A Legal Problem

There is an ongoing debate in legal communities as to the best method of accommodating emerging technologies, such as artificial intelligence (AI), under the law. There is a question of whether these technologies are adequately accommodated for under existing laws. Or instead, whether such technologies are incompatible with existing legal paradigms, prompting the need for the law to adapt and evolve to accommodate new forms of technology. This book looks at an issue at the heart of this debate – one that is increasingly becoming urgent to address in our modern society. The development of AI has advanced exponentially in the past decade. Not only has the technology advanced, but importantly, the technology has shifted from being confined primarily to scientific communities to being accessible by broader society. AI as a technology holds the potential to radically improve global society, yet the pace of its advancement and increased accessibility far outstrips the pace at which legal systems are responding creating legal uncertainty.

Consider the following scenario. If a doctor negligently misdiagnoses your loved one with dire consequences, this gives rise to a course of action against the medical professional. Similarly, if, in a car accident, another driver's carelessness causes you injury, you could seek legal redress against the driver. The same could be true in instances where an adverse decision against you is reached – the decision could be subject to a review. Alternatively, where a contract is entered on your behalf without your authority or someone copies or imitates an artist's music without consent, both give rise to the possibility of a legal dispute.

Imagine, though, if these avenues of redress were not available or they were severely obfuscated. How could you seek to have your grievance resolved? The deployment of modern AI poses this exact challenge. Although it is an emerging technology, its proliferation is rapid. AI is already in use, for example,

DOI: 10.4324/9781003617549-1

in the above identified scenarios.[1] This technology's proliferation is widely labelled as the 'next industrial revolution'. Like the past industrial revolution, AI holds the potential to change global society and will, along the way, raise several legal and ethical issues. Yet, despite this, consideration as to the legal consequences of its use is still largely in the nascent stages of development. Modern forms of AI, especially the forms that can act with some degree of autonomy, create new legal uncertainties, as it is unclear who should be legally responsible for the actions of these systems and under what circumstances they should be held liable. It is further unclear, what the interaction should be between any liability and regulatory responses to AI. There is a need for clarity surrounding the legal implications associated with a deployed AI system to improve certainty for actors engaging with AI.

The central objective of this book therefore is to address the issue of how liability should be assigned in contexts where modern forms of AI are deployed. There exists a need to provide a legal framework addressing how legal liability should be assigned, especially in instances where AI systems form, act and/or execute decisions. Such a framework should be flexible with scope to consider the type of AI and the context in which it is deployed. Additionally, there is a need to consider how any such framework would complement regulatory responses to AI. The goal of this book is to therefore propose one such liability framework and consider its relationship to relevant regulatory measures.

0.2. What Is Modern AI?

Before considering a possible liability response to AI and how this should interact with regulatory measures, it is first prudent to consider the varying forms of modern AI, as this in turn will enable a more focused consideration of relevant legal issues concerning AI in this book. The concept of what is AI is not entirely settled. There is a distinction between AI and algorithms. Algorithms are mathematical equations capable of self-executing predefined instructions.[2] AI uses algorithms as internal building blocks, but unlike algorithms, AI is capable of adaptation, which can involve the generation of new algorithms.[3] Algorithms are therefore not by themselves AI.

1 For the use of AI in medical diagnosis see: Vivek Kaul, Sarah Enslin, Seth A. Gross, 'History of artificial intelligence in medicine' (2020) 92 (4) *Gastrointestinal Endoscopy* 807. For the use of AI in autonomous cars see: Yifang Ma, Zhenyu Wang, Hong Yang, and Lin Yang, 'Artificial Intelligence Applications in the Development of Autonomous Vehicles: A Survey' (2020) 7(2) *Journal of Automatica Sinica* 315. For AI used to make automated decisions see: Order of Davies J in *Amato v Commonwealth of Australia* (Federal Court of Australia, VID611/2019, 27 November 2019). For AI in the automated formation of contracts see: *B2C2 Ltd v Quoine Pte Ltd* [2019] SGHC (1) 03 ('*B2C2 Ltd v Quoine Pte Ltd*'). For consideration of AI emulating the works of music artists see: Marcel Danesi, 'AI-Generated Music' in *AI-Generated Popular Culture: A Semiotic Perspective* (Palgrave Macmillan, 2024), 59.

2 Philip Sales, 'Algorithms, Artificial Intelligence, and the Law' (2021) 105(1) *Judicature* 23, 24.

3 Philip Sales, 'Algorithms, Artificial Intelligence, and the Law' (2021) 105(1) *Judicature* 23, 24.

It is useful to also understand the type of AI under consideration before commencing an analysis concerning its legal implications. There is an acknowledgement that there is a distinction between *classical* and *modern* forms of AI.[4] 'Modern AI' in this context is not confined to recent developments in AI, but rather it is a term of art: indeed, some forms of modern AI date back decades and are not modern in terms of 'recent' developments. Importantly though, modern forms of AI exhibit different capacities to classical forms. They are capable of a greater degree of independence relative to classical forms; they are also better at drawing upon and adapting from previously 'learnt' experiences.[5] Due to their relative degree of independence and heightened sophistication, my focus is on modern forms of AI because when these forms of AI are deployed, they are more likely than classical forms of AI to pose interesting legal conundrums in relation to liability.

Within modern AI, there exists three generally accepted categories: Artificial Narrow Intelligence (ANI), Artificial General Intelligence (AGI) and Artificial Super Intelligence (ASI).[6] ANI is the weakest of these forms of AI, as ANI consists of systems primarily designed to achieve a set task.[7] AGI, if fully achieved, would be akin to human-level intelligence and ASI, if achieved, would surpass this level of intelligence.[8] AGI and ASI are therefore in contrast to ANI, as these systems, if realised, are designed to complete multiple or varied tasks.[9] Most forms of modern AI currently in deployment are ANI, but given the rapid proliferation of AI and the rate at which it is advancing in society, a robust liability response ought to accommodate the possibility of AGI and ASI.

0.2.1 Types of Modern AI

Considering these distinctions, I now turn to identify types of technologies that could be categorised as modern AI and consider why these technologies pose legal uncertainty.

4 For consideration of the nature of *classical* and *modern* forms of AI see: Kevin Warwick, *Artificial Intelligence: The Basics* (Routledge, 2012) 31–59, 88–115, Erik J. Larson, *The Myth of Artificial Intelligence: Why Computers Can't Think the Way We Do* (Harvard University Press, 2021) 106–132; Margaret A Boden, *Artificial Intelligence: A Very Short Introduction* (Oxford University Press, 2nd ed., 2018) 5–6.

5 Warrick (n 4) 88–89, 108–109.

6 See: Boden (n 4) 18–49, 130–150; J. E. (Hans), Korteling et al., 'Human- versus Artificial Intelligence' (2021) 4 *Frontiers in Artificial Intelligence* 1–3, 8.

7 Korteling (n 6) 8.

8 See: Boden (n 4) 18–49,130–150; Korteling (n 6).

9 Boden (n 4) 18–49,130–150; Korteling (n 6).

0.2.1.1 Machine Learning

The broadest of the forms of modern AI I consider is machine learning. It is worth noting that within the field of machine learning, there are types of machine learning styles. These include supervised machine learning, unsupervised machine learning, semi-supervised machine learning and reinforcement learning. I consider each of these forms of AI in turn and examine the degree to which these systems act autonomously in making decisions. Excluded from examination are the technical complexities of these AI systems, such as the mathematics of the underlying algorithms, as what is key to a legal analysis is the ability of these systems to reason and act.

A key element of the reasoning process in a *supervised* machine learning AI system is that a natural person must oversee its function in the initial stages. That is, the system is 'taught' to identify and distinguish between diverse types of data.[10] To achieve this, a natural person 'labels' data into distinct categories so that the system can learn to emulate this reasoning process.[11] As the system strives to mirror this process, the natural person supplies ongoing feedback about the system's performance so that it can adapt accordingly.[12] What is key about this form of machine learning is that a natural person is directly involved in shaping the reasoning process of the system. The parameters set by the natural person 'teaching' the system therefore limit the system's autonomy.

In contrast, *unsupervised* machine learning AI systems have a greater degree of autonomy in terms of their ability to make decisions. Unsupervised machine learning systems must sort and label data by themselves, setting up their own framework for doing so through trial and error.[13] A natural person engaging with these systems does not supply ongoing feedback in the way that they would for a supervised system,[14] nor do they set an end objective for the system. Instead, the system is free to make its own 'discoveries'.[15] Natural persons are significantly less engaged in the development of these systems' internal reasoning processes. The degree of autonomy in decision-making executed by these systems is therefore higher than their supervised counterparts.

If supervised machine learning denotes the lowest degree of autonomy in decision-making and unsupervised machine learning marks the highest, *semi-supervised* sits in the middle of the continuum. Semi-supervised machine learning AI systems consist of both supervised and unsupervised learning processes.[16] A natural person provides the system with labelled and unlabelled

10 Boden (n 4) 40.
11 Boden (n 4) 40; X Zhu and A Goldberg, *Introduction to Semi-Supervised Learning* (Springer Nature, 2022) 4.
12 Boden (n 4) 40.
13 Boden (n 4) 40–41; Goldberg (n 11) 2.
14 Boden (n 4) 40–41.
15 Boden (n 4) 40–41.
16 Goldberg (n 11) 9.

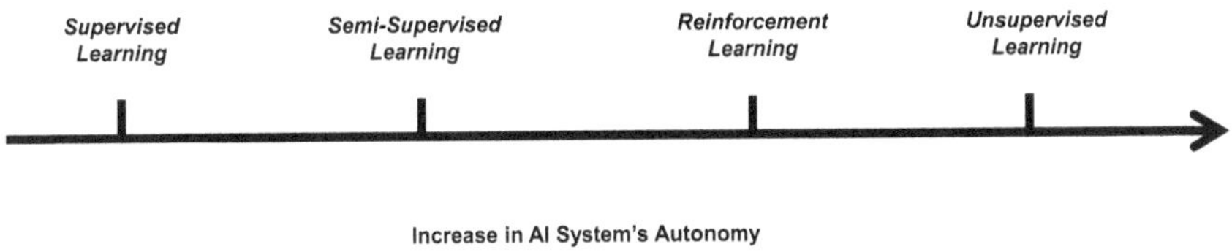

Figure 0.1 Autonomy Spectrum of AI Learning Style

data and then 'teaches' the system how to process the labelled data; however, the system engages in autonomous reasoning in terms of the unlabelled data.[17] On this basis, there is a mixed degree of natural person interaction with a semi-supervised machine learning system and, therefore, a mixed degree of influence over the end outcome.

Lastly, reinforcement machine learning also sits in the middle of the autonomy continuum. This model of machine learning relies upon feedback loops that teach the system how to reason based on a reward-and-punishment model.[18] Importantly, reinforcement, this notion of reiterating learning habits through reward and punishment, can apply to both single decisions and to the outcome of decisions in a series.[19] A reinforcement machine learning system therefore has a degree of autonomy over data but within set parameters.

The variation in autonomy of these AI learning styles is depicted in *Figure 0.1.*

0.2.1.2 Neural Networks

Neural networks also fit within the ambit of modern forms of AI. Neural networks consist of interconnected units that individually complete simple tasks but, when combined, work together in parallel to achieve complex ends.[20] Being a subset of modern AI, these systems are also subject to the same types of learning (supervised, unsupervised, reinforced) as the more simplistic 'machine learning' systems considered in Section 0.2.1.1.[21] Additionally, components of the network are weighted differently.[22] As the system learns, within the parameters of its learning style (supervised, etc.), the weights are adjusted to accommodate adaptive changes to the system as a whole.[23] These systems are therefore capable of achieving more complex tasks, but they are still subject to varying permutations of human input or control. These systems

17 Goldberg (n 11) 9, 11.
18 Boden (n 4) 41.
19 Boden (n 4) 41.
20 Boden (n 4) 69–70.
21 Boden (n 4) 75.
22 Boden (n 4) 74–75.
23 Boden (n 4) 74–75.

are more complex in nature than the broader category of machine learning but are subject to the various downfalls of each learning style considered above (supervised, etc.). Neural networks raise the same legal ambiguities as machine learning discussed above but with an amplified risk of consequences due to the increased complexity of these systems.

0.2.1.3 Deep Learning

Deep learning is another type of modern AI. It is a further subset of modern AI again – one that is based on layering of networks to achieve an end or objective.[24] Deep learning systems are premised on the notion of an advanced layering of multiple networks such that they produce a hierarchy of network levels.[25] In this respect, deep learning is yet again more complex in nature and set to achieve more complex ends than neural networks. However, unlike neural networks, which are subject to the different learning styles common to machine learning and neural networks (supervised, etc.), deep learning systems are typically ***unsupervised*** and therefore have relatively limited input from human actors and are more likely to set their own ends.[26] These systems not only achieve more complex ends but do so with less human oversight relative to their other modern AI counterparts. The risk of legal uncertainties attached to the consequences of deep learning is amplified further than other forms of modern AI.

By first considering what is modern AI as a theory, I have highlighted that AI is not a single concept. Rather, there are varying degrees of complexity of AI, with some forms capable of a greater degree of autonomy than others. This is important when conceiving of a liability response, as the varying degrees of AI capacity are likely to yield varying outcomes associated with a deployed AI. In turn what arises are key practical enforcement challenges under the law. For it becomes difficult to apply and enforce private law principles that do not accommodate the varied capacities of modern AI. Understanding the permutations in the reasoning processes of different modern AI systems and their relevant degree of autonomy is therefore important to understanding legal responses to AI more broadly. It aids in devising an appropriate liability framework that can fully accommodate modern AI and that complements regulatory measures for AI.

24 Boden (n 4) 42; for more detail on deep learning see also: Stuart J Russell, Peter Norvig et al., *Artificial Intelligence: A Modern Approach* (Pearson Education, 4th ed., 2022) 819–820.
25 Boden (n 4) 42.
26 Boden (n 4) 79.

0.3. Regulation versus Liability

There is a need for a more robust liability framework for AI as current approaches to AI liability are confined in their scope. For example, they might focus *civil* law liability responses to AI, address individual narrow aspects, components or elements of liability or, instead, address how AI should be regulated.[27] In addition to focusing on narrowed aspects of liability, there is a propensity to not fully acknowledge the varying permutations of AI with different functionalities and capacities. Instead, what often transpires is one of two common assumptions: (a) that all AI is the same and that there are not different types of AI or (b) that all AI, regardless of whether there is an acknowledgement of the different types of AI, ought to be viewed in a fixed manner. Modern forms of AI however have varying capacities and limitations influenced by the context in which they are deployed, necessitating an *adaptive* private law liability response.

The varied nature of modern forms of AI therefore poses a unique legal challenge in that predicting outcomes derived from these AI systems becomes dependent upon the *type* of modern AI and the *context* in which it is deployed. This raises the question then of how should the uncertainties posed by modern AI be managed legally. One possible response is to offer legal regulations managing the design and deployment of AI. This alone I contend is not a robust legal response to AI. I consider how AI is, or ought to be, regulated an important issue, but I am also of the view that many AI systems are already in use, increasingly giving rise to legal uncertainty surrounding their deployment. This necessitates establishing not only a regulatory response but also a liability response to AI.

By way of analogy, consider a regular non-autonomous vehicle. The production and use of such a vehicle is commonly regulated, but this regulation alone is insufficient in managing how these vehicles are deployed. Often, it is common for there to also be private law liability rules managing the negative outcomes associated with how these vehicles are deployed. In this regard, a liability response could be considered one half of the legal response to managing such vehicles, with the other half being a regulatory response. The rapid proliferation of modern forms of AI needs a robust legal response that addresses these two halves: regulation and liability.

27 For examples of literature focused on AI liability in a *civil* law context see: Sebastian Lohsse, Reiner Schulze, and Dirk Staudenmayer (eds), *Liability for Artificial Intelligence and the Internet of Things* (Bloomsbury Publishing, 2019); Mark A Geistfeld, Ernst Karner, Bernhard A Koch, and Christiane Wendehorst (eds), *Civil Liability for Artificial Intelligence and Software* (Walter de Gruyter GmbH & Co KG, 2022). For examples of literature focused on aspects or components of AI-related liability see: Ernest Lim and Phillip Morgan (eds), *The Cambridge Handbook of Private Law and Artificial Intelligence* (Cambridge University Press, 2024); Larry A DiMatteo, Cristina Poncibò and Michel Cannarsa (eds), *The Cambridge Handbook of Artificial Intelligence: Global Perspectives on Law and Ethics* (Cambridge University Press, 2022).

The primary focus of this book is directed towards the second of these two halves – the liability response. In addressing this objective, this book offers a flexible overarching framework – the *Tri-Phase AI Liability Model*. The proposed model offers a unique way of acknowledging the different permutations of modern AI, their varied capacities and contexts in which it can be deployed. It moves beyond the limited view of arguing that AI should *always* be viewed simplistically as 'a tool' whilst still acknowledging there is a role in certain contexts for this approach. This book therefore offers a more nuanced understanding of private law AI liability. In providing a comprehensive overarching framework, the book prevents ad hoc, fragmented or reactive liability approaches. Through offering an overarching framework, the aim is to prevent the likelihood of inconsistent approaches to AI and potential subsequent injustices. The aim of the *Tri-Phase AI Liability Model* is to offer an adaptive, context-aware approach to private law liability, one that moves beyond looking at individual aspects of liability. It therefore fills a critical gap in existing legal scholarship through offering a comprehensive and robust approach to AI liability that will hold guidance on the future of AI governance within private law.

Here, it is worth pausing to outline the adopted notion of private law as relied upon in this book. The parameters of private law as a concept, especially in relation to public law, are not clearly delineated. Whether there ought to be a divide between public law and private law in common law jurisdictions is an ongoing discussion and among theorists subscribing to imposing a divide, where the divide ought to be drawn between these two areas of law is subject to much debate.[28] Such discussions have been influenced by economic, realism and utilitarian theories, among others.

The role of private law, however, holds important implications for commercial arrangements. For private law is often accepted as encompassing key areas of law impacting business operations, including tort, contract, corporation's law and intellectual property. In this respect, private law therefore encapsulates the key legal mechanisms underpinning global market arrangements and is a vehicle for supporting commercial operations. An analysis of the relationship between AI and private law mechanisms is therefore fundamental to supporting commercial activity involving AI.

In this book I subscribe to the normative legal theory of the *correlative justice* approach to defining the scope of private law. Correlative justice theories historically have been championed in relation to tort law principles.[29] Ernest

28 For an overview of key considerations behind the private-public law divide see: Thomas W Merrill, 'Private and Public Law', in Andrew S Gold et al. (eds), *The Oxford Handbook of the New Private Law* (Oxford University Press, 2020) 575.

29 Benjamin C Zipurksy, 'Philosophy of Private Law', in Jules Coleman and Scott Shapiro (eds), *The Oxford Handbook of Jurisprudence and Philosophy of Law* (Oxford University Press, 2002) 623, 627–628.

Weinrib, however, has advocated for correlative justice to serve as a guiding framework for managing liability responses more broadly; that is, beyond solely tortious wrongdoings.[30]

Several key tenants lie at the core of Weinrib's account of a correlative justice interpretation of private law, which informs the view I adopt in this book. Firstly, he considers that under correlative justice, individual parties are capable of taking positive actions and directing these towards their own goals.[31] An injustice arises when the positive action of one party prevents another party from pursuing their own goals or objectives.[32] A corresponding liability follows then between the infringing party and the infringed upon party.[33] At its core, liability is therefore explained in terms of the relationship between parties in which an injustice arises.[34] The relationship between the parties in connection to a legal harm alone however is insufficient. According to Weinrib, to provide a robust account of private law correlative justice needs to accommodate not just the circumstances in which an injustice arises but also the corresponding remedy to correct or repair the injustice.[35] Correlative justice therefore places a strong emphasis on understanding the internal reasons and justifications used to facilitate a liability response to an injustice.[36]

Informed by Weinrib's views, I adopt a *correlative justice* approach to defining private law. More specifically, I implicitly rely upon two key aspects of correlative justice when considering private law liability in this book. Firstly, private law liabilities are defined by the relationship between the parties in which a harm arises because one party infringes upon the rights of another. Placing an emphasis on the relationship between parties in the context of an injustice inherently encapsulates areas of law such as tort law, contract law and property law, among others (areas of law key to commercial arrangements). The primary focus is therefore the relationship between private parties but does not preclude the possibility of a relationship between a private party and a government actor. In instances between a private party and a government actor, I consider this relationship will be captured by a private law liability response when an injustice arises because one party acts and infringes upon the rights of the other party. This contrasts with instances where one party acts and breaches a regulatory rule, which may or may not infringe upon the rights of another party but does result in a regulatory breach against society. Such regulatory breaches I would not deem fitting within a private law analysis. The second aspect I implicitly rely upon is that it is not sufficient to merely identify that a legal wrong has occurred between parties; there needs to also

30 Ernest J Weinrib, *Corrective Justice* (Oxford University Press, 2012) 37.
31 Ernest J Weinrib, *Corrective Justice* (Oxford University Press, 2012) 25.
32 Ernest J Weinrib, *Corrective Justice* (Oxford University Press, 2012) 25.
33 Ernest J Weinrib, *Corrective Justice* (Oxford University Press, 2012) 25–26.
34 Ernest J Weinrib, *Corrective Justice* (Oxford University Press, 2012) 36.
35 Ernest J Weinrib, *Corrective Justice* (Oxford University Press, 2012) 36.
36 Ernest J Weinrib, *Corrective Justice* (Oxford University Press, 2012) 35–36.

be a means for responding to that injustice, such as identifying the relevant standard of liability.

Viewing private law through a *correlative justice* lens aligns with commercial practices. Consider how business activities are often performed through contractual arrangements. Whilst many commercial arrangements supported by contract are completed appropriately, on rare occasions adverse circumstances can arise. A situation could arise, for example, where one party to a contract does not perform their obligations or does not perform their contractual obligations to the requisite standard. In such instances, a private law liability would arise for a breach of contract. This aligns with the *correlative justice* view that an injustice arises when one party prevents another party from pursuing their own goals. If one party fails to perform their contractual obligations as expected, this prevents the other from obtaining what they were expecting from the contractual arrangement. Under a *correlative justice* view, this commercial scenario amounts to a private law liability.

On this basis, the primary focus of the book is to therefore consider and propose an appropriate private law liability response to AI; this, however, does not outright exclude consideration of regulatory measures. Regulation as it relates to AI is considered in this book but to a lesser extent; it is considered insofar as it relates to and complements the considered private law liability response to AI. Consideration is not given to deployed AI systems in a public law context, such as military Lethal Autonomous Weapons Systems ('LAWS').

0.4. Overview of Chapters

Before turning to an overview of the chapters in this book, it is worth pausing at this juncture to offer an observation about some key terms used throughout this book. Firstly, for ease of reference, I use the terms AI and AI system interchangeably.[37] I also consider that algorithms are not AI but may form the underlying components of AI. I therefore reject using the term 'AI algorithm' to denote an AI system.[38] Secondly, I favour describing AI as being 'deployed' rather than 'used', as I consider that the latter inadvertently suggests that AI is only a product or property that can be used. As I come to explore, AI can indeed be a product or property on some occasions, but, depending on the type of AI, it could also be construed in other capacities, such as a service. For this reason, I prefer the term 'deployed'. Lastly, I use the phrase 'threshold issue' throughout this book to refer to elements that ought to be considered as part of the process of assigning liability. I note that these could be viewed as considerations of liability or elements of individual liability rules. I have instead adopted this phrase to better reflect that liability cannot be assigned

37 I explore the types of AI I address in this book at [2].

38 I explore the distinction between AI and algorithms at [2].

until such issues are first resolved, which is why, at least in relation to AI, I favour the phrase 'threshold issue'.

In responding to the macro question of how to assign private law liability in the context of modern AI, this book is broadly divided into four parts. In Part I, which is comprised of Chapter 1, I evaluate current regulatory responses to AI and current proposed theoretical legal responses to AI. Parts II and III explore several secondary questions I consider important to address in responding to the primary question of how to assign liability in response to a deployed AI. Part II, comprised of Chapters 2 to 5, addresses the question of how modern forms of AI should be characterised legally. There is division in the literature as to whether AI should be viewed as a legal person, an agent or property. The question of how AI ought to be characterised is an important threshold issue as part of the process of assigning liability, for it shapes the parameters in which we view and consider AI legally. For example, if AI is best characterised as merely property, then this could give rise to the use of a product liability framework.

One of the challenges of modern forms of AI, which I explore at Section 2, and at several junctures throughout the book, is that not all types of modern AI are the same. There are varying degrees of independence and autonomy among these AI systems giving rise to the need for an adaptive method of characterising AI legally – one that considers the type of modern AI being deployed. It is this objective, secondary to the primary question, that is the subject of Part II. In Part II, I extrapolate key themes needed to propose a more robust characterisation model. Chapter 5, relying upon these themes and observations, proposes a new model for how AI should be legally characterised that is best suited and adaptive to modern forms of AI: the *Hierarchical Legal Personality* model. The legal characterisation of AI is, in my view, one of the key threshold issues that ought to be addressed as part of the process of assigning liability, and it is for this reason that it is predominantly the focus of Part II.

How AI should be legally characterised is an imperative threshold issue to consider as part of the process of assigning liability, but there are other threshold issues and, therefore, other considerations secondary to the primary question of how to assign liability in an AI context. These additional threshold issues are my initial focus in Part III. Part III is comprised of Chapters 6 to 8. It begins by addressing additional threshold issues that I view ought to be considered in the process of assigning liability. Chapter 6 raises the first of these additional threshold issues by exploring the notion of causation and links this issue back to the *Hierarchical Legal Personality* model proposed in Part II, Chapter 5. Chapter 7 then expands upon my considerations of issues that must be addressed as part of assigning liability and seeks to consider how the context in which an AI system is deployed, together with the scope of actions of an AI system, can narrow the scope of liability. Chapter 7 also addresses the issue of 'who' could be liable for the consequences arising from the deployment of AI.

Part III then turns to propose a theoretical liability model for AI. In Chapter 8, I seek to draw upon the discussions in Chapters 6 and 7, addressing liability threshold issues, and incorporate the overarching conclusions from these chapters with those in Chapter 5 into a new theoretical model for assigning liability in the context of modern AI. In doing so, it is in Chapter 8 that I propose a new three-phase theoretical model to assigning liability in response to the deployment of AI: the *Tri-Phase AI Liability Model.*

The goal of the new liability model is to provide a theoretical approach to managing liability in response to modern forms of AI being deployed – one that considers AI *situationally*. As common law principles hold great influence over international commercial law, the views offered in this book are grounded in a common law approach, rather than a civil law approach. Whilst the focus of the book is on a common law response to AI liability – filling a crucial gap in the literature – key civil law approaches, such as that of the European Union are not ignored. Instead, macro concepts are extracted from these approaches to inform the *Tri-Phase AI Liability Model.* The new liability model is therefore ultimately proposed as a solution for common law jurisdictions, but it might inform considerations in other jurisdictions. Its potential applicability to non-common law jurisdictions, however, will not be addressed in this book. In doing so, the aim is to contribute to a discourse informing how we respond to AI and reduce the uncertainties arising in what is a rapidly evolving area of technology and law.

Part IV, comprised of Chapter 9, then turns to consider the relationship between the proposed *Tri-Phase AI Liability Model* and regulatory measures. What emerges is that to some extent there is an interdependent relationship between regulatory and liability measures. Developing a robust legal response to AI therefore requires not only acknowledging this interdependence but also, ideally, co-ordinating both regulatory and liability measures. Following this discussion, the chapter then moves to explore the parts of the proposed model that would benefit from being supported by a regulatory response including the circumstances and types of regulatory measures needed to complement the *Tri-Phase AI Liability Model* to ensure a robust solution to the legal uncertainties posed by AI. Part IV also explores how the proposed model could inform practical responses to AI. A particular emphasis is placed on the benefits for emerging policy and law reform responses to AI. Such discussion holds value for policymakers together with academics and practitioners considering novel situations involving AI.

0.5. A Need for Flexibility

Modern forms of AI with their variability in capacity for actions and the degree to which control can be exerted over these systems pose unique challenges in responding to the private law liability implications connected to these technologies. The lack of uniformity in these systems combined with the fact that they can be deployed in a variety of contexts creates practical challenges with applying and enforcing existing liability principles in AI-related scenarios. Parallels can be drawn between existing challenges faced in intellectual property rights enforcement together with enforcement issues in other novel digital environments, such as issues of contracting in the metaverse.

What emerges in response is that there is a need for a flexible approach to responding to private liabilities raised in the context of modern AI. For an AI system deployed in one context may not act or be capable of submitting to the same level of control in another context. It is incompatible with modern forms of AI to mandate a uniform liability response. A central tenet of this book is therefore flexibility. By striving to propose a resolution that is adaptable in nature, I thus offer a theoretical framework to assist with navigating liability issues related to AI, one aimed at overcoming the practical challenges associated with enforcing existing private law liability responses to AI. In turn, this book seeks to provide a comprehensive account of private law governance mechanisms as they relate to AI.

References

A Articles/Books/Reports

Boden, Margaret A, *Artificial Intelligence: A Very Short Introduction* (Oxford University Press, 2nd ed, 2018).

Danesi, Marcel 'AI-Generated Music' in *AI-Generated Popular Culture: A Semiotic Perspective* (Palgrave Macmillan, 2024), 59.

DiMatteo, Larry A, Cristina Poncibò and Michel Cannarsa (eds), *The Cambridge Handbook of Artificial Intelligence: Global Perspectives on Law and Ethics* (Cambridge University Press, 2022).

Geistfeld, Mark A, Ernst Karner, Bernhard A. Koch and Christiane Wendehorst (eds), *Civil Liability for Artificial Intelligence and Software* (Walter de Gruyter GmbH & Co KG, 2022).

Kaul, Vivek, Sarah Enslin, Seth A. Gross, 'History of artificial intelligence in medicine' (2020) 92 (4) *Gastrointestinal Endoscopy* 807.

Korteling, J. E. Hans, G. C. van de Boer-Visschedijk, R. A. M. Blankendaal, R. C. Boonekamp and A. R. Eikelboom, 'Human- versus Artificial Intelligence' (2021) 4 *Frontiers in Artificial Intelligence* 1.

Larson, Erik J., *The Myth of Artificial Intelligence: Why Computers Can't Think the Way We Do* (Harvard University Press, 2021).

Lim, Ernest and Phillip Morgan (eds), *The Cambridge Handbook of Private Law and Artificial Intelligence* (Cambridge University Press, 2024).

Lohsse, Sebastian, Reiner Schulze and Dirk Staudenmayer (eds), *Liability for Artificial Intelligence and the Internet of Things* (Bloomsbury Publishing, 2019).

Ma, Yifang, Zhenyu Wang, Hong Yang, and Lin Yang, 'Artificial Intelligence Applications in the Development of Autonomous Vehicles: A Survey' (2020) 7(2) *Journal of Automatica Sinica* 315.

Merrill, Thomas W. 'Private and Public Law' in Andrew S. Gold et al. (eds), *The Oxford Handbook of the New Private Law* (Oxford University Press, 2020) 575.

Russell, Stuart J., Peter Norvig et. al, *Artificial Intelligence: A Modern Approach* (Pearson Education Limited, 4th ed, 2022).

Sales, Philip, 'Algorithms, Artificial Intelligence, and the Law' (2021) 105(1) *Judicature* 23.

Warwick, Kevin, *Artificial Intelligence: The Basics* (Routledge, 2012).

Weinrib, Ernest J. *Corrective Justice* (Oxford University Press 2012).

Zhu, X and A Goldberg, *Introduction to Semi-Supervised Learning* (Springer Nature Switzerland AG, 2022).

Zipurksy, Benjamin C, 'Philosophy of Private Law' in Jules Coleman and Scott Shapiro (eds), *The Oxford Handbook of Jurisprudence and Philosophy of Law* (Oxford University Press, 2002) 623.

B Cases

B2C2 Ltd v Quoine Pte Ltd [2019] SGHC (1) 03 ('B2C2 Ltd v Quoine Pte Ltd')

C Other

Order of Davies J in *Amato v Commonwealth of Australia* (Federal Court of Australia, VID611/2019, 27 November 2019)

Part I

1 Understanding the AI Legal Landscape

1.1. Evaluating Legal Approaches to Artificial Intelligence

The *Introduction* identified that there is a need for an overarching framework that provides a theory for unifying the different fragmented approaches to AI liability: the *Tri-Phase AI Liability Model.* Before turning to Part II and exploring foundational issues behind this model, it is important to first gain an understanding of the existing private law governance mechanisms responding to AI. For these mechanisms are the individual or fragmented approaches that the *Tri-Phase AI Liability Model* will seek to unify.

Many of the legal approaches to AI are focused on either regulatory responses or where they do address liability, they are often based on the underlying assumption that all forms of AI are the same or ought to be viewed legally as the same. As considered in the *Introduction* this is not always an accurate assumption; for there is a great degree of variance in terms of capacity and control over modern forms of AI. This chapter therefore assesses the emerging legal approaches to AI. More specifically, the aim is to evaluate relevant responses to AI and consider the controversies, issues and limitations these approaches raise. Both emerging regulatory approaches and approaches responding to the liability implications arising from AI being deployed are considered.

This chapter therefore has two focus points. Firstly, emerging regulatory responses to AI that are relevant to common law jurisdictions will be evaluated. A particular emphasis is placed on whether these regulatory responses provide scope to accommodate the liability implications of AI and if so to what extent. This is especially important in terms of understanding the divide between regulatory and liability responses to AI (considered further in Chapter 9). The chapter then moves to evaluate theoretical approaches relevant to the liability implications of a deployed AI. Understanding the liability implications associated with this form of technology is becoming increasingly important to determine the appropriate liability response to modern forms of AI. The considerations in this chapter in turn lay the foundations for discussions that follow in Parts II and III.

DOI: 10.4324/9781003617549-3

1.2. Regulatory Responses to Artificial Intelligence

I begin by evaluating current and emerging regulatory approaches that specifically target AI. It is worth noting at the outset that these approaches are evolving rapidly and consist of varying degrees of enforceability.

1.2.1 Legislative Regulatory Responses

1.2.1.1 European Union

Although not a common law jurisdiction, as one of the first legislative responses to AI, the European Union's (EU) approach to regulating AI is noteworthy. The EU's Artificial Intelligence Act ('EU AI Act'), among other things, establishes harmonised rules pertaining to how AI systems are brought to market and how they should be monitored together with governance and enforcement regulations once an AI system is on the market.[1] It also outlines transparency rules for AI systems along with specific requirements for high-risk AI systems and prohibitions on certain AI practices.[2] The EU AI Act regulates AI systems utilising a risk-based approach with higher risk systems being subject to more stringent regulations.[3] The Act, for example, outlines prohibited practices using AI systems, such as the exploitation of vulnerabilities (disabilities, minority status) and the expansion of facial recognition databases among other practices.[4] The EU AI Act imposes consequences for breaching these regulations;[5] however, these are primarily directed towards the developers, manufacturers and deployers of AI systems who fail to meet the imposed standards. Notably the Act does not outline the liability implications for individuals who have suffered a harm in response to a deployed AI. The options available to individuals instead form part of the proposed EU AI Liability Directive[6] and the EU's Product Liability Directive amended in

1 *Regulation (EU) 2024/1689 of the European Parliament and of the Council of 13 June 2024 laying down harmonised rules on artificial intelligence and amending Regulations (EC) No 300/2008, (EU) No 167/2013, (EU) No 168/2013, (EU) 2018/858, (EU) 2018/1139 and (EU) 2019/2144 and Directives 2014/90/EU, (EU) 2016/797 and (EU) 2020/1828 (Artificial Intelligence Act)* [2024] OJ L 1689/1 (the 'EU AI Act'), art 1.

2 *Regulation (EU) 2024/1689 of the European Parliament and of the Council of 13 June 2024 laying down harmonised rules on artificial intelligence and amending Regulations (EC) No 300/2008, (EU) No 167/2013, (EU) No 168/2013, (EU) 2018/858, (EU) 2018/1139 and (EU) 2019/2144 and Directives 2014/90/EU, (EU) 2016/797 and (EU) 2020/1828 (Artificial Intelligence Act)* [2024] OJ L 1689/1 (the 'EU AI Act'), art 1.

3 For the foundations of the risk-based approach see: the EU AI Act (n 1), arts 5–7, with 'High-Risk AI Systems' defined in Annex III. Notably the regulations imposed on these systems are outlined in arts 8–15.

4 For the full range of prohibited practices see: the EU AI Act (n 1), art 5.

5 For penalties see: the EU AI Act (n 1), art 99.

6 European Union, *Proposal for a Directive on Adapting Non-Contractual Civil Liability Rules to Artificial Intelligence* (28 September 2022) <https://eur-lex.europa.eu/legal-content/EN/TXT/PDF/?uri=CELEX:52022PC0496> 'EU AI Liability Directive'.

March 2024 to accommodate AI systems.[7] The latter of these options is based on the notion that AI must always be characterised as a product, which as I come to explore in Part II is not necessarily the best approach to legally characterising AI. The former, being the EU AI Liability Directive, I discuss in this chapter in Section 1.3.

1.2.1.2 Canada

Canada is another jurisdiction looking to provide AI-specific regulations through a proposed framework which is in many aspects like the EU AI Act. At the time of writing the proposed Artificial Intelligence and Data Act ('AIDA')[8] is still in development. The version of the draft bill as of its first reading however is framed around the notion of 'high-impact' AI systems. The draft does not define what is a high-impact AI system; instead meaning is to be ascribed by regulations to be created by the Governor in Council post the enactment of AIDA.[9] Given that one of the purposes of AIDA is to place prohibitions on conduct involving AI systems that could cause individuals or their interests serious harm,[10] it is likely then that in this context high-impact AI systems could be interpreted as systems that have the capacity to trigger this level of harm. The significance of this observation is twofold. Firstly, there are some more simplistic forms of AI that are not likely to be subject to key provisions in AIDA, if enacted. Secondly, the EU AI Act is also based on a risk assessment profile of AI systems, but the 'high-risk' AI systems under this framework are relatively prescriptive in nature. It remains to be seen if any regulations defining 'high-impact' AI systems under the AIDA approach will also be ascribed with similar level of specificity.

The proposed AIDA framework also includes mandatory requirements and consequences for breaching these requirements. The proposal places an emphasis on transparency through requiring that persons making high-impact

7 European Parliament, *European Parliament legislative resolution of 12 March 2024 on the proposal for a directive of the European Parliament and of the Council on liability for defective products (COM(2022)0495 – C9-0322/2022 – 2022/0302(COD))*, P9_TA(2024)0132, 14 March 2024.

8 For the wording of the proposed Artificial Intelligence and Data Act (AIDA) see: C-27, *An Act to enact the Consumer Privacy Protection Act, the Personal Information and Data Protection Tribunal Act and the Artificial Intelligence and Data Act and to make consequential and related amendments to other Acts*, 1st Sess, 44th Parl, 2021 pt 3 (first reading 16 June 2022).

9 C-27, *An Act to enact the Consumer Privacy Protection Act, the Personal Information and Data Protection Tribunal Act and the Artificial Intelligence and Data Act and to make consequential and related amendments to other Acts*, 1st Sess, 44th Parl, 2021 pt 3, s 36 (first reading 16 June 2022).

10 C-27, *An Act to enact the Consumer Privacy Protection Act, the Personal Information and Data Protection Tribunal Act and the Artificial Intelligence and Data Act and to make consequential and related amendments to other Acts*, 1st Sess, 44th Parl, 2021 pt 3, s 4(b) (first reading 16 June 2022).

AI systems available for use publish a plain language description of the intended use of the system, its intended outputs and any mitigation steps taken in relation to the system.[11] Similar requirements are imposed upon persons who manage these systems only instead of foreshadowing how the system could be used, they must disclose how it is actually used.[12] Importantly, the proposed approach creates an offence where a person knowingly or recklessly uses an AI system to cause damage to another which includes physical and psychological damage together with and economic loss.[13] The consequences for committing such an offence include fines and potential terms of imprisonment.[14] Unlike the EU AI Act, the form of AIDA proposed in the first reading captures more actors; that is, it is not primarily directed towards the developers or manufacturers of an AI system but instead has a broader ambit covering users of these systems. Additionally, AIDA seeks to address harms arising from a deployed AI system but does so through designating such conduct as an offence – a *public* law response – and imposing fines or imprisonment as the legal consequences for a breach of this offence. AIDA in this form does not provide scope for individuals to correct injustices against them. It therefore does not address how private law liabilities involving AI ought to be addressed.

1.2.2 Policy-Based Approaches

Below I consider the key emerging non-legislative approaches to AI regulation responsive to common law jurisdictions.

1.2.2.1 United States

In recent years, US approaches to AI policy have evolved rapidly. Under President Biden, October 2023 marked the release of United States (US) Presidential Executive Order 14110 regarding the *Safe, Secure, and Trustworthy*

11 C-27, *An Act to enact the Consumer Privacy Protection Act, the Personal Information and Data Protection Tribunal Act and the Artificial Intelligence and Data Act and to make consequential and related amendments to other Acts*, 1st Sess, 44th Parl, 2021 pt 3, s 11(1) (first reading 16 June 2022).

12 C-27, *An Act to enact the Consumer Privacy Protection Act, the Personal Information and Data Protection Tribunal Act and the Artificial Intelligence and Data Act and to make consequential and related amendments to other Acts*, 1st Sess, 44th Parl, 2021 pt 3, s 11(2) (first reading 16 June 2022).

13 C-27, *An Act to enact the Consumer Privacy Protection Act, the Personal Information and Data Protection Tribunal Act and the Artificial Intelligence and Data Act and to make consequential and related amendments to other Acts*, 1st Sess, 44th Parl, 2021 pt 3, s 39 (first reading 16 June 2022).

14 C-27, *An Act to enact the Consumer Privacy Protection Act, the Personal Information and Data Protection Tribunal Act and the Artificial Intelligence and Data Act and to make consequential and related amendments to other Acts*, 1st Sess, 44th Parl, 2021 pt 3, s 40 (first reading 16 June 2022).

Development and Use of Artificial Intelligence (the '2023 Executive Order').[15] This Executive Order set out guiding principles for US federal agencies in engaging with AI.[16] The principles covered a broad array of topics such as: addressing algorithmic discrimination, ensuring AI research advancement in the US together with supporting groups impacted by AI, such as consumers, patients, students and workers.[17] It also set out an aim to increase international engagement and cooperation regarding appropriate use and governance of AI.[18] Like the EU and Canadian approaches the 2023 Executive Order placed an emphasis on improving AI safety and security.[19] It also acknowledged the potential adverse impacts of AI on individual privacy and sought to foster responsible and ethical use of AI within US government agencies.[20] The breadth of the 2023 Executive Order is a notable distinction from other emerging approaches to AI for it could be conceived of as aiming for a holistic response to the legal uncertainties posed by AI.

It is worth observing that the 2023 Executive Order was revoked by President Trump on his first day as President in 2025.[21] President Trump later in the first week of his second term then signed a new Executive Order (the '2025 Executive Order') marking a revision in the US' approach to AI policy.[22] The 2025 Executive Order seeks to ensure AI systems are developed in a manner 'free from ideological bias or engineered social agendas'.[23] It also sets the policy that the US will further its AI leadership at global level through focusing on 'human flouring, economic competitiveness, and national security'.[24] The exact particulars of how this goal is to be achieved will be proposed within 180 days of the 2025 Executive Order.[25] Consideration must also be given to any implications arising from Biden's 2023 Executive Order that are inconsistent with the goals of the 2025 Executive Order. President Trump's approach to AI policy early in his second term therefore reflects a different emphasis from

15 Exec. Order No. 14110, 3 C.F.R. 75191 (2023).
16 Exec. Order No. 14110, 3 C.F.R. 75191 (2023) s 2.
17 Exec. Order No. 14110, 3 C.F.R. 75191 (2023) ss 2(b) – (e).
18 Exec. Order No. 14110, 3 C.F.R. 75191 (2023) s 2(h).
19 Exec. Order No. 14110, 3 C.F.R. 75191 (2023) s 2(a).
20 Exec. Order No. 14110, 3 C.F.R. 75191 (2023) ss 2(f) – (g).
21 For an information regarding President Trump's revocation of the 2023 Executive Order see: White House, 'Initial Rescissions of Harmful Executive Orders and Actions' (Web Page, 20 January 2025) <https://www.whitehouse.gov/presidential-actions/2025/01/initial-rescissions-of-harmful-executive-orders-and-actions/>.
22 See: White House, 'Removing Barriers to American Leadership in Artificial Intelligence' (Web Page, 23 January 2025) <https://www.whitehouse.gov/presidential-actions/2025/01/removing-barriers-to-american-leadership-in-artificial-intelligence/>.
23 See: White House, 'Removing Barriers to American Leadership in Artificial Intelligence' (Web Page, 23 January 2025) s 1.
24 See: White House, 'Removing Barriers to American Leadership in Artificial Intelligence' (Web Page, 23 January 2025) s 2.
25 See: White House, 'Removing Barriers to American Leadership in Artificial Intelligence' (Web Page, 23 January 2025) ss 4–5.

that of President Biden. His focus seems to be directed towards ensuring the benefits associated with AI are realised. Notably though, by its very nature as an executive order this approach has key limitations namely that its application is confined to US federal agencies and also that it is subject to the possibility of easily being revoked by future executive orders. The 2025 Executive Order does not offer the same level of 'permanence' that a legislative response such as the EU and proposed Canadian approaches offer. It remains to be seen what legislative responses to AI may be pursued under President Trump's second term.

1.2.2.2 United Kingdom

Although its stance is still in development, the United Kingdom (UK) has signalled it will adopt a pro-innovation approach to regulating AI. In March 2023 the UK Government outlined its proposed approach, highlighting that it would not mandate specific rules or designate specific AI systems to be of a certain risk level, rather the approach will seek to consider the context in which an AI system is deployed and regulate the *outcomes* associated with a deployed AI.[26] The effect of this being then that the UK approach in 2023 was less focused on regulating AI technologies and more directed towards the outcomes associated with such technologies.[27] To support this approach, the government proposed a principles-based approach where key overarching principles would be used by existing regulators within the UK to interpret how they should respond to AI-related issues.[28] The five overarching principles included themes common to the approaches considered earlier: safety and security, transparency and explainability of AI systems, fairness, AI governance and accountability together with contestability and redress.[29] What is key to the 2023 approach though is that there was no proposal for an AI-specific regulator, rather to equip existing regulators with principles to assist in interpreting existing regulator obligations in an AI landscape.

One strength of this 2023 approach is to acknowledge that the effect of a deployed AI system is very much context specific. At the same time, however, the approach has the limitation of assuming these varied outcomes can adequately be managed through existing regulatory responses but with the addition of an AI 'overlay' in the form of AI-specific principles. In February 2024, the UK Government released its report in response to consultations

26 For an overview of the UK approach see: Department for Science, Innovation & Technology, *A Pro-Innovation Approach to AI Regulation* (No CP 815, 2023), 25.

27 For an overview of the UK approach see: Department for Science, Innovation & Technology, *A Pro-Innovation Approach to AI Regulation* (No CP 815, 2023), 25.

28 For an overview of the UK approach see: Department for Science, Innovation & Technology, *A Pro-Innovation Approach to AI Regulation* (No CP 815, 2023), 26.

29 For an overview of the UK approach see: Department for Science, Innovation & Technology, *A Pro-Innovation Approach to AI Regulation* (No CP 815, 2023), 26.

regarding its proposed approach. Interestingly, the report revealed that a concern expressed in the public consultation phase is that the proposed 2023 approach might not adequately accommodate liabilities arising from a deployed AI system.[30] In response the UK Government identified that allocating liability in an AI context does not invoke a simple solution and acknowledged that more complex forms of AI only compound issues associated with allocating liability.[31] Further, the Government conceded the need to develop a liability response to AI which would complement the proposed approach.[32] On this basis there exists a need for a context-focused approach to assigning liability that accommodates for the varied nature of AI and the varied scenarios in which it could be deployed. In January 2025, the UK Government, under a new administration, released a new report signalling its intention to develop binding AI regulations in the form of AI-specific legislation.[33] This marks a key shift away from the previous administration's principles-based approach layered over existing regulations. While proposals for a UK AI-specific legislative response are still in development, it will be interesting to see if any proposal incorporates a context-aware approach to AI liability.

1.2.2.3 Singapore

Singapore's approach to regulating AI is largely similar to that of the UK Government's initial position. Singapore, like the UK, has adopted a pro-innovation approach to supporting the use and development of AI development.[34] Unlike the UK, however, which is moving towards implementing AI-specific regulations, Singapore is yet to propose a legislative response. Instead, in February 2025, the Singaporean Government sought to introduce AI testing and collaboration initiatives aimed at enhancing AI safety at a foundational level through industry and international partnerships.[35] Singapore has also relied upon its 'Model Artificial Intelligence Governance Framework'. This voluntary framework offers guidance on key AI-related issues such as how

30 Department for Science, Innovation & Technology, *A pro-innovation approach to AI regulation: Government response to consultation* (No CP 1019, February 2024) 56–57.

31 Department for Science, Innovation & Technology, *A pro-innovation approach to AI regulation: Government response to consultation* (No CP 1019, February 2024) 57–58.

32 Department for Science, Innovation & Technology, *A pro-innovation approach to AI regulation: Government response to consultation* (No CP 1019, February 2024) 58.

33 Science, Innovation and Technology Committee, *Governance of Artificial Intelligence (AI): Government Response* (2024–25, HC 591) 2–3, 23.

34 Government of the Republic of Singapore, *NAIS 2.0 Singapore National AI Strategy: AI for the Public Good: For Singapore and the World* (Report, 4 December 2023) <https://file.go.gov.sg/nais2023.pdf> ('Singapore National AI Strategy') 11.

35 Government of the Republic of Singapore, 'Singapore Announces New AI Safety Initiatives at the Global AI Action Summit in France', *Infocomm Media Development Authority* (Web page, 11 February 2025) <https://www.imda.gov.sg/resources/press-releases-factsheets-and-speeches/press-releases/2025/singapore-ai-safety-initiatives-global-ai-summit-france>.

AI systems can be developed, the level of human involvement in AI decisions together with factors to consider as part of incorporating AI into processes.[36] What is interesting is that this soft regulatory approach expressly excludes responding to liability issues raised by AI and notes the need for a separate more expansive consideration on this topic.[37] Despite the lack of a specific AI liability response, Singapore's approach does acknowledge the need for a context-specific, tiered risk-based response to AI.[38] Acknowledging the need for a 'context-specific' approach to AI is arguably a unique approach adopted by Singapore when compared with the other policy-based approaches discussed earlier. Singapore's approach to AI therefore impliedly acknowledges that not all forms of AI are the same nor do they function the same in all contexts. In this respect, Singapore's underlying policy as a theory at least is better placed to responding to the variances in forms of modern AI.

1.2.3 Observations Regarding AI-Specific Regulatory Measures Relevant to Liability

Regulatory responses that are specific to AI are still largely under development and even when complete their impacts will remain to be seen for some time. What is emerging is that there are more formalistic methods of regulating AI through adopting a legislative approach to responding to AI. The alternative is to offer guiding principles that are not formalistic in nature but are instead designed to complement established legal principles. Regardless of the approach – formalistic or principles-based – what is emerging is that the accounts so far do not adequately accommodate for liabilities in response to AI. The principles-based approach, more so than the formalistic approach, aligns with this observation. Regardless, what becomes clear is that there is a need therefore for a robust liability response, especially a private law liability response, to address the implications from a deployed AI system.

1.3. Evaluation of Proposed Legal Responses to a Deployed AI

I now turn to consider the theoretical approaches to managing modern forms of AI, as this will inform the discussions in Part III. I discuss next that I am of the view that these approaches could be broadly grouped into four categories of responses to addressing the legal issues arising from the deployment of modern AI. An overview of these approaches is given in Table 1.1. The

36 Personal Data Protection Commission Singapore, *Model Artificial Intelligence Governance Framework* (2nd ed., 21 January 2020) <https://www.pdpc.gov.sg/-/media/Files/PDPC/PDF-Files/Resource-for-Organisation/AI/SGModelAIGovFramework2.pdf> ('Model AI Governance Framework') 13, 21, 28, 35.

37 Personal Data Protection Commission Singapore, *Model Artificial Intelligence Governance Framework* (2nd ed., 21 January 2020) 11.

38 Singapore National AI Strategy n (34) 57.

Table 1.1 A Comparison of Existing Legal Responses to AI

	General Principles (Tort or Contract)				*Shared Liability*		*Imposed Liability*			*Insurance-Mandated Liability*		
Approach	Negligence-based response	Non-delegable duty with contract (potentially supplemented by insurance)	Adaptations to existing obligation laws	Amendments to existing burdens of proof	Association risk and enterprise liability	Tiered product liability	Autonomy risk and vicarious liability	Digital Peculium [backed by insurance]	Harmonised strict liability [and mandatory insurance]	Legal personhood with insurance	Interconnectivity risk and collective fund liability	Liability complemented by insurance schemes

four overarching categories are: (a) general principles, (b) shared liability, (c) imposed liability and (d) insurance-mandated liability. In evaluating the theoretical responses to AI, I first consider each proposed solution in turn as it relates to one of the above four categories.

1.3.1 Proposed Solutions: General Principles

I commence my review of the existing theoretical responses to legally managing AI by considering the views comprising a general-principles approach – that is, managing AI through existing principles of law.

1.3.1.1 Negligence-Based Response

Ryan Abbott poses a liability solution for AI that is rooted in tortious – more specifically, negligence-based – principles. He is one of the leading theorists proposing a response to AI rooted in tortious principles. In Chapter 6, I explore his approach relates to issues of causation. Here, I consider his approach as it relates to the broader issue of liability for AI.

To an extent, Abbott's view is persuasively informed by historical liability approaches to new technological developments. He conducts a useful discussion considering how, historically, there has emerged a trend, at least in common law jurisdictions, to manage the harm from the use of new technologies in tort law, which in turn has provided an incentive for safer use of these technologies.[39]

Applying negligent standards to AI is what Abbott ultimately settles upon in terms of liability. Central to his argument is the view that AI systems are: (a) capable of being tortfeasors, (b) that torts involving AI should be based in negligence (and not another form of tort, such as an intentional tort) and (c) that there is a need for a new standard objective test for determining liability in instances involving AI – the 'Reasonable Robot' test.[40] I now explore how each of these components of Abbott's argument ultimately informs his approach to liability for AI. In terms of (a), Abbott considers that AI is at least capable of being a tortfeasor as, unlike traditional 'products', there are varying degrees of independence and control surrounding AI. Such systems are not just utilised by individuals as confined tools.[41] This is a persuasive argument, for AI is more complex than a product, with some forms of AI even seeking to define their own end goals or objectives. So, it is not inconceivable that AI as a form of actor could indeed therefore be a tortfeasor.

39 Ryan Abbott, *The Reasonable Robot: Artificial Intelligence and the Law* (Cambridge University Press, 2020) 52–55.
40 Ryan Abbott, *The Reasonable Robot: Artificial Intelligence and the Law* (Cambridge University Press, 2020) 50–70.
41 Ryan Abbott, *The Reasonable Robot: Artificial Intelligence and the Law* (Cambridge University Press, 2020) 59–60.

In terms of (b), Abbott justifies his approach by drawing upon the historical considerations mentioned above. He views negligence as serving a dual function: seeking to deter harm suffered by individuals and ensure manufacturers are held accountable for suffered harms.[42] Whilst this is an admirable goal, and one I agree with in principle, it is the latter part – holding only manufacturers to account – with which I have concerns. As I explore in Chapter 7, it is not always pragmatic or equitable to hold manufacturers to account. Consideration needs to be given to other actors and the degree of influence and control they have over an AI system. Additionally, my focus is on the accountability aspect and not the harm prevention, as I consider harm *prevention* to fit more within the ambit of regulation, which I consider in Chapter 9.

Lastly, in terms of (c), this is a central and novel aspect of Abbott's overall approach. As I consider in Chapter 6 in relation to causation, Abbott seeks to adjust the traditional reasonable person test, common to negligent actions, and replace it with the 'Reasonable Robot' test to encompass AI actors.[43] Central to his test is considering whether the AI system's act was negligent and not whether the AI was designed or manufactured negligently.[44] If the key issue is how and why an AI system acted and not whether there is an issue with production, then does this not imply, to a degree, an element of autonomy on the part of the AI system? This potential element of autonomy is why I find it concerning to have manufacturers as the only or primary option as to who is liable for the actions associated with AI. Admittedly, Abbott does acknowledge that other actors in the supply chain pertaining to an AI system could be held accountable.[45] However, he is still focused on liability derived from the production of an AI system when his own test seeks to examine the actions of an AI system and not its design. I consider Abbott's Reasonable Robot objective test useful; it is who he deems ought to be accountable for the AI system that I query.

1.3.1.2 Non-Delegable Duty with Contract

Simon Chesterman also offers a theoretical approach to AI that could be deemed as relying on general legal principles. Before turning to Chesterman's approach, however, I first raise his objections to other potential methods for resolving legal responsibility in the context of AI, viz. (a) negligence, (b) strict

42 Ryan Abbott, *The Reasonable Robot: Artificial Intelligence and the Law* (Cambridge University Press, 2020) 50.

43 Ryan Abbott, *The Reasonable Robot: Artificial Intelligence and the Law* (Cambridge University Press, 2020) 60–63.

44 Ryan Abbott, *The Reasonable Robot: Artificial Intelligence and the Law* (Cambridge University Press, 2020) 62.

45 Ryan Abbott, *The Reasonable Robot: Artificial Intelligence and the Law* (Cambridge University Press, 2020) 62.

liability, (c) product liability and (d) insurance schemes. Understanding his objections will further an understanding of his views.

Chesterman arguably considers that a negligence-only approach is not without limitations. I mentioned above that Abbott favours utilising negligence principles to best resolve responsibility issues in relation to AI. Chesterman seemingly acknowledges that such an approach has its merits.[46] He suggests, though, that to ensure greater levels of human control over AI and transparency in relation to AI, negligence alone as a guiding legal response is insufficient.[47] Chesterman's concerns with a purely negligence-based approach are not that dissimilar from my own. He considers that such an approach poses challenges for identifying who should be liable for the actions of AI systems, as it can be difficult to identify who is the key actor.[48] He purports that some of these issues could be resolved depending on whether the AI system exists physically or instead in an online format.[49] He considers that it is easier to identify a clear actor in instances where the AI system has a physical presence, such as arises in the context of a robot.[50] This is especially interesting when viewed in relation to my discussion in Chapter 3 regarding that any property characterisation of AI needs to be reconciled with issues of how integrated an AI system is with, or dependent upon, corporeal objects.

Next are Chesterman's considerations as they relate to strict and product liability. He acknowledges that there is an intersection between these two forms of liability.[51] He considers a strict liability approach applied to the users of an AI system, based on the system being hazardous, as an error because AI often strives to improve safety.[52] What is emerging as a common trend in the literature is that strict liability principles are problematic in the context of AI. This is due to factors such as what Chesterman espouses but also the potential for such an approach to have a chilling effect on the use of AI. Additionally, considering Chesterman's views, another problem with strict liability is who should this standard be imposed upon. Imposing this standard on manufacturers in all instances is potentially problematic, not only due to a chilling effect but also as it would fail to acknowledge that there are varying degrees of com-

46 Simon Chesterman, *We, The Robots? Regulating Artificial Intelligence and the Limits of the Law* (Cambridge University Press, 2021) 193.
47 Simon Chesterman, *We, The Robots? Regulating Artificial Intelligence and the Limits of the Law* (Cambridge University Press, 2021) 193.
48 Simon Chesterman, *We, The Robots? Regulating Artificial Intelligence and the Limits of the Law* (Cambridge University Press, 2021) 88.
49 Simon Chesterman, *We, The Robots? Regulating Artificial Intelligence and the Limits of the Law* (Cambridge University Press, 2021) 88.
50 Simon Chesterman, *We, The Robots? Regulating Artificial Intelligence and the Limits of the Law* (Cambridge University Press, 2021) 88.
51 Simon Chesterman, *We, The Robots? Regulating Artificial Intelligence and the Limits of the Law* (Cambridge University Press, 2021) 92.
52 Simon Chesterman, *We, The Robots? Regulating Artificial Intelligence and the Limits of the Law* (Cambridge University Press, 2021) 92–93.

plexity in relation to AI. This is an important point that Chesterman acknowledges when considering the merits of strict liability for the users of AI.[53]

Product liability poses similar challenges to strict liability, as between the two there is arguably a degree of overlap. Chesterman raises an interesting question in relation to product liability: is AI a product or a service?[54] There is a view that AI could be construed in either capacity.[55] This raises an interesting point, which integrates well with my arguments in Chapter 5: is it possible for AI to be characterised in more than one way and, consequently, is a degree of flexibility required in shaping a liability framework? Such a framework needs to have the capacity to acknowledge that sometimes AI will indeed be acting in the capacity of a product and, at other times, a service, or it may even hold the potential for a heightened degree of autonomy and behave as a legal person. It is for these reasons that I agree with the perspective that whilst product liability may be a viable liability option for AI in some circumstances, it does not hold for all forms of AI. As such, a more robust resolution is required.

The varied nature of AI also poses challenges from an insurance perspective. As Chesterman highlights, the ability for AI to be viewed as either a product or a service, depending on the AI system itself, can create 'gaps' or uncertainty in the insurance landscape.[56] This creates difficulties for insurers to adequately insure AI systems. Arguably, there are other industries with a high degree of variability that are still insurable. What makes the varied nature of AI distinct or unique is the potential lack of predictability associated with these forms of technology. Insurance, to Chesterman, is better suited to a form of regulation rather than a means for uniformly determining liability.[57] I find I too am persuaded by this consideration, although I do acknowledge that insurance could be used to address the issue of financial consequences for liability in some circumstances.

To resolve the liability uncertainty associated with AI, Chesterman offers a dual-faceted proposal. He considers that existing liability models and insurance regimes ought to be adapted to accommodate AI, and that it may be necessary to identify responsibility, even if doing so is not the most efficient

53 Simon Chesterman, *We, The Robots? Regulating Artificial Intelligence and the Limits of the Law* (Cambridge University Press, 2021) 93.

54 Simon Chesterman, *We, The Robots? Regulating Artificial Intelligence and the Limits of the Law* (Cambridge University Press, 2021) 93–95; Jacob Turner also raises the question of whether AI is a product or a service; see: Jacob Turner, *Robot Rules: Regulating Artificial Intelligence* (Palgrave Macmillan, 2019) 95–98.

55 Turner (n 54) 95–98; Chesterman, *We, The Robots? Regulating Artificial Intelligence and the Limits of the Law* (n 46) 93–95.

56 Chesterman, *We, The Robots? Regulating Artificial Intelligence and the Limits of the Law* (n 46) 99–101.

57 Chesterman, *We, The Robots? Regulating Artificial Intelligence and the Limits of the Law* (n 46) 100.

way to resolve an uncertain outcome.[58] To that end, he proposes a response that focuses on two key lines of reasoning: non-delegable duties and command responsibility.[59] In relation to non-delegable duties, Chesterman proposes that, with respect to AI, there should sit an overriding primary obligation to ensure no harm arises from its use.[60] Here, he draws an analogy with existing special relationships, such as between a hospital and a patient or between a school and its students.[61] He acknowledges that the role of such a duty is to require that the duty holder ensures adequate measures are adopted in the first instance to attempt to reduce harm.[62] Additionally, he maintains that such an approach requires foresight, as for this approach to function effectively, duty holders would need to enter into contractual arrangements that apportion liability between parties.[63] There is a concern that this approach could, albeit to a lesser degree than strict liability, have some chilling effect on the use of AI. Individuals seeking to engage with AI would need to have the foresight to prepare an agreement covering all potential outcomes associated with the AI system in question. This might not be feasible for all parties seeking to engage with AI. At a broad level, however, this is quite a persuasive approach, as it could be used to require all or, at a minimum, *key* parties involved with the use of AI to take all reasonable measures to prevent harm.

In contemplating this approach, I first consider the concept of non-delegable duties without a linked contractual arrangement for the proportioning of liability. As Chesterman highlights, central to the concept of a non-delegable duty is the special relationship between the duty holder and the person (or persons) to whom they owe the duty.[64] This special relationship aspect of the duty is arguably somewhat analogous to the concept of a class of persons to whom a duty is owed in negligence actions. It requires foresight to consider all persons who could potentially be construed as part of the special relationship and all actions required to prevent harm to these persons. Without coupling this duty with a secondary aspect, the duty alone is therefore potentially exposed to similar issues as a purely negligence-based approach, such as what happens if the AI system interacts with a person outside the scope of the spe-

58 Chesterman, *We, The Robots? Regulating Artificial Intelligence and the Limits of the Law* (n 46) 100–101, 244.
59 Chesterman, *We, The Robots? Regulating Artificial Intelligence and the Limits of the Law* (n 46) 101–109.
60 Chesterman, *We, The Robots? Regulating Artificial Intelligence and the Limits of the Law* (n 46) 101–103.
61 Chesterman, *We, The Robots? Regulating Artificial Intelligence and the Limits of the Law* (n 46) 101–103.
62 Chesterman, *We, The Robots? Regulating Artificial Intelligence and the Limits of the Law* (n 46) 103.
63 Chesterman, *We, The Robots? Regulating Artificial Intelligence and the Limits of the Law* (n 46) 103.
64 Chesterman, *We, The Robots? Regulating Artificial Intelligence and the Limits of the Law* (n 46) 101–103.

cial relationship or if the AI system acts in an unforeseeable way in light of its potential ability to evolve and adapt as it collects more data.

As such, a duty seeks to pre-emptively address behaviour or manage behaviour with the aim of reducing overall harm, while a non-delegable duty by itself could also be construed as a regulatory measure, not just solely a liability principle. Indeed, Chesterman acknowledges such a view when considering that tort law is regarded as entailing a regulatory aspect.[65] If we consider that a regulatory response in this context means measures to prevent harm occurring in the first instance rather than a regulatory policy (a topic I consider in Chapter 9 insofar as it relates to liability measures), this adds another layer of utility to Chesterman's account. It is the latter part of Chesterman's proposal – the contractual arrangement for apportioning liability (while admittedly brief) – that I consider necessitates further reflection. In a sense, by linking a contractual arrangement to a non-delegable duty, it is as if the duty itself is insufficient to adequately apportion responsibility between actors and therefore appropriately address issues of liability. Overcoming these challenges, in addition to the scoping issues I addressed above, largely turns on the specific terms of a contract used to address these points. This raises an interesting policy issue: should such auxiliary aspects of liability be managed by contract only? Or should there instead be a more robust framework that accommodates these aspects in a uniform, yet flexible, approach?

There is merit in Chesterman's view, especially when one considers how confining only the auxiliary aspects of liability to contract allows persons to tailor their relationships to suit their needs. The concern I have, however, is that if we confine liability to a creature of tort alone – the non-delegable duty – and then use contract to supplement this arrangement, this facilitates the possibility of a gap in liability. The parties may elect to exclude or fail to contract in relation to key aspects of liability, to the extent they are permitted (noting that jurisdictions often have provisions preventing contractual parties from opting out of some tortious principles, such as personal injury liability). When this is combined with the complexities of AI, it could give rise to further uncertainty. Additionally, such an approach would necessitate that if a harm has occurred to a third party, then they would need to sue both parties to the contract if they were to blame each other, which is not entirely practical.[66] Chesterman does suggest that one way around these uncertainties is to rely upon insurance to supplement a general principles approach.[67] There is another concern with Chesterman's approach though, which is a recurring concern in the literature:

65 Chesterman, *We, The Robots? Regulating Artificial Intelligence and the Limits of the Law* (n 46) 101–103.

66 This is a view that is, to an extent, shared by Jacob Turner. Additionally, he maintains that the use of contracts holds the possibility of liability distributions being kept secret between the parties. See: Turner (n 43) 109–112.

67 Chesterman, *We, The Robots? Regulating Artificial Intelligence and the Limits of the Law* (n 46) 244.

what if the AI system becomes the primary actor and is not a secondary actor? How do we establish a non-delegable duty in this scenario and define the special relationship? I find Chesterman's approach persuasive; yet, like the other theoretical approaches I consider, it is not suited to *all* situations involving AI. Determining the appropriate response to AI therefore needs to be viewed situationally.

1.3.1.3 Adaptations to Existing Obligation Laws

Baris Soyer and Andrew Tettenborn offer a relatively conservative approach to the legal response to AI. They consider that any legal response to AI should be managed through existing obligation laws with amendments required only in instances where these laws cannot adequately accommodate AI.[68] It is for this reason that I have suggested they should be viewed in relation to the general-principles grouping. Yet, they propose supplementing this general-principles approach by imposing standards of liability, potentially also lending them to the imposed-liability grouping. They favour imposing a strict liability standard for personal injury or death caused by AI and a fault-based standard for reputational damages caused by AI. [69] In this respect, their view gives rise to an interesting point of tension. For they advocate in favour of current general principles while also acknowledging the need for imposing standards of liability. This gives rise to interesting questions about the functional scope of existing general principles governing the deployment of AI. I explore the appropriate standards of liability for AI in depth in Chapter 8.

1.3.1.4 Amendments to Existing Burdens of Proof

In September 2022, the European Union proposed a directive for adapting non-contractual liability rules to artificial intelligence ('EU AI Liability Directive').[70] The EU AI liability directive, however, specifically seeks to propose a liability response to the deployment of AI. One very important observation raised is that without a specific AI response, there is the potential for an extemporaneous response to liability issues involving AI, which could give rise to inconsistencies and, therefore, injustices.[71] The EU AI Liability Directive proposes a two-stage response to managing liability issues related to AI. Stage

68 Baris Soyer and Andrew Tettenborn, 'Artificial Intelligence and Civil Liability—Do We Need a New Regime?' (2022) 30(4) *International Journal of Law and Information Technology* 385, 397.

69 Baris Soyer and Andrew Tettenborn, 'Artificial Intelligence and Civil Liability—Do We Need a New Regime?' (2022) 30(4) *International Journal of Law and Information Technology* 385, 397.

70 'EU AI Liability Directive' (n 6).

71 European Union, *Proposal for a Directive on Adapting Non-Contractual Civil Liability Rules to Artificial Intelligence* (28 September 2022) <https://eur-lex.europa.eu/legal-content/

1 consists of amending existing legal liability mechanisms to respond to AI.[72] For example, the EU AI Liability Directive requires that Member States are empowered to order disclosure of evidence, at a claimant's request from providers or users of high-risk AI systems (as defined in the EU AI Act) where they are suspected of causing damage (or harm) to the claimant and have refused disclosure of evidence.[73] In such circumstances, the claimant must first prove the plausibility of being able to claim damages, thereby necessitating the order for evidence.[74] If a defendant, a provider or user of a high-risk AI system suspected of causing harm, fails to comply with an order to disclose evidence, then a rebuttable presumption is established that the defendant has not complied with a relevant duty of care.[75] The significance of these proposed requirements under the EU AI Liability Directive is that it would shift the burden of proof away from a claimant to a defendant, reducing the difficulty for a claimant to establish harm arising from a high-risk AI system. This is furthered through the proposed rebuttable presumption establishing a causal link between a damage (harm) suffered by a claimant and an AI system when specific conditions are met.[76] I explore the topic of causation extensively in Chapter 6. For now, what is interesting about this approach is that it seeks to amend existing laws to accommodate a liability response to AI. Additionally, it is worth noting that these amendments are proposed in negligence-based principles. It is for these reasons that stage 1 fits within the general-principles grouping, for it seeks to rely upon existing legal responses but acknowledges they require amendment. A discussion of stage 2 follows in Section 1.3.3.3.

EN/TXT/PDF/?uri=CELEX:52022PC0496> Explanatory Memorandum 2, 7 ('EU AI Liability Directive Explanatory Memorandum').

72 European Union, Proposal for a Directive on Adapting Non-Contractual Civil Liability Rules to Artificial Intelligence (28 September 2022) <https://eur-lex.europa.eu/legal-content/EN/TXT/PDF/?uri=CELEX:52022PC0496> Explanatory Memorandum ('EU AI Liability Directive Explanatory Memorandum') 6–7.

73 'EU AI Liability Directive' (n 6) art 3(1).

74 'EU AI Liability Directive' (n 6) art 3(1).

75 'EU AI Liability Directive' (n 6) art 3(5).

76 'EU AI Liability Directive' (n 6) art 4; it is worth noting that the proposed EU AI Liability Directive fames this causal link as between a fault and an AI output. It has been suggested a new presumption should be added to Article 4 establishing a causal link in instances where there has been non-compliance with the EU AI Act Articles 14 and 26(2) and an output of an AI system resulting in harm. See: Philipp Hacker, *Proposal for a Directive on Adapting Non-Contractual Civil Liability Rules to Artificial Intelligence: Complementary Impact Assessment* (Study, September 2024) 17 <https://www.europarl.europa.eu/RegData/etudes/STUD/2024/762861/EPRS_STU(2024)762861_EN.pdf>.

1.3.2 Proposed Solutions: Shared Liability

The next groupings of possible solutions seek to share liability between actors rather than necessarily manage the legal response to AI through purely general principles.

1.3.2.1 Association Risk and Enterprise Liability

Anna Beckers and Gunther Teubner seek to offer a liability framework that is inherently linked to the concept of social and legal institutions and evaluated through the level of perceived risk. To Beckers and Teubner, there are three scenarios in which AI poses a substantial legal risk. These risks give rise to increased gaps in legal liability and responsibility if not adequately addressed.[77] In considering multiple scenarios involving AI, their view is therefore somewhat flexible and adaptable to the varied nature of AI, which is in line with my own proposed response.[78] Beckers and Teubner's second identified risk, which I consider first out of their three risks, is what they deem 'association risk'. This type of risk arises in instances where an AI system is so interconnected in its cooperation with a human that it is difficult to discern which party – the AI system or the human – is liable for the outcomes arising from this relationship.[79] They consider that it is difficult in such situations to hold either the AI or natural person liable for the actions in which they cooperatively engage.[80] For this reason, they propose a joint form of liability in this category, viz. 'enterprise liability'.[81]

Similar to their proposal in relation to vicarious liability (considered in Section 1.3.3.1), Beckers and Teubner outline a set of requirements that must be met in order to necessitate the response of enterprise liability. They consider that this response is appropriate in instances where there exists such a degree of cooperation between humans and machines that their actions are intertwined and, consequently, neither AI nor humans can easily be liable for a wrongful decision or outcome.[82] They also incorporate a causation requirement. More specifically, for enterprise liability to be required, the causal links between individual actors and a harm incurred need to be damaged, or they must be unable to be established.[83] Causality between the intertwined decisions of the natural person and that of an AI system, referred to as a *collective decision*, can be established and linked to the arising damage.[84] Combined, to

77 Anna Beckers and Gunther Teubner, *Three Liability Regimes for Artificial Intelligence: Algorithmic Actants, Hybrids, Crowds* (Hart Publishing, 2021) 2–5.
78 See Chapter 8 for a detailed overview of my own proposed response.
79 Beckers and Teubner (n 77) 21.
80 Beckers and Teubner (n 77) 21.
81 Beckers and Teubner (n 77) 139.
82 Beckers and Teubner (n 77) 139.
83 Beckers and Teubner (n 77) 139.
84 Beckers and Teubner (n 77) 139.

Beckers and Teubner, these elements give rise to the need to impose enterprise liability.

To Beckers and Teubner, enterprise liability has precise implications. In the above outlined 'collective decision' scenario, they consider that, in such situations, the entity who initiates the intertwined human–AI relationship is primarily liable for the consequences arising from this relationship.[85] Under this account, it is the producers or programmers of AI that ought to be considered primarily liable.[86] At first observation, this may seem akin to product liability principles, where the manufacturer is held to account for the actions of an AI system. However, Beckers and Teubner's system differs from traditional product liability accounts, for they acknowledge that there exists a relationship between the natural person actors and AI and that the effects of this relationship can be difficult to 'detangle' and assign to individual actors. Such an approach marks a distinction from product liability, which does not seemingly seek to acknowledge that AI is an actor capable of being liable for key actions. The precursor to the enterprise liability proposed by Beckers and Teubner, however, does at least, by implication, acknowledge that AI is an actor rather than viewing AI as a 'tool', which is a common assumption of product liability.

Beckers and Teubner do not confine liability to actors responsible for instigating a relationship between natural persons and AI. Rather, their notion of enterprise liability extends to encapsulate other actors contributing to the intertwined relationship between a natural person and AI, leading to harm. Central to their view is the notion that instigators of a relationship leading to a *collective decision* can in turn pursue other actors in their network who contributed to the relationship.[87] To Beckers and Teubner, liability can be based on a *network share* where this secondary concept is influenced by the degree of economic benefit and control associated with the intertwined relationship.[88] It seems that they suggest enterprise liability consists of a network apportionment of legal responsibility.

From a practical approach, I find myself contemplating an alternative perspective. Rather than a network of responsibility, I consider instead that enterprise liability, as proposed, rather consists of *layers* of responsibility. If, in apportioning liability, the primary instigator of the relationship leading to a collective decision then needs to seek redress from other actors, this in effect would instigate a chain of litigation, with each plaintiff onwards seeking to apportion liability further. Whilst this does not entirely contradict or undermine the network principle, it is perhaps more indicative of how the network would be called upon practically to apportion liability. There is the additional concern with viewing AI in this context primarily through the lens

85 Beckers and Teubner (n 77) 139.
86 Beckers and Teubner (n 77) 139.
87 Beckers and Teubner (n 77) 139.
88 Beckers and Teubner (n 77) 139.

of economic benefit, for some forms of AI could be used to achieve non-economic but social benefits, such as AI deployed in a medical context. Granted, there are financial considerations to medical procedures, but there is also a social utility aspect where AI could be deployed for the benefit of society more broadly. Consider, for example, AI systems used to find new strains of antibiotics that are impervious to antibiotic-resistant bacteria. A robust liability response to AI needs to acknowledge that there are non-economic benefits associated with AI.

1.3.2.2 Tiered Product Liability

Frank Pasquale's approach acknowledges that there are layers of actors involved in the use of AI. He considers that when a manufacturer develops an AI device, they are potentially liable for harm imposed by the system.[89] Pasquale acknowledges, however, that users of AI can materially influence its outputs, thereby potentially influencing the degree and shape of harm suffered.[90] He considers a solution to this scenario is simply to discourage the development of AI in instances where its liable effects cannot be assigned to a person.[91] This solution presupposes that to determine accountability for AI, the effects of an AI system are foreseeable. Some effects, however, are not always foreseeable. Consider, for example, the public release of ChatGPT in 2022. This large-language model (LLM) generative from of AI was designed to produce material in written form only, such as draft documents or emails. One of the emerging uses of ChatGPT, however, is that people are utilising the technology to seek mental health advice as they would from a professional advisor.[92] This is an unforeseen use of this generative form of AI. Here is a form of AI whose liable outputs could be assigned to a legal person – ChatGPT's developer, OpenAI – but the scenario posed results in an interesting question: should the AI system's developer be held liable if the system is being used for unforeseen or unintended uses?

Pasquale proposes one view in response to such a question. He considers that the developer ought not necessarily always be held liable – or solely liable – in these situations.[93] He contends that the user of the system ought

89 Frank Pasquale, 'Data-Informed Duties in AI Development' (2019) 119 *Colombia Law Review* 1917, 1937–1939.

90 Frank Pasquale, 'Data-Informed Duties in AI Development' (2019) 119 *Colombia Law Review* 1917, 1937–1939.

91 Frank Pasquale, 'Data-Informed Duties in AI Development' (2019) 119 *Colombia Law Review* 1917, 1937–1939.

92 Lance B Eliot, 'People Are Eagerly Consulting Generative AI ChatGPT For Mental Health Advice, Stressing Out AI Ethics And AI Law', *Forbes* (online, 1 January 2023) <https://www.forbes.com/sites/lanceeliot/2023/01/01/people-are-eagerly-consulting-generative-ai-chatgpt-for-mental-health-advice-stressing-out-ai-ethics-and-ai-law/?sh=4e82769e2643>.

93 Pasquale (n 89) 1937–1939.

to be subject to what he deems a 'duty of competence', a secondary duty that requires the user of the system to be aware of the legal implications of its use.[94] Holding manufacturers liable is essentially a form of product liability. Introducing this secondary duty upon users of an AI system therefore initiates a *two-tiered* product liability framework. This is an interesting notion, as it acknowledges the limitations of a product liability approach specifically in relation to forms of AI that could evolve and adapt in ways unforeseen to the manufacturer. In some respects, this tiered approach is consistent with my own view about layers of responsibility considered in Chapter 7. Pasquale's approach seemingly acknowledges that users of an AI system can influence the end output despite not being involved in the systems manufacturing phase, which is a key strength of the account. Yet, at its core, it is still an iteration of product liability and is therefore subject to the key criticism of a product liability approach explored earlier: it fails to acknowledge that an AI system itself, depending on the type of AI, could potentially evolve and adapt, thereby influencing its own impacts in ways unforeseen or uninfluenced by natural person actors. Pasquale's account is interesting and holds value in instances when product liability is the most appropriate liability framework for a given type of AI.

1.3.3 Proposed Solutions: Imposed Liability

A third option exists in dealing with the legal implications from AI: imposed liability. This group of responses seeks to resolve the legal uncertainty created by AI through imposing liability on parties.

1.3.3.1 Autonomy Risk and Vicarious Liability

The first of the key legal risks Beckers and Teubner consider, which I address second, is what they deem the 'autonomy risk', which arises when AI systems are capable of independent decisions.[95] In response to this legal risk, Beckers and Teubner propose to resolve the uncertainty created through utilising a shared form of liability: vicarious liability.[96] More specifically, they outline key circumstances that, when collectively met, warrant the response of vicarious liability.[97] They consider that vicarious liability arises in instances where a natural person delegates a task to an algorithm that has sufficient capacity to independently form a decision and subsequently does so in a manner that lacks foreseeability or explainability.[98] Additionally, they hold that this deci-

94 Pasquale (n 89) 1939.
95 Beckers and Teubner (n 77) 21.
96 Beckers and Teubner (n 77) 139.
97 Beckers and Teubner (n 77) 139.
98 Beckers and Teubner (n 77) 139.

sion amounts to a breach of a tortious or contractual duty and that causation can be sufficiently established.[99] In such circumstances, they deem that the natural person acting in the role of principal is vicariously liable via established tortious or contractual principles.[100] They favour vicarious liability, for this class of risk, in their view, seeks to address the decision risks of actors rather than necessarily the end outcome of legal objects.[101]

Importantly, Beckers and Teubner consider that socio-legal institutions respond to this situation by engaging with such machines as 'actants' rather than actors in their own right with fully fledged capacity.[102] These actants fall into a principal–agent relationship, with the actant situated as the agent; further, such actants lack a degree of certainty surrounding their actions, giving rise to uncertainty and a lack of predictability.[103] In some respects, this raises a similar issue to what I consider in Chapter 2 with regard to AI's potential characterisation as a legal agent. A key point of differentiation, however, is that Beckers and Teubner's argument directly correlates to the three socio-legal institutions they propose (viz. digital assistance, human–machine association and interconnectivity), which they then link to their individual liability responses.[104] In this respect, their approach is grounded in socio-legal institutions rather than focused on a situational approach between actors. Beckers, Teubner and I are aligned insofar as we do not think typecasting AI into one option is a feasible approach to managing a liability response. Instead, some degree of flexibility is required to fully accommodate the varying types of modern AI considered in the *Introduction* in Section 0.2.1. My own approach differs from Beckers and Teubner's, however, in that it is not inherently linked to institutions but, rather, is grounded in a situational approach as I explore further in Part III.

1.3.3.2 Digital Peculium

Drawing upon concepts from Roman law, Ugo Pagallo poses a novel legal approach for AI systems. He proposed adapting the Roman concept of *peculium* to the digital sphere. Pagallo highlights that historically a *peculium* was a limited quantity of assets (typically in the form of money or other property) bestowed upon a slave for the purpose of assuring transactions conducted on behalf of their master.[105] In such instances the *peculium* remained the property of the slave's master but enabled the slave to act on behalf of their master with

99 Beckers and Teubner (n 77) 139.
100 Beckers and Teubner (n 77) 139.
101 Beckers and Teubner (n 77) 84.
102 Beckers and Teubner (n 77) 21.
103 Beckers and Teubner (n 77) 21.
104 Beckers and Teubner (n 77) 139.
105 Ugo Pagallo, *The Laws of Robots: Crimes, Contracts and Torts* (Springer, 2013) 104.

a limited degree of liability.[106] Pagallo adapts this concept as a mechanism for responding to a deployed AI system (specifically, he narrows his focus to robots).[107] He considers that in contractual situations the liabilities of manufacturers, operators and users of robots should be confined to that which has been guaranteed through a *digital peculium*.[108] In this respect a robot could be held liable for any breach of contract and the liability of the human parties would be limited. [109] The *digital peculium* is a unique creature in that it seeks to limit liability in a manner akin to corporate legal personality, but the structure arises in agency-based relationships.

To accommodate instances beyond mere contractual liabilities, Pagallo considers that the *digital peculium* should be accompanied by a requirement of insurance in instances where a tortious wrong may arise.[110] He offers that in instances of a tortious wrongdoing, the *digital peculium* to hold strict liability is the subsequent necessary standard of liability which should be imposed.[111] The *digital peculium* is therefore a novel account of liability for AI as it accommodates viewing robots, at least, as a legal agent of another legal person. It also accommodates the notion that legal persons in the position of the 'master' ought not *always* be held liable for the actions of an AI and that at times it may even be preferable for an AI system itself to be held to account. At its core though, the approach is centred on the notion of an AI system being characterised as a legal agent which as I explore in Part II; this should not *always* be the case.

1.3.3.3 Harmonised Strict Liability

Earlier, under the general-principles grouping, I considered the proposed EU AI Liability Directive stage 1, which seeks to work with, but amend slightly, general tortious liability principles. The second stage of the proposed EU AI Liability Directive, to be actioned at a date to be specified, requires a review of whether strict liability principles should be imposed on AI systems that are deemed high risk.[112] It is worth noting that it was proposed in September 2024, in a complementary impact assessment, that the proposed EU AI Liability Directive should be amended to incorporate strict liability principles for banned forms of AI from the outset of the Directive rather than waiting for the fault-based or tortious liability approach to be reviewed after stage 1.[113]

106 Ugo Pagallo, *The Laws of Robots: Crimes, Contracts and Torts* (Springer, 2013) 104.
107 Ugo Pagallo, *The Laws of Robots: Crimes, Contracts and Torts* (Springer, 2013) 105–106.
108 Ugo Pagallo, *The Laws of Robots: Crimes, Contracts and Torts* (Springer, 2013) 105.
109 Ugo Pagallo, *The Laws of Robots: Crimes, Contracts and Torts* (Springer, 2013) 105.
110 Ugo Pagallo, *The Laws of Robots: Crimes, Contracts and Torts* (Springer, 2013) 133.
111 Ugo Pagallo, *The Laws of Robots: Crimes, Contracts and Torts* (Springer, 2013) 133.
112 'EU AI Liability Directive (n 6) art 5.
113 See: Philipp Hacker, *Proposal for a Directive on Adapting Non-Contractual Civil Liability Rules to Artificial Intelligence: Complementary Impact Assessment* (Study, September 2024)

Further, the complementary impact assessment also recommended amending the proposed Directive to impose joint liability for sharing the burden of responsibility for harms along an AI value chain.[114] Stage 2, together with the suggested amendments to the proposed EU AI Liability Directive, suggests that a general-principles approach grounded in tort law alone may not be sufficient to address liability; additional responses may be required. The necessity of multiple liability standards is explored in Chapter 8. It is worth noting that stage 2 of the EU AI Liability Directive also potentially infiltrates the next grouping, for there is some consideration that the imposition of a strict liability standard could also be accompanied by mandated insurance.[115] Mandated insurance is the next possible grouping, but it is worth acknowledging that stage 2 could potentially blur into this group.

1.3.4 Proposed Solutions: Insurance-Mandated Liability

The last groupings of responses are what I deem insurance-mandated responses. This group seeks to reduce the legal uncertainty associated with AI through requiring insurance in certain contexts.

1.3.4.1 Legal Personhood with Insurance

Jacob Turner views legal personality as central to resolving legal responsibility for AI. Turner considers that there are two key reasons for recognising AI systems as capable of baring legal rights viz. moral and pragmatic reasons.[116] To Turner, these reasons are potentially opposed to each other; this opposition is resolved through ascribing AI with legal personality.[117] He considers that legal personality could function as a 'firewall' between an AI system and current legal persons, potentially minimising harm suffered by the persons behind the AI system (owners, designers, etc.).[118] In this respect, his approach is arguably somewhat analogous to corporate legal personality. Indeed, Turner even considers the merits of corporate legal personality for AI and argues that such a firewall (perhaps akin to a corporate veil[119]) is even more imperative in

i–iv, 33 <https://www.europarl.europa.eu/RegData/etudes/STUD/2024/762861/EPRS_STU(2024)762861_EN.pdf>.

114 See: Philipp Hacker, *Proposal for a Directive on Adapting Non-Contractual Civil Liability Rules to Artificial Intelligence: Complementary Impact Assessment* (Study, September 2024) iv, 34–35.

115 See: Philipp Hacker, Proposal for a Directive on Adapting Non-Contractual Civil Liability Rules to Artificial Intelligence: Complementary Impact Assessment (Study, September 2024) iv, 34–35, art 5(2); 'EU AI Liability Directive Explanatory Memorandum' (n 71) 6.

116 Turner (n 54) 184–186.

117 Turner (n 54) 186.

118 Turner (n 54) 187.

119 The concept of a corporate veil is a legal fiction common to corporate law, originally derived from *Solomon v Solomon & Co Ltd* [1897] AC 22 ('*Solomon v Solomon & Co Ltd*'). Broadly,

the context of AI than for corporations, as AI can act independently of human actors, unlike corporations.[120] He draws upon the established view that where an actor can determine its own approach, it ought to be held accountable for the independent actions it takes in relation to its own end.[121] In this respect, Turner accepts that AI ought to be viewed as a legal person but also, and perhaps more importantly, that AI ought to be held to account for its own actions.

Turner proposes a legal personhood model for AI like corporate legal personality. Sophisticated legal personality akin to a corporation is not always needed to assign liability; nor is it necessarily the best vehicle for achieving this goal in *all* circumstances. Whilst it is true that some more complex forms of AI, like deep learning AI, hold the potential to act independently, it is not reasonable to assume that *all forms* of AI act with a degree of independence. There are also relatively more simplistic forms of AI reliant on input from natural persons, such as 'human-in-the-loop' or supervised forms of modern AI (see the *Introduction* Section 0.2.1). Such forms of AI, in which a natural person can exhibit a greater degree of control over their function, decrease the need for a sophisticated form of legal personhood. In Chapter 5, I consider that these more simplistic forms of AI ought to be viewed in relation to complex AI but ranked at a lower level in my proposed hierarchical account of legal personhood. In instances where an AI system is relatively simple and easier for a natural person to exert control over, legal personality with a sophisticated structure is potentially unnecessary. Legal personality with a relatively more complex structure, such as a veil or 'firewall' between the legal person and the natural persons sitting behind it, may not be required in instances where there is greater human control over an AI system. It is for this reason that, although Turner's approach holds great utility for complicated forms of AI, his view could be expanded to accommodate more 'simplistic', more readily controlled forms of AI.

There is the additional question of how remedies for harm inflicted by an AI system ought to be financially compensated. I address this question broadly in Chapters 7 and 8. Here, however, I briefly evaluate Turner's consideration concerning this issue. As Turner's solution to liability is predicated on AI holding legal personality akin to corporate legal personality, he considers that it is imperative that AI ought to have the ability to hold funds in order to make payment for any imposed legal remedies, such as damages.[122] To this

---

the case gave rise to the concept that a company is a legal person separate from the persons behind the company, such as director, separated by a corporate veil. The company as a separate legal person is primarily responsible for any liabilities it incurs, save for in egregious circumstances when the corporate veil is 'pierced' so that the individuals behind the company, for example directors, may be held to account.

120 Turner (n 54) 187.

121 Turner (n 54) 187–188.

122 Turner (n 54) 193–194.

end, he proposes the use of insurance as a means to ensure such entities have funds to draw upon to offset any imposed remedies.[123] Yet, as Turner acknowledges, this would allow an insurer to set the boundaries of their liability.[124] He highlights that insurers may seek to exclude liability for conduct by an AI system outside of a set of parameters acceptable to the insurer.[125] This raises an interesting policy consideration: should the parameters of liability largely be defined by one sector and its business objectives? The concern with this approach is that insurers may not seek to cover scenarios involving AI that are perceived by them as posing too much financial risk arising from the potential of harm.[126] One possible solution would be to regulate so that insurers must cover AI systems in instances outside what they would otherwise be willing to insure. The role of regulations and insurance as it relates to a liability response is a topic I consider in Chapter 9. I merely pause and acknowledge how liability and regulatory responses to AI potentially work together.

1.3.4.2 Interconnectivity Risk and Collective Funds Liability

Beckers and Teubner's third risk identifies what they deem an 'interconnectivity risk'. Such a risk arises in instances where algorithms are so interconnected with other algorithms that they create a new entity with 'collective properties'.[127] They consider that the interconnected nature of these algorithms results in an opacity of actors, thereby reducing the ability to readily separate out such individual actors for the purpose of assigning liability, giving rise to a collective social responsibility.[128] This raises an interesting observation: the more interaction between advanced technologies, the harder it is to discern individual actors. I am broadly in agreement with this preliminary view. I note, however, as a technical aspect, that Beckers and Teubner have framed this argument in relation to algorithms and not expressly AI. As I acknowledged in the *Introduction* Section 0.2.1, algorithms by themselves are distinct from AI. For Beckers and Teubner's argument to hold in relation to AI, I am considering then that they are referring to the layers of algorithms that, when amalgamated, can form more complex types of AI. Based on this reasoning, I will be considering Beckers and Teubner's interconnectivity risk as applying to complicated forms of AI, or when AI systems work in concert with other AI systems.

In instances where risk is interconnected, Beckers and Teubner consider that liability should be resolved through what they term 'fund liability'.[129] They

123 Turner (n 54) 115–117, 193–194.
124 Turner (n 54) 116–117.
125 Turner (n 54) 117.
126 Turner (n 54) 117.
127 Beckers and Teubner (n 77) 21.
128 Beckers and Teubner (n 77) 21.
129 Beckers and Teubner (n 77) 139.

consider that fund liability ought to be the avenue of redress in instances where vicarious liability or enterprise liability cannot be successfully established.[130] A prerequisite to this form of liability is the existence of a compensation fund that persons seeking legal redress can draw upon.[131] Central to their view is that such a fund would be administered by a regulatory body or agency based in the relevant industry responsive to a claim.[132] This agency would determine (a) which actors ought to finance the fund based on their market share and (b) who would be liable for an incident involving AI.[133] As a guiding principle, they consider that for liability to be triggered under this approach, there must be a violation of a tortious or contractual duty by an interconnected form of AI resulting in damage.[134] Therefore, this approach arguably seeks to account for all instances not covered by Beckers and Teubner's notions of autonomy or association risk.

This third option of liability, fund liability, is greatly intertwined with regulatory principles. This approach seeks to establish a regulatory body unique to each sector. I do not proceed to examine the merits of Beckers and Teubner's regulatory proposals at this juncture for I consider relevant regulatory issues in Chapter 9. I am not opposed to utilising a fund mechanism in some circumstances to account for liability, and I elaborate further in this regard in Chapters 7 and 8. What concerns me at this juncture is that a fund mechanism must always be the accepted response to complex forms of AI, for as I consider in Chapter 8, an AI system may have complex functionality, but it may not necessarily be acting in a complex manner necessitating such a response.

1.3.4.3 Liability Complemented by Insurance Schemes

Lyria Moses looks at liability responses and their relationship with insurance regimes. Broadly, she considers the merits of proportionate liability, strict liability, product liability and non-fault-based liability each in turn before examining the role of insurance.[135] She regards proportionate liability as a valid mechanism for distributing liability between actors in instances where multiple parties have contributed to a loss suffered.[136] She considers, though, that a key limitation of this response is that apportioning liability sufficiently between parties can only be achieved through firstly litigating a liability dispute and secondly through ensuring that all potential contributors to a harm suffered are

130 Beckers and Teubner (n 77) 139.
131 Beckers and Teubner (n 77) 139.
132 Beckers and Teubner (n 77) 139.
133 Beckers and Teubner (n 77) 139–140.
134 Beckers and Teubner (n 77) 139.
135 Lyria Moses, 'Liability and Insurance' in Michael Guihot and Lyria Bennett Moses (eds), *Artificial Intelligence, Robots and the Law* (LexisNexis, 2020) 229, 229–253.
136 Lyria Moses, 'Liability and Insurance' in Michael Guihot and Lyria Bennett Moses (eds), *Artificial Intelligence, Robots and the Law* (LexisNexis, 2020) 239.

parties to the litigation.[137] There are financial and time constraints associated with this mechanism for apportioning liability, which could make it prohibitively expensive, both financially and in terms of delayed access to justice for the aggrieved parties.

In relation to strict and product liability, Moses' views are broadly like those already considered in this section, these key arguments being that strict liability is costly to manufacturers and does not adequately apportion liability between liability contributors and that product liability fails to consider that AI could evolve in ways not reasonably foreseeable to the manufacturer.[138] In perhaps a less common approach for the context of AI, Moses also evaluates a no-fault liability regime.[139] She draws upon examples of no-fault liability schemes in the context of traffic accidents, considering that such an approach could provide compensation to parties without imposing the rigours of proving fault on aggrieved parties.[140] However, she notes that this response is not without a cost – for who bears the cost of establishing and maintaining the fund utilised for compensation payments.[141]

This is a similar approach to Beckers and Teubner's fund liability, but, in contrast, Moses does not tie a no-fault approach to a particular risk base induced by an AI system of a given level of complexity. Additionally, she does not provide consideration regarding the intricacies of who should manage the fund and from where its resources should be garnered. To Moses, the role of insurance serves as a counterpoint to each of these liability responses. Moses considers that each of the above only partially responds to liability.[142] Further, she posits that insurance evolves in tandem with liability approaches for the ultimate purpose of redistributing liability losses between parties involved in generating the caused harm.[143] I consider what ought to be the role of insurance further in Chapters 7 and 8.

137 Lyria Moses, 'Liability and Insurance' in Michael Guihot and Lyria Bennett Moses (eds), *Artificial Intelligence, Robots and the Law* (LexisNexis, 2020) 239.
138 Lyria Moses, 'Liability and Insurance' in Michael Guihot and Lyria Bennett Moses (eds), *Artificial Intelligence, Robots and the Law* (LexisNexis, 2020) 240, 243–244.
139 Lyria Moses, 'Liability and Insurance' in Michael Guihot and Lyria Bennett Moses (eds), *Artificial Intelligence, Robots and the Law* (LexisNexis, 2020) 244–245.
140 Lyria Moses, 'Liability and Insurance' in Michael Guihot and Lyria Bennett Moses (eds), *Artificial Intelligence, Robots and the Law* (LexisNexis, 2020) 244–245.
141 Lyria Moses, 'Liability and Insurance' in Michael Guihot and Lyria Bennett Moses (eds), *Artificial Intelligence, Robots and the Law* (LexisNexis, 2020) 245.
142 Lyria Moses, 'Liability and Insurance' in Michael Guihot and Lyria Bennett Moses (eds), *Artificial Intelligence, Robots and the Law* (LexisNexis, 2020) 253.
143 Lyria Moses, 'Liability and Insurance' in Michael Guihot and Lyria Bennett Moses (eds), *Artificial Intelligence, Robots and the Law* (LexisNexis, 2020) 253.

1.3.5 Key Observations Relevant to Liability from Proposed Legal Responses

The above discussion emphasises that theoretical approaches to how AI ought to be managed legally could broadly be grouped into four approaches. The four groupings I have suggested acknowledge the similarities in liability responses between the approaches within the groupings. This reveals that there is a trend among such views to often strive towards, or favour, one liability response to AI. Yet, as I considered in the *Introduction* there are varying types of modern AI, and these systems have differing degrees of independent capacity. Some liability responses may be better suited than others to particular types of modern AI. There exists a need, therefore, to view AI situationally and consider how it is being deployed in trying to decide which approach is best suited to AI.

1.4 The Need for an Overarching Liability Framework

The focus of this chapter has been to understand the emerging legal landscape as it relates to AI with a particular emphasis on private law governance. Understanding this landscape is integral to offering an informed private law liability response to AI. This chapter has therefore sought to evaluate emerging regulatory responses relevant to common law jurisdictions. It has also sought to categorise theoretical approaches to AI liability.

In response to the analysis in this chapter, what emerges is that both regulatory measures and theoretical approaches to managing modern forms of AI that are relevant to common law jurisdictions do not yet adequately accommodate the private law liability implications of a deployed AI. Of the emerging regulatory measures in response to AI that do not fully accommodate private law liabilities, principles-based approaches to regulation are less accommodating than emerging formalistic approaches. There is a need for a robust private law liability response to AI to complement emerging regulatory measures, for regulation alone is insufficient at responding to the legal implications arising from a deployed AI.

Among the theoretical approaches having regard to deployed AI systems there is often an underlying assumption that there must be but one liability response applicable to AI. This is not congruent with the varied nature of modern forms of AI considered in the *Introduction*. One liability response alone is insufficient for accommodating the varied permutations of modern AI and the varied contexts in which these systems can be deployed. There are varying degrees of complexity of AI, with some forms capable of a greater degree of autonomy than others. This is important when conceiving of a liability response, as the varying degrees of AI capacity are likely to yield varying outcomes associated with AI. What is subsequently discernible is that there exists a need not only for a private law liability response to complement the regulatory efforts but also for a liability framework that is flexible to accommodate the varying permutations of AI-related outcomes.

In Part III, I turn to propose one such liability framework: the *Tri-Phase AI Liability Model.* The observations in this chapter inform the discussion of foundational issues in Parts II and III that are then drawn upon in offering the proposed liability model. In turn, the model becomes an overarching framework that provides a theory for unifying the different approaches to AI considered in this chapter. Before this can be offered, there are additional threshold issues that must be considered. Part II next begins by exploring one such issue: the legal characterisation of AI.

References

A Articles/Books/Reports

Abbott, Ryan, *The Reasonable Robot: Artificial Intelligence and the Law* (Cambridge University Press, 2020).

Beckers, Anna and Gunther Teubner, *Three Liability Regimes for Artificial Intelligence: Algorithmic Actants, Hybrids, Crowds* (Hart Publishing, 2021).

Chesterman, Simon, *We, The Robots? Regulating Artificial Intelligence and the Limits of the Law* (Cambridge Univertiy Press, 2021).

Moses, Lyria, 'Liability and Insurance' in Michael Guihot and Lyria Bennett Moses (eds), *Artificial Intelligence, Robots and the Law* (LexisNexis, 2020) 229.

Pagallo, Ugo, *The Laws of Robots: Crimes, Contracts and Torts* (Springer, 2013).

Pasquale, Frank , 'Data-Informed Duties in AI Development' (2019) 119 *Colombia Law Review* 1917.

Soyer, Baris and Andrew Tettenborn, 'Artificial Intelligence and Civil Liability—Do We Need a New Regime?' (2022) 30(4) *International Journal of Law and Information Technology* 385.

Turner, Jacob, *Robot Rules: Regulating Artificial Intelligence* (Palgrave Macmillan, 2019).

B Cases

Solomon v Solomon & Co Ltd [1897] AC 22

C Other

C-27, An Act to enact the Consumer Privacy Protection Act, the Personal Information and Data Protection Tribunal Act and the Artificial Intelligence and Data Act and to make consequential and related amendments to other Acts, 1st Sess, 44th Parl, 2021 pt 3 (first reading 16 June 2022)

Department for Science, Innovation & Technology, A pro-innovation approach to AI regulation: Government response to consultation (No CP 1019, February 2024)

Eliot, Lance B, 'People Are Eagerly Consulting Generative AI ChatGPT For Mental Health Advice, Stressing Out AI Ethics And AI Law', *Forbes* (online, 1 January 2023) <https://www.forbes.com/sites/lanceeliot/2023/01/01/people-are-eagerly-consulting-generative-ai-chatgpt-for-mental-health-advice-stressing-out-ai-ethics-and-ai-law/?sh=4e82769e2643>

European Parliament, European Parliament legislative resolution of 12 March 2024 on the proposal for a directive of the European Parliament and of the Council on liability for defective products (COM(2022)0495 – C9-0322/2022 – 2022/0302(COD)), P9_TA(2024)0132, 14 March 2024

European Union, 'Proposal for a Directive on Adapting Non-Contractual Civil Liability Rules to Artificial Intelligence' (28 September 2022) <https://eur-lex.europa.eu/legal-content/EN/TXT/PDF/?uri=CELEX:52022PC0496>

Government of the Republic of Singapore, 'NAIS 2.0 Singapore National AI Strategy: AI for the Public Good: For Singapore and the World' (Report, 4 December 2023) <https://file.go.gov.sg/nais2023.pdf>

Government of the Republic of Singapore, 'Singapore Announces New AI Safety Initiatives at the Global AI Action Summit in France', *Infocomm Media Development Authority* (Web page, 11 February 2025) <https://www.imda.gov.sg/resources/press-releases-factsheets-and-speeches/press-releases/2025/singapore-ai-safety-initiatives-global-ai-summit-france>

Hacker, Philipp, 'Proposal for a Directive on Adapting Non-Contractual Civil Liability Rules to Artificial Intelligence: Complementary Impact Assessment' (Study, September 2024) <https://www.europarl.europa.eu/RegData/etudes/STUD/2024/762861/EPRS_STU(2024)762861_EN.pdf>

Personal Data Protection Commission Singapore, 'Model Artificial Intelligence Governance Framework' (2nd ed, 21 January 2020) <https://www.pdpc.gov.sg/-/media/Files/PDPC/PDF-Files/Resource-for-Organisation/AI/SGModelAIGovFramework2.pdf>

Regulation (EU) 2024/1689 of the European Parliament and of the Council of 13 June 2024 laying down harmonised rules on artificial intelligence and amending Regulations (EC) No 300/2008, (EU) No 167/2013, (EU) No 168/2013, (EU) 2018/858, (EU) 2018/1139 and (EU) 2019/2144 and Directives 2014/90/EU, (EU) 2016/797 and (EU) 2020/1828 (Artificial Intelligence Act) [2024] OJ L 1689/1

Science, Innovation and Technology Committee, Governance of Artificial Intelligence (AI): Government Response (2024–25, HC 591)

White House, 'Initial Rescissions of Harmful Executive Orders and Actions' (Web Page, 20 January 2025) <https://www.whitehouse.gov/presidential-actions/2025/01/initial-rescissions-of-harmful-executive-orders-and-actions/>

White House, 'Removing Barriers to American Leadership in Artificial Intelligence' (Web Page, 23 January 2025) <https://www.whitehouse.gov/presidential-actions/2025/01/removing-barriers-to-american-leadership-in-artificial-intelligence/>

Part II

2 Reevaluating Legal Personality for AI

2.1. AI as a Legal Person?

In determining how to assign liability in the context of modern forms of artificial intelligence ('AI'), Part II addresses what can be viewed as a key threshold issue: how should modern forms of AI be legally characterised? This chapter contributes to addressing this question by examining in depth the possibility of characterising AI as a legal person. The notion of ascribing legal personality to AI challenges the view that AI should always be considered merely a 'tool' or consumer good. Whilst emerging regulatory responses do not treat AI as a legal person, such a characterisation for private law liability purposes is not necessarily incompatible with these responses. As emphasised from the outset, this book focuses on *private law* liability responses to AI, which are distinct from, yet complementary to, regulatory approaches.

Characterising AI as a legal person has been subject to much discussion in AI literature, with recent works advocating for the need to view AI as a legal person either currently or in the future when more advanced forms of AI arise.[1] This approach has further informed debates on policy responses to AI.[2] It also aligns with emerging industry views, such as Microsoft AI CEO Mustafa Suleyman's 2024 TED Talk, in which he posited that we should think of AI as something completely new, proposing we view AI as a 'digital species'.[3] Legal personality offers a way to ascribe rights and obligations to an entity and, depending on the form, to apportion liability among actors connected to the legal person. On this basis, its potential applicability to AI warrants in-depth examination.

1 See: Jacob Turner, *Robot Rules: Regulating Artificial Intelligence* (Palgrave Macmillan, 2019); Simon Chesterman, *We, The Robots? Regulating Artificial Intelligence and the Limits of the Law* (Cambridge Univertiy Press, 2021).

2 For example: *European Parliament Resolution of 16 February 2017 with Recommendations to the Commission on Civil Law Rules on Robotics* (2015/2103(INL) [2018]) OJ C 252/239 ('Resolution Civil Law Rules on Robotics').

3 Mustafa Suleyman, 'What Is an AI Anyway?', *TED* (TED Talk, TED Conferences LLC, April 2024) 0.4.52, 0.12.25 <https://www.youtube.com/watch?v=KKNCiRWd_j0>.

DOI: 10.4324/9781003617549-5

This chapter therefore explores whether modern forms of AI ought to be characterised as a legal person. It examines the parameters of legal personality and their potential application to modern AI. The chapter also considers the socio-legal background to legal personhood status, viz. the notion that legal personhood is but a fiction or a tool that can be used to bestow legal rights and duties on entities within society. As a legal concept and creation of law, it is informed by its socio-legal background and can be used pragmatically to resolve legal uncertainties. In adopting this view, the chapter considers that legal personhood as a concept is malleable and capable of expansion.

This is further underpinned through an analysis of the parameters and components of legal personality revealing that these elements are non-binary capable of existing on a spectrum. Distinct from other legal personality for AI approaches, the chapter proposes ranking these components based on their direct correlation to an actor's autonomy. This is key in that it encourages viewing the components of legal personhood as potentially hierarchical, laying the foundation for a new approach where legal personhood itself is viewed as existing in a hierarchical structure. In relation to AI not only is it possible to characterise AI as a legal person but that there are varying degrees of legal personality. These degrees of legal personality should be viewed hierarchically. The importance of this hierarchical structure to the legal characterisation of modern AI is explored further in Chapter 5 which ultimately influences the analysis in Part III.

2.2. Legal Personhood Approaches to AI

The legal personhood view considers that AI systems, such as modern AI, should be given 'legal personhood' status. This school of thought subscribes to the view that AI systems are viewed as an entity before the law for the purpose of assigning legal rights and duties. To test the parameters of legal personality and assess whether AI could be accommodated under the approach, it is first prudent to examine theories looking at the possible relationship between AI and legal personality.

One perspective arising from the literature is to view legal personality as a theoretical framework. What emerges from this approach is that legal personality is a flexible concept within legal systems.[4] Throughout history certain classes within society (viz. slaves and women) have been included or excluded from the concept of legal personality at various points in history demonstrating the malleability of legal personality as a concept.[5] Other scholars have

4 Robert van den Hoven van Genderen, 'Do We Need New Legal Personhood in the Age of Robots and AI?' in Marcelo Corrales et al. (ed.), *Robotics, AI and the Future of Law* (Springer Nature, 2018) 15, 22.

5 van Genderen (n 4) 15, 26; Samir Chopra and Laurence White, *A Legal Theory for Autonomous Artificial Agents* (University of Michigan Press, 4th ed., 2014) 156–157.

considered the malleable nature of legal personality through offering that it consists of two key subcategories: dependent and independent personality.[6] They argue that some classes in society, for example children, hold dependent legal personality as they must rely on a legal agent exercising rights on their behalf.[7] Independent legal personality is free of the need to rely upon another legal actor to exercise rights.[8] In adapting this concept to AI, it has been suggested that AI systems can be bestowed dependent legal personality and that this option is more pragmatic than ascribing independent legal personality to AI.[9]

An alternative perspective arising from the literature is to view legal personality as a pragmatic tool. A theme arising is that AI is varied in nature and, as such, has the potential to be characterised in different methods (object, subject, thing or person).[10] In response, legal personality is conceived of as a 'tool' that can be used in society to achieve different aims.[11] In this respect, legal personality is viewed as a potential mechanism to resolve legal issues rather than being a concept solely unique to either natural persons or corporations. When viewing legal personality through this pragmatic lens, there is also a debate about how legal personality for AI should be structured.[12] If AI is to be ascribed legal personality, in what form it should be structured is a topic I address in Chapter 5.

Others regarding the practical implications of legal personality for AI have considered its potential adverse effects. It has been suggested that legal personality holds the potential to be used by natural persons to escape accountability if it is modelled in a similar manner to corporate legal personality.[13] Further that of approaches looking at ascribing legal personality to AI, there is a concern that this imposes one type of legal personality in turn overlooking the varying nature of AI.[14] That is, typecasting AI into one form of legal personality does not necessarily accommodate the differing types of AI.

The role of legal personality for AI has also been considered by legislators. In 2017, the EU passed a resolution with recommendations to the Commission on Civil Law Rules on Robotics.[15] Importantly, the resolution proposed

6 Ugo Pagallo, *The Laws of Robots: Crimes, Contracts and Torts* (Springer, 2013) 153–155, 165; Chopra and White (n 5) 159–163.
7 Chopra and White (n 5) 159.
8 Chopra and White (n 5) 162–163.
9 Pagallo (n 6) 165; Chopra and White (n 5) 160–162.
10 Turner (n 1) 132.
11 Turner (n 1) 205.
12 Turner (n 1) 205.
13 Simon Chesterman, 'Artificial Intelligence and the Limits of Legal Personality' (2020) 69 (October) *International and Comparative Law Quarterly* 819, 826; Chesterman, *We, The Robots? Regulating Artificial Intelligence and the Limits of the Law* (n 1) 121.
14 Chesterman, *We, The Robots? Regulating Artificial Intelligence and the Limits of the Law* (n 1) 141.
15 'Resolution Civil Law Rules on Robotics' (n 2).

instituting a form of 'electronic personhood' status for more advanced forms of robots in the longer term.[16] One of the identified goals for this 'electronic personhood' status was to ensure that the robots could be deemed responsible for any damage they caused.[17] This 'electronic personhood' could be deemed to fit within the notion of legal personality. The policy position of the EU evolved away from the concept of electronic personhood, towards a risk-based approach, as it has not been incorporated into the EU's proposed AI Liability Directive (discussed in Chapter 1 in Section 1.3.1.4 and 1.3.3.3).[18] The importance of this resolution, though, is that it demonstrates a propensity to at least consider legal personality as a policy response to managing AI.

Whilst these approaches hold merit, they do not adequately accommodate for the potential proprietary nature of an AI system. Nor do they consider that legal personality could instead be viewed as a tiered model – that is, a tiered model of rights and obligations that, in turn, hold benefits for establishing a framework for assigning liability arising in the context of modern AI. The question remains then as to whether the current legal personhood characterisations of AI systems could be developed further to draw from other legal models to address issues of legal liability.

2.3. Socio-Legal Background of Legal Personhood

To understand legal personhood better as part of testing its potential utility for AI, it is prudent to examine further the socio-legal background of legal personhood. In doing so, I consider the relationship between the concept of legal personality and three distinct groups: marginalised individuals in society, animals and corporations. These three groups have been selected for two reasons. Firstly, unlike other subjects of legal personality, such as rivers in nature,[19] and much like modern AI, these three groups are capable of decision-making and executing actions to some extent. Secondly, these groups are, to some extent, examined in existing literature in relation to legal personality for AI.[20] I commence my analysis with these three distinct groups to directly respond to the

16 'Resolution Civil Law Rules on Robotics' (n 2) at [59, f].

17 'Resolution Civil Law Rules on Robotics' (n 2) at [59, f].

18 For further insights into the EU's risk based approach to AI see: *Regulation (EU) 2024/1689 of the European Parliament and of the Council of 13 June 2024 laying down harmonised rules on artificial intelligence and amending Regulations (EC) No 300/2008, (EU) No 167/2013, (EU) No 168/2013, (EU) 2018/858, (EU) 2018/1139 and (EU) 2019/2144 and Directives 2014/90/EU, (EU) 2016/797 and (EU) 2020/1828 (Artificial Intelligence Act)* [2024] OJ L 1689/1 (the 'EU AI Act'),

19 Kate Evans, 'The New Zealand River that Became a Legal Person', *BBC Travel* (Web Page, 21 March 2020) <https://www.bbc.com/travel/article/20200319-the-new-zealand-river-that-became-a-legal-person>; Sylwia Wojtczak, 'Endowing Artificial Intelligence with Legal Subjectivity' (2020) 37 *AI & Society* 205, 206–207.

20 See, for example: van Genderen (n 4) 15, 21–22; Chesterman, *We, The Robots? Regulating Artificial Intelligence and the Limits of the Law* (n 1) 114–143.

existing literature that seeks to characterise AI as a legal person based on a socio-legal lens. This is an important step to addressing if the socio-legal lens is the best way to conceive of AI as a legal person before turning to assess if AI ought to be characterised as a legal person based on an alternative line of reasoning.

2.3.1 Marginalised Individuals

Historically, four key factions of society, each of which I consider briefly, have had strenuous relationships with the concept of legal personhood.

2.3.1.1 Women

Women historically have struggled to gain legal and political recognition. The recognition of women as legal equals to their male counterparts is ever evolving, with significant obstacles being overcome – in some jurisdictions more than others. Van Genderen and others consider that women have not historically always been granted legal personhood status and have been reduced to the status of merely being the property of their husbands and male relations.[21] The case of Sophia the robot, powered by artificial intelligence, provides an interesting contrast to this position. In 2018, Sophia was the first 'humanoid' to be granted legal citizenship, which was bestowed by Saudi Arabia.[22] Sophia has also been granted other rights and privileges: she was granted an immigration visa by Azerbaijan[23] and has even been granted a credit card in her own name.[24] The rationale for granting Sophia these rights is not entirely clear, save for the presumed novelty factor.

The contrast between Sophia's legal personhood status and the struggle of women historically to gain the same recognition is important for several reasons. Firstly, it illustrates that legal personhood is an abstract concept that can be conferred upon an entity. It also demonstrates that the parameters of legal personhood are dictated by societal norms and expectations.[25] This is apparent

21 Andrew Cowie, 'A History of Married Women's Real Property Rights' (2009) 6 *Australian Journal of Gender Law* 4; van Genderen (n 4) 21.

22 Andrew Griffin, 'Saudi Arabia Grants Citizenship to a Robot for the First Time Ever', *The Independent* (online, 26 October 2017) <https://www.independent.co.uk/life-style/gadgets-and-tech/news/saudi-arabia-robot-sophia-citizenship-android-riyadh-citizen-passport-future-a8021601.html>; van Genderen (n 4) 16.

23 Paul Armstrong, 'AI Humanoid "Sophia" Is Granted First Ever Robot Visa, Speaks With President', *Forbes* (online, 27 October 2018) <https://www.forbes.com/sites/paularmstrongtech/2018/10/27/ai-humanoid-sophia-is-granted-first-ever-robot-visa-speaks-with-president/#45c0158f1f39>.

24 Aurel Dragan, 'UniCredit becomes the First Bank in the World with a Robot Customer', *BR Business Review* (online, 11 May 2018) <https://business-review.eu/news/unicredit-is-the-first-bank-in-the-world-that-has-a-robot-sophia-as-a-customer-169290>.

25 A view shared by Robert van den Hoven van Genderen, see: van Genderen (n 4) 18.

through considering how women have, over time, slowly and incrementally gained rights associated with legal personhood status,[26] versus Sophia's blanket endowment of rights. Lastly, it demonstrates that legal personhood status exists on a spectrum of rights and obligations. It is both an abstract and, importantly, fluid concept that can evolve.

2.3.1.2 Racial Minorities

Like women, persons of non-white ethnicities have struggled historically to obtain legal personhood. The slave trading of centuries past only further undermined the legal status of these persons. When slavery was first found to not be legally sanctioned in England and Wales, judgment was mute as to whether the same principle applied in the British colonies.[27] In the British colonies, and later the United States in its formative years, an interesting line of jurisprudence emerged considering whether or not slaves could be viewed as legal persons, property or a combination of the two.[28] The renowned 1841 case of *Groves v Slaughter*[29] is an illustrative example. The decision upheld a contract for the sale of slaves.[30] In doing so, the Court abhorrently deemed that these individuals were not to be viewed under the law as legal persons but as tradeable property.[31] What these cases illustrate is that legal personhood status is not a rigid concept, as is evidenced by the natural person legal personality now encompassing persons regardless of their ethnicity. The flexibility of legal personality based on slave trading is a view supported in the literature.[32] Legal personality is therefore a concept in which the parameters are malleable and susceptible to evolutionary change.

2.3.1.3 Persons with Intellectual Disabilities

Persons with intellectual disabilities have not historically been denied legal personality like some groups above but have instead been permitted a lesser engagement with the concept. Legal capacity is central to this concept, which, as I explore in detail in Section 2.5, is an inherent part of some conceptions of legal personality. Most jurisdictions inhibit the legal capacity of persons with disabilities, especially those with impaired cognitive abilities or ability to understand legal consequences. Importantly, these factions in society are

26 Cowie (n 21).
27 *Somerset v Stewart* (1772) 98 ER 499 ('*Somerset v Stewart*').
28 Paul Finkelman, 'Slavery in the United States: Persons or Property?' in Jean Allain (ed.), *The Legal Understanding of Slavery: From the Historical to the Contemporary* (Oxford University Press, 2012) 105, 123–124.
29 *Groves v Slaughter* 40 US (15 Pet.) 449 (1841).
30 *Groves v Slaughter* 40 US (15 Pet.) 449 (1841).
31 *Groves v Slaughter* 40 US (15 Pet.) 449 (1841).
32 See: the discussions of the Digital Peculium in Chapter 1 in Section 1.3.3.2.

not excluded from being legal persons in the way that others have been historically. Rather, their ability to function as full legal persons in society by themselves is limited but still capable of being achieved with the aid of a third person acting in the role of legal guardian.[33]

2.3.1.4 Legal Minors

Legal minors are another example where we limit the degree of their legal personality, at least until they reach the age of majority. For example, under certain circumstances, we restrict the ability of minors to enter contracts or consent to medical treatment.[34] Instead, we defer to those acting *in loco parentis* to account for their actions – legally, at least – whilst they are minors.[35] An important distinction can be made here in contrast to persons with intellectual disabilities. Individual minors may have the capacity to act with the full legal capacity of a person in the majority but, for policy reasons, are often prevented from doing so until they reach the majority. Persons with intellectual disabilities, however, lack an underlying capacity and therefore often require ongoing limitations on the extent of their legal personality. Both persons with intellectual disabilities and minors have their legal personality curtailed to some, but differing, extents due to a need to protect these vulnerable members of society and prevent forms of abuse. An individual's engagement with the concept of legal personhood is therefore in part shaped by the accepted underlying degree of capacity – a notion explored further in Section 2.5. What is apparent is that, even within the sphere of legal personhood, there exists a variance in the rights and obligations assigned to legal persons and those through whom these are exercised.

2.3.2 Animals

Whether animals fall within the concept of legal personhood is paradoxical historically. In the Middle Ages, animals were deemed to be entities that could be held to account for their supposed crimes – disobeying their masters, attacking humans, destruction of property, etc.[36] These animals were put on trial for their actions before being dealt their punishment.[37] Putting aside the issue of whether the trial was fair or the underlying purpose of such a trial, these animals arguably had more rights before the law than animals of today. In granting trials to the accused, it could be said that these animals were considered

33 This view is acknowledged by other authors too, see: Pagallo (n 6) 153.

34 Consider, for example, the restrictions imposed in the Australian state of Victoria through the *Guardianship and Administration Act 2019* (Vic).

35 Van Genderen (n 4) 21; Chopra and White (n 5) 159–163; Pagallo (n 6) 153.

36 Jen Girgen, 'The Historical and Contemporary Prosecution and Punishment of Animals' (2003) 9 *Animal Law* 97; van Genderen (n 4) 18, 21, 29, 35; Pagallo (n 6) 36–40.

37 Girgen (n 36).

entities accountable for their actions. This notion of accountability for actions is central to the modern notion of legal personhood.

Fast forward to the modern era, the rights of animals have significantly devolved. Animals are no longer enveloped into the concept of legal personhood. Consider, for example, the case of Tommy the Chimpanzee in New York.[38] In 2016, the New York Supreme Court Appellate Division was asked to consider the merits of a *Habeas Corpus* writ that had been filed on Tommy's behalf.[39] Tommy's petitioners alleged that he was falsely imprisoned and that, as a complex sentient being, he was entitled to basic rights afforded to humans.[40] They submitted that Tommy should be recognised as a 'non-human legal person', thereby seeking to expand the concept of legal personhood. The Court in this instance did not agree with the submission, but it raised some interesting points for consideration, which are addressed in Section 2.4.1.2.

2.3.3 Corporations

The notion of corporate entities being granted legal personhood status is less controversial; however, it nonetheless raises important questions in terms of the underlying functionality of legal personhood. Corporate legal personality was born from a pragmatic necessity. *Solomon v Solomon & Co Ltd*[41] demonstrates this best. The case is renowned in common law jurisdictions, but it is worth revisiting its reasoning. Mr Solomon incorporated his leather and wholesale boot-making business as a limited liability company, of which he was the majority shareholder.[42] Put simply, when an order was made for the company's compulsory liquidation, it became a question of whether Mr Solomon was personally liable for the company's debts.[43] In considering this point, Halsbury J made key findings in terms of legal personality. Importantly for our purposes, he found that upon incorporation, a company is a separate

38 The case of Tommy has been considered by several scholars in contemplating the scope of legal personhood. See, in particular: S M Solaiman, 'Legal Personality of Robots, Corporations, Idols and Chimpanzees: A Quest for Legitimacy' (2017) 25 *Artificial Intelligence Law* 155; Visa A J Kurki, 'Why Things Can Hold Rights: Reconceptualizing the Legal Person' in Visa A J Kurki and Tomasz Pietrzykowski (eds), *Legal Personhood: Animals, Artificial Intelligence and the Unborn* (Springer International Publishing AG, 2017) 69; Tomasz Pietrzykowski, *Personhood Beyond Humanism: Animals, Chimeras, Autonomous Agents and the Law* (Springer Briefs in Law, 2018).

39 *Nonhuman Rights Project, Inc. ex rel. Tommy v. Lavery*, 152 A.D. 3d 73 (Webber J) (NY Ct App, 2017); Steven Wise, 'Why the First Department's Decision In Our Chimpanzee Rights Cases Is Wildly Wrong' (Blog Post, 22 June 2017) <https://www.nonhumanrights.org/blog/first-department-wildly-wrong/>; Kurki (n 38); Solaiman (n 38).

40 *Nonhuman Rights Project, Inc. ex rel. Tommy v. Lavery* (n 39).

41 *Solomon v Solomon & Co Ltd* [1897] AC 22 ('*Solomon v Solomon & Co Ltd*').

42 *Solomon v Solomon & Co Ltd* [1897] AC 22 ('*Solomon v Solomon & Co Ltd*').

43 *Solomon v Solomon & Co Ltd* [1897] AC 22 ('*Solomon v Solomon & Co Ltd*').

independent person capable of rights and liabilities.[44] In doing so, Halsbury J expanded the concept of legal personhood to non-natural persons to address a practical concern – the question of liability from incurred debts. What is key here is that legal personality was used as a practical solution to a problem incurred. Ascribing AI legal personality based on this model is one that is supported in the literature.[45] In the early cases, the expansion of legal personhood did not arise from other considerations based on normative values such as morality or human rights.

If legal personhood is a fictional construct,[46] then the above case studies illustrate that it is a malleable construct. Legal personality can envelop a variety of subject entities and bestow a variance of rights and obligations upon entities deemed 'persons'. If legal personality is artificial, then it can change and evolve to encompass new actors, such as potentially modern AI artificial intelligence systems.

2.4. Elements of Legal Personhood: Legal Rights and Duties

Having observed the flexible nature of legal personhood as a concept through real-world examples of historical iterations of its expansion and retraction, I now move to examine two key elements underpinning this concept: legal rights and legal duties. I examine the other key element, capacity, in Section 2.5. Considering these elements is especially important given the notion that legal personhood is a fiction, comprised of both legal rights and duties. Here, I consider whether these underlying concepts can be expanded to extend to artificially intelligent actors.

2.4.1 Legal Rights

In considering whether artificially intelligent systems, such as modern AI systems, can be viewed as legal rights holders, I compare two models of legal rights: the will theory and interest theory of legal rights.

2.4.1.1 Will Theory of Legal Rights

The will theory of legal rights is based on a notion of dominance. Proponents of the view, such as Hart, contend that legal rights come into being through the ability of an individual to assert control, or influence, over the affairs of

44 *Solomon v Solomon & Co Ltd* [1897] AC 22 ('*Solomon v Solomon & Co Ltd*') per Halsbury J.

45 Jacob Turner, *Robot Rules: Regulating Artificial Intelligence* (Palgrave Macmillan, 2019) 184–187; Chopra and White (n 5) 183; van Genderen (n 4) 22.

46 Chopra and White, together with van Genderen, support the view that legal personhood is a fictional construct. See: Chopra and White (n 5) 182–3; van Genderen (n 4) 22.

another.[47] The individual whose affairs are being controlled in turn owes the 'controller' a duty.[48] It is this interconnected relationship that allows the controller to become a legal right holder.[49] Under this model, legal rights are dependent upon the creation of a legal obligation in the form of a duty. Yet, at the same time, a right entails an expression of dominance over another actor. On this basis, then, we could say that the will theory of rights gives rise to an imbalanced symbiotic relationship between legal rights and duties, with the weight of the relationship being skewed towards legal rights over duties.

Corporate legal entities exemplify problems with the will theory model. The *Solomon* case in Section 2.3.3 shows that a corporation is viewed as a separate legal entity to the persons who form the company. Thus, the company itself is a legal person, albeit one artificially constructed. Importantly, the natural persons behind the corporate veil dictate the direction of the company. According to orthodox views of the corporation, the company as a legal person does not engage in the reasoning process behind its own legal actions. This is significant in terms of the will theory. When viewed as separate from the persons behind the company, it is difficult to consider the company as a legal person exercising its will over others. The deliberations behind a company's actions are not made by the legal person but instead by the natural persons behind it. There is a disjointedness between the decision-making process and the effect of that decision. So, even if a company effectively had control over another legal person's affairs, this disjointed approach could be viewed as unsupported by the will theory. Key here is that the legal person with control is different from the natural person choosing to exercise control. In this respect, the will theory of rights could be viewed as confined in its scope.

2.4.1.2 Interest Theory of Legal Rights

In contrast to the will theory, duties are secondary to legal rights under an interest-theory model. Duties do not share the same interdependent relationship in this model as they do under the will theory. Broadly, the interest theory is centred on the notion that a duty towards another gives rise to a legal right and that this legal right is borne by the person to whom the duty is owed.[50] On this basis, rights function to further the interests of right holders.[51] This

47 Solaiman (n 38); Paul Graham, 'The Will Theory of Rights: A Defence' (1996) 15 *Law and Philosophy* 257.

48 Solaiman (n 38); Paul Graham, 'The Will Theory of Rights: A Defence' (1996) 15 *Law and Philosophy* 257.

49 Solaiman (n 38); Paul Graham, 'The Will Theory of Rights: A Defence' (1996) 15 *Law and Philosophy* 257.

50 Matthew H. Kramer, 'Refining the Interest Theory of Rights' (2010) 55 *The American Journal of Jurisprudence* 31, 32.

51 Matthew H. Kramer, 'Refining the Interest Theory of Rights' (2010) 55 *The American Journal of Jurisprudence* 31, 32.

furtherance of interests marks a shift in the *direction* of an obligation to act, which commentators have observed marks a key difference between the two theories.[52] As we have seen in the will theory, it is the legal right holder who must positively assume or influence control over the affairs of another, whereas under the interest theory, it is the duty holder who must engage in a positive action towards the right holder. This is an important distinction, the weight of which is considered more fully in Section 2.4.2.2.

The utility of the interest theory can be seen through considering the Tommy case discussed in Section 2.3.2. In deciding whether Tommy could be deemed a legal person, Webber J. considered submissions that Tommy, as a chimpanzee, was a legal right holder entitled to certain freedoms, such as 'bodily liberty'.[53] In considering this petition, Webber J. looked to the meaning of the term 'person' in the relevant New York statute,[54] finding that there was no evidence supporting the view that it expanded to non-human persons, such as Tommy. By implication, it was found then that Tommy was not entitled to the right to freedom from false imprisonment. In reaching this conclusion, Webber J. could be said to follow a will theory of rights, for it is assumed that only natural persons have the capacity to exert their interests and hold rights. The interest theory is perhaps more useful in extending the scope of legal rights – for, in the case of Tommy, if it could be established that his 'captors' were not acting in his best interests, then he could be ascribed legal rights under their duties towards him.

In viewing legal personhood through the 'rights and duties' framework, it is apparent that, to expand legal personhood as a concept, we need to consider the flexibility of legal rights. The will and interest theories of legal rights offer another layer to this framework of legal personhood. The interest theory of rights is more malleable than the will theory. For this reason, it is in turn better suited to expanding the rights aspect of legal personhood to potentially encompass artificially intelligent actors.

2.4.2 Legal Duties

Having considered the nature of legal rights underpinning the rights–duties model of legal personhood, I now turn to the duties aspect of this framework. Again, I draw upon an analysis of both will and interest theories.

52 Matthew H. Kramer, 'Refining the Interest Theory of Rights' (2010) 55 *The American Journal of Jurisprudence* 31, 32.
53 *Nonhuman Rights Project, Inc. ex rel. Tommy v. Lavery* (n 39); Wise (n 39).
54 *Nonhuman Rights Project, Inc. ex rel. Tommy v. Lavery* (n 39); Wise (n 39).

2.4.2.1 Will Theory of Rights' Relationship to Duties

Legal duties are intrinsically linked to the concept of legal rights when viewed through the lens of will theory. Recalling that Hart, for example, views legal rights as the ability to assert control over another's obligations,[55] we can see that, under this account, legal duties are not separate from the notion of legal rights. Instead, they form a symbiotic relationship. Neil MacCormick raises an interesting objection to this account. He notes that, under this approach, duties can only exist if an individual has the capacity to exercise their will over another, thereby creating a duty.[56] He comments that this is not always possible for some groups within society.[57] He observes that legal minors, as a result of legally constructed paradigms, are typically prevented from exhibiting such behaviour.[58] This artificial limitation over their rights occurs regardless of whether they would otherwise have the autonomous capability to control the obligations of another person, giving rise to a legal duty. I consider the issue of capacity more fully in Section 2.5. For now, this objection provides a useful illustration of the limited scope of the will theory in contributing to an overarching model of legal personhood. By implication, it suggests that an artificially intelligent system could not, or should not, be viewed as being a legal right holder unless it can assert control over another legal person to the extent that this gives rise to a legal duty in response.

2.4.2.2 Interest Theory of Rights' Relationship to Duties

Unlike in the will theory of legal rights, duties for the interest theory are primary to rights, not symbiotic. Under this framework, rights seek to ensure the protection and interests of individuals; a duty is largely viewed, then, as an obligation that must be fulfilled in order to meet the interests of an individual.[59] Matthew Kramer observes that there is a difference in direction of action between the will and interest theories.[60] That is, he emphasises that, under the will theory, it is the right holder who must exert influence over another to ensure their duty.[61] By contrast, the direction of obligation under the interest theory is inversed – that is, the individual with a duty must act positively towards a right holder for the rights–duties relationship to function.[62] Under

55 Solaiman (n 38); Graham (n 47).

56 Neil MacCormick, 'Rights in Legislation' in P M S Hacker and J Raz (eds), *Law, Morality and Society: Essays in Honour of HLA Hart* (Clarendon Press, 1977) 189.

57 Neil MacCormick, 'Rights in Legislation' in P M S Hacker and J Raz (eds), *Law, Morality and Society: Essays in Honour of HLA Hart* (Clarendon Press, 1977) 189.

58 Neil MacCormick, 'Rights in Legislation' in P M S Hacker and J Raz (eds), *Law, Morality and Society: Essays in Honour of HLA Hart* (Clarendon Press, 1977) 189.

59 Kramer (n 50).

60 Kramer (n 50) 32–33.

61 Kramer (n 50) 32–33.

62 Kramer (n 50) 32–33.

an interest model, duties are therefore primary to rights. This directional shift is key when considering the potential rights and duties of entities with a lesser ability to assert control over another. If we consider legal minors again, the interest theory lends itself better to accounting for the legal rights of minors who cannot control the obligations of others. It is the actions of others towards these minors that give rise to a duty. This directional difference and role of duties hold value when considering whether artificially intelligent systems can be ascribed legal rights and duties.

Like legal rights, the interest theory is more adaptable to expanding the notion of legal duties. Viewing legal personhood through a rights–duties framework, the interest theory holds greater utility than the will theory for expanding both legal rights and legal duties. On this basis, the interest theory is perhaps better suited to expanding the concept of legal personhood to encapsulate artificially intelligent actors. In permitting flexibility of expansion, the theory, by implication, suggests that both legal rights and duties could exist on a spectrum. However, legal rights and duties are not the only prerequisite to expanding legal personhood – capacity must also be considered.

2.5. Elements of Legal Personhood: Capacity

In assessing whether artificially autonomous systems are most aptly characterised as legal persons, we must look further at legal capacity. More specifically, it is necessary to determine whether AI actors can have a legal capacity. I only consider capacity here as it relates to legal personhood. In Chapter 3, I consider capacity further but in relation to agency.[63]

2.5.1 Defining Legal Capacity

Ngaire Naffine outlines that legal capacity is a core element of legal personhood. In doing so, she considers three commonly held views of what forms legal capacity. Firstly, she considers that capacity entails the ability to bear both legal rights and duties.[64] From the analysis above in Section 2.4, the interest theory allows the expansion of these concepts to envelop artificially intelligent actors, thereby meeting this first criterion. Secondly, Naffine outlines that inbuilt into the concept of legal capacity is the notion that an individual has a capacity for legal relations.[65] By this, she means that an individual has the capacity to form binding legal obligations. The ability to do so combines the first element, bearing legal rights and duties, with the soon-to-be-discussed

63 See Chapter 3 Section 3.3.1.

64 Ngaire Naffine, *Ngaire Naffine Law's Meaning of Life—Philosophy, Religion, Darwin and the legal Person* (Hart Publishing, 2009) 1, 7–10, 21,32–36, 49, 54–56.

65 Ngaire Naffine, *Ngaire Naffine Law's Meaning of Life—Philosophy, Religion, Darwin and the legal Person* (Hart Publishing, 2009) 1, 7–10, 21,32–36, 49, 54–56.

third element – the ability to reason and process decisions. Forming legal relations entails a cognitive capacity to understand that an individual is agreeing to become the bearer of legal rights and obligations.

Naffine thirdly considers that legal capacity is comprised of a mental element. She acknowledges that legal capacity entails the ability to reason and process decisions.[66] This is especially apparent if we reconsider the example of persons with intellectual disabilities mentioned in Section 2.3.1.3. A widely common feature of both common and civil law jurisdictions is that the legal capacity of persons with intellectual disabilities is often limited, to varying degrees, due to diminished abilities to engage in cognitive reasoning processes. In the Australian state of Victoria, the *Guardianship and Administration Act 2019* (Vic) is a useful illustrative example. Section 8 provides that one of the general principles of this Act is to ensure 'practicable and appropriate support' to a person with a disability 'who requires support to make decisions'. If we view legal capacity as entailing the ability to reason and process decisions, the issuing of a guardianship order under this model could be said to limit this ability. In turn, the legal capacity of these individuals is limited by the order and displaced onto their legal guardians.

The problem with this approach to legal capacity is that, by implication, it suggests that in instances where capacity is limited or displaced, the individual is somehow less of a legal person. We therefore need to consider if there are alternative methods for categorising legal capacity in order to accommodate artificially intelligent actors.

2.5.2 Legal Capacity in Application

To understand the importance of legal capacity as it relates to legal personhood, I now briefly consider the legal tests in four areas of the law[67] in which legal capacity is considered. In doing so, I identify distinctive characteristics of legal capacity and categorise these for further analysis.

2.5.2.1 Contract Law

There is a common law presumption that an individual who enters a contract has the capacity to do so unless proven otherwise.[68] That is, there is a presumption that an individual has the requisite intention to create legal relations. Although the presumption can be overturned, it is interesting to note that, from a practical point of view, capacity is assumed in the first instance.

66 Ngaire Naffine, *Ngaire Naffine Law's Meaning of Life—Philosophy, Religion, Darwin and the legal Person* (Hart Publishing, 2009) 1, 7–10, 21,32–36, 49, 54–56.

67 Here, I have not considered capacity as it relates to the law of agency, as I address this topic in the context of my wider agency considerations in Chapter 3.

68 For an example of the presumption of legal capacity in contractual formation, see: *Borthwick v Carruthers* (1787) 99 ER 1300 ('*Borthwick v Carruthers*').

This, as we will see, holds potential when considering the capacity of artificially intelligent actors. It is also worth observing that this presumption has a limitation in that it assumes that the underlying entity being bestowed with legal capacity can rebut the presumption of capacity. This approach is less likely to be of utility in relation to entities that are bestowed legal capacity as a way of regulating human relations (such as legal personhood bestowed on rivers). It does, however, hold utility in instances where the underlying entity has the capacity to rebut the presumption. If we were to categorise this type of capacity, it could be said that, given the emphasis on the creation of legal relations – rights and obligations – this form of capacity is interlinked with the earlier notion of rights and duties. In turn, I view this form of legal capacity as a *rights–duties capacity*.

2.5.2.2 *Criminal and Tort Law*

Criminal law issues pertaining to capacity tend to focus on whether an individual had the cognitive capacity to form the requisite *mens rea* at the time of an offence. Broadly, capacity in a criminal law context is centred on the notion of cognitive abilities. Similarly, tort law requires an objective consideration of what a person knew or ought to have known in deciding to act. Legal capacity here is closer to the issues raised in relation to persons with cognitive disabilities in Section 2.3.1.3. In this context, capacity looks at an individual's ability to reason, form and act on decisions. Given this, I consider that legal capacity in such a context is a form of *cognitive capacity*.

2.5.2.3 *Succession Law*

Often, the test for capacity in succession law is also centred on the notion of cognitive capacity.[69] An individual must understand the nature and effect of their will at the time of its formation and execution. Yet, testamentary capacity is also coupled with other requirements, such as age requirements. Commonly, testators must have reached the age of legal majority for their wills to be binding. This form of capacity is like what I have deemed *cognitive capacity* in Section 2.5.2.2, except that it is qualified. For this reason, I view this form of capacity as *qualified cognitive capacity*.

In considering the different tests for legal capacity in application, I have offered three key types of legal capacity: rights–duties capacity, cognitive capacity and qualified cognitive capacity. I now turn to consider these further, in addition to the implications they hold for a legal personhood characterisation of artificial intelligence.

69 For case law concerning the importance of cognitive capacity in relation to testamentary capacity, see: *Banks v Goodfellow* (1870) LR 5 QB 549 ('*Banks v Goodfellow*').

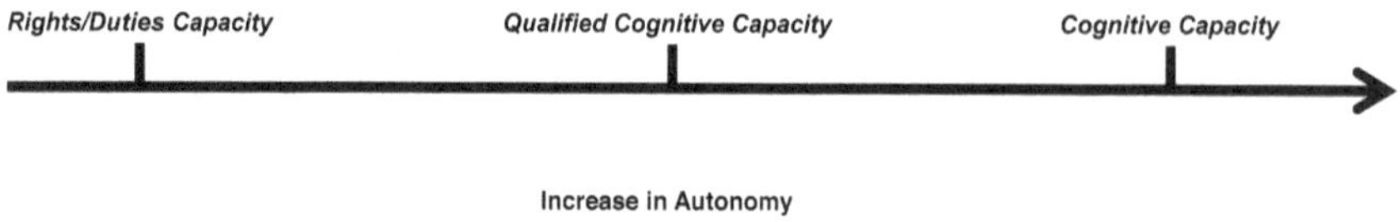

Figure 2.1 Spectrum of Legal Capacity

2.5.3 Spectrum of Legal Capacity

Considering how capacity is addressed in the application of the law allows an important observation: legal capacity is a wide and varied concept. In turn, we could rank the varying forms of capacity on a spectrum based on the associated degree of autonomy. Drawing on *Figure 2.1*, I outline an overview of a possible capacity spectrum.

Cognitive capacity consists of the most unfettered form of autonomy. It is an assessment of an individual's abilities to reason and process decisions. Its limits are defined internally by the individual. It is for this reason that this form of capacity sits on one end of the spectrum – the 'highest degree of autonomy' end. In the middle, we should place qualified cognitive capacity. The limits of this form of legal capacity are both internally and externally defined. It is internally defined in the same manner as cognitive capacity, yet it is also subject to external qualifications, such as the previously considered age requirements imposed upon the concept of capacity. Qualified cognitive capacity could be said to acknowledge that an entity may have the capacity to act autonomously. Yet, this autonomy must be exercised within defined parameters.

At the opposite end of the spectrum, the end representing the least degree of autonomy, we should place rights–duties capacity. This is a form of capacity that is externally assumed unless proven otherwise. By this, I mean to suggest that the rights–duties capacity is a form that is *bestowed* upon entities rather than one that is derived from the inherent abilities of an individual actor, like with cognitive capacity. The rights–duties capacity is formulated based on norms external to the cognitive state of an individual. That is not to say that this external bestowment cannot be rebutted, for it can. Rather, there is a baseline assumption that actors subject to this form of capacity (a) have cognitive capacity and (b) that this capacity entails that they are the bearer of legal rights and duties. It is this underlying base assumption that renders this form of legal capacity more useful to artificially intelligent actors. It does not require looking behind the complex algorithmic reasoning of such actors to prove capacity, as would be needed under the cognitive or qualified cognitive forms of capacity.[70] Rather, legal capacity is objectively assumed unless proven otherwise. If we recall that legal capacity is an element of legal personhood,

70 There are other reasons to not look behind these algorithms, such as potentially undermining the proprietary value of these systems. This is considered in further in Chapter 4.

then to characterise artificially intelligent actors in this manner, it must be established that they can have legal capacity. A rights–duties form of capacity is one method of establishing this requirement.

The concepts of automation and involuntariness could be considered as a possible objection to this proposed spectrum, yet this does not consider that legal capacity involves more than simply action. In criminal law, there are dual concepts of automation and voluntariness regarding the mental state of an actor at the time of their actions. Automation is deemed to arise when the mental state of an individual does not occur simultaneously with a person's action,[71] such as a reflex action induced by a state beyond an individual's control (such as a seizure, for example). This is particularly significant if we view legal capacity as being confined to cognitive capacity, in which the mental state of an actor alone defines an individual's capacity – that is, where capacity is shaped internally by an actor. Yet, the spectrum of capacity outlined considers more than just this narrow form of capacity, which could arguably be undone through the concept of automation. The spectrum I have outlined also introduces external influences on the notion of capacity and acknowledges instances when capacity may be objectively assumed. Criminal law introduces another concept that potentially poses an objection to the proposed spectrum: involuntariness. Involuntariness – or the state in which the actions of an individual do not match the intended will of that individual – could again seek to undermine legal capacity but only if legal capacity is assumed to be defined as cognitive capacity. Yet, as I have highlighted, there are other external or objective factors that can affect legal capacity and therefore call for the notion of legal capacity to be defined more broadly than just cognitive capacity alone.[72]

The spectrum of capacity outlined is therefore more expansive than just cognitive capacity. As such, legal capacity is defined by more than just the notion of an individual's internal mental state. This is important when considering the relationship of legal capacity to legal personhood – that is, as an element underpinning the concept.

2.6 Viewing Legal Personality Hierarchically

I have considered legal personhood as being comprised of legal rights, duties and capacity. Additionally, I have outlined that these elements of personhood are non-binary and can therefore exist on a spectrum. However, it is necessary – especially when considering non-traditional actors, such as modern AI – to

71 *Ryan v R* (1967) 121 CLR 205 ('*Ryan v R*') at 214.

72 Further, to rely on cognitive capacity alone would arguably imply that only forms of personality that are typically plenary, such as natural personality, are legal persons. It would incorrectly suggest that forms of legal personality that are not plenary by lacking 'cognitive capacity', such as corporate legal personality, would be excluded from being characterised as a legal person. This distinction is especially relevant in criminal and tort law where corporations can still be found liable despite not having 'cognitive capacity'.

question whether a spectrum alone is a sufficient way of viewing legal personhood. An alternative way of viewing legal personhood could be to view it according to a hierarchy rather than a spectrum.

Steven Wise has offered a hierarchical model of animal rights. His model is an interesting starting point for considering whether legal personhood could and should also be viewed in a hierarchical manner. Wise argues that animal rights are divided into a four-tiered pyramid. At the base of the pyramid, he places legal personhood, as he contends that this is representative of the basis upon which all rights are built.[73] In the pyramid hierarchy, legal personhood is then followed by 'legal rights possessed', of which he argues that legal persons can possess unlimited quantities.[74] At this level, he outlines that an entity may possess legal rights but also lack standing to sue in order to uphold these rights.[75] Incrementally following this is his notion of the 'private right of action', in which he considers rights bestowed through legal instruments.[76] Wise's approach is, however, more expansive and arguably permits the obtaining of legal rights through mechanisms other than at law, such as accepted social norms. Lastly, 'standing' is included at the top of Wise's pyramid and refers to whether the entity is granted *locus standi* (the right to bring a legal action in court) as the final layer of rights.[77] The purpose of Wise's pyramid is to provide a model to analyse how legal rights could be obtained for animals. Yet, the model could serve as a basis for ascribing rights to other entities, such as AI. His model allows us to see that rights can be ranked into a hierarchical structure but, more importantly, that these rankings can be weighted with different degrees of importance.

In light of Wise's views, we could consider a similar hierarchical ranking of the elements of legal personhood. I address the utility of this ranking later. First, I consider ranking legal rights theories. As discussed in Section 2.4.1, there are two theories of legal rights that could encompass artificially intelligent systems: the will theory and the interest theory of legal rights. Here, it is first worth recalling from our earlier considerations that (a) the will theory requires the rights holder to positively assert dominance over another individual and (b) the interest theory requires positive action by a duty holder towards another individual to give form a right.

73 Steven M Wise, 'Legal Personhood and the Nonhuman Rights Project' (2010) 17(1) *Animal Law* 1.
74 Steven M Wise, 'Legal Personhood and the Nonhuman Rights Project' (2010) 17(1) *Animal Law* 1.
75 Steven M Wise, 'Legal Personhood and the Nonhuman Rights Project' (2010) 17(1) *Animal Law* 1.
76 Steven M Wise, 'Legal Personhood and the Nonhuman Rights Project' (2010) 17(1) *Animal Law* 1.
77 Steven M Wise, 'Legal Personhood and the Nonhuman Rights Project' (2010) 17(1) *Animal Law* 1–2.

As previously discussed, this difference in direction of obligation gives rise to a difference in the flexibility of the legal rights created under the theory. That is, legal rights created by the will theory are potentially more restrictive than those created under the interest theory; therefore, the latter is probably better suited to potential non-traditional legal persons, such as artificially intelligent actors.[78] These theories yield a variance in rights that could be ranked based on who must be the positive actor in the rights–duty holder relationship. That is, the interest theory is more adaptive than the will theory in terms of its ability as a framework to support the view that legal personhood can be extended to actors other than natural persons. The interest theory of rights could therefore rank lower than the will theory of rights in terms of an expansion of legal personhood. That is to say, the interest theory should be placed at the bottom of a legal rights pyramid, as it is a more expansive notion of legal rights than the will theory.

Yet, it is not the ranking of legal rights alone that can give rise to a hierarchical model of legal personhood. The other elements of legal personhood must also be considered. I now turn to whether legal duties should be ranked rather than viewed on a spectrum. From the discussion in Section 2.4.2, it is clear that the direction of action influences the scope of a legal duty. For example, under the will theory, if a rights holder exerts dominance over another individual, the right bearer sets the parameters of the duty in question. The reverse is true under the interests theory in that the duty holder sets the parameters of a legal right borne from their obligation to another. This marks an interesting and contrasting nexus between the two theories. That is, the ratio of duties to rights under the interest theory could be said to be weighted towards the duties. The inverse could be said of the same ratio under the will theory. It becomes a question then as to which weighted ratio is key for expanding legal personhood to non-human agents. As we have already seen, the interest theory is better suited to expanding the parameters of the legal rights part of legal personhood. It is similarly suited to expanding the legal duties aspect. For this reason, in a pyramid of legal duties, the interest theory account of these obligations is better suited to being placed below the will theory of duties. Again, the interest theory offers a more expansive account of this element of legal personhood and is therefore suited to the wider base of the pyramid. An overview of the rankings as they relate to legal rights and duties is outlined in *Figure 2.2.*

We have considered how legal rights and duties can be ranked hierarchically to demonstrate the degree of flexibility in expanding legal personhood to support actors such as artificially intelligent systems. I now turn to the last element of legal personhood – capacity. In Section 2.5.3, I found legal capacity could be viewed on a spectrum based on the relevant degree of autonomy possessed by an individual actor. Rather than perceiving this spectrum linearly, I now progress this concept further and propose that the spectrum should be

78 See discussion in Section 2.4.

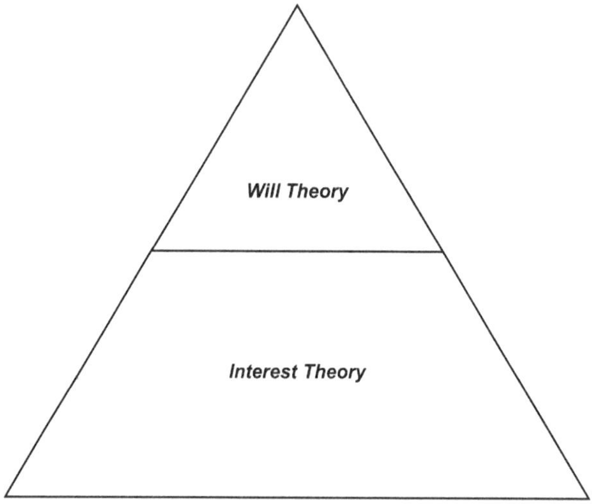

Figure 2.2 Hierarchical Ranking of Legal Rights and Duties

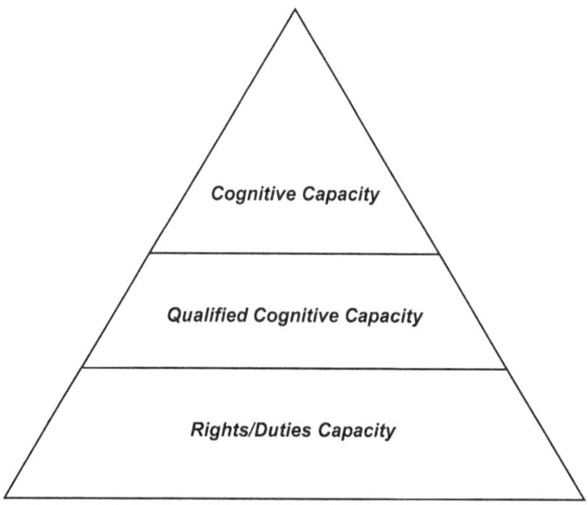

Figure 2.3 Hierarchical Account of Legal Capacity

considered *vertically*. The three previously identified categories of legal capacity build upon each other incrementally and so could also be placed in a pyramid structure, represented next in *Figure 2.3*. For example, cognitive capacity is the broadest form of legal capacity and is the least restricted in terms of the autonomy of individual actors. Given this, it should be placed at the top of the pyramid. As previously discussed, qualified cognitive capacity draws upon the notion of cognitive capacity in that it is both internally and externally defined. Considering this, it should be placed at the next level in the pyramid. At the bottom sits rights–duties capacity, as this form of capacity is underpinned by two baseline assumptions (cognitive capacity and bearer of legal rights and duties). This structure therefore acknowledges the spectrum of legal capacity but, furthermore, also accepts that the varying forms of legal capacity are conceptually connected to each other.

Ranking legal rights, duties and capacity in pyramid structures is key to expanding the notion of legal personhood more broadly, as each of these elements contributes to the formation of legal personhood as a concept. Viewing its components in a hierarchical form allows for a more expansive form of legal personhood – one that is not binary (person versus not person). It allows for the consideration that legal personhood as a concept exists in *degrees of personhood*. That is, an entity may exhibit characteristics that can be perceived as part legal person and part another concept, such as property.[79] This is particularly apparent if we return to the concept of past slavery jurisprudence, in which humans were viewed, to some degree, as both legal persons and property; the same could also be said of animals. A binary, non-hierarchical model of legal personhood would fail to accommodate the concept of slaves as a restricted form of legal personhood. Whilst this is ideal in terms of contributing to the prohibition of slavery, it is not pragmatic for addressing other legal issues to which solutions could be offered based on a more expansive notion of legal personhood.

Viewing the elements of legal personhood as hierarchical allows us to construct a model of legal personhood that is also hierarchical to accommodate varying forms of legal persons. The advantage of such a structure is that it can accommodate varying degrees of autonomy for not only natural persons but other entities as well, such as the differing forms of modern AI systems discussed in the *Introduction* in Section 0.2.1. In Chapter 5, I propose in more detail a hierarchical model of legal personhood. For now, my goal is to demonstrate that there exists a need for such a model to expand the notion of legal personhood further. As we have seen, the current forms of legal personhood do not fully accommodate the varying forms of modern AI, the result being that a legal personhood characterisation of artificial intelligence is lacking in depth.

2.7. Legal Personhood: An Adaptable Concept

In considering the parameters and components of legal personhood, along with its socio-legal background, what becomes apparent is that, as a concept, legal personhood is malleable and capable of expansion. This is particularly apparent when considering the components most commonly associated with legal personhood – legal rights, duties and capacity. In regarding legal rights

79 Whether a legal person can, or should, also be characterised as property is explored further in Chapter 4.

and duties through a lens of the interests theory rather than the will theory, these components are perhaps more flexible and capable of expanding to accommodate artificially intelligent actors. Additionally, considering the concept of legal capacity in application reveals that this component is also flexible and capable of expansion.

In finding that the components of legal personhood are non-binary and exist on a spectrum, it is possible to then rank these components based on their direct correlation to the autonomy of an actor. This is key in that it encourages viewing the components of legal personhood as potentially hierarchical. By viewing its components in this way, we can in turn begin to consider legal personhood as also existing in a hierarchical structure. Exactly what this structure may look like and its importance to the characterisation of modern AI is a topic I explore in Chapter 5.

A core point is that if we are to characterise modern AI as a legal person, this is not a binary question. If the legal personhood characterisation is the best option for modern AI, we will need to consider where on the hierarchical spectrum it fits. That is, we will need to address what *type* or *degree* of legal person we should be classifying modern AI. This is another issue that I explore in Chapter 5.

Lastly, if we proceed with this form of characterisation, there are other issues that will need to be reconciled. For example, modern AI systems also hold strong proprietary value. The proprietary nature of these systems is explored in Chapter 4. The relationship between proprietary and legal personhood characterisations of these systems is considered in Chapter 5. Additionally, there is the question that if legal personhood for AI is accepted to some extent, then does this give rise to the potential for AI to act as an agent of another legal person? Whether AI is best characterised as a legal agent, or if it ought to be characterised as such, I consider next in Chapter 3.

For now, what is key is that legal personhood as a construct does hold the potential to expand and encompass artificially intelligent actors. Whether it should be expanded – and if so, how – are points I explore in later chapters, as I determine the best legal characterisation of modern AI. Determining how AI should be legally characterised is an important threshold issue that needs to be resolved as part of the process of assigning liability, for how AI is characterised shapes the legal relations between an AI system and other entities. Understanding the likely framework in which AI operates is important, as it sets the parameters for devising an appropriate liability response to the deployment of AI. For this reason, I continue with my considerations of how AI ought to be characterised in the remaining chapters of Part II (Chapters 3–5) before turning to other threshold issues that need to be considered as part of the process of assigning liability in Part III.

References

A Articles/Books/Reports.

Chesterman, Simon, 'Artificial Intelligence and the Limits of Legal Personality' (2020) 69(October) *International and Comparative Law Quarterly* 819.
Chesterman, Simon, *We, The Robots? Regulating Artificial Intelligence and the Limits of the Law* (Cambridge Univertiy Press, 2021).
Chopra, Samir and Laurence White, *A Legal Theory for Autonomous Artificial Agents* (The University of Michigan Press, 4th ed, 2014).
Cowie, Andrew, 'A History of Married Women's Real Property Rights' (2009) 6 *Australian Journal of Gender Law* 4.
Finkelman, Paul, 'Slavery in the United States: Persons or Property?' in Jean Allain (ed), *The Legal Understanding of Slavery: From the Historical to the Contemporary* (Oxford University Press, 2012) 105.
Girgen, Jen, 'The Historical and Contemporary Prosecution and Punishment of Animals' (2003) (9) *Animal Law* 97.
Graham, Paul, 'The Will Theory of Rights: A Defence' (1996) 15 *Law and Philosophy* 257.
Kramer, Matthew H., 'Refining the Interest Theory of Rights' (2010) 55 *The American Journal of Jurisprudence* 31.
Kurki, Visa A J, 'Why Things Can Hold Rights: Reconceptualizing the Legal Person' in Visa A J Kurki and Tomasz Pietrzykowski (eds), *Legal Personhood: Animals, Artificial Intelligence and the Unborn* (Springer International Publishing AG, 2017) 69.
MacCormick, Neil, 'Rights in Legislation' in P M S Hacker and J Raz (eds), *Law, Morality and Society: Essays in Honour of HLA Hart* (Clarendon Press, 1977) 189.
Naffine, Ngaire, *Ngaire Naffine Law's Meaning of Life—Philosophy, Religion, Darwin and the legal Person* (Hart Publishing, 2009).
Pagallo, Ugo, *The Laws of Robots: Crimes, Contracts and Torts* (Springer, 2013).
Pietrzykowski, Tomasz, *Personhood Beyond Humanism: Animals, Chimeras, Autonomous Agents and the Law* (Springer Briefs in Law, 2018).
Solaiman, S M, 'Legal Personality of Robots, Corporations, Idols and Chimpanzees: A Quest for Legitimacy' (2017) 25 *Artificial Intelligence Law* 155.
Turner, Jacob, *Robot Rules: Regulating Artificial Intelligence* (Palgrave Macmillan, 2019).
van Genderen, Robert van den Hoven, 'Do We Need New Legal Personhood in the Age of Robots and AI?' in Marcelo Corrales et al. (ed), *Robotics, AI and the Future of Law* (Springer Nature Singapore Pte Ltd, 2018) 15.
Wise, Steven M, 'Legal Personhood and the Nonhuman Rights Project' (2010) 17(1) *Animal Law* 1.
Wojtczak, Sylwia, 'Endowing Artificial Intelligence with Legal Subjectivity' (2020) (37) *AI & Society* 205.

B Cases

Banks v Goodfellow (1870) LR 5 QB 549
Borthwick v Carruthers (1787) 99 ER 1300
Groves v Slaughter 40 US (15 Pet.) 449 (1841)

Nonhuman Rights Project, Inc. ex rel. Tommy v. Lavery, 152 A.D. 3d 73 (Webber J) (NY Ct App, 2017)
Ryan v R (1967) 121 CLR 205
Solomon v Solomon & Co Ltd [1897] AC 22
Somerset v Stewart (1772) 98 ER 499

C Legislation

Guardianship and Administration Act 2019 (Vic)

D Other

Armstrong, Paul, 'AI Humanoid "Sophia" Is Granted First Ever Robot Visa, Speaks With President', *Forbes* (online, 27 October 2018) <https://www.forbes.com/sites/paularmstrongtech/2018/10/27/ai-humanoid-sophia-is-granted-first-ever-robot-visa-speaks-with-president/#45c0158f1f39>
Dragan, Aurel, 'UniCredit becomes the First Bank in the World with a Robot Customer', *BR Business Review* (online, 11 May 2018) <https://business-review.eu/news/unicredit-is-the-first-bank-in-the-world-that-has-a-robot-sophia-as-a-customer-169290>
European Parliament Resolution of 16 February 2017 with Recommendations to the Commission on Civil Law Rules on Robotics (2015/2103(INL) [2018]) OJ C 252/239
Evans, Kate, 'The New Zealand River that Became a Legal Person', *BBC Travel* (Web Page, 21 March 2020) <https://www.bbc.com/travel/article/20200319-the-new-zealand-river-that-became-a-legal-person>
Griffin, Andrew, 'Saudi Arabia Grants Citizenship to a Robot for the First Time Ever', *The Independent* (online, 26 October 2017) <https://www.independent.co.uk/life-style/gadgets-and-tech/news/saudi-arabia-robot-sophia-citizenship-android-riyadh-citizen-passport-future-a8021601.html>
Regulation (EU) 2024/1689 of the European Parliament and of the Council of 13 June 2024 laying down harmonised rules on artificial intelligence and amending Regulations (EC) No 300/2008, (EU) No 167/2013, (EU) No 168/2013, (EU) 2018/858, (EU) 2018/1139 and (EU) 2019/2144 and Directives 2014/90/EU, (EU) 2016/797 and (EU) 2020/1828 (Artificial Intelligence Act) [2024] OJ L 1689/1
Suleyman, Mustafa, 'What Is an AI Anyway?', *TED* (TED Talk, TED Conferences LLC, April 2024) 0.4.52, 0.12.25 <https://www.youtube.com/watch?v=KKNCiRWd_j0>
Wise, Steven, 'Why the First Department's Decision In Our Chimpanzee Rights Cases Is Wildly Wrong' (Blog Post, 22 June 2017) <https://www.nonhumanrights.org/blog/first-department-wildly-wrong/>

3 AI as a Legal Agent

Strengths, Limitations and Situational Applicability

3.1. The AI Legal Agent

With the aim of resolving how AI ought to be legally characterised, this chapter examines the possibility that modern AI systems ought not be characterised as legal persons. Instead, it considers whether we should view them as the legal agents of natural or legal persons, as the characterisation of AI informs the liability rules with which it correlates. The advancement of AI and the emerging roles for 'AI agents' and 'AI avatars' further emphasise the importance of AI possibly being characterised as a legal agent.

This chapter therefore explores whether agency as a theory can potentially, or ought to, accommodate modern forms of AI. For such an approach holds that if an AI system is an agent, then the natural or legal person for whom it acts ultimately bears liability for its actions. After considering if AI as a legal agent is theoretically possible, the chapter then examines the commonly accepted elements of an agency relationship and whether modern AI can meet the required thresholds for characterisation as an agent.

In testing the robustness of the agency characterisation approach a view is offered: the concepts of agency and AI do not *always* align. Although we can theoretically characterise modern AI as a legal agent of another legal person, this does not necessarily mean we should *consistently* characterise such systems as agents. In turn, this chapter proposes that we should characterise AI as a legal agent on a *situational* basis, thereby offering that agency is a partial solution to the question of how AI ought to be legally characterised. This chapter therefore furthers a central tenet of this book: that the law should respond to AI on a *situational* basis. We need a more robust way of characterising AI, one that accommodates the varied nature of AI and the varied contexts in which it is deployed.

3.2. Theories of Agency and Their Applicability to AI

There is a well-established body of law that governs agency models involving only natural or corporate legal persons (traditional agency). The agency characterisation of AI systems seeks to adapt the traditional agency model to

DOI: 10.4324/9781003617549-6

assign legal liability for the actions of AI systems. Such a characterisation recognises that an AI system can autonomously decide and execute actions in the name of achieving an assigned goal. In examining whether the agency is the best method for legally characterising AI, I commence by considering agency for AI before then turning to critically examine the potential applicability of agency theories not previously applied to AI.

3.2.1 *Agency for AI*

Chopra and White offer an approach to characterising AI as a legal agent. A key pillar of their account is that they draw upon the work of the theorist Daniel Dennett, who proposed the concept of an 'intentional stance', and seek to adopt this stance towards the actions of artificial agents.[1] For Chopra and White's purposes, they utilise the intentional stance as a method of objectively looking at an entity and viewing it as a rational actor when prognosticating about it as an actor.[2] They consider that the actions of such agents ought to be viewed as based on reason and directed towards an end – that is, that the actions of these systems are not blind but designed for a purpose.[3] In this sense, Chopra and White propose to look at the actions of 'artificial agents' objectively, which in turn shapes their perspective of the agency in relation to such actors and liability for their actions.

By adopting an intentional stance towards artificially intelligent actors, Chopra and White subsequently develop an account of agency in relation to these systems that is somewhat constrained. They contend that an 'intentional stance' offers one mechanism of interpreting agency models involving only natural or corporate legal persons (traditional agency) to accommodate artificial agents or actors.[4] Chopra and White consider that a legal agency relationship entails four key characteristics: (1) consent between the parties, (2) that one party acts on behalf of or represents the other party (the agent), (3) that the agent has the legal power to affect the legal rights and duties of the party they are representing and (4) that the party being represented (the principal) has the right to control the agent.[5] In applying the intentional stance to these four elements, Chopra and White consider that this allows for artificial

1 Samir Chopra and Laurence White, *A Legal Theory for Autonomous Artificial Agents* (University of Michigan Press, 4th ed., 2014) 11–12.
2 Samir Chopra and Laurence White, *A Legal Theory for Autonomous Artificial Agents* (University of Michigan Press, 4th ed., 2014) 11–17.
3 Samir Chopra and Laurence White, *A Legal Theory for Autonomous Artificial Agents* (University of Michigan Press, 4th ed., 2014) 12.
4 Samir Chopra and Laurence White, *A Legal Theory for Autonomous Artificial Agents* (University of Michigan Press, 4th ed., 2014) 18.
5 Samir Chopra and Laurence White, *A Legal Theory for Autonomous Artificial Agents* (University of Michigan Press, 4th ed., 2014) 18, 20.

agents to fit into existing legal doctrines.[6] In response to the potential for more autonomous forms of AI than considered, Chopra and White are of the view that new categories of agency could be developed as and when the need arises.[7]

Whilst there are practical considerations for favouring an intentional stance interpretation of agency, the approach is less compatible with more complex forms of modern AI. For example, the intentional stance seeks to consider the effect or output of the actions of entities, such as modern AI, by relying upon an objective interpretation of the system's actions. In doing so, the approach calls for us to attribute the knowledge and actions of such systems, as can be objectively discerned, to the principals for whom they act. This poses two key problems. Firstly, there is an underlying assumption that these systems will act to achieve a pre-determined objective or end. As I have discussed, more complex forms of modern AI are not only capable but are *expected* to determine their own end. This is potentially at odds with element (4) considered above, viz. that the principal has the *right* to control the agent. If more complex AI systems, such as *unsupervised* and *reinforcement* learning, are to be considered an agent, the principal must have the *right* to control these systems. Yet, having a right alone is insufficient; it must also be capable of being expressed. These more complex systems potentially pose a scenario where a principal may have the right to control them under an agency relationship but in which their reasoning processes, and ultimately their output, cannot be controlled due to the very nature of these systems. If we consider that the *right* to control an agent also implies that the principal has the *ability* to control the agent, then more complex forms of modern AI challenge the effectiveness of their approach.

3.2.2 Other Agency Theories

I will now expand my considerations to agency theories not yet applied to modern AI and evaluate their potential applicability to such systems.

3.2.2.1 Consent Theory

Gerard McMeel outlines that one key model of agency, the normative 'consent theory', explores the notion that agency as a concept is underpinned by consent. More specifically, he observes that there is a long line of jurisprudence

6 Samir Chopra and Laurence White, *A Legal Theory for Autonomous Artificial Agents* (University of Michigan Press, 4th ed., 2014) 23.

7 Samir Chopra and Laurence White, *A Legal Theory for Autonomous Artificial Agents* (University of Michigan Press, 4th ed., 2014) 24; other scholars also support the view that traditional agency principles should be adapted to accommodate the autonomy of AI systems, or digital agents. See: Anna Beckers and Gunther Teubner, *Three Liability Regimes for Artificial Intelligence: Algorithmic Actants, Hybrids, Crowds* (Hart Publishing, 2021) 56–57.

in common law jurisdictions that focuses on the degree of consent between a principal and an agent.[8] Central to this dynamic is the notion that the relationship is one where a clear agreement is consensually reached by the parties and that the respective rights and obligations of each party are derived from this consensual agreement.[9] McMeel highlights that, under this theory, the trust-based nature of the principal–agent model is akin to the common law doctrine of contractual formation in that whether consent exists between the parties is determined objectively.[10]

The consent theory of agency prompts questions that must be addressed to test the effectiveness of categorising AI as an agent of natural or legal persons. Firstly, by focusing on the underlying contractual nature of the principal–agent relationship, the theory assumes that consent must flow bidirectionally between the principal and the agent. More specifically, both parties to the agency agreement must consent to their respective rights and obligations within the arrangement.[11] Yet, this raises the question of whether an agency relationship could exist in instances where consent flows monodirectionally – such as from a 'principal' who is a natural person to an AI agent. Does an AI agent need to be capable of consent, and must they consent for an agency relationship to arise when AI is in use? Answering these questions requires that we consider the nature of 'consent' in the context of agency more closely and test this against the capabilities, or potential capabilities, of AI systems, for surely a principal–agent relationship involving AI under the consent theory could not exist without resolving such issues.

Given these considerations, I now turn to examine the nature of consent and the potential implications it poses in the AI context. Consent in the principal–agent relationship ('the relationship') has been interpreted in common law jurisdictions as providing *assent* to a set of instructions.[12] Importantly, embedded into this notion of assent is an *intention*[13] by the principal for the agent to undertake the issued instructions.[14] Indeed, it has been held in case law that assent manifests itself as a nexus between the principal's intention for an action

8 Gerard McMeel, 'Philosophical Foundations of the Law of Agency' (2000) 116 (July) *Law Quarterly Review* 387, 387.

9 Gerard McMeel, 'Philosophical Foundations of the Law of Agency' (2000) 116 (July) *Law Quarterly Review* 387, 387–389.

10 Gerard McMeel, 'Philosophical Foundations of the Law of Agency' (2000) 116 (July) *Law Quarterly Review* 387, 387–389.

11 Gerard McMeel, 'Philosophical Foundations of the Law of Agency' (2000) 116 (July) *Law Quarterly Review* 387, 387.

12 G E Dal Pont (ed.), *Law of Agency* (LexisNexis Butterworths, 2nd ed., 2008) 91.

13 Intention in this context is distinct from the intentional stance relied upon by Chopra and White. The intentional stance considered earlier is about objectively looking at an entity and assuming it is a rational actor when contemplating its actions. See: Chopra and White (n 1) 11–17. By contrast, intention in this context contributes to an understanding of consent in the principal–agent relationship.

14 Dal Pont (ed) (n 12) 91.

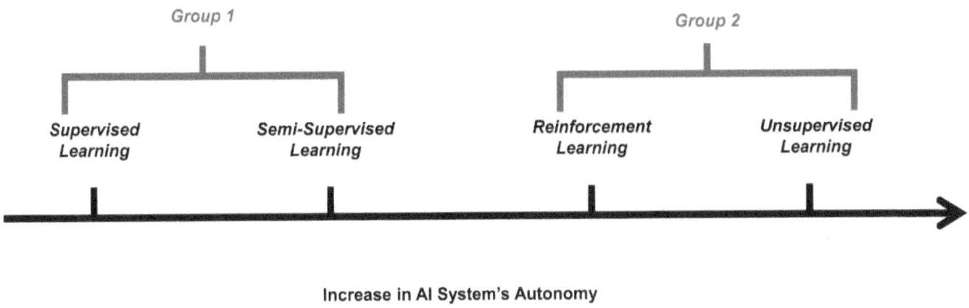

Figure 3.1 Categorised Continuum of AI Autonomy

to be undertaken by an agent and the agent, in response, actually partaking in that action.[15] If we distil consent to the notion of intention, the issue then arises as to whether it is sufficient for intention to flow monodirectionally from the principal to the agent or if it must flow bidirectionally between the parties. Again, there is common law precedent that provides that the agent must also intend to accept the principal's authority and to act upon their instructions.[16] On this basis, consent is reduced to an intention, and this intention must be exhibited by both parties for the consent theory to hold true.

If we assume that, in the context of modern AI, the principal is a natural person or traditional legal person[17] and the AI system is the agent, then whether the principal intends for the agent to act upon the instructions provided is relatively straightforward to determine. What is more controversial is whether the AI system can subsequently act in a manner that evidences an *intention* of the AI system to *accept* the principal's authority and act upon their instructions. As McMeel highlights under the consent theory, consent is determined objectively, like how it is determined in contract formation.[18] By this account, whether an AI system intends to accept the instructions of the principal would also be determined objectively.

However, it is worth recalling here the distinct types of modern AI outlined in the *Introduction*. More specifically, it is worth noting the continuum of autonomy these systems exhibit, as represented in *Figure 0.1* in the *Introduction* and adapted as *Figure 3.1*. Modern AI systems at the left of this figure, such as the *supervised* or *semi-supervised* systems (Group 1), are designed to achieve an objective or 'end' set by the user of these systems. The systems on the right of *Figure 3.1* are more complicated. These systems, viz. *reinforcement* and *unsupervised* learning (Group 2), design and achieve their

15 Dal Pont (ed) (n 12); see also *Launchbury v Morgans* [1973] AC 127.
16 Dal Pont (ed) (n 12); see also *Field v Shoalhaven Transport Pty Ltd [1970] 3 NSWR 96.*
17 By 'traditional legal person', I mean to suggest a corporation that has natural persons sitting behind it making decisions rather than the potential for a new form of legal person, such as an AI legal person.
18 McMeel (n 8) 387–389.

own ends. The relatively controlled forms of modern AI where the output can be predicted – that is, Group 1 systems – are more likely to be able to respond to an objective test of intention. One of the purposes of a Group 2 system, a form of modern AI that has a greater degree of autonomy over their end, is that it might be able to achieve ends not predicted or foreseen by an individual. This ability renders such systems less likely to be compatible with an objective test of intention. By their very nature, these systems are designed to produce outcomes that are less predictable to natural persons, which is why they are deployed in the first instance. The lack of compatibility of such systems with an objective test of intention suggests that the consent theory of agency is not suited to all modern AI systems.

3.2.2.2 Power–Liability Model

An alternative to the consent theory is the power liability model of agency ('Model'). McMeel highlights that the Model stems from the works of Wesley Hohfeld.[19] McMeel summarises the Model as being an ontological account where agency arises when an agent is empowered to alter a principal's legal relations with a third party. [20] Additionally, this empowerment gives rise to a correlative liability on the part of the principal that alters their legal relations.[21] That is, the principal is ultimately liable for the actions of the agent. The rights and duties of the principal and agent are therefore intrinsically linked, but perhaps more importantly, the legal actions of the agent not only impact but bind the principal, especially in terms of liability.

The Model, when considered in relation to modern AI, poses several challenges. In some respects, the Model is like the common law accounts of agency where 'within scope' actions of the agent bind the principal. There are two issues with this account of agency when considered in relation to modern AI. Firstly, the Model implicitly assumes that the agent must be a legal person to accept the authority of the principal and, in turn, bind the principal. For the Model to work then in terms of modern AI, this form of AI must be capable of being characterised as a legal person. Whether this is achievable was considered in Chapter 2, but it is not without its complications. It follows then that for the power–liability model to extend to AI, modern AI must be categorised as a legal person. Exactly what form of legal person, under what circumstances the status can be ascribed to AI, and whether the rights and obligations of a modern AI system should be diminished in comparison to other legal persons are all issues I address in Chapter 5. For now, though, it is worth identifying that the Model assumes a degree of legal personality that is ascribed to all agents within its ambit.

19 McMeel (n 8) 389.
20 McMeel (n 8) 389, 391–392.
21 McMeel (n 8) 389.

Secondly, the Model fails to consider the consequences of an agent acting outside the scope of their authority. It falls short of accounting for liability when an agent fails to act in accordance with the authority bestowed upon them by the principal. In the Model, there is the potential for this to arise in instances where the agent is not empowered to act but purports to a third party that they are empowered to act, thereby seemingly inducing a correlative liability for the principal. This scenario poses several challenges for characterising modern AI as a legal agent. This is an issue that I consider in more detail in Section 3.3.3, but it is worth noting for now that there is the potential for AI agents under the Model to act outside the scope of their authority.

The Model therefore offers an additional method by which AI could be characterised as a legal agent. Yet, due to the shortfalls of the Model, it is not necessarily apparent that AI should always be characterised as an agent.

3.2.2.3 Cost–Benefit Internalisation Theory

In addition to the theories of agency discussed above, there exists a third theory that is based on moral and economic principles. Paula Dalley espouses a theory of agency, the 'cost–benefit internalisation theory', which largely centres on the notion that an individual actor is responsible for the *foreseeable* consequences of their actions.[22] In terms of the principal–agent relationship, Dalley contends that a principal is therefore liable for the *foreseeable harm* that might arise from the use of an agent and their potential engagement in any unauthorised acts.[23] Dalley constrains her theory to instances where a principal uses an agent 'in business'. In terms of AI, this poses a challenge, as modern AI can be deployed in non-commercial settings.[24] For the theory to be an effective mechanism for legally characterising modern AI, it would need to expand beyond principal–agent relationships arising solely in commercial contexts.

In terms of what is a *foreseeable harm* under the theory, Dalley considers two approaches: the moral and the economic. The economic approach focuses on what *costs* are reasonably foreseeable.[25] As discussed, the use of modern AI extends beyond simply commercial and economic situations, and so this definition of 'foreseeable harm' is not always suited to the AI context. Morally foreseeable harm, in Dalley's view, requires the exercising of both reason and free will.[26] Whether or not AI is capable of free will is a loaded question. For Chopra and White, the notion of free will applies in relation to artificial agents

22 Paula J Dalley, 'A Theory of Agency Law' (2011) 72(3) *University of Pittsburgh Law Review* 495, 498.

23 Paula J Dalley, 'A Theory of Agency Law' (2011) 72(3) *University of Pittsburgh Law Review* 495, 498.

24 For examples of how modern AI is utilised in non-commercial settings, see the *Introduction* to this book.

25 Dalley (n 22) 502.

26 Dalley (n 22) 501–502.

if free will is viewed as the ability to learn from experience through reason about the past, adapt behaviour and plan for the future – all actions they note AI is capable of executing.[27] The issue of free will is raised under Dalley's account of agency, as she aligns moral agency with that of legal agency.[28] Importantly, she finds that the commonly replied-upon 'reasonable person test' in law utilises the concept of reasonable foreseeability, which leads her to conclude that a principal ought to be liable for the foreseeable consequences arising from relying upon an agent.[29] Dalley's account of agency therefore relies upon the notion of foreseeability, which is predicted through reasonableness. Additionally, this notion of foreseeability is human-centric and does not necessarily accommodate instances where an AI system may become more sophisticated than us, thereby requiring a different measure of foreseeability. I consider the notion of foreseeability further in Chapters 6 and 8. For now, in order for the theory to be applicable to modern AI, an AI system must be capable of acting reasonably. There are varying degrees in which modern AI systems can exercise reason, as is noted by the distinction between the Group 1 and Group 2 systems. In turn, there are varying degrees to which AI can meet this reasonableness threshold.

The last element of the cost–benefit internalisation theory is that of 'causation'. I consider the issue of causation in depth in Chapter 6. Here, however, it is prudent to note that central to Dalley's argument is that there must be a causal link between an outcome and the principal in order to hold the principal to account.[30] Her definition of causation is self-acknowledged to be broad and based on moral considerations.[31] She considers that an outcome can be achieved by a variety of acts, some of which are more proximate to the principal than others, including the use of an agent.[32] She holds the principal to account for the actions of an agent in a broad variety of situations. For AI to be considered an agent under this theory, there must therefore be a causal link between AI acting as the agent and the principal deploying the AI system. The establishing of causal links between an AI system and an individual is considered in Chapter 6.

On this basis, there are three possible theoretical foundations for characterising modern AI as a legal agent: the Chopra and White account, the approach offered by the power–liability model and the cost–benefit internalisation theory. The first two of these theories fail to consider who ought to be held to account in scenarios where an agent acts outside of its authority. The latter requires expansion to accommodate the situations in which AI can be

27 Chopra and White (n 1) 175.
28 Dalley (n 22) 501–502.
29 Dalley (n 22) 502.
30 Dalley (n 22) 502–503.
31 Dalley (n 22) 502–503.
32 Dalley (n 22) 503.

deployed. What these approaches reveal is that it is theoretically possible for modern AI to be characterised as a legal agent. Whether AI should be characterised as such will depend upon whether modern AI systems can *consistently* meet the accepted elements of an agency relationship.

3.3. Key Elements of a Principal–Agent Relationship

For modern AI to be truly characterised as a legal agent, there are three commonly accepted minimum criteria that must be met by the technology. Whether modern AI systems are capable of consistently meeting these criteria will impact whether the technology should always be characterised as a legal agent; and so, I consecutively evaluate each criterion's compatibility with AI.

3.3.1 Capacity to Act as an Agent

One of the key characteristics of agency is that the agent must have the legal capacity to act as an agent. In light of the observations arising from the discussion in Section 3.2, it is worth pausing to note that a point of commonality between the considered theories is the underlying assumption that an agent must be a legal person of sorts. It follows then that for an agent to have capacity, they must have a type of capacity exhibited by a legal person. Consequently, if a modern AI system is a legal agent, it must therefore also be a legal person that is capable of such capacity. I have considered the issue of capacity in depth as it relates to legal personhood status in Chapter 2. Additionally, I offered in Chapter 2 that capacity in this context ought to be viewed in a hierarchical or pyramid structure based on the degree of autonomy and the correlating level of internal and external influences.

This pyramid structure of capacity is key in considering the relationship between capacity and agency. Furthermore, it is compatible with current approaches that characterise AI as legal agents. Chopra and White also acknowledge that capacity is a fluid concept.[33] Yet, where they differ is in their deployment of the intentional stance.[34] Adopting an intentional stance narrows what they consider to be the ideal form of legal capacity that ought to be used in relation to AI legal agents. Although they acknowledge that capacity is fluid, their intentional stance creates a situation where they constrain the capacity of artificial agents to what can only objectively be determined.[35] On this basis, it is as if they confine capacity in relation to AI to that of the far end of Figure 3.2 (from Chapter 2) – that is, their views agree with the *rights–duties* form of capacity.

33 Chopra and White (n 1) 57.
34 Chopra and White (n 1) 57.
35 Chopra and White (n 1) 57.

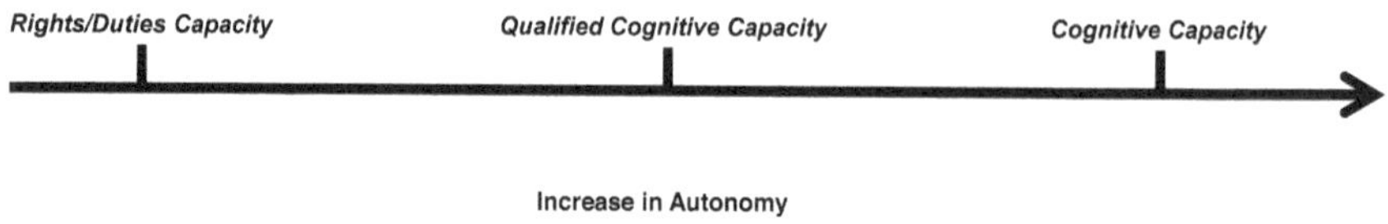

Figure 3.2 Spectrum of Legal Capacity

As discussed in Chapter 2, this form of capacity is *externally bestowed* upon an agent and therefore more easily applied to modern AI systems. I am of the view that confining the issue of capacity to only a *rights/duties* approach overlooks the varying permutations in AI complexity. More specifically, it holds the potential to overlook the complex and more autonomous forms of AI, which indeed pose a challenge to traditional notions of legal capacity.

Capacity in relation to AI legal agents therefore can and ought to mirror capacity as measured for legal persons. For modern AI to be characterised as a legal agent, it needs to consistently be able to meet the requirements of legal personhood capacity. On this basis, AI therefore needs to consistently be viewed as a legal person. This could be a legal person akin to a typical plenary legal person, such as a natural person, or instead a juridical person. Regardless, to establish the agency relationship a degree of legal personality is required.

3.3.2 Creation of the Relationship

The method by which a principal–agent relationship arises will inform whether AI can sufficiently be characterised as a legal agent. There are three commonly accepted methods of agency formation under common law. I now consider the implications of each in turn.

3.3.2.1 Agreement

One accepted method for agency formation is by agreement. Formation by this method entails the parties involved – both principal and agent – consenting to the formation of the agency relationship.[36] Such consent can be granted either expressly or impliedly.[37] The agreement approach to agency formation is unsurprisingly in line with the consent theory of agency discussed in Section 3.2.2.1. This approach therefore poses several challenges in relation to characterising AI, such as those discussed above in relation to intention. In light of the issues raised in Section 3.2.2.1, the agreement method of agency formation, in the context of modern AI, is therefore not best suited to characterising AI as a legal agent.

36 Dal Pont (ed) (n 12) 87–90.
37 Dal Pont (ed) (n 12) 87–90.

3.3.2.2 Ratification

Agency formation by ratification arises in a scenario where a principal retrospectively authorises the actions of another, thereby creating a principal–agent relationship.[38] There are two benefits of this approach. Firstly, it allows for the actions of putative agents to be 'claimed' by a principal and, therefore, the legal consequences of these actions to rest with the principal.[39] Secondly, in instances where an agency relationship arises via other methods, such as by consent, and the agent acts outside the scope of their authority, the ratification process allows for a principal to retroactively authorise 'out of scope' actions.[40] Initially, this approach may seem appropriate for modern AI actors, as it does not necessarily give rise to the issues surrounding the intention considered above; yet, upon further examination, it becomes clear that the approach is not entirely compatible with modern AI.

The method by which ratification occurs poses issues when viewed in relation to AI. There are several widely accepted elements required for ratification to be effected. There is one I intend to focus on due to the potential obstacles it poses for AI. In common law, there exists a principle that for ratification to occur, at a time an action is completed, the putative agent must disclose their *intention* that the benefit of their actions will be bestowed upon a third party (the principal upon ratification).[41] This approach again raises the issue of intention and the subsequent difficulties discussed above that this poses for Group 2 systems in *Figure 3.1*. For ratification to legally hold under this principle, both Group 1 and Group 2 systems would need to be constructed so that they include a mechanism that allows for the disclosure of the benefits of the system. In the context of AI, this is not always practical. Consider, for example, a driverless car. Cars in general on the road encounter numerous other actors – other drivers (or driverless vehicles), cyclists, pedestrians, etc. How could the disclosure requirement be effected in such a contemporaneous and ever-changing environment? This element of ratification is therefore not always feasible in the context of AI; thus, this method of agency formation is not well suited in the context of potential modern AI agents.

3.3.2.3 Operation of Law

The final method of agency formation is when a principal–agent relationship arises by operation of law. In emergency circumstances, or out of necessity, the law will impose rights and obligations on one party in relation to the property of another.[42] It has long been held that an agency relationship arises out of an

38 Dal Pont (ed) (n 12) 112–113.
39 Dal Pont (ed) (n 12) 113.
40 Dal Pont (ed) (n 12) 112–113.
41 Dal Pont (ed) (n 12) 116–118
42 Dal Pont (ed) (n 12) 149–150.

operation of law in shipping transactions.[43] In bills of exchange, the master of the ship assumes the role of agent in taking carriage of goods and executing contracts on behalf of the owner of the goods at various stages of the shipping process.[44] The growing emergence of autonomous, unmanned ships, however, poses legal difficulty in terms of the role of the master of the ship.[45] If there is no human, or natural person, as master of the ship, who will assume the role of agent? One theory is that the autonomous system will eventually need to assume this role.[46] If such a circumstance were to arise, this would result in the imposition of agency on an AI actor by operation of law. An agency relationship involving an AI actor created by operation of law is therefore not improbable.

This form of agency creation in relation to AI, however, is not without its difficulties. If modern AI is to be legally characterised as an agent, the creation of a principal–agent relationship by operation of law may initially seem to be the most appealing method of instigating this relationship, as it potentially avoids the issues associated with *intention* discussed previously. Yet, the concept is underpinned by the concept of necessity – that is, agency by this formation can only arise in instances of necessity – and the courts have been reluctant to extend the concept of necessity beyond emergency or commercially necessary situations.[47] For AI to functionally be categorised as a legal agent, short of the introduction of legislative provisions, agency jurisprudence concerning the concept of necessity would need to expand to include modern AI systems under the classification of agents by necessity. This would be a slow and incremental process that could potentially create uncertainty around when modern AI is and is not to be categorised as a legal agent.

Whether AI can consistently meet the requirements of agency formation, and be characterised as an agent, will depend upon the accepted classes of necessity arising in relation to agency by operation of law or, alternatively, whether the issues of intention can be overcome so that agency involving modern AI can be formed through agreement.

3.3.3 Scope of Authority

The last threshold requirement I discuss is the scope of an agent's authority and how far this ought to extend if AI is to be characterised as an agent. The very nature of a principal–agent relationship entails the agent, to some extent,

43 Dal Pont (ed) (n 12) 149–150.
44 Dal Pont (n 12) 149–150; Simon Baughen, 'Who Is the Master now? Regulatory and Contractual Challenges of Unmanned Vessels' in Baris Soyer and Andrew Tettenborn (eds), *New Technologies, Artificial Intelligence and Shipping Law in the 21st Century* (Informa Law from Routledge, 2020) 129, 141–147.
45 Baughen (n 44) 141–147.
46 Baughen (n 44) 146–147.
47 Dal Pont (ed) (n 12) 153.

being granted authority to act on behalf of the principal and legally bind the principal. There are varying degrees of authority that can be bestowed on an agent. Broadly, authority can be viewed in two categories – actual or ostensible – each of which I now consider as they potentially relate to modern AI.

3.3.3.1 Actual Authority

Actual authority is a consensual agreement between the principal and agent where the agent accepts the scope of the authority bestowed upon them.[48] Actual authority can be *express* – that is, manifested in either written or oral form.[49] Where express authority is granted in oral form, the exact scope of that authority is discerned based on the circumstances surrounding the agency relationship and in light of the purpose of the agency relationship.[50] In terms of modern AI, it is difficult to foresee a situation in which a principal and an agent could distil express authority in a written form unless that written form was extended to non-traditional mediums.[51] If express authority in written form could be extended to technology that could co-ordinate between a principal and an AI agent, then perhaps this form of authority would be feasible in terms of AI systems such as modern AI.

As an alternative approach, it could be argued that the algorithms behind a modern AI system could constitute a clear set of instructions or parameters of functioning for the system and therefore be deemed a form of express authority between the principal and the agent. This approach is flawed, for several reasons. Firstly, the creator of the modern AI system responsible for the establishment of such algorithms may not also be the person deploying the system and, therefore, may not be the putative principal in such a relationship. Secondly, the scope of an agent's authority must be discernible so that instances where an agent potentially acts outside its scope can be ascertained. If the principal is not the creator of the system and does not have the requisite algorithmic literacy or means to access the algorithms, then they cannot, in such a situation, discern the scope of the authority purportedly bestowed upon the system in such a scenario. Another view is that such an approach reduces AI to the status of a tool rather than an independent actor. I consider the flaws of this view in Chapter 5. For now, actual authority in express form is not suited to modern AI.

Actual authority, however, can also be *implied*. Implied actual authority, by contrast, is discerned based on the conduct of both the principal and the agent.[52] This is more applicable to instances involving modern AI, as the

48 Dal Pont (ed) (n 12) 161–162.
49 Dal Pont (ed) (n 12) 162–163.
50 Dal Pont (ed) (n 12) 163.
51 By 'non-traditional forms of express written authority', I mean to suggest documents not in the nature of written contracts or deeds.
52 Dal Pont (ed) (n 12) 162–163.

relevant conduct of the parties could be examined considering each other to determine if there is the requisite interconnectedness to give rise to a situation of implied authority. Yet, this approach is not without its flaws either, for agency by ratification and by operation of law are forms of implied authority. As discussed, these forms of agency are not entirely suited to modern AI either. If actual ***implied*** authority is to hold and be applicable to modern AI, the issues pertaining to intention need to be resolved in favour of such systems.

3.3.3.2 Ostensible Authority

The second category for defining an agent's scope of authority is ostensible authority. Ostensible authority arises in situations where an agent has not been granted actual authority by a principal but the principal's ***conduct*** represents the agent as having authority.[53] Or, it occurs in instances where an agent has been granted actual authority but their actions exceed this authority, yet the principal purports that the authority of the agent nonetheless extends to the overreach.[54] Importantly, it is the principal's conduct that gives rise to the presumption that the agent has authority they have not actually been granted. Common scenarios in which ostensible authority arises from representations by a principal are during the course of dealings, when an agent is granted an office or title, or when an agent is permitted to sign a document.[55] In terms of AI, the most likely scenario where ostensible authority would arise is in the course of dealings. If AI is regularly deployed in the course of dealings, such as the replacement 'master of a ship' in the autonomous shipping example mentioned earlier, then a scenario could arise in which such a modern AI system could be inadvertently bestowed with ostensible authority. Ostensible authority in relation to AI would be determined by the conduct of the principal and, to a lesser extent, the purported (AI) agent, as it is the principal's conduct that represents whether the modern AI system is an agent.[56]

For a modern AI system to consistently be characterised as a legal agent, it must be able to meet the above threshold elements. More specifically, it must be able to exhibit the capacity of a legal person, and its existence as an agent must arise either by operation of law or by agreement in instances where the issues pertaining to intention are combatted. Additionally, such systems need to be bestowed with authority, most likely in the form of ostensible authority unless the mediums of express authority can be expanded to accommodate AI. If these elements cannot consistently be met, then it is not possible for modern AI to always be characterised as a legal agent. Instead, characterising modern AI as a legal agent will become ***situational***.

53 Dal Pont (ed) (n 12) 513.
54 Dal Pont (ed) (n 12) 517.
55 Dal Pont (ed) (n 12) 524–527.
56 This is a view shared by Beckers and Teubner. See: Beckers and Teubner (n 7) 63.

3.4. Problems with Modern AI as a Legal Agent

Despite that modern AI systems can situationally be characterised as legal agents, I now turn to consider whether they ought to be, given two potential problems.

3.4.1 Actions Outside the Scope of Authority

One key issue with characterising modern AI as a legal agent is what happens in situations where, as an agent, it acts outside the scope of its authority within the principal–agent relationship? Here, it is worth recalling the Group 2 modern AI systems referred to above that can exercise some degree of independence in setting ends and executing actions. More importantly, it is worth noting that these systems, by their very nature, are designed to act independently and achieve objectives not determined or *foreseen* by any principal. These systems lack a degree of predictability and, therefore, could quite easily act outside the scope of their authority.

Chopra and White have predicted the possibility of some artificial agents acting outside the scope of their authority. Whilst they do not focus on the specific forms of AI defined in Group 2, they have considered that it is at least possible for 'artificial agents' to potentially exceed the scope of their authority.[57] In response to such a scenario, they are of the view that, in these instances, the principal should not be liable for the actions of the agent.[58] This is not opposed to agency theories involving only natural persons. Yet, in theories involving only natural persons, the agent themselves is held liable for their out-of-scope actions, and so there is still a course of redress for an aggrieved party. This approach, together with that of the power liability model discussed in Section 3.2.2.2, arguably does not provide an avenue for redress in instances of out-of-scope actions. In contrast, the cost–benefit internalisation theory assumes that the principal ought to be liable regardless of the agent's actions – in or out of scope – so long as they are reasonably foreseeable.[59] Some scholars note that there are limited circumstances in which an AI agent can exceed its authority and consider ostensible authority can be relied upon in instances where the AI system acts outside the scope of its authority.[60] As been raised at previous junctures, some AI systems by their very nature are designed to act in ways that are unforeseeable. An AI system acting in an unforeseeable manner makes it more difficult for a principal to act as if, or purport that, the AI system has authority in advance of an action taken by the AI system exceeding its scope. The ostensible authority argument is therefore more likely to hold in instances where an AI system has exceeded the scope of its authority

57 Chopra and White (n 1) 48–49, 60–61.
58 Chopra and White (n 1) 60–61.
59 Dalley (n 22) 498.
60 Beckers and Teubner (n 7) 63.

through undertaking actions that were *foreseeably* (not unforeseeably) within its capabilities. This still poses the question of who could be held liable for unforeseeable out-of-scope actions by an AI agent. This is a question I address in Part III (Chapter 7). For now, it is prudent to identify that unforeseeable out-of-scope actions pose a challenge to characterising modern AI as an agent in all circumstances and, instead, a relativist or situational approach might be more appropriate.

3.4.2 Multiple Actors

Another potential challenge to modern AI agents arises in instances where there are multiple actors. Our discussions so far have been on the basis that there is but one 'principal' and one 'agent'. What happens if there is more than one principal or if there is more than one agent? How would this impact the ability of a modern AI system to be characterised and to function as a legal agent?

3.4.2.1 More than One Principal

A scenario with more than one principal could pose two key difficulties – firstly, in terms of agency formation. Where formation occurs by agreement, a consensus is reached between the parties as to what the objective of the agency relationship is. Impliedly, there must be a uniformity in approach agreed between the parties. In situations where there are multiple principals, this potentially poses an issue for the agent if the principals are not in agreement as to the objective purpose of the agency relationship. Secondly, and related to the first issue, is that multiple principals have the potential to give rise to a conflicting scope of authority bestowed upon the agent. Both issues have the potential to become even more problematic in instances where the agent is an artificial agent. Here, it is worth recalling the discussion in Section 3.3.3.1 in relation to whether an artificial agent can receive express authority. It is important to understand that the intentions of the principals must be received in a manner computable to the AI system. Considering this, where there is more than one principal in an agency relationship involving an AI actor, the principals must reach a uniform consensus that is *translatable* to the AI system, in both the process of agency formation – if by agreement – and defining the scope of the agent's authority. Failure to do so could result in conflicting approaches, which are likely to result in conflicting outputs by the AI agent.

3.4.2.2 More than One Agent

Scenarios where there is more than one agent, especially more than one AI agent, are more complex. The theories discussed in Section 3.2 largely rely on a uniformed approach to agency. By this, I mean to suggest that a point of commonality between the theories is that each assumes a particular degree of legal capacity is possessed by the agents under their consideration. Admittedly, there is some variance *between* the theories as to what degree of capacity is applicable. As I have already espoused, however, there can be varying degrees of legal capacity *within* a single theory of agency.[61] What happens to the principal–agent relationship if there is more than one agent and each agent exhibits different degrees of legal capacity?

A variation in capacity between agents is likely to affect the agency relationship. Firstly, it is likely to impact the scope of authority that could reasonably be granted to each agent. Modern AI agents with a greater degree of cognitive capacity, and, in turn, higher potential degrees of legal capacity are likely to be permitted a wider scope of authority within which to act. Although the scope of the agent with the more sophisticated level of capacity could potentially be limited to mirror that of its agent counterpart with a lesser capacity, this might not be desirable. It is conceivable that a principal could deploy two different forms of modern AI systems with varying capacities to act together to achieve a common goal and thereby act as joint agents. Consider again the example of an autonomous ship engaged in shipping transactions. It is conceivable that such a transaction could consist of multiple AI systems – one for navigation, one for steering, one acting as the 'master' of the ship, etc. Each of these systems could be acting in concert to achieve the end objective of shipping an owner's goods from one destination to another and transferring title of the goods to a new owner. Here, a joint agency situation could arise, with the individual agents having varying degrees of capacity and, in turn, scope. This may become an issue in instances where one agent within the joint agency relationship acts outside the scope of their authority or gives rise to an ostensible authority scenario – for how could the agent with a lesser capacity be jointly held to the standard of the system with the more sophisticated level of capacity? It would defeat the purpose of the joint agency relationship from the outset. Complicating the utility of an agency approach further is the possibility that distributed forms of AI systems, or AI systems comprised of multiple parts, might not fit neatly into an agency relationship. The possibility of multiple actors, or AI systems with multiple parts, therefore poses a challenge to the utility of characterising modern AI systems as legal agents and reinforces the view that such a classification ought not be constant but instead situational.

3.4.3 Complex AI

Another objection to only viewing AI as an agent is that agency as a concept has its limits. As Simon Chesterman highlights, when AI becomes complex and holds a degree of opacity and autonomy, this tests the limits of the utility

61 For a discussion on the varying degrees of legal capacity within agency, see Section 2.3.1 and Chapter 2.

of an agency account.[62] In such instances, AI is behaving as more than a mere tool and potentially beyond the control of the person deploying the system (or principal in a principal–agent relationship).[63] More complex forms of AI that are difficult for a natural person to exert control over may not be suited to being characterised as an agent, whilst more simplistic forms with increased transparency and less autonomy may be suited to an agency characterisation. AI therefore needs to be viewed situationally.

3.5. Agency and Situational Utility

In testing the robustness of the agency characterisation approach, it becomes apparent that agency and AI are not *always* compatible. What becomes clear is that although modern AI can theoretically be characterised as a legal agent of another legal person, this does not necessarily mean such systems should *consistently* be characterised as agents. The lack of consistency is especially apparent when commonly accepted criteria for agency are considered in the context of AI and how modern AI systems can fall short of these thresholds. This is key in that it encourages us to consider that AI is best characterised as a legal agent on a *situational* basis, thereby suggesting that agency is a partial solution to the question of how AI ought to be legally characterised.

Subsequently, there are other issues that will also need to be reconciled before determining the best method of characterisation – issues such as: if these systems are characterised as agent, when are they an agent and when are they not? When they are not an agent, are they to be characterised as a legal person, as property or as a combination of any one of these forms? These are issues I address in Chapter 5. Before doing so, however, I continue with my analysis of one of the key threshold issues that needs to be resolved in the process of assigning liability: how should AI be legally characterised? Therefore, I turn next to considering the potential for AI to be characterised as property in Chapter 4.

For now, what *is* discernible is that if modern AI is legally characterised as an agent, it cannot consistently be characterised as such, and so this form of characterisation alone is deficient. A more robust way of characterising AI is needed before turning to the remaining threshold requirements for assigning liability, addressed in Part III of this book.

62 Simon Chesterman, *We, The Robots? Regulating Artificial Intelligence and the Limits of the Law* (Cambridge University Press, 2021) 89.
63 Simon Chesterman, *We, The Robots? Regulating Artificial Intelligence and the Limits of the Law* (Cambridge University Press, 2021) 89–90.

References

A Articles/Books/Reports

Baughen, Simon 'Who Is the Master now? Regulatory and Contractual Challenges of Unmanned Vessels' in Baris Soyer and Andrew Tettenborn (eds), *New Technologies, Artificial Intelligence and Shipping Law in the 21st Century* (Informa Law from Routledge, 2020).

Beckers, Anna and Gunther Teubner, *Three Liability Regimes for Artificial Intelligence: Algorithmic Actants, Hybrids, Crowds* (Hart Publishing, 2021).

Chesterman, Simon, *We, The Robots? Regulating Artificial Intelligence and the Limits of the Law* (Cambridge University Press, 2021).

Chopra, Samir and Laurence White, *A Legal Theory for Autonomous Artificial Agents* (The University of Michigan Press, 4th ed, 2014).

Dal Pont, G E (ed), *Law of Agency* (LexisNexis Butterworths, 2nd ed, 2008).

McMeel, Gerard, 'Philosophical Foundations of the Law of Agency' (2000) 116(July) *Law Quarterly Review* 387.

Paula J Dalley, 'A Theory of Agency Law' (2011) 72(3) University of Pittsburgh Law Review 495.

B Cases

Field v Shoalhaven Transport Pty Ltd [1970] 3 NSWR 96

Launchbury v Morgans [1973] AC 127

4 AI as Property

A Limited View?

4.1. Proprietary Nature of AI

This chapter continues considering how AI ought to be legally characterised but seeks to evaluate a third option: that we could simply view modern forms of AI as property. This is important in determining the appropriate liability response because if AI can simply be viewed as property it could be subject to tort or product liability frameworks negating the need for other liability responses. Determining if AI can or should be viewed as property is important as a proprietary characterisation offers the possibility of liability responses different to an agency or legal personhood characterisation. This chapter tests whether AI amounts to property in some degree and under what circumstances. It considers the strengths and limitations of viewing AI as property and argues that AI should not *always* be typecast as property but may under certain conditions be viewed as such. It offers a situational account of whether AI is property. The significance of the view is relied upon in Chapter 5, where a situational approach to characterising AI is offered as a solution to the question of how AI ought to be characterised legally.

The legal personhood and agency characterisations considered in previous chapters are based on the premise that AI systems are capable of legal actions. Whilst this may be true, such characterisations do not sufficiently address the notion that AI systems could also be property. Debates have ensued as to whether AI systems can be characterised as property through copyright or patents.[1] Additionally, approaches seeking to apply a product liability framework to AI largely assume that AI is a consumer good.[2] What is clear, though, is that there is some consensus to characterise AI systems as property. Such a characterisation however is at odds with the autonomous decision-making nature of modern AI systems. In terms of characterising AI systems for the purpose of

1 For a discussion concerning if AI is subject to copyright or patent laws see: Swapnil Tripathi and Chandni Ghatak, 'Artificial Intelligence an Intellectual Property Law' (2018) 7(1) *Christ University Law Journal* 83.

2 Jacob Turner, *Robot Rules: Regulating Artificial Intelligence* (Palgrave Macmillan, 2019) 95–96.

DOI: 10.4324/9781003617549-7

assigning liability, there is a need to reconcile the views that such systems can be both property *and* capable of executing legal actions.

In reviewing whether AI can be characterised as property, this chapter adopts a comprehensive approach, which is possible due to the overall structure of Part II where different chapters review various characterisation methods. The chapter first considers non-intellectual property ('IP') forms of property. It considers whether AI systems in their entirety amount to property or if, instead, AI can partially be classified as property through its individual elements, such as its underlying algorithms. To engage in a robust consideration of whether AI can be characterised as property consideration is given to both tangible and intangible property. AI can take on a variety of forms; consider an autonomous car, which is a physical thing, in contrast to an AI system used to approve bank loans. It is for this reason that, in this chapter, I therefore first undertake a comparative analysis of property law to consider if AI may be attributed a proprietary status outside of IP. The chapter also offers a critical evaluation of arguments surrounding whether AI is a consumer good ('AI as a tool' view).

Whilst viewing AI as but merely a tool or a consumer product is one accepted method of characterising AI as property, it is not the only proprietary consideration in relation to this technology. Any chapter considering the proprietary implications of AI would be remiss to not also address relevant IP in relation to AI. In understanding if AI can be characterised as property, it is important to consider if AI can be viewed as either corporeal or non-corporeal property. To that end, this chapter also evaluates the merits of AI in terms of patents, copyright and the trade secret principle. This analysis informs the survey of whether AI is proprietary in nature.

The limitations of viewing AI as property are also addressed. In doing so consideration is given to the relationship between AI and data governance. The chapter also contemplates whether AI can *create* property drawing upon a series of patent applications and their correlating judicial decisions. To offer a holistic perspective and facilitate the integration if concepts from preceding chapters, the chapter briefly addresses the question of whether this view is compatible with legal personhood status before turning to evaluate whether characterising AI as property is sufficient. That is, if AI can be characterised as property, should it be? In doing so, it is proposed that yes, AI can be classified as property, but that does not mean that it should *always* be characterised *solely* as property. There are also circumstances, especially where AI systems are more sophisticated exhibiting greater degrees of autonomy, where we ought not view AI *solely* as property. Whether the approach of characterising AI with dual or multifunctionality (such as a hybrid of property and legal personhood) is feasible is not a topic explored in this chapter; instead, it is explored in Chapter 5.

4.2. Can AI Be Construed as Non-IP Property?

To determine if AI can be considered as a non-IP form of property, it is important to initially test if these systems can be established as having proprietary characteristics. Given that the potential non-IP proprietary status of AI (other than as a consumer product, which I explore below) is somewhat unexplored, I therefore engage in a comparative analysis of how different jurisdictions approach the question of managing forms of property.[3] In particular, I examine what rights and obligations these forms of property may attract. Here, I utilise a *functional comparative approach*,[4] which I adopt to identify the macro themes of commonality that transcend beyond individual jurisdictional families. It is for this reason that I consider the approach of both common law and the general European Union approach to managing forms of property. In turn, I intend to make observations about dealing with novel forms of property, which leads to the view that there is scope for AI to be characterised as a form of intangible property.

4.2.1 Comparative Approaches

In considering whether AI can be characterised as a non-IP form of property, I evaluate the approach of a variety of jurisdictions. The jurisdictions I have chosen for my analysis represent a broad cross-section of jurisdictional approaches to the issue of responding to the societal problem of classifying new technologies under the law. This allows me to identify macro themes of commonality, which are useful in my analysis of whether AI can be characterised as a non-IP form of property.

4.2.1.1 Australia

The Australian jurisdiction distinguishes between *real property (reality)* and *personal property (personality)*, with the former being land and the latter being property other than land.[5] AI is arguably not land. Although I acknowledge that there are various AI systems that interact with land for specific objectives, such as improving agricultural practices, I consider these systems to be independent of land, as they hold objectives that merely interact with land rather than integrating with it. It is not inconceivable that AI systems may reach a point where they are integrated with land or buildings, but as these are not widespread practice as yet, I do not consider real property in my analysis.

3 In terms of searches relating to AI as a form of property that is not 'intellectual property', I conducted various searches across legal encyclopaedias (such as *Halsbury's Laws of Australia*, *Halsbury's Laws of England*), legal databases (such as Lexis Advance, Westlaw), journal platforms (such as HeinOnline) and Google Scholar utilising variations of the following terms: "AI" OR "Artificial Inteligen!" OR "machine learn!" w/10 "property" OR "chattel".

4 For further detail about a functional comparative approach, see: Ralf Michaels, 'The Functional Method of Comparative Law' in Mathias Reimann and Reinhard Zimmermann (eds), *Oxford Handbook of Comparative Law* (Oxford Academic, 2nd ed., 2019) 345.

5 LexisNexis, *Halsbury's Laws of Australia*, vol. 1 (online at 3 October 2021) 315 Personal Property '(A) Introduction—Meaning and Classification of Personal Property' [315-1].

Instead, I focus on personal property and the rights and obligations to which this gives rise and their potential applicability to AI. Within personal property, there are additional sub-categories, each bestowing different rights and obligations. Broadly, personal property can be divided into *chattels real* – interests in land – and *chattels personal*.[6] Similarly, for the reasons mentioned relating to real property, I am not focusing on chattels real in my analysis. Instead, I consider chattels personal and the various categories of this form of property.

Within chattels personal there are two key categories. The first is *incorporeal personal property* (*chose in action*).[7] These are forms of personal property that are incapable of actually being possessed – that is, they are not physical forms of personal property.[8] Instead, this form of property is intangible and protected through the allocation of legal rights and remedies to this form or property.[9] I delve deeper into this form or property shortly, but first I want to identify the second form of personal property: *corporeal personal property* (*chose in possession*). Corporeal personal property, in contrast, entails tangibility – that is, this is a form of property that is physically capable of being possessed. Depending on how AI is deployed, it is potentially possible for this technology to, at times, be classified as either incorporeal or corporeal personal property. I now turn to considering the merits of each account in relation to AI.

In evaluating whether AI could be construed as either category of chattels personal, it is important to explore the notion of possession in more depth. First, I focus on possession as it relates to choses in possession. Legal possession as a concept is still not always clearly defined, yet it can be broadly divided into *actual* and *constructive possession*.[10] *Legal possession* arises when a person in possession of tangible property is of the mindset that they are entitled to exclusive control of that property and are free to use the property without interference from others.[11] It is therefore a legal relationship between a legal person and other legal persons in relation to a corporeal object.[12] Actual and constructive possession differs in terms of the relationship the possessor has with other people regarding the rights associated with the corporeality of property. Actual possession arises when a possessor takes physical possession of a chattel, thereby putting other persons on notice that they, the possessor,

6 LexisNexis, *Halsbury's Laws of Australia*, vol. 1 (online at 3 October 2021) 315 Personal Property '(A) Introduction—Meaning and Classification of Personal Property' [315-1].

7 LexisNexis, *Halsbury's Laws of Australia*, vol. 1 (online at 3 October 2021) 315 Personal Property '(A) Introduction—Meaning and Classification of Personal Property' [315-1].

8 LexisNexis, *Halsbury's Laws of Australia*, vol. 1 (online at 3 October 2021) 315 Personal Property '(A) Introduction—Meaning and Classification of Personal Property' [315-1].

9 LexisNexis, *Halsbury's Laws of Australia*, vol. 1 (online at 3 October 2021) 315 Personal Property '(A) Introduction—Meaning and Classification of Personal Property' [315-1].

10 Possession is a debated topic still—see *Introduction to Property and Commercial Law*, Scott Grattan and Sheelagh McCracken (eds) (Thomson Reuters (Professional) Australia Limited, 2016) 197.

11 Grattan and McCracken (n 10) 197; see also *Knapp v Knapp* [1944] SASR 257 at 265.

12 Grattan and McCracken (n 10) 198.

have rights in that chattel.[13] Actual possession could not therefore be applied to intangible property. Constructive possession, in contrast, arises when the possessor puts other persons on notice that they *intend* to possess the object and take control over that object, even though they do not actually possess the object.[14] In essence, constructive possession puts other persons on notice that the possessor has a legal right to possession,[15] even though they do not have actual corporeal possession of the property.

I next want to contrast possession as it relates to choses in possession against that of the situation relating to choses in action. Like choses in possession, choses in action are a legal relationship between a legal person and other legal persons in relation to property – but here, it refers to *intangible* property. The lack of corporeality in choses in action, however, marks a key differential point between the rights these forms of property attract, for an intangible, non-corporeal form of property cannot be physically possessed. The method by which rights are ascribed to this form of property therefore cannot be by actual or constructive possession. Instead, choses in action give rise to an *in personam* bare right of action (or litigation).[16] This marks a key point of differentiation between choses in possession, which attract rights *in rem*. This *in personam* vs *in rem* classification of rights is particularly important when considering the potential proprietary status of AI.

There is a question of whether AI is best characterised as a chose in action or a chose in possession. In terms of how AI could be classified, this will depend on whether an AI system can be viewed as independent of any host technology. There exists a divide between AI systems that operate with or without additional data being provided to the AI system through a physical object that hosts the system. Consider, for example, a driverless car in contrast to an AI system deployed by a bank to approve or decline loan applications. A driverless car operates with the use of AI but via a physical object – a car – that informs the operation of the AI system. The car is central to the operation of the AI system because, as it operates, the car itself provides feedback data to the AI system, which it then uses in its processes. In this respect, the AI system underpinning an autonomous car is inherently linked to the physical object hosting the system – the car – for additional data to operate. This raises the question of whether the AI system underpinning the car's decision-making processes can be viewed independently of the car itself or, instead, if the AI system must be viewed as part of the car. From this, I mean to suggest that whether the AI system can be physically possessed by a legal person will determine its potential classification.

13 Grattan and McCracken (n 10) 197.
14 Grattan and McCracken (n 10) 197–198.
15 Grattan and McCracken (n 10) 201.
16 Grattan and McCracken (n 10) 326.

To underscore my point, by way of contrast in the loan example, this AI system would not necessarily be dependent upon a physical object to operate but could operate solely in an intangible form independent of feedback from a physical object's interaction with the world around it. That is, the computer or device linked to the system in this intangible example does not provide additional data that is used by the AI system and is necessary for it to operate. In other words, unlike the autonomous car example, the loan AI system is not inherently linked or dependent upon a physical object to provide it with data essential to its operation. There is no car with cameras collecting road traffic data, for example, to inform the operation of the system. If, in my loan example, the AI system can be viewed as operating independently from a physical object (or without additional input data that is derived from a connected physical object that is essential for the system to operate), then a case could be made that AI systems, if classified as property, ought only to be classified as choses in action and never as choses in possession.

It is not inconceivable, however, that in instances where AI systems are integrated into a physical object, such as a car, they are largely dependent upon the object to operate (because, as noted earlier, the driverless car itself provides feedback data to the AI system, which it then uses in its processes). On this basis, it is unlikely that such AI systems could be separated from their physical hosts. Rather, they are integrated and dependent upon their physical hosts to operate. It could be said, then, that whether an AI system is a chose in action or a chose in possession depends on the degree to which such systems are independent from physical objects in their ability to operate. The degree to which an AI system is reliant upon a physical object to operate or integrated into a physical object is therefore important, as it influences whether an AI system can be classified as either a chose in action or a chose in possession.

4.2.1.2 New Zealand

New Zealand's common law approach to personal property in most respects mirrors that of other common law jurisdictions. It is for this reason that I do not intend to labour the particulars of personal property law. Instead, I am of the view that it is useful to consider developments in New Zealand case law, the principles of which could be applied to the question of whether AI may be classified as property. Here, I extrapolate macro themes to identify key qualities that are essential to characterising AI as property.

A New Zealand case considering the potential proprietary nature of crypto assets, such as Bitcoin, offers a useful point of comparison. The case in question, *Ruscoe v Cryptopia Ltd (in liq)* ('*Ruscoe*'),[17] adjudicates the issue of whether cryptocurrencies are considered property. Given the digital nature of these currencies, which are governed by algorithms, they are in some ways

17 *Ruscoe v Cryptopia Ltd (in liq)* [2020] NZHC 728 ('*Ruscoe*').

analogous to AI systems. AI systems, like cryptocurrencies, are assets found in the form of a digital medium that are 'powered' or underpinned by algorithms. My comparison of AI and cryptocurrencies is confined to these points of similarity. I do, however, acknowledge that AI also has a 'cognitive' aspect not common to cryptocurrencies (that is, the algorithms underpinning AI use reasoning processes to achieve a goal, or an end, in a way that the algorithms behind cryptocurrencies do not). In considering whether AI can be construed as property, it is therefore worth examining the salient features of this case.

Before turning to the specifics of the *Ruscoe* case, I pause to provide a *brief* overview of cryptocurrency technology so that I can later draw an analogy between this technology and the intangible nature of AI. Cryptocurrencies are a digital form of currency. Importantly, these currencies are stored in digital 'wallets' and are protected by algorithms that act as 'keys' to unlock or lock the wallets and prevent non-owners from accessing the currency. Cryptocurrency transactions are conducted on a peer-to-peer basis and are openly recorded on a centralised distributed ledger known as blockchain; therefore, it is clear when ownership of such currencies transfers to a new owner.

In 2020, the New Zealand High Court was asked to consider if cryptocurrencies could be characterised as property and, additionally, if such a currency is capable of being held on trust. There is limited case law addressing this issue,[18] yet it is an interesting question, as cryptocurrencies, like AI systems, are a digital medium. In considering whether cryptocurrencies constitute property, Gendall J ultimately applied the indicia from *National Provincial Bank Ltd v Ainsworth* ('*Ainsworth*').[19] Broadly, Lord Wilberforce identified in *Ainsworth* that for a 'thing' to be deemed property, it must adhere to four indicia: firstly, that a right or interest in relation to the thing must be definable (first indicia); secondly, that this must be 'identifiable by third parties' (second indicia); thirdly, that it must be 'capable in its nature of assumption by third parties' (third indicia); and lastly, that there must be 'a degree of permanence or stability' associated with the right or interest (fourth indicia) (together, the *Ainsworth Indicia*).[20]

Gendall J ultimately concluded that each of the Ainsworth Indicia was met in relation to cryptocurrencies, but his underlying reasoning is useful in considering the proprietary status of AI. In relation to the first indicia, Gendall J found that the fact cryptocurrencies are recordable in a blockchain – a

18 There are two notable cases outside of New Zealand that also address the question of whether crypto assets are property: the English case of *AA v Persons Unknown* [2019] EWHC 3556 and also the Singaporean case of *B2C2 Ltd v Quoine Pte Ltd* [2019] SGHC (1) 03 ('*B2C2 Ltd v Quoine Pte Ltd*'). I consider the latter of these in depth in this chapter but do not review the English case, for I note its reasoning largely mirrors that of the Singaporean case.

19 *National Provincial Bank Ltd v Ainsworth* [1965] 1 AC 1175 ('*National Provincial Bank Ltd v Ainsworth*'), in particular at 1247–1248.

20 *National Provincial Bank Ltd v Ainsworth* [1965] 1 AC 1175 ('*National Provincial Bank Ltd v Ainsworth*'), in particular at 1247–1248.

distributive ledger of sorts – means that although intangible, these forms of technology are clearly definable.[21] Here, it is worth recalling the varying forms of AI discussed in the *Introduction*. Regardless of the form of AI (supervised, unsupervised, etc.), these are clearly defined systems that are underpinned by a set of algorithms that power their operation. It could be said, then, that AI systems are also intangible but defined by clear parameters, meeting the first indicia.[22]

In terms of the second indicia, Gendall J largely relied upon the nature of blockchain technology to meet the required threshold. He argued that the public visibility of a blockchain – meaning that transactions are traceable on the platform – meant that cryptocurrencies are identifiable to third parties.[23] AI systems are not as readily identifiable as cryptocurrencies on a blockchain platform. The commercial value in AI systems is often derived from protecting the algorithms that underpin this technology from disclosure to the general public. AI systems are therefore *prima facie* less transparent than cryptocurrencies – a potential obstacle to establishing the second indicia in favour of AI systems. Instead, it perhaps should become a question not of whether AI systems are *identifiable* by third parties but, rather, whether the technology is *capable* of being identified by third parties. The owners of AI systems could increase the transparency of their systems so that they are examinable and, therefore, more readily identifiable by third parties. On this basis, AI systems could meet the second indicia.

The third indicia is perhaps not as easily met for AI as it is for cryptocurrencies, but it is not necessarily insurmountable. The third indicia requires that for something to be considered property, it must be transferable or assignable to another.[24] That is, for AI to be conceived of as property under the *Ainsworth Indicia*, it must be capable of being transferred between owners. Gendall J found that this threshold was clearly met in terms of cryptocurrencies based on the notion that there is a clearly defined and established market for the exchange of these currencies.[25] There is not such an apparent market for the exchange of AI systems. Despite this, that is not to say that AI systems cannot be transferred between persons or possession of such systems transferred between persons. Consider, for example, the *Oral-B iO series 9* electronic toothbrush, which Oral-B purports is supported by *genius* artificial intelligence that analyses a user's brushing habits and, in response,

21 Paul Babie, David Brown, Ryan Catterwell and Mark Giancaspro, 'Cryptocurrency as Property: Ruscoe v Cryptopia Ltd (in liq) [2020] NZHC 728' (2020) 28 *Australian Property Law Journal* 106, 114.

22 The only exception to the notion that AI algorithms are a set of clearly defined parameters is the notion of black-box and deep-learning forms of AI, for which one cannot, by the very nature of the technology, trace the algorithms.

23 Paul Babie (n 21).

24 Paul Babie (n 21).

25 Paul Babie (n 21).

offers cleaning recommendations.[26] This device is not only useful for cleaning one's teeth but is also useful as an illustrative example of the proprietary qualities of AI. Assuming the 'genius' AI system is inbuilt into the toothbrush and not hosted on another platform[27], ownership of that AI system could be conceived of as being passed from Oral-B to the purchaser of the electronic toothbrush.[28] Alternatively, if ownership does not pass outright to the purchaser of the toothbrush, the AI system could be said to be *in the possession* of the purchaser but for a specific purpose (such as assisting with tooth brushing and not redistribution of the AI system). What is key here is that there exists the *potential* for AI systems to be assumed by third parties, thereby meeting the requirements of the third indicia to be classified as property.

Lastly, in terms of the fourth indica, Gendall J found this bore little weight in considering the proprietary nature of cryptocurrencies. His Honour observed that there are varying forms of assets that are fleeting, citing an example of concert tickets, which have an expiration date; additionally, he indicated that circulating assets, such as currency in a bank account, are not permanent assets either.[29] In this respect, he found that the degree of permanence of the asset is not central to the question of whether cryptocurrencies can be characterised as property. Given the similarities between cryptocurrencies and AI systems, it is reasonable to view the degree of an AI system's permanence as also not being material to whether such systems constitute property.

The application of the *Ainsworth Indica* to a novel technology, viz. cryptocurrencies, in the *Ruscoe* case highlights several key themes about what constitutes 'property' when confronted with new forms of technology. Two key themes emerge. Firstly, the legal interaction with the technology must give rise to both legal rights and duties for the persons engaging with the technology. For example, legal persons holding title to the technology could have the right to *exclusive possession* of the technology. Conversely, this in turn would impose a duty of *non-interference* on others so that they do infringe upon the property holders' rights. In this regard, for an AI system to be deemed property, it must be a 'thing' capable of invoking legal rights and duties in relation to how persons engage with the system.

26 See: 'Oral-B iO™, The Biggest Innovation in Oral Care History Is Now Available Nationwide', *businesswire.com* (Web Page, 20 August 2020) <https://www.businesswire.com/news/home/20200820005069/en/Oral-B-iO™-The-Biggest-Innovation-in-Oral-Care-History-Is-Now-Available-Nationwide>.

27 Assuming the AI system is inbuilt into the toothbrush and not hosted on another platform controlled by Oral-B, such as a cloud-based platform.

28 I acknowledge that there are a variety of potential legal mechanisms, such as contractual clauses, copyright, licencing arrangements, etc., that could potentially be used by Oral-B to prevent ownership of their AI system passing outright to a purchaser of the toothbrush. I merely wish to use the toothbrush as an illustrative example of the *potential* for AI systems to be passed between individuals and thereby demonstrate their proprietary capacity.

29 Paul Babie (n 21).

The second key theme arising from this case is that for new forms of technology to constitute property, it must be capable of assumption: that is, the rights and interests in the technology must be capable of passing from one person – legal or natural – to another. For now, what is discernible from the *Ruscoe* case is that there are two key requirements for new technology to be classified as property: a rights–duty and an assumption requirement.

4.2.1.3 Singapore

Singapore, as a jurisdiction, largely subscribes to the same delineation of personal property law that other common law jurisdictions follow – in particular, the division between corporeal and incorporeal property. Tan Yock Lin[30] provides a useful overview of not only Singapore's municipal property law but also the debates surrounding intangible property more specifically. Given the large practical similarities between common law approaches to personal property law, it is this latter point of Tan's – the debates – that I now proceed to consider, as I am of the view that these discussions will contribute to addressing the question of whether AI can or ought to be classified as property.

Tan's overview provides both a doctrinal and theoretical overview of Singaporean approaches to intangible property. It is his consideration of the theoretical approaches that I am more interested in for my purposes. Tan concludes that doctrinal accounts often result in non-flexible approaches to defining intangible property; that is, doctrinal views are less accommodating of new potential forms of intangible property.[31] In terms of theoretical approaches to intangible property, he considers three forms of this type of property: choses in action, securities and intellectual property. I do not focus on his considerations of securities as, being specific financial instruments, these are not likely to capture AI. I do, however, consider choses in action and, later, intellectual property in Section 4.3.

Tan considers that choses in action as a concept hold a greater degree of flexibility than other forms of intangible property. He notes that, as a concept, choses in action have traditionally been confined to personal property rights that manifest as enabling an individual to bring a legal action or having the right to sue.[32] Tan does, however, highlight that choses in action have since evolved and expanded in meaning to encapsulate rights that cannot be physically possessed but can be protected by legal action.[33] In support of this view, he cites several examples of recently recognised choses in action, such as interests in partnerships, permits and admission tickets, among others.[34]

30 Tan Yock Lin, *Personal Property Law* (Singapore Academy of Law, 2014).
31 Tan Yock Lin, *Personal Property Law* (Singapore Academy of Law, 2014) 778–782.
32 Tan Yock Lin, *Personal Property Law* (Singapore Academy of Law, 2014) 820.
33 Tan Yock Lin, *Personal Property Law* (Singapore Academy of Law, 2014) 824.
34 Tan Yock Lin, *Personal Property Law* (Singapore Academy of Law, 2014) 824.

This expansion of the concept of choses in action is an important theoretical observation. It then becomes a question as to whether AI can fit into this expanded concept.

Determining whether AI is compatible with an expanded form of choses in action requires a closer examination of the concept of AI with regard to key proprietary principles. Recalling Tan's expanded account of a chose in action, for AI to be classified as such a form of property, two key elements are required: (1) that it is not capable of being physically possessed and (2) that it can be protected by legal action. I now consider each of these elements in turn. The first element, incorporeality, may initially seem a straightforward observation if we take the view that AI is, in essence, confined to merely being the underlying algorithms responsible for the operation of each AI system. According to this view, AI would surely be incorporeal. Yet, as previously discussed above, there is the possibility for an AI system to be dependent upon a physical object, such as a car or robot. If the AI system is dependent upon a physical object, then the first element of incorporeality is not met, furthering the view that these forms of AI ought to be classified as a chose in action. In instances where AI is not dependent upon a physical object, the first threshold can be established.

From here, it then becomes a question of whether the second threshold – protection by legal action – can be met in relation to AI. More pointedly, is AI something legally worth protecting by legal action? That is, does AI as a 'thing' give rise to rights and obligations capable of being protected or upheld by legal action? Here, Tan offers additional useful commentary. He notes that intangible property rights are not derived from dominion and control but, rather, are created through personal relationships.[35] More specifically, he notes that intangible property obtains value through an exchangeable social abstraction.[36] By this account, for AI to hold proprietary value, such value would be derived through a form of social relationship between persons in which AI is recognised as property and, in exchange, the AI system is treated as a thing of value. Although seemingly a somewhat abstract concept, there are numerous examples of this already occurring in practical contexts: recall the Oral B toothbrush mentioned earlier.

In 2019, the Singaporean International Commercial Court also considered a case involving automated decisions. In *B2C2 Ltd v Quoine Pte Ltd*,[37] B2C2 traded cryptocurrencies using the Singaporean currency exchange platform 'Quoine'. Importantly, the platform did not operate as intended and executed trades that were distinctively advantageous to B2C2. After uncovering these defective trades, Quoine reversed the exchanges. In the first instance, Thorley IJ was subsequently asked to consider several issues in response to these defec-

35 Tan Yock Lin, *Personal Property Law* (Singapore Academy of Law, 2014) 777.
36 Tan Yock Lin, *Personal Property Law* (Singapore Academy of Law, 2014) 777.
37 *B2C2 Ltd v Quoine Pte Ltd* [2019] SGHC (I) 03 ('*B2C2 Case*').

tive trades. Firstly, whether the defective trades amounted to a breach of contract and if so, whether the trades could be void on the grounds of mistake. Secondly, whether the cryptocurrencies could be construed as property held on trust and, therefore, whether Quoine's reversal of the trades constituted a breach of trust. It is in considering the first issue that Thorley IJ's opinion is particularly interesting. Notably, he found that the algorithms in this instance were set to achieve an end goal and only that end goal.[38] Additionally, he observed that the systems did not have any independent thought processes.[39] Importantly, the platform was structured in a way that did not grant the system a degree of autonomy in achieving its end goal.

The reasoning of this Singaporean case is confined. Thorley IJ tends to view the automatic decision-making platform as a tool. The problem with this approach is that although it rightfully considers the technology in dispute, it also seems to assume that, as a broader rule, AI systems do not have the ability to reason autonomously. It is problematic that Thorley IJ seemingly type-casted all AI systems in this role, as it ignores the distinctly different systems like those considered in the *Introduction*. On appeal, that majority upheld Thorley IJ's decision in relation to the first issues, thereby endorsing this reasoning.[40]

It is worth pausing to note then that Thorley IJ reached a similar view to that established in the New Zealand *Ruscoe* case discussed above.[41] Importantly, Thorley IJ applied the *Ainsworth Indicia* and held that cryptocurrencies, although intangible, are a thing that is clearly identifiable and attracts value.[42] This in turn allowed him to conclude that they are proprietary in nature.[43]

4.2.1.4 European Union

European Union (EU) law, as a community body, is generally accommodating of intangible property as a concept. There is a view that defining a uniformed set of property rules at an EU level is difficult, as it is still a largely developing area of EU law.[44] One view is that, at an EU level, most property law focuses

38 *B2C2 Ltd v Quoine Pte Ltd* [2019] SGHC (1) 03 ('*B2C2 Case*') at [208].

39 *B2C2 Ltd v Quoine Pte Ltd* [2019] SGHC (1) 03 ('*B2C2 Case*') at [208].

40 *Quoine Pte Ltd v B2C2 Ltd* [2020] SGCA(I) 2.

41 It is worth acknowledging for completeness that the *B2C2 Ltd v Quoine Pte Ltd* case was decided *before* the *Ruscoe*, but they both follow similar lines of reasoning.

42 *B2C2 Ltd v Quoine Pte Ltd* (n 17) at [142]–[143]; Gwen Wackwitz and Jenna Rennie, 'Cryptocurrencies: Property, Trust and Mistake', *White & Case* (Web Page, 10 April 2019) <https://www.whitecase.com/publications/alert/cryptocurrencies-property-trust-and-mistake>.

43 It is worth pausing to note that reasoning adopted in *B2C2 Ltd v Quoine Pte Ltd* (n 17) was also applied in the English case of *AA v Persons Unknown* [2019] EWHC 3556.

44 Eveline Ramaekers, 'The Development of EU Property Law' (2015) 3 *European Review of Private Law* 437, 443.

on considering what is an object of property law.[45] As a general principle, EU law will accept intangible forms of property, providing there is an underlying economic value to this property.[46] Based on this account, one prerequisite for AI to be recognised as property is that it must hold value in an economic sense. Meeting this threshold is not implausible, given that these systems can attain strong commercial value.[47] The overall approach of EU law, at this stage, is to recognise intangible forms of property, even if the recognition of intangible forms of property are still, as a concept, open for debate within individual member states.[48] On this account, even if a generalised EU property law approach is still in development, its rudimentary stages are therefore supportive of intangible forms of property that hold commercial value. In this respect, assuming that AI meets this threshold, EU law would be accommodating of recognising AI as intangible property. French law, to an extent, mirrors that of the EU general approach.

4.2.1.5 Observations Arising from the Comparison

The above analysis yields several key themes in response to the social problem of how novel forms of property can be managed. Firstly, characterising AI as property will depend on the degree of corporeality of a system and whether such a system can be viewed independently from physical objects or is instead reliant upon a physical object for additional data to operate.[49] In this respect, it is possible that AI could exist as two varying forms of property: either as a chose in action or a chose in possession, depending on the level of independence the system exhibits from a physical object. When AI lacks a degree of independence from a physical object an analogy could be drawn with other digital assets. Digital assets, like software, have been considered corporeal in nature due to being stored on physical devices or hardware.[50] Secondly, for AI to be considered a chose in action, it is necessary to expand on traditional forms of choses in action to include newer intangible property that is of

45 Eveline Ramaekers, 'The Development of EU Property Law' (2015) 3 *European Review of Private Law* 437, 443.

46 Eveline Ramaekers, 'What is Property Law?' (2017) 37(3) *Oxford Journal of Legal Studies* 588, 604.

47 Jaques Bughin et al., 'Notes from the AI Frontier: Modelling the Impact of AI on the World Economy', *McKinsey Global Institute* (September 2018) <https://www.mckinsey.com/featured-insights/artificial-intelligence/notes-from-the-ai-frontier-modeling-the-impact-of-ai-on-the-world-economy>.

48 Ramaekers (n 44).

49 Jacob Turner acknowledges that, for most current forms of AI, it is distinct from the physical hardware it requires to operate. See: Jacob Turner, *Robot Rules: Regulating Artificial Intelligence* (Palgrave Macmillan, 2019) 198. The degree of corporeality of an AI system will become increasingly important as AI evolves.

50 Sarah Green and John Randall, *The Tort of Conversion* (Hart Publishing, 2009) 118–119.

value.[51] Thirdly, AI gains recognition as property as a result of the relationship an owner of AI has with other persons where these other persons are put on notice that the owner has rights in the AI system, such as the right to control the use of the system, and these rights are recognised in reciprocation. Lastly, AI must be capable of assumption for it to be considered property. From the discussions above, it is apparent that AI could, in certain circumstances, meet these requirements and therefore be considered as property. Whether AI *ought* to be considered property is another question, and it is one I address in part below in Section 4.5 and further in Chapter 5.

4.2.2 AI as a Consumer Good (the 'AI as a Tool' Approach)

Another way in which AI could be conceived of as property is for it to be viewed as a consumer good. As Jacob Turner identifies, the literature typically focuses on whether product liability is an appropriate liability framework for AI and often assumes that AI is capable of being viewed as a consumer product.[52] Whether product liability is the most appropriate liability framework for AI is a topic I consider at other junctures in this book.[53] There are problems with this assumption. Firstly, as Turner and Simon Chesterman both acknowledge, AI could be conceived of as a product, but it could also be regarded as a service.[54] Simply assuming that AI is but a consumer product may be valid for some types of AI, but it is an insufficient assumption in relation to *all types* of AI. Doing so equates AI to the status of a 'mere tool'.

The concept of autonomy is an important part of the debate for advocates of the AI-as-a-tool approach. AI-as-a-tool proponents, such as Eliza Mik, contend that there is a difference between how autonomy is conceived in legal, political and philosophical disciplines, in contrast to how it is viewed by AI or computer scientists.[55] Mik notes that, in law, autonomy concerns whether an

51 Expanding on traditional forms of choses in action to include newer intangible property that is of value is a view that is shared by other commentators in relation to different forms of digital technologies. See for example the discussion of Green and Randall in relation to 'digital assets' or 'software' although they place a stronger emphasis on whether these forms of technology have value than whether they are a chose in possession or action: Green and Randall (n 50) 128–131.

52 Turner (n 1) 95–96.

53 For discussion concerning if product liability is an appropriate framework for AI, see the discussions in Chapters 1, 6, 7 and 8 together with: Anna Beckers and Gunther Teubner, *Three Liability Regimes for Artificial Intelligence: Algorithmic Actants, Hybrids, Crowds* (Hart Publishing, 2021) 74–79; Ryan Abbott, *The Reasonable Robot: Artificial Intelligence and the Law* (Cambridge University Press, 2020) 50–58; Turner (n 1) 91–98; and Simon Chesterman, *We, The Robots? Regulating Artificial Intelligence and the Limits of the Law* (Cambridge University Press, 2021) 93–97.

54 Turner (n 1) 95–98; Chesterman (n 53) 95.

55 Eliza Mik, 'AI as a Legal Person?' in Jyn-An Lee et al. (ed.), *Artificial Intelligence and Intellectual Property* (Oxford University Press, 2021) 419, 422–3.

entity has the capacity to engage in self-governance or self-rule.[56] In contrast, in an AI technical context, autonomy assumes a different meaning – one that is defined by the interactions between a human actor and an AI system.[57] More specifically, autonomy is defined in terms of the degree of automation in which an AI system engages.[58] That is, the greater the degree to which an AI system automates its actions, the more 'autonomous' the system is considered.

The AI-as-a-tool view considers that autonomy is largely informed by the degree of control a human exerts over an AI system, rather than the degree to which an AI system is capable of exhibiting independence in executing actions. Core to this approach is the notion of control, which AI-as-a-tool contemporaries, such as Mik, acknowledge is complex and largely context based. There may be merit in viewing AI as a tool under *some* circumstances but not when the AI system is more complex and capable of acting with some degree of independence. Characterising AI as a mere tool therefore overlooks the varying complexities of this technology.[59] Whilst there are problems with this approach, I pause here to acknowledge that there is at least the possibility of AI being viewed as a consumer good, furthering the notion that AI could be characterised as property.

4.3. AI as Intellectual Property

I now turn to evaluate the view that AI can be classified as intellectual property. I continue my comparative approach in contemplating whether AI meets the requirements of patent and copyright law together with examining the relevancy of trade secrets. I then move to evaluate the merits of these approaches.

Adopting the view that trademarks are an identifying sign or feature capable of distinguishing between classes of goods and services,[60] I do not consider trademark law in my analysis. Here, it is important to recall from the discussions of the types of modern AI in the *Introduction* that AI are systems designed to 'reason' towards set outcomes or, instead, to even achieve their own ends through a process of discovery. As such, I view AI as being more complex than simply a sign or feature alluding to the differences between goods and services, and so I will be excluding trademark law from my considerations.

56 Eliza Mik, 'AI as a Legal Person?' in Jyn-An Lee et al. (ed.), *Artificial Intelligence and Intellectual Property* (Oxford University Press, 2021) 419, 422.

57 Eliza Mik, 'AI as a Legal Person?' in Jyn-An Lee et al. (ed.), *Artificial Intelligence and Intellectual Property* (Oxford University Press, 2021) 419, 423.

58 Eliza Mik, 'AI as a Legal Person?' in Jyn-An Lee et al. (ed.), *Artificial Intelligence and Intellectual Property* (Oxford University Press, 2021) 419, 423.

59 For further discussions concerning the complex nature of AI, see the *Introduction*.

60 'Trademarks: What Is a Trademark?', *World Intellectual Property Organisation* (Web Page) <https://www.wipo.int/trademarks/en/>.

4.3.1 Patents

The patentable status of AI across jurisdictions is largely questionable. It is worth noting that inventions by AI systems have also been considered as potentially patentable. I do not consider that issue here but do so in Section 4.4. Here, I consider the approaches of the UK, EU, US and Australia in determining whether AI is patentable.

4.3.1.1 United Kingdom (UK) and European Union

The *Patents Act 1977* (UK) was amended to mirror that of the *European Patent Convention 1973*,[61] and so it is sensible to consider the approach of the UK and the EU in parallel. In both jurisdictions, there is a presumption at law that AI is non-patentable.[62] Consider s 1(2) of the *Patents Act 1977* (UK) and article 52 (2) of the *European Patent Convention*, both of which provide that, among other things, the following are specifically non-patentable forms of property: 'schemes, rules and methods for performing mental acts, playing games or doing business', 'programs for computers' and 'mathematical methods'.[63] Each of these prohibitions provides a *prima facie* presumption that AI is not patentable property in the UK or EU, as each of these could be said to be elements that underpin AI, viz. 'mathematical methods', or instead, if not elements of AI, they could represent objectives of an AI system, viz. 'performing mental acts'.

The EU has cemented the presumption that AI is non-patentable through providing additional guidelines regarding the question of AI patentability.[64] The guidelines provide that as AI is of 'an abstract mathematical nature', it is not patentable unless it falls into an exception provided for in the guidance for 'mathematical methods'. [65] The guidance for mathematical methods outlines that, in very limited circumstances, an exemption exists permitting their patentability.[66] To engage this exemption, the methods need to be deployed via technical means, such as a computer, and address a subject matter that is technical in nature.[67] That is, the mathematical methods underpinning an AI

61 *Convention on the Grant of European Patents* ('*European Patent Convention*'), European Union signed 5 October 1973 EPC (entered into force 7 October 1977).

62 Justice of the Supreme Court Lord Kitchin, 'UKIPO—WIPO Conference Keynote Speech' (UKIPO—WIPO Conference Keynote Speech, UKIPO—WIPO Conference, 18 June 2019) <https://www.supremecourt.uk/docs/speech-190618.pdf>.

63 '*European Patent Convention*' (n 61) art. 52 (2); *Patents Act 1977* (UK) s1(2)(b).

64 Lord Kitchin (n 62); European Patent Office, '*Guidelines for Examination in the European Patent Office 2023*', *EPO* (Document, March 2023) Art 52(2)(a) <https://link.epo.org/web/epo_guidelines_for_examination_2023_hyperlinked_en.pdf> ('*Guidelines for Examination in the European Patent Office 2023*').

65 '*Guidelines for Examination in the European Patent Office 2023*' (n 64).

66 '*Guidelines for Examination in the European Patent Office 2023*' (n 64).

67 '*Guidelines for Examination in the European Patent Office 2023*' (n 64).

system need a technical purpose, and any successful patent of these methods would be confined in its scope to that technical purpose identified.[68]

Therefore, the method for considering AI as patentable property under the EU regime is very confined and, arguably, somewhat flawed. Firstly, the presumption that AI cannot be patented is rebuttable only in a very specific and narrowed set of circumstances. It ignores the possibility that an AI system seeking to perform a mental act or do business, for example, could also be addressing a technical purpose. Additionally, the exception to the rebuttable presumption is weighted towards the end objective of an AI system – the technical purpose. This is problematic, as some forms of modern AI are structured in such a way that the end objective is not clearly defined; rather, the objective of the system is to make its own 'discoveries'. By this account, under the narrowed exception, such forms of AI would not be patentable. This begs the question, then, of what happens if an AI system learns or evolves beyond the original technical purpose. In such instances, would the system no longer be deemed patented, losing its property status? Or would the system retain its patent status in relation to the original technical purpose but not in terms of the new developments achieved by the system's 'development'? In some ways, the narrowed circumstances in which the presumption that AI is not patentable can be rebutted creates more uncertainty than if AI was simply not patentable under any circumstances.

4.3.1.2 United States (US)

The United States patent regime is more accommodating of AI than the UK or EU. Indeed, the US Patent Office has specifically denoted AI with a classification class,[69] the effect of this classification being that AI, as a form of technology, is recognised as being a potential high-volume category of patents requiring their own identification class. Yet, the impetus is on 'potential', for AI is not automatically patentable under US Code.[70] There are threshold requirements that must be met before AI can be patented, and these requirements, it has been suggested,[71] are not without their ambiguities. The relevant section of US Code, § 101, outlines what is patentable property and provides that this extends to 'new processes', 'machines', 'manufacture', the 'composition of a matter' or a 'new and useful improvement'.[72] The US Supreme

68 '*Guidelines for Examination in the European Patent Office 2023*' (n 64).

69 Thomson Reuters Westlaw, *Practice Note* (at 7 February 2022) Practical Law Intellectual Property & Technology, 'Artificial Intelligence Key Legal Issues: Overview' ('*Thomson Reuters Westlaw, Practice Note*'); 'Class 706, Data Processing—Artificial Intelligence', *Classification Definitions* (Web Page, 7 February 2022) <https://www.uspto.gov/web/patents/classification/uspc706/defs706.htm> ('*Classification Definitions*').

70 *Patents* 35 USC § 101 (2011).

71 *Thomson Reuters Westlaw, Practice Note* (n 69); *Classification Definitions* (n 69).

72 *Patents* 35 USC § 101 (2011).

Court has interpreted this section as preventing the laws of nature, physical phenomena and, importantly, abstract ideas from being considered as patentable property.[73] Mathematical algorithms, computer code and the like could all be construed as an abstract idea and thus, under this approach, would be excluded from being deemed patentable property.

Until relatively recently, this was the approach. However, a decision from the US Supreme Court blurred the line between deeming abstract ideas non-patentable and property that is actually patentable. In *Alice Corp. Pty. Ltd. v CLS Bank International*, the Court held that where an abstract idea is connected to other elements in a manner that provides additional meaning to the idea, the abstract idea becomes more than simply that. Instead, it becomes what the Court deemed an 'inventive concept'.[74] Under these limited circumstances, when an abstract idea takes on more meaning, it becomes patentable property.[75] For AI to be patentable under this account, the technology needs to be demonstrable as more than a mere idea. This could potentially be challenging for forms of AI designed to make their own discoveries, where the value of the system lies in its internal 'reasoning' processes rather than in an end objective being achieved. Indeed, when considering the minutiae of both the UK/EU and US approaches to patenting AI, there appear to be similarities in the challenges facing both patent regimes. The fact that both legal systems require proof that AI is more than simply a technical or theoretical system, but also entails an 'inventive' element, has been noted in judicial observations.[76] Expanding on the notion of an abstract idea is not the only threshold requirement that must be met for AI to be successfully patented in the US. There are novelty and additional subject-matter requirements, but I do not consider these elements, as they do not concern the primary issue of whether AI is patentable property, which is instead addressed by the jurisprudence surrounding § 101. For now, what is key is that AI is deemed as *potentially* patentable property in the US under limited, and perhaps in somewhat ambiguous, circumstances.

4.3.1.3 Australia

Australian patent law faces similar AI eligibility issues as the US but with a heightened degree of confusion. What is deemed patentable property (or a

73 *Thomson Reuters Westlaw, Practice Note* (n 69); *Classification Definitions* (n 69); *Diamond v. Chakrabarty*, 447 US 303 (1980).

74 *Thomson Reuters Westlaw, Practice Note* (n 69); *Classification Definitions* (n 69); *Alice Corp. Pty. Ltd. v CLS Bank International*, 134 S. Ct. 2347 (2014) ('*Alice Corp. Pty. Ltd. v CLS Bank International*').

75 *Thomson Reuters Westlaw, Practice Note* (n 69); *Classification Definitions* (n 69); *Alice Corp. Pty. Ltd. v CLS Bank International*, 134 S. Ct. 2347 (2014) ('*Alice Corp. Pty. Ltd. v CLS Bank International*').

76 Lord Kitchin (n 62).

patentable subject matter) in Australia is provided for in section 18(1) *Patents Act 1990* (Cth) and extends to inventions that are: (a) novel, (b) involve an inventive step, (c) are useful and, importantly, (d) 'a manner of manufacture within the meaning of s 6 of the Statute of Monopolies'. There are also requirements that the invention not be secretly used in Australia by or with the patentee's authority prior to the patent date.[77] This latter requirement is less important to determining whether AI is patentable, as it relates to the use of an established patent. It is element (d) above, the 'manner or manufacture', that is key. The 'manner of manufacture', as within the meaning of the *Statute of Monopolies 1623* (UK), has been held within Australia to be interpreted with consideration to broader policy, or the purpose of the Act, rather than a literal interpretation of the words.[78] The explanatory memorandum to the *Patents Act 1990* (Cth) indicates that the fundamental purpose of the 'manner of manufacture' test is to ensure that a patentable invention belongs 'to the useful arts rather than the fine arts'.[79] In other words, the manner of manufacture must give rise to inventions with a practical nature in order to be patentable. On this basis, it would seem that there would be scope for AI to be eligible as a patentable subject matter, providing the AI system holds a practical benefit. The requirement of 'something more' than mere technology is akin to that expected under the US system.

Unlike the US patent process, however, the Australian process is more ambiguous when considered in relation to whether AI is a patentable subject matter. In a recent appeal case, *Commissioner of Patents v Rokt Pte Ltd*,[80] the Full Federal Court of Australia was asked to consider a patent application that involved an advertising system that operated by being linked to a computerised system.[81] The Court was asked to consider whether or not a computer-implemented invention, such as the marketing system, was a manner of manufacture

77 *Patents Act 1990*(Cth) ('*Patents Act*') s18(1); LexisNexis, *Halsbury's Laws of Australia* (online at 7 February 2022) Patents, Trade Marks & Related Rights, '5 Requirements for a Valid Patent' [[12,000], [12,510], [12,535]] ('*Halsbury's Laws of Australia*, Requirements for a Valid Patent').

78 *National Research Development Corp v Commissioner of Patents* (1959) 102 CLR 525 at 276–7; 'Patentable Subject Matter', *Australian Law Reform Commission* (Web Page, 2 August 2010) <https://www.alrc.gov.au/publication/genes-and-ingenuity-gene-patenting-and-human-health-alrc-report-99/6-patentability-of-genetic-materials-and-technologies/patentable-subject-matter/#:~:text='Invention'%20is%20defined%20in%20the,and%20includes%20an%20alleged%20invention>.

79 Explanatory Memorandum, *Patents Bill 1990* (Cth); *Halsbury's Laws of Australia*, Requirements for a Valid Patent (n 77).

80 *Commissioner of Patents v Rokt Pte Ltd* (2020) 379 ALR 86 ('*Commissioner of Patents v Rokt Pte Ltd*').

81 *Commissioner of Patents v Rokt Pte Ltd (2020) 379 ALR 86 ('Commissioner of Patents v Rokt Pte Ltd')* at [1]–[2].

for the threshold requirements under s 18(1) of the *Patents Act 1990* (Cth).[82] Importantly, the Full Federal Court upheld recent patent decisions[83] and found that where a computer or computerised system merely implements the function of an invention, this is not sufficient to meet the threshold requirements.[84] As in the US, a mere abstract idea is non-patentable; the computerised element must be integrated into the invention and be integral to its operation in order to meet the patentability threshold requirement.[85] This line of reasoning did not provide binding authority to the effect that computer-implemented inventions are patentable in Australia. Yet, it arguably provides persuasive authority that AI *may* be patentable *if* it can be demonstrated that this form of technology is integral to the functioning of an invention. On this basis, the position in Australia is more ambiguous than the position in the US, for AI is at least recognised in the US as a patentable subject matter, whereas the position is still evolving in Australia to date.

4.3.2 Copyright

I now move to briefly consider copyright principles in the same jurisdictions as I reviewed in Section 4.3.1. Here, I pause to acknowledge that source code is a recognised form of work that can be protected by copyright. In Australia, source code and object codes have been held to be forms of 'literary work' under the *Copyright Act 1968* (Cth) and are therefore eligible for copyright protection.[86] Similarly, in the US, these forms of code have also been held to be literary works capable of copyright protection, providing they can be distilled into a tangible medium (paper or hard drive, for example).[87] The US approach is narrower than the Australian approach in that the copyright only extends to the original expressions of the code and not the individual algorithms embedded within the code.[88] That is, the copyright protects how the code works as a whole to form a 'literary work' of expression that is copyrightable but not the individual elements of the code themselves. The UK, like

82 *Commissioner of Patents v Rokt Pte Ltd (2020) 379 ALR 86 ('Commissioner of Patents v Rokt Pte Ltd')* at [65]–[69].

83 *Research Affiliates LLC v Commissioner of Patents* (2014) 316 ALR 135; *Commissioner of Patents v RPL Central Pty Ltd* (2015) 328 ALR 458; *Encompass Corporation Pty Ltd v InfoTrack Pty Ltd* (2019) 372 ALR 646.

84 *Commissioner of Patents v Rokt Pte Ltd* (n 80) at [1], [68], [69]; [74]–[81]; [83]–[89], [114], [115].

85 *Commissioner of Patents v Rokt Pte Ltd* (n 80) at [1]–[2].

86 *Star Micronics Pty Ltd v Five Star Computers Pty Ltd* (1990) 18 IPR 225; *Computer Edge Pty Ltd v Apple Computer Inc* (1986) 161 CLR 171; LexisNexis, *Halsbury's Laws of Australia* 240 Intellectual Property, '3 Copyright' [240–1559].

87 *Thomson Reuters Westlaw, Practice Note* (n 69); *Classification Definitions* (n 69); *Sega Enters. v. Accolade, Inc.*, 977 F.2d 1510.

88 *Thomson Reuters Westlaw, Practice Note* (n 69); *Classification Definitions* (n 69).

Australia and the US, also recognises that code and object code are capable of copyright protection.[89]

There are several issues with copyrighting AI, which I consider shortly in Section 4.3.4. What I do note here though is that this form of an IP right in relation to AI extends only to the underlying code. It does not deem other aspects of an AI system, such as its objectives or methods of operation, as property. Copyright is therefore a very narrow approach to viewing AI as property.

4.3.3 Trade Secrets

Before turning to evaluating the merits of AI as IP, I will briefly consider one last form of IP protection in relation to AI – trade secrets. It is widely reported that Google's algorithms underpinning not only its search functionality but also what content it directs at users is not protected by any of the above IP measures; rather, it is protected by trade-secret mechanisms.[90] In the US, trade secrets are protected by legislative instruments. At a federal level, the US criminal code provides that theft of a trade secret is a criminal offence.[91] A trade secret is defined as including, among other things, all forms and types of 'methods, techniques, processes, procedures, programs or codes, whether tangible or intangible' in instances where (a) the owner has taken reasonable steps to keep the information secret and (b) the information is of independent economic value.[92] The US approach arguably represents the most staunch level of protection for trade secrets.

At the other end of the spectrum sits the less formalised Australian approach to trade secrets. In contrast to the US, Australia does not seek to protect such information through the imposition of criminal sanctions. The Australian approach is instead governed by common law and equitable principles. Trade secrets have been held to include information used in business or trade that has been kept secret but, if widely shared, especially to a commercial competitor, would cause harm to the keeper of the secret.[93] It is not inconceivable that AI could meet this threshold. If this is so, such information is protected by an action in a breach of confidence, which is recognised in equity in Australia.[94]

89 *Ibcos Computers Ltd v Barclays Mercantile Highland Finance Ltd* [1994] FSR 275; *John Richardson Computers Ltd v Flanders* [1993] FSR 497; *Halsbury's Laws of England*, vol. 23 (online at 7 February 2022) 2 Copyright, '566 Copyright in Computer Programs'.

90 John Naughton, 'Good Luck in Making Google Reveal its Algorithm', *The Guardian* (online, 13 November 2016) <https://www.theguardian.com/commentisfree/2016/nov/13/good-luck-in-making-google-reveal-its-algorithm>.

91 *Crimes and Criminal Procedure* 18 USC § 1832 (2009) ('*Crimes and Criminal Procedure*').

92 *Crimes and Criminal Procedure* (n 91) § 1839(3).

93 *Lansing Linde Ltd v Kerr* (1990) 21 IPR 529 at 536; *Halsbury's Laws of England*, vol. 19 (online, 7 February 2022) 3 Categories confidential information, '1 Confidence' ('*Halsbury's Laws of England*, Confidence').

94 *Mainbridge Industries Pty Ltd v Whitewood* (1984) 3 IPR 97 at 102–103 per McLelland J; affirmed in *Mainbridge Industries Pty Ltd v Whitewood* (1985) 6 IPR 239.

Alternatively, such information could be protected through contractual obligations. The Australian approach is therefore more centred on deriving meaning from the personal relationships between legal persons connected to the information, unlike the US approach, which, being rooted in criminal law, offers a more society-wide focus on protecting such information.

If the US approach to trade secrets is at one end of the spectrum and the Australian approach is at the other end, then the UK and EU sit in the middle. In the UK, trade secrets are defined in a similar manner to Australia and are also protected by common law and contractual principles.[95] The UK holds a similar action for a breach of confidence, which protects information that has a quality of confidence, that is disclosed in circumstances that impose a degree of confidentiality and where the information is later used without authorisation.[96]

In addition to a breach of confidence action providing protection to trade secrets, the UK also follows the EU directive regarding trade secrets. More specifically, EU Directive 2016/943[97] has been transposed into UK law through the *Trade Secrets (Enforcement, etc) Regulations 2018* (UK) SI 2018/597. These instruments together provide a more formalised and more regulated method of protecting trade secrets. A 'trade secret' in this context is defined more narrowly than 'confidential information' in a breach of confidence action. Trade secrets under this approach are defined as information that is secret – that is, not commonly known to persons who normally deal with such information, that has commercial value by virtue of its secrecy and that the person who is lawfully in control of has taken reasonable steps to maintain its secrecy.[98] This definition of trade secrets is more confined than what is protected by a breach of confidence action. Information protected under this approach must entail a degree of commercial value, which is not necessarily a requirement to establish a breach of confidence.

4.3.4 Merits of AI as IP

Each of the above IP measures establish to some extent that AI can be characterised as intellectual property; yet they are not without their flaws, bringing into question whether an IP characterisation is the best method of viewing AI. Putting aside the ambiguous and non-uniform approach to threshold issues surrounding patents, there are also other concerns associated with patenting AI, the most notable being that patents create an exclusive licence over these systems, and this is not always in the public interest. Here, an analogy could be drawn between patenting AI and patenting lifesaving medicines. This is a

95 *Halsbury's Laws of England*, 1 Confidence (n 93).

96 *Coco v A.N. Clark (Engineers) Limited* [1968] FSR 415 at 419–420.

97 See: *Council Directive 2016/943 of 8 June 2016 on the Protection of Undisclosed Know-How and Business Information (Trade Secrets) Against their Unlawful Acquisition, Use and Disclosure* [2016] OJ L 157/1.

98 *Trade Secrets (Enforcement, etc) Regulations 2018* (UK) SI 2018/597, reg. 2.

well-worn debate. On one side of the debate there needs to be an incentive for pharmaceutical companies to develop new medicines – the incentive being exclusivity over the drug once patented. On the other side of the debate sits the notion that such medicines as property form a public good that is in the interests of being shared with the wider community. This line of reasoning could be extended to patenting AI. AI systems are often constructed with goals that benefit persons beyond the individual owner of a system. This is especially true for AI systems deployed in relation to public health or security, which although privately developed and owned under a patent system, also hold a benefit for the wider community. If patenting AI is to be considered the favoured form of IP rights over these systems, a balance needs to be reached between private and public interests in relation to this form of property.

As identified earlier, copyright is also an ineffectual method of characterising AI as property. This is because the approach applies only to the code underlying AI and does not protect a system's outward expressions or actions. Trade secrets also pose challenges. Trade secrets are perhaps the most straightforward method of characterising AI as IP, for the threshold requirements are relatively uncomplicated and the IP right, once obtained, applies to the AI system in its entirety. Yet, this approach is less desirable in terms of issues of explainability. To obtain a patent or copyright of AI, the system needs to be made publicly available, either fully or partially, as part of the IP recognition process. In doing so, the underlying elements of the AI system can be publicly reviewed if needed for other reasons, such as issues of determining causation (which I explore further in Part II in Chapter 6) or when individuals are entitled to understand how a decision that impacts them has been reached. Trade secrets are, by their nature, entirely secret; as such, they prevent information of this nature from being considered by non-owners or non-approved users of the information.

Regardless of the flaws associated with an IP approach to AI, what is clear is that this is a rapidly evolving area of IP law. As such, it is likely that there will be ongoing recognition of AI as intellectual property in some form or another.

4.4. Other Important Considerations

As part of evaluating whether AI can or ought to be characterised as property, it is important to consider the limitations of this approach. To that end, I turn now to consider other important aspects influencing the legal response to AI including its relationship with data governance and whether AI can create property. These considerations are still part of the survey of whether AI is best characterised as property.

4.4.1 Data Governance and AI

Briefly, the role of data governance and competition law raises interesting questions about the limitations of viewing AI solely as property. To consider this further, it is first important to understand the relationship between AI and data. Data is foundational to the functioning of AI. Analysts have observed, however, that the relationship between AI and data has evolved alongside the evolution of AI systems.[99] Modern forms of AI – such as neural networks and deep learning – are capable of processing data in distinct ways. These forms of AI have been observed as capable of processing complex multi-layer data models.[100] As we move towards more advanced forms of AI, it has been suggested that there is a need for relying on more than just data, that these more advanced forms will also require explicit knowledge to function.[101] From this it becomes clear that for AI to function – regardless of its level of sophistication – it is dependent upon the data fed into the system. Its interactions with this data, however, are likely to vary depending on the level of sophistication associated with the AI system.

What emerges in response are several interesting questions about the impact of data governance on AI. This relationship is becoming the subject of increased attention, especially given new regulatory measures aimed at managing data. Consider for example, the European Union's raft of data regulations that aim to regulate the acceptable use of data beyond merely personal information that is the primary focus of the GDPR.[102] Although not targeted at common law jurisdictions, the introduction of these data regulations is indicative of an appetite to expand the regulation of data.[103] Additionally, there is an emerging interest in amending competition laws to better respond to the potential of cartel-like behaviour in relation to capturing, storing and managing datasets to be utilised by AI systems.[104] In response to these examples of AI data governance practices – via data regulations or competition law mechanisms – an argument could be made that regulating data in turn holds implications for AI liabilities.

Whilst data undoubtedly influences the operations of AI, a misuse of data does not necessarily give rise to an AI liability *directly*. My own view is that

99 Amit Sheth and Krishnaprasad Thirunarayan, 'The Duality of Data and Knowledge Across the Three Waves of AI' (2021) 23(3) *IT Professional* 1, 1–7.

100 Amit Sheth and Krishnaprasad Thirunarayan, 'The Duality of Data and Knowledge Across the Three Waves of AI' (2021) 23(3) *IT Professional* 1, 5.

101 Amit Sheth and Krishnaprasad Thirunarayan, 'The Duality of Data and Knowledge Across the Three Waves of AI' (2021) 23(3) *IT Professional* 1, 14.

102 See: *Regulation (EU) 2023/2854 of the European Parliament and of the Council of 13 December 2023 on harmonised rules on fair access to and use of data and amending Regulation (EU) 2017/2394 and Directive (EU) 2020/1828 (Data Act)* [2023] OJ L 1/71 ('EU Data Act') ; *Regulation (EU) 2022/868 of the European Parliament and of the Council of 30 May 2022 on European data governance and amending Regulation (EU) 2018/1724 (Data Governance Act)* [2022] OJ L 152/1 ('EU Data Governance Act').

103 It is worth noting that common law jurisdictions are considering expanding their data governance regulations. See for example: Data (Use and Access) HL Bill (2024–2025) 179.

104 See for example the considerations raised by Suzanne Rab in: Suzanne Rab, 'Competition Law' in Charles Kerriagan (ed.), *Artificial Intelligence: Law and Regulation* (Edward Elgar Publishing Limited, 2022) 197.

data holds a *secondary* relationship with AI. By which I mean to suggest that any regulatory response specifically aimed at data, and not AI, will have only a secondary impact on the management of AI and a secondary impact on any subsequent liability arising from an AI system. For example, the GDPR regulates acceptable uses of personal information and this in turn shapes the parameters of data that can be fed into an AI system for it to function. The GDPR does not directly regulate how or in what context an AI system could be deployed, which is ultimately what is likely, I consider, to give rise to a private law liability in response to a deployed AI system.

In considering the relationship between AI and data, the more interesting question is perhaps whether data is in itself property? I do not intend to explore this topic in depth here as I note it is the subject of much academic debate.[105] Instead, I raise this point to observe that the property status of data is debatable, and this in turn further shapes the relationship between AI and data. For if whether or not data is property raises similar issues in response to the question of whether or not AI is property and if so what form? The importance of this observation lies in that how both data and AI are characterised restricts or narrows the private law mechanisms that can be applied. By this I mean to suggest that if they are conceived of as property – rather than another characterisation, such as a legal agent in the case of AI – then this restricts the private law mechanisms to proprietary considerations that must be applied in response. In the case of data, however, it may be defined, I still contend holds a *secondary* impact in relation to AI. For I consider that private law liabilities arising in relation to AI will stem from how an AI system is deployed an in what context. The private law applications to data therefore only indirectly shape AI liabilities.

4.4.2 AI as a Creator of Property

I pause to observe that AI, unlike traditional forms of property, holds a 'cognitive' aspect. The potential cognitive capacities of AI systems beg the question then, can AI *create* property?

4.4.2.1 Can AI Be a Creator of Property?

Seminal IP case law addresses the question of whether AI can create property, and it raises interesting points of consideration. Consider for example, the Australian case of *Thaler* v Commissioner of Patents ('Thaler')[106] considered

105 See for example: James Grimmelmann and Christina Mulligan, 'Data Property' (2023) 72 *American University Law Review* 829; Jeffrey Ritter and Anna Mayer, 'Regulating Data as Property: A New Construct for Moving Forward' (2017–2018) 16 *Duke Law & Technology Review* 220.

106 *Thaler v Commissioner of Patents* [2021] FCA 879 ('*Thaler*') at [3].

the status of AI as an inventor in patent law. In the first instance, Beach J of the Federal Court of Australia was asked to judicially review the decision of the Deputy Commissioner of Patents. In 2019, Dr Stephan Thaler filed for a patent and did not list a natural or legal person as the inventor; rather, he listed 'DABUS, The invention was autonomously generated by an artificial intelligence' as the inventor on the application.[107] Beach J needed to consider if the term 'inventor' under the *Patents Act 1990* (Cth) could include an artificially intelligent system.[108] He reached the conclusion that an AI system could be an inventor of a patentable invention based on three key aspects.[109] Firstly, he concluded that the term 'inventor' is a noun that encapsulates 'a person or a thing that invents'.[110] Secondly, that there are instances where an invention cannot sensibly be invented by a human, and so the definition of inventor needs to be accommodating of this fact.[111] Lastly, including AI under the definition of an inventor, he found, was not contrary to the legislation.[112] Although an AI system could be found to be an inventor of a patent, it could not be the owner of the patentable property.[113] This approach, in the first instance, provides a unique consideration of the possibility that AI could be a creator of property. Importantly, this decision was not upheld. On appeal, the decision was overturned, and an 'inventor' was found to be a natural person.[114] Despite this, the case still provides useful consideration of the possibility that AI could be more than a mere tool to be used by natural person actors.

Dr Thaler applied for the same patent in other jurisdictions. The issue of whether AI could be an inventor of patentable property has therefore been considered by more than one jurisdiction in parallel. Except for in South Africa, where the Companies and Intellectual Property Commission (CIPC) reached a controversial decision to approve the filed patent with DABUS listed as the inventor;[115] the net outcome of the considerations from other jurisdictions has largely been similar to the final conclusion reached in Australia.[116] In England and Wales for example, it was held on appeal that it was impossible legally for

107 *Stephen L. Thaler* [2021] APO 5 ('*Stephen L. Thaler*').
108 *Thaler v Commissioner of Patents* (n 106) at [6].
109 *Thaler v Commissioner of Patents* (n 106) at [10].
110 *Thaler v Commissioner of Patents* (n 106) at [10].
111 *Thaler v Commissioner of Patents* (n 106) at [10].
112 *Thaler v Commissioner of Patents* (n 106) at [10].
113 *Thaler v Commissioner of Patents* (n 106) at [193]–[194].
114 *Commissioner of Patents v Thaler* [2022] FCAFC 62 ('*Commissioner of Patents v Thaler*') at [119]–[121].
115 For further information, see: Desmond Osaretin Oriakhogba, 'DABUS Gains Territory in South Africa and Australia: Revisiting the AI-Inventorship Question' (2021) 9 *South African Intellectual Property Law Journal* 87.
116 See: Desmond Osaretin Oriakhogba, 'DABUS Gains Territory in South Africa and Australia: Revisiting the AI-Inventorship Question' (2021) 9 *South African Intellectual Property Law Journal* 87, 89–92.

an AI system to be an inventor of patentable property.[117] Further, that as section 13 of the *Patents Act 1977* (UK), requires the patent applicant to name the person or persons believed to be the inventor, the implication being that legal personhood status is a necessary prerequisite for inventor recognition.[118]

At this point, it is worth emphasising that the Australian case in the first instance did (albeit temporarily) acknowledge the possibility of an AI system being deemed the legal creator of property before the decision was ultimately overturned.[119] In South Africa, the relevant AI system, DABUS, was recognised as the inventor of the filed patent when the application was approved in this jurisdiction.[120] However, the outcome of this application is somewhat dubious given that the South African patent examination system is not as robust as other jurisdictions.[121] Nonetheless, what this establishes is that it is at least theoretically possible for an AI system to be deemed a creator of property.[122]

4.4.2.2 Can Property Create Property? Or Is Legal Personhood Necessitated?

Thus far, I have considered that AI could potentially be characterised as property and, further, that there is an emerging argument that AI can invent property. Looking at these two issues together, it follows logically that if both hold true, can property create property, or is an element of legal personhood status required? I do not fully address the interplay with the notion of legal personhood here, as this is a topic I cover in Chapter 5. For now, I wish to note two key examples of property with questionable legal personhood status creating property. The first are instances where animals, often elephants in zoos, paint paintings, which are then sold for the purpose of charitable fundraising. There is much debate about the legal personhood status of animals, but it is also acknowledged that animals are property that can be owned. Indeed, my dog is recognised as a mere chattel despite how much I may 'parent' her. The second example I wish to consider are rivers – or water bodies – that are used to create electricity. Although rivers cannot be owned in a private capacity like AI or animals can, there is much commentary recognising that these bodies of water can be owned by people, most often indigenous persons. Without

117 *Thaler v Comptroller-General of Patents, Designs and Trade Marks* [2021] EWCA Civ 1374 at [143].
118 *Thaler v Comptroller-General of Patents, Designs and Trade Marks* [2021] EWCA Civ 1374 at [122].
119 In the first instance, see: *Thaler v Commissioner of Patents* [2021] FCA 879; and in the second instance, see: *Commissioner of Patents v Thaler* [2022] FCAFC 62.
120 Michelle Lavrichenko, 'Thaler v. Vidal: Artificial Intelligence—Can the Invented Become the Inventor' (2022) 44(2) *Cardozo Law Review* 699, 708.
121 Michelle Lavrichenko, 'Thaler v. Vidal: Artificial Intelligence—Can the Invented Become the Inventor' (2022) 44(2) *Cardozo Law Review* 699, 708–709.
122 See also: Abbott (n 53) 71–91.

delving into how rivers are owned and the intricacies of their proprietary status, this is another example of property creating property – more importantly, property that has, in some instances, been recognised as a legal person creating property. On this preliminary basis, it is possible for property to be both property and a legal person of sorts and, further, for this property to create new or additional property. The decision in *Thaler* is therefore not necessarily incompatible with the notion that AI can be a legal person as well as property. The intersection of AI as property and legal personhood is something I consider in Chapter 5.

4.5. Characterising AI as Property: Sufficient?

Having established that it is at least possible for AI to be characterised as property and that AI can create property, I now turn to the question of whether such a characterisation alone is sufficient – that is, whether AI ought to be viewed as property alone.

Characterising AI as property has several benefits. Firstly, and not necessarily most importantly, it acknowledges and protects the commercial value of these systems. Granted, there are instances where these systems are not always developed with a purely capitalist goal in mind, such as systems used in public administration, which still hold financial value but are not always privately funded. They are nonetheless systems that do hold great proprietary value that might not be protected if they could not be recognised as such.

There are also reasons against characterising AI as only property and not a hybrid of characterisations. If the proprietary nature of the algorithms behind these systems is robustly protected through property law, it holds the potential to reduce the permissible instances in which these algorithms can be exposed as part of seeking liability for the consequences of using such a system. For example, an individual negatively impacted through the use of an AI system could not seek to examine the underlying algorithms for further information without first gaining a court order in instances where such algorithms are protected by robust IP measures such as trade secrets. This information is needed, for example, to achieve a greater understanding of why an AI system acted in the way that it did or reached a certain decision, an understanding that could be necessary to address issues of causation.[123] The disadvantage of this approach is that it tends to favour a notion of property that is owned by individuals rather than a community or acknowledge that there are instances of individual property ownership that can have an impact on communities at large. Consider examples of flag burnings. An individual may individually own a flag and may individually choose to destroy their property, but, depending on the circumstances, such actions can have a significant impact on the wider community. Lastly, and perhaps most importantly, recognising AI as property

123 For a discussion on issues of causation, see Chapter 6.

alone tends to treat this technology as merely a tool to be deployed by natural and legal persons. Whilst this may be true for some simplistic forms of AI, such a characterisation fails to acknowledge that there are forms of AI that have a degree of 'cognitive' independence. There are therefore some forms of AI that could act in ways not reasonably foreseen or intended by the person deploying these systems. On this basis, yes, AI can be characterised as property, but it does not follow that it ought to always, or solely, be characterised as such.

4.6. Artificial Intelligence: More than Merely Property

I have tested whether AI can be found to possess a proprietary nature. In doing so, it is apparent that a property characterisation of AI is not an impossibility, especially in relation to intellectual property. Such a characterisation does, however, need to be reconciled with issues of how dependent upon or integrated an AI system is with corporeal objects. It is worth noting that just because AI can, under certain circumstances, be construed as property, it is not clear that it should always be viewed as such.

It then becomes a question of how to adequately balance the need of acknowledging AI as property, to some degree, against the issues with this approach. There are further aspects to consider, such as how we account for property that can *think* for itself. Does this give rise to the need for a new form of legal characterisation, such as a hybrid of legal personhood and property? This is an issue that I consider in Chapter 5. If a hybrid model can be established, what would be the legal consequences of this model – and how does this assist with assigning liability? These are questions I address in Part III.

In the interim, it is worth acknowledging that it would be myopic to overlook the importance of AI as property entirely, as these systems are, in essence, things of value. But it would be equally foolish to solely characterise AI as property alone, especially given the potential cognitive capacities of these systems. It is apparent, then, that a more fulsome, possibly hybrid method of characterisation is needed to sufficiently characterise AI legally.

References

A Articles/Books/Reports

Abbott, Ryan, *The Reasonable Robot: Artificial Intelligence and the Law* (Cambridge University Press, 2020).

Babie, Paul, David Brown, Ryan Catterwell and Mark Giancaspro, 'Cryptocurrency as Property: Ruscoe v Cryptopia Ltd (in liq) [2020] NZHC 728' (2020) 28 *Australian Property Law Journal* 106.

Beckers, Anna, and Gunther Teubner, *Three Liability Regimes for Artificial Intelligence: Algorithmic Actants, Hybrids, Crowds* (Hart Publishing, 2021).

Chesterman, Simon, *We, The Robots? Regulating Artificial Intelligence and the Limits of the Law* (Cambridge University Press, 2021).

Grattan, Scott and Sheelagh McCracken (eds), *Introduction to Property and Commercial Law* (Thomson Reuters (Professional) Australia Limited, 2016).
Green, Sarah and John Randall, *The Tort of Conversion* (Hart Publishing, 2009).
Grimmelmann, James, and Christina Mulligan, 'Data Property' (2023) 72 *American University Law Review* 829.
Lavrichenko, Michelle , 'Thaler v. Vidal: Artificial Intelligence—Can the Invented Become the Inventor' (2022) 44(2) *Cardozo Law Review* 699.
Michaels, Ralf, 'The Functional Method of Comparative Law' in Mathias Reimann and Reinhard Zimmermann (eds), *Oxford Handbook of Comparative Law* (Oxford Academic, 2nd ed, 2019).
Mik, Eliza, 'AI as a Legal Person?' in Jyn-An Lee et al (eds), *Artificial Intelligence and Intellectual Property* (Oxford University Press, 2021) 419.
Oriakhogba, Desmond Osaretin, 'DABUS Gains Territory in South Africa and Australia: Revisiting the AI-Inventorship Question' (2021) 9 *South African Intellectual Property Law Journal* 87.
Rab, Suzanne, 'Competition Law' in Charles Kerriagan (ed), *Artificial Intelligence: Law and Regulation* (Edward Elgar Publishing Limited, 2022).
Ramaekers, Eveline, 'The Development of EU Property Law' (2015) 3 *European Review of Private Law* 437.
Ramaekers, Eveline, 'What is Property Law?' (2017) 37(3) *Oxford Journal of Legal Studies* 588.
Ritter, Jeffrey and Anna Mayer, 'Regulating Data as Property: A New Construct for Moving Forward' (2017–2018) 16 *Duke Law & Technology Review* 220.
Sheth, Amit and Krishnaprasad Thirunarayan, 'The Duality of Data and Knowledge Across the Three Waves of AI' (2021) 23(3) *IT Professional* 1.
Tan, Yock Lin, *Personal Property Law* (Singapore Academy of Law, 2014).
Tripathi, Swapnil and Chandni Ghatak, 'Artificial Intelligence an Intellectual Property Law' (2018) 7(1) *Christ University Law Journal* 83.
Turner, Jacob, *Robot Rules: Regulating Artificial Intelligence* (Palgrave Macmillan, 2019).

B Cases

AA v Persons Unknown [2019] EWHC 3556
AA v Persons Unknown [2019] EWHC 3556
Alice Corp. Pty. Ltd. v CLS Bank International, 134 S. Ct. 2347 (2014)
B2C2 Ltd v Quoine Pte Ltd [2019] SGHC (1) 03
Coco v A.N. Clark (Engineers) Limited [1968] FSR 415
Commissioner of Patents v Rokt Pte Ltd (2020) 379 ALR 86
Commissioner of Patents v RPL Central Pty Ltd (2015) 328 ALR 458
Commissioner of Patents v Thaler [2022] FCAFC 62
Computer Edge Pty Ltd v Apple Computer Inc (1986) 161 CLR 171
Diamond v. Chakrabarty, 447 US 303 (1980)
Encompass Corporation Pty Ltd v InfoTrack Pty Ltd (2019) 372 ALR 646
Ibcos Computers Ltd v Barclays Mercantile Highland Finance Ltd [1994] FSR 275
John Richardson Computers Ltd v Flanders [1993] FSR 497
Knapp v Knapp [1944] SASR 257
Lansing Linde Ltd v Kerr (1990) 21 IPR 529
Mainbridge Industries Pty Ltd v Whitewood (1984) 3 IPR 97

Mainbridge Industries Pty Ltd v Whitewood (1985) 6 IPR 239
National Provincial Bank Ltd v Ainsworth [1965] 1 AC 1175
National Research Development Corp v Commissioner of Patents (1959) 102 CLR 525
Quoine Pte Ltd v B2C2 Ltd [2020] SGCA(I) 2
Research Affiliates LLC v Commissioner of Patents (2014) 316 ALR 135
Ruscoe v Cryptopia Ltd (in liq) [2020] NZHC 728
Sega Enters. v. Accolade, Inc., 977 F.2d 1510
Star Micronics Pty Ltd v Five Star Computers Pty Ltd (1990) 18 IPR 225
Stephen L. Thaler [2021] APO 5
Thaler v Commissioner of Patents [2021] FCA 879
Thaler v Comptroller-General of Patents, Designs and Trade Marks [2021] EWCA Civ 1374

C Legislation

Crimes and Criminal Procedure 18 USC § 1832 (2009)
Patents 35 USC § 101 (2011)
Patents Act 1977 (UK)
Patents Act 1990 (Cth)

D Treaties

Convention on the Grant of European Patents ('*European Patent Convention*'), European Union signed 5 October 1973 EPC (entered into force 7 October 1977)

E Other

'Oral-B iO™, The Biggest Innovation in Oral Care History Is Now Available Nationwide', *businesswire.com* (Web Page, 20 August 2020) <https://www.businesswire.com/news/home/20200820005069/en/Oral-B-iO™-The-Biggest-Innovation-in-Oral-Care-History-Is-Now-Available-Nationwide>
'Patentable Subject Matter', *Australian Law Reform Commission* (Web Page, 2 August 2010) <https://www.alrc.gov.au/publication/genes-and-ingenuity-gene-patenting-and-human-health-alrc-report-99/6-patentability-of-genetic-materials-and-technologies/patentable-subject-matter/#:~:text='Invention'%20is%20defined%20in%20the,and%20includes%20an%20alleged%20invention>
'Trademarks: What Is a Trademark?', *World Intellectual Property Organisation* (Web Page) <https://www.wipo.int/trademarks/en/>
Bughin, Jaques et al., 'Notes from the AI Frontier: Modelling the Impact of AI on the World Economy', *McKinsey Global Institute*, September 2018) <https://www.mckinsey.com/featured-insights/artificial-intelligence/notes-from-the-ai-frontier-modeling-the-impact-of-ai-on-the-world-economy>
Class 706, Data Processing—Artificial Intelligence', *Classification Definitions* (Web Page, 7 February 2022) <https://www.uspto.gov/web/patents/classification/uspc706/defs706.htm>

Council Directive 2016/943 of 8 June 2016 on the Protection of Undisclosed Know-How and Business Information (Trade Secrets) Against their Unlawful Acquisition, Use and Disclosure [2016] OJ L 157/1

Data (Use and Access) HL Bill (2024–2025) 179

European Patent Office, '*Guidelines for Examination in the European Patent Office 2023*', *EPO* (Document, March 2023) Art 52(2)(a) <https://link.epo.org/web/epo_guidelines_for_examination_2023_hyperlinked_en.pdf>

Explanatory Memorandum, *Patents Bill 1990* (Cth)

Halsbury's Laws of England, vol 19 (online 7 February 2022) 3 Categories confidential information, '1 Confidence'

Halsbury's Laws of England, vol 23 (online 7 February 2022) 2 Copyright, '566 Copyright in Computer Programs'

Justice of the Supreme Court Lord Kitchin, 'UKIPO—WIPO Conference Keynote Speech' (UKIPO—WIPO Conference Keynote Speech, UKIPO—WIPO Conference, 18 June 2019) <https://www.supremecourt.uk/docs/speech-190618.pdf>

LexisNexis, *Halsbury's Laws of Australia* (online 7 February 2022) Patents, Trade Marks & Related Rights, '5 Requirements for a Valid Patent'

LexisNexis, *Halsbury's Laws of Australia* 240 Intellectual Property, '3 Copyright'

LexisNexis, *Halsbury's Laws of Australia*, vol 1 (online 3 October 2021) 315 Personal Property '(A) Introduction—Meaning and Classification of Personal Property'

Naughton, John, 'Good Luck in Making Google Reveal its Algorithm', *The Guardian* (online, 13 November 2016) <https://www.theguardian.com/commentisfree/2016/nov/13/good-luck-in-making-google-reveal-its-algorithm>

Regulation (EU) 2022/868 of the European Parliament and of the Council of 30 May 2022 on European data governance and amending Regulation (EU) 2018/1724 (Data Governance Act) [2022] OJ L 152/1

Regulation (EU) 2023/2854 of the European Parliament and of the Council of 13 December 2023 on harmonised rules on fair access to and use of data and amending Regulation (EU) 2017/2394 and Directive (EU) 2020/1828 (Data Act) [2023] OJ L 1/71

Thomson Reuters Westlaw, *Practice Note* (7 February 2022) Practical Law Intellectual Property & Technology, 'Artificial Intelligence Key Legal Issues: Overview'

Trade Secrets (Enforcement, etc) Regulations 2018 (UK) SI 2018/597

Wackwitz, Gwen and Jenna Rennie, 'Cryptocurrencies: Property, Trust and Mistake', *White & Case* (Web Page, 10 April 2019) <https://www.whitecase.com/publications/alert/cryptocurrencies-property-trust-and-mistake>

5 A New Legal Characterisation

'Hierarchical Legal Personality' for AI

5.1. Artificial Intelligence: What Should It Be Legally?

In Part II, the focus until this point has been to consider how AI ought to be legally characterised and whether, as a technology, AI is compatible with existing methods of characterisation, viz. legal personhood, agency and property. What this focus has revealed is that AI is at least capable of exhibiting key elements of *each* of these characterisations. It is not simply just one – rather, it crosses boundaries. The challenge is to therefore synthesise a new method of characterising AI, which will assist in determining exactly what rights and obligations an AI system can attain. This is an imperative first step in the process of determining the end goal of assigning liability – for how can we determine who is legally liable for the actions of an AI system, or the actions involving the use of an AI system, if the legal status of such technology is in doubt? How AI is classified and under what circumstances is therefore integral to addressing this broader question of liability.

The objective of this chapter is therefore to consider the best method to legally characterise AI and, ultimately, to propose a new characterisation model that accommodates modern AI.[1] To do so, this chapter first considers the unique nature of AI and why the methods of characterisation in the preceding chapters are alone insufficient. The focus then shifts more specifically to legal personhood as a concept. If legal personhood is considered a method of assigning rights and duties to entities within a society, it follows then that, as a concept, it is a useful tool in determining how rights and duties might be assigned in the context of AI. The approach regarding legal personhood is thus to firstly consider why it is insufficient to consider AI merely as a 'tool'[2] and why legal personhood is an appropriate starting point for characterising AI. The chapter then moves to consider the need for a hierarchical account of legal personhood before proposing a new model: the *Hierarchical Legal*

1 For a definition of modern AI, see the *Introduction*.

2 Eliza Mik, for example, argues in favour of reducing AI to a tool. See: Eliza Mik, 'AI as a Legal Person?' in Jyn-An Lee et al. (ed.), *Artificial Intelligence and Intellectual Property* (Oxford University Press, 2021) 419, 422–3.

DOI: 10.4324/9781003617549-8

Personality Model. The chapter next examines how the components of this model interact before layering the concepts of property and agency into the proposed model to provide a robust account capable of accommodating the spectrum of modern forms of AI. How this relates to liability and an overview of how liability ought to be assigned in the context of AI is the focus of Part III of this book.

5.2. The Unique Characteristics of AI

There is a temptation to treat modern AI as simply another computer program, a tool to be used by natural persons, and assume that the law will, or ought to, adapt in response to the deployment of AI in our society. Indeed, some writers looking at AI and the law have advocated for this approach.[3] I am of the view, however, that this approach overlooks the uniqueness of modern AI and, perhaps more importantly, the potential challenges it poses to a legal system.

In the preceding chapters, I have explored the extent to which AI may fit into more traditional legal paradigms through considering how AI can be legally characterised, viz. legal personhood, agency and property. For the reasons discussed in the previous chapters, none of these forms of characterisation is entirely compatible with AI. There is no perfect 'fit'. In advocating for a new form of legal personhood for AI, I therefore first explore the unique nature of AI as a type of technology and why this necessitates a new legal characterisation.

5.2.1 Cognitive Capacity of AI

In considering the uniqueness of modern AI, I begin with the now infamous Turing Test. Alan Turing is considered a founder of the school of AI. Put briefly, Turing posed the renowned challenge of the 'Imitation Game', in which he foresaw computers as being able to imitate the intelligence of humans.[4] He proffered that, in time, this imitation would be so successful that a human would not be able to discern between the intelligence of another human and that of a computer evidencing a human level of intelligence.[5] Although modern AI developments have not yet practically reached such a level of human intelligence, the Turing Test arguably sparked the quest

3 David J Gunkel, 'Both/And', *Person, Thing, Robot: A Moral and Legal Ontology for the 21st Century and Beyond* (MIT Press, 2023).

4 Philip C Jackson, *Introduction to Artificial Intelligence* (Dover Publications Inc., 3rd ed., 2019) 1–4.

5 Philip C Jackson, *Introduction to Artificial Intelligence* (Dover Publications Inc., 3rd ed., 2019) 1–4.

to do so.[6] Perhaps more importantly, however, the Turing Test set out the notion that intelligent computer systems – now modern AI – will not be able to exhibit intelligence through utilising the same mechanisms that underpin human intelligence; rather, such AI systems will require new mechanisms to generate this level of intelligence.[7]

Why is this important? Because, put crudely, it outlines one of the underlying objectives of AI research: to strive towards achieving a level of intelligence akin to that of human intelligence. If one of the goals is to achieve a level of intelligence comparable to humans, it follows then that the actions of such AI systems will exhibit a degree of sophistication comparable to those of humans. Admittedly though, the actions of an AI system may not take the same shape as a human engaging in such activities but will instead be achieved via new mechanisms. Consider Google's smart assistant, Google Duplex, which is being developed to make telephone appointments on behalf of natural persons.[8] This technology requires an AI system to locate a telephone number, dial it, have a conversation with persons on the other end of the line and cross-check calendar data to ensure appointments do not clash. The functionality of this system is set to achieve the same role as a personal assistant, but the system does not conduct itself in the same manner as a human personal assistant (there are, for example, no fingers used to dial a phone number, etc). In such instances, the AI system seeks to achieve the same end goal as a human but strives towards this goal utilising different means or alternative mechanisms. And this is a key point: the AI system is expected to achieve tasks that are ordinarily completed by a human, or accepted category of legal person like a corporation, but without utilising the same 'reasoning' processes. It is this expectation, combined with the alternative non-human 'cognitive' processes of AI, that makes it truly unique. We do not typically expect consumer products to reason by themselves and achieve the same, or a better, outcome than humans would. The fact that modern forms of AI can reason and react, albeit at varying levels, is in part why this technology necessitates a new type of legal response.

It is not enough to acknowledge that modern AI has a cognitive capacity, unlike other forms of technology. Within modern forms of AI to date, there are also varying *degrees* of cognitive capacities. Modern AI has not yet reached

6 Philip C Jackson, *Introduction to Artificial Intelligence* (Dover Publications Inc., 3rd ed., 2019) 1–4.

7 Philip C Jackson, *Introduction to Artificial Intelligence* (Dover Publications Inc., 3rd ed., 2019) 1–4.

8 Brian X Chen and Cade Metz, 'Google's Duplex Uses A.I. to Mimic Humans (Sometimes)', *The New York Times* (online, 22 May 2019) <https://www.nytimes.com/2019/05/22/technology/personaltech/ai-google-duplex.html>; Yaniv Leviathan and Yossi Matias, 'Google Duplex: An AI System for Accomplishing Real-World Tasks Over the Phone', *Google AI Blog* (Blog Post, 8 May 2018) <https://ai.googleblog.com/2018/05/duplex-ai-system-for-natural-conversation.html>.

a level of intelligence akin to that of human intelligence; importantly, however, there exists the potential to reach a human-level intelligence and this is uncommon to other forms of technology.[9] Additionally, there are varying levels of 'intellectual' independence exhibited by AI – consider, for example, the different forms of modern AI discussed in the *Introduction*. By this account, it is possible to rank the extent to which an AI system is deemed to be intelligent in a hierarchy. As I explore further in Section 5.3, this is essential in determining the extent to which an AI system acts independently. The variation in levels of 'intelligence' exhibited by these systems only further contributes to the uniqueness of AI as a technology – this is a form of technology expected to achieve human tasks, but the extent to which this is possible differs based on the variation in capacities of these systems.

With the rapid evolution of this technology, and varying intellectual capacities of these systems, it is imperative to lay the foundation for a legal model that recognises this uniqueness of AI. A model is required that looks beyond viewing AI as a mere product in all the circumstances in which it is deployed. Whilst there are instances where AI will undoubtedly be utilised as a product, there are, and will increasingly be, instances where such an approach is insufficient. Given that the law is intrinsically slow to respond to new developments, I therefore consider that a proactive approach will need to be taken to accommodate these forms of technology as they are increasingly integrated into the lives of natural and corporate legal persons. It is for these reasons that I propose a new legal model for responding to modern forms of AI.

5.3. A Hierarchical Model of Legal Personhood

In offering a new model of legal personhood status, several considerations are required. First, I address why viewing AI solely as a tool, and not a more sophisticated form of legal characterisation, is insufficient. I then turn to outlining the need for a hierarchical model of legal personhood before proposing one such model and examining the relationship between the components of this model.

5.3.1 Against the View that AI Is Always a Tool

In Chapter 2, I outlined that there is a growing consensus in legal literature in support of granting AI legal personhood status. The counterview is to consider AI as equivalent to a mere tool.[10] Although it is not entirely without merit, I submit that this view largely oversimplifies the significance of legal personhood status and tends to ignore its flexible nature as a concept. In Chapter 4, I introduced the 'AI as a tool' view and outlined that autonomy and control are

9 Jackson (n 4) xlix.
10 I first introduced the concept of AI being viewed as a tool in Chapter 4.

central to this approach. I explore my objections to this approach shortly, but before I do so, I consider it important to firstly dissect the concept of 'control' under the AI-as-a-tool account.

Control as it relates to autonomy is complex, and this complexity is not lost on proponents of the AI-as-a-tool approach. The complexity is rather a key tenet of their argument. Eliza Mik, a proponent of the AI-as-a-tool view, for example, differentiates between theories of control and control as deployed in a practical setting.[11] She favours a practical account of control and argues that control is defined based on a specific relationship between a human actor and an AI system; that is, control is a context-based concept when viewed through a practical lens.[12] Additionally, she highlights that underscoring control is whether there are channels of communication between a human actor and an AI system, for she contends that there can be no control over an AI system if a human actor cannot communicate their instructions (or the parameters of operation) to an AI system.[13] It would logically follow that an AI system acts autonomously, then, when the relationship between a system and a human actor is such that the AI system can act without instruction from a human. Mik does, however, caution against leaping to this conclusion by noting that there can be instances where control is exercised either indirectly or through delayed mechanisms, giving rise to the appearance that an AI system is acting autonomously through what she contends is a misguided illusion that the system is 'beyond' human control.[14] I do not seek to contradict this account, as I view this reasoning as logical – if you accept the premise that autonomy is inherently linked to the concept of control in the first instance.

Where I differ in perspective is in relation to the point at which control by a human actor ends. I consider that, at least theoretically, there are instances where an AI system can engage in independent actions, or self-determination, as a baseline underpinning a system's autonomy. Recalling the varying forms of modern AI explored in the *Introduction*, I consider that autonomy, as it relates to AI, ought to exist on a spectrum. I accept that at one end of this spectrum there will undoubtedly be instances where AI is utilised in a more simplistic manner that is akin to using a mere tool. I do not accept, however, that all forms of modern AI will act or be deployed in such a manner. In this respect, I view the AI-as-a-tool approach to autonomy as having value in instances where AI systems are more highly controlled by a human. At this end of the spectrum, I accept that there are instances where a human actor can shape an AI system's actions and thereby limit its autonomy by exercising control over the system and limiting the scope in which it can act. This is particularly apparent in relation to forms of AI such as supervised machined

11 Mik (n 2) 425.
12 Mik (n 2) 425–427.
13 Mik (n 2) 426.
14 Mik (n 2) 426–427.

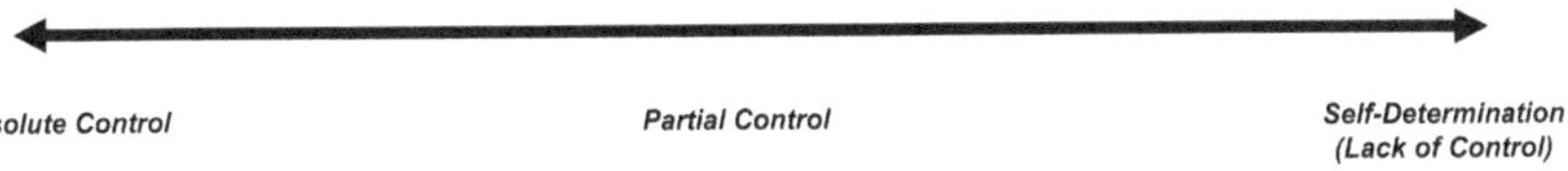

Figure 5.1 Spectrum of Control

learning. In my view, it is plausible for there to be AI systems over which human actors will exercise either absolute or partial control. This control may be either real or in deployed time. Consider more autonomous modern forms of AI, such as neural networks and deep learning.[15] These pose a significant challenge to the AI-as-a-tool account of autonomy derived from the concept of control because these forms of modern AI can exercise a degree of independence in executing actions. By their very nature, they are subject to less control than other forms of modern AI, such as supervised machine learning, that necessitate more control or human intervention to function. It is at the point where external control over an AI system diminishes and the AI system starts to act independently of ineffective control that I consider there should be a shift towards a more traditional or legal-based notion of autonomy (a 'self-determination approach').

Following on from this, I consider that control could be viewed on a spectrum: at one end, absolute control; in the centre, partial control; and at the opposite end, no human control (see *Figure 5.1*). I consider that, as we move away from absolute control towards the other end of the spectrum, we shift from viewing autonomy in relation to AI as being defined by the level of human control and move towards the more traditional self-determination models of autonomy.

This more fluid account of autonomy is key to being able to accommodate the varying forms of AI.[16] Not all AI systems are alike, and not all AI systems will lend themselves to the notion that a human can always exercise control over the system, albeit at varying degrees. Additionally, this model of autonomy is more likely to accommodate instances where an AI system may have control over another AI system (which I explore further in Part III). It is naïve to think that AI systems cannot be layered and respond to other AI systems. This latter point is especially important in relation to issues of causation, which I explore further in Chapter 6. It is for these reasons that a fluid notion of autonomy also informs the Hierarchical Legal Personality model I

15 Recall from the *Introduction that* 'Modern AI' in this context is not confined to recent developments in AI, but rather it is a term of art: indeed, some forms of modern AI date back decades and are not modern in terms of 'recent' developments.

16 Chopra and White also consider the need for a spectrum in relation to AI – one based on the level of autonomy of an AI system. See: Samir Chopra and Laurence White, *A Legal Theory for Autonomous Artificial Agents* (The University of Michigan Press, 4th ed., 2014) 121. I consider this as distinct from control, for an AI system might be autonomous but also capable of being controlled in some situations.

propose in Section 5.3.4. For now, what is key is that I agree that there are *some* instances in which AI behaves like a mere tool, but I do not accept that AI systems *always* and *will always* act as a tool.

5.3.2 Other Objections to Legal Personhood

Other objections have been raised against bestowing legal personality on AI. Ryan Abbot, for example, considers that legal personality for AI akin to a natural person would be inappropriate and suggests that if AI was to be given legal personality, it could be bestowed with obligations only and not rights.[17] Despite this, he considers that granting such a form of legal personality to AI could lead to a 'rights creep' as AI is anthropomorphised.[18] This view does, however, fail to consider the utility of legal personality as a tool that could be subjected to express limitations preventing such a rights creep.

In Chapter 1, I highlighted two concerns of Simon Chesterman's in adopting legal personality for AI. Firstly, we agree that many models of legal personality are not suited to accommodating the varied nature of AI.[19] The model of legal personality I propose below in Section 5.3.4 is designed to be flexible in structure to accommodate the varied nature of AI. Chesterman also raises the concern that if legal personality is too complex, it holds the potential to follow the 'android fallacy', where AI is anthropomorphised.[20] He seeks to overcome these concerns through adopting an approach that adopts general legal principles whilst considering that legal personality may be appropriate later.[21] The model I propose addresses these concerns. It is a model of legal personality, but it is a tiered approach where, as I explore in Part III of this book, each tier is ultimately reflective of an AI system's abilities and how it is functioning in context. Additionally, it is structured based on the degree to which an entity can hold rights and duties relative to the level of control that can be exerted over the entity and is therefore not human centric in structure but does accommodate natural persons. In this respect, each tier represents a narrowed set of circumstances working to simplify the proposed model.

17 Ryan Abbott, *The Reasonable Robot: Artificial Intelligence and the Law* (Cambridge University Press, 2020) 127.

18 Ryan Abbott, *The Reasonable Robot: Artificial Intelligence and the Law* (Cambridge University Press, 2020) 127–128.

19 For further information about Chesterman's concerns with the limits of legal personality for AI, see: Simon Chesterman, *We, The Robots? Regulating Artificial Intelligence and the Limits of the Law* (Cambridge University Press, 2021) 141–143.

20 Simon Chesterman, *We, The Robots? Regulating Artificial Intelligence and the Limits of the Law* (Cambridge University Press, 2021) 141–143.

21 Simon Chesterman, *We, The Robots? Regulating Artificial Intelligence and the Limits of the Law* (Cambridge University Press, 2021) 244.

5.3.3 Need for a Hierarchical Model of Legal Personhood

Before turning to my proposed hierarchical model, it is important to consider the underlying importance of why legal personhood ought to exist in a hierarchy. I address the importance of a vertical structure to some extent in Section 5.3.4. I explore this relationship in more depth here by first outlining why a continuum approach to legal personhood status will not suffice.

Some analysts have attempted to acknowledge the malleability of legal personhood as a concept through viewing legal personhood categories as either capable of being bundled together (bundle theory)[22] or existing on a continuum (gradient theory).[23] However, neither approach adequately considers conceptions of control or the independent actions of an entity. The bundle theory of legal personhood, first devised by Visa Kurki, broadly considers that the elements of legal personhood are interconnected.[24] For Kurki, legal personhood as a concept is underpinned by two key notions: firstly, that legal personhood can be viewed as cluster property that is comprised of 'incidents' that are both interconnected and separate; and secondly, that the 'incidents' involve endowing a legal person with types of claim rights and obligations.[25] This view is arguably complex, but, at its core, and for the purposes of this discussion, it marks a key shift in the way legal personhood as a concept could be viewed. Some analysts view this theory as a positive move away from orthodox legal personhood approaches that consider a binary approach whereby a thing or a person can only be or not be a legal person.[26] The cluster approach, which accepts varying *degrees* of legal personhood, is in contrast more accommodating of a flexible method for determining if new technologies, such as AI, can be deemed legal persons.

The bundle theory approach is not as accepting of the notion that types of legal persons can be related or interconnected. Diana Mocanu seeks to build upon the bundle theory and proposes a *gradient* approach to legal personhood. Her approach accepts the underlying premise of the bundle theory – that is, rejecting the binary nature of orthodox legal personhood approaches. She argues that legal persons are not always clearly delineated but can instead blur or bleed into one another.[27] Her view is more expansive in that she considers rights and obligations can be added to or subtracted from bundles to create a more nuanced approach that could be viewed on a gradient.[28] Her

22 Visa A J Kurki, *A Theory of Legal Personhood* (Oxford University Press, 2019) 91–152; Jacob Turner also explores the bundle theory. See: Jacob Turner, *Robot Rules: Regulating Artificial Intelligence* (Palgrave Macmillan, 2019) 175–176.

23 Diana Mocanu, 'Gradient Legal Personhood for AI Systems—Painting Continental Legal Shapes Made to Fit Analytical Molds' (2022) 8 *Frontiers in Robotics and AI* 1, 9.

24 Gunkel (n 3) 155–165; Kurki (n 22).

25 Kurki (n 22) 5; Gunkel (n 3) 155–165.

26 Gunkel (n 3) 155–165.

27 Mocanu (23) 9.

28 Mocanu (23); Gunkel (n 3) 157–159.

approach is, however, suggestive of a view that places legal personhood on a continuum. A continuum, by its very nature, suggests that any categories the continuum represents are not clearly delineated, save for the two distinct categories at opposing ends of the spectrum. In other words, categories along the spectrum are not clearly distinct from one another but rather blur into each other along the continuum. It is the opposing ends of the continuum that mark a clearly separate approach.

The strength in Mocanu's argument lies in acknowledging the potential for legal personhood status to exist in multiple permutations, but her gradient approach creates ambiguity. Such ambiguity is especially apparent when considering what the criteria would be to move from one end of the continuum to the other. In other words, what bundle combination causes a particular legal person to be placed at a particular juncture on the gradient, and how does this relate to other bundles on the gradient? Mocanu has offered that bundles of the same kind can be added to and subtracted from to form separate like entities; she draws an analogy with colour spectrum models to explain how this may be represented.[29] Although it is an interesting starting point, this account still does not yet adequately address the positioning of specific legal persons on a gradient, nor does it overcome the problems associated with a lack of clear delineation between types of legal persons. Mocanu further contends that the placement of a legal person ought to be determined by its *function*, or how it is utilised within society or what end the AI system is directed towards.[30] This is an interesting notion, and one that I find moderately persuasive in terms of where a legal person can be placed within an overall structure that seeks to accommodate *degrees* of legal persons (rather than just viewing legal personhood as a binary construct). However, this book advocates for a framework that can allow legal personhood status to be used as an instrument in the process of assigning liability. Therefore, I consider it important to evaluate not only the *social* function of how legal personhood status is being deployed but how its deployment relates to its *legal* function.

Here, I wish to pause to acknowledge that I have argued previously in favour of a continuum for the *components* of legal personhood.[31] It does not automatically follow, however, that because the components of legal personhood can exist on a continuum, legal personhood itself ought to also be viewed in such a manner. The components of legal personhood that I considered in Chapter 2 – capacity, legal rights, legal duties – can exist on a continuum within a defined category of legal person. By this, I mean to suggest that I am supportive of the bundle theory insofar as it groups elements of legal personhood status together into a clearly defined category. I am of the view

29 Mocanu (n 23).

30 Mocanu (23); Gunkel (n 3) 157–159.

31 For a discussion about the components of legal personhood existing on a spectrum, see Chapter 2 and the notion of a capacity spectrum.

that within an individual bundle (or what I refer to as a 'level' in my model in Section 5.3.4) of legal person, there is room for some variation. Consider, for example, corporations. In most jurisdictions, corporate entities are endowed with legal personhood status, yet there are varying types of corporations (such as proprietary limited, limited, etc.) that are all accepted as corporate legal persons. I therefore consider that *within* a bundle (or level), the individual elements can exist on a spectrum without infringing on a clear delineation between types of legal persons.

In a hierarchical approach, as I demonstrate with my proposed model in Section 5.3.4, however, there is a clear delineation between categories, rather than a gradual blurring of categories along the continuum. The ability to identify clear categories of legal personhood status is crucial to the utility of legal personhood as a concept in resolving liability for AI. As considered in Chapter 2, legal personhood is but an artificial construct used to organise what legal rights and duties are allocated to different entities within a society. A clear delineation of legal personhood categories is thus integral to understanding how such rights and obligations are distributed within a society. Such an approach enables identification of the legal personhood status of entities capable of legal actions whilst acknowledging some flexibility within a category. Yet, the distinct categories inhibit the legal personhood status of entities blurring into one another, thereby preventing a rights creep.

A hierarchical approach does not only clearly differentiate between categories – in effect, it also ranks these categories. Sylwia Wojtczak critiques one such hierarchical model of *legal subjectivity* incorporating AI. At the core of the view she considers is the underlying notion that entities ought to be placed within the hierarchy in accordance with 'their degree of similarity to human beings'.[32] She offers a four-tiered hierarchical approach, placing animals – she does not distinguish between animal types – at the bottom of the hierarchy due to their lack of reason, followed by contemporary forms of AI with imperfect forms of reasoning.[33] Second from the top of the hierarchy, she places 'collective entities',[34] as these have the ability to engage in collective reasoning. Humans are positioned at the highest level due to their sentient nature

32 Sylwia Wojtczak, 'Endowing Artificial Intelligence with Legal Subjectivity' (2020) 37 *AI & Society* 205, 207.

33 Sylwia Wojtczak, 'Endowing Artificial Intelligence with Legal Subjectivity' (2020) 37 *AI & Society* 205, 207.

34 When discussing 'collective entities', Wojtczak refers to 'juristic persons' or 'collective subjects' without providing explicit definitions. See: Sylwia Wojtczak, 'Endowing Artificial Intelligence with Legal Subjectivity' (2020) 37 *AI & Society* 205, 206–207. For the purposes of my discussion, I am adopting the view that Wojtczak is referring to legal entities that are not comprised of one natural person but may be a collective of natural persons or an artificial legal person (like a corporation), though this interpretation extends beyond Wojtczak's explicit statements.

and ability to reason.[35] Wojtczak acknowledges this approach is flawed. One problem with this hierarchical account is that it is framed in terms of human beings[36] and does not consider that legal personality itself is a useful 'tool' or framework for ascribing the components of legal personhood to various entities within a society. Such an approach therefore fails to consider the pragmatic nature of legal personhood, explored in Chapter 2.

The view considered by Wojtczak also potentially leads to a value judgment of which type of legal person is superior to another (and therefore more highly placed in the hierarchy). Wojtczak acknowledges this as a possibility in her critique.[37] In favouring a hierarchical approach, I do not intend to cast such a value judgement. Instead, in my view, the purpose of a hierarchy is to: (a) clearly delineate between categories, for the reasons discussed above, and b) to demonstrate the relationship between control and cognitive independence. It is this latter point, (b), that I explore in Section 5.3.4 in more depth, as these elements I consider are essential to utilising legal personhood as an instrument in the process of assigning liability.

5.3.4 A New Model: Hierarchical Legal Personality

Having established the need for a new model to manage forms of AI, I now turn to outlining the intricacies of the model I am proposing. In particular, I outline a hierarchical structure of legal personhood that accommodates notions of control. In Chapter 2 Section 2.5, I considered that the elements comprising legal personhood, viz. rights, duties and capacity, could be ranked in a hierarchical spectrum to allow for *degrees of legal personhood*. The model I propose – the Hierarchical Legal Personality model – draws upon and expands this analysis. More specifically, I propose a seven-tiered pyramid model of legal personhood. The model is confined to seven tiers as tiers one to six accommodate existing notions of legal personality and tier seven offers a 'placeholder' for future possibilities. My contention is that a move *up* between each tier marks an increase in both an entity's legal capacity and its legal rights and duties. Equally, I am of the view that movement *down* a tier denotes an increase in the ability for a human actor to exert control over an entity. In other words, the higher the tiered level, the greater the legal capacity of an entity and its ability to hold rights and duties but the less likely this entity could be controlled by a human actor.[38] It is important to note that, in this section, I use the

35 Wojtczak (n 32) 206–207.

36 By framing its considerations in terms of human beings, the view critiqued by Wojtczak arguably falls into the 'android fallacy' that Simon Chesterman discusses. See: Chesterman (n 19) 141–143.

37 Wojtczak (n 32) 207–208.

38 A note about 'capacity': I acknowledge that there is the difference between having a formal legal capacity to complete an action (i.e. you are legally permitted to do so) in contrast to having the capability to do something. An individual may have capacity but not the capability, for

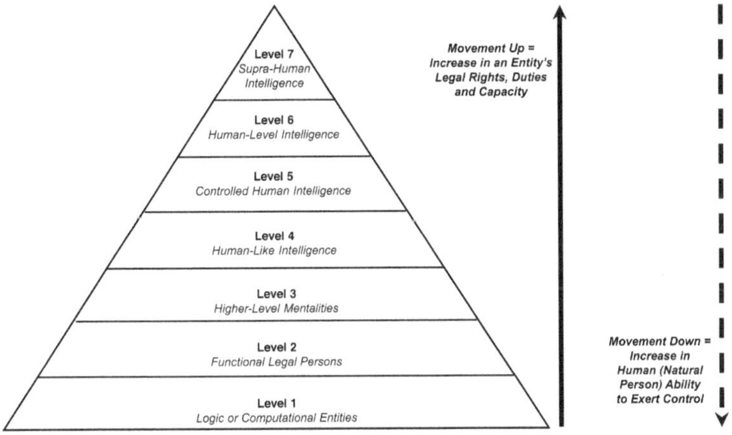

Figure 5.2 Hierarchical Model of Legal Personhood

word 'entity' and its derivatives in the broadest sense to encapsulate objects or things as well as current or potential legal persons.[39] The importance of this tiered approach is better understood through outlining the function and limitations of each tier (see also *Figure 5.2*).

5.3.4.1 Level 1: Logic or Computational Entities

Level 1 is located at the base of my proposed pyramid. This level accommodates entities with the least legal rights and duties. These entities also have minimal to no legal capacity. Additionally, entities at this level are the most likely to be capable of being controlled by natural persons. For example, Level 1 accommodates simple logic or computational systems. These are more traditional computing systems, which rely upon mere logic-based or computational reasoning processes. To be clear, I do not mean 'computational' in a computer science jargonistic account; rather, I mean to suggest entities that can utilise computational reasoning in the ordinary sense of the word, based on mathematics. Level 1 therefore accommodates more traditional computer reasoning processes, such as PCs or laptops and devices such as calculators – the most simplistic form of computer-based reasoning in widespread use. This level accommodates simplistic reasoning processes, as Level 1 does not allow for independent thought. The level therefore does not tend to encompass

example, to undertake an action. I have framed my considerations in terms of 'capacity' and not 'capability', as I consider it important to conceive of a framework in terms of legal permissions, noting that capability debates can then sit within such considerations.

39 It is also important to note that although a hierarchical account of legal personhood is proposed, this is not intended to endorse slavery or any notions of colonialism that might inadvertently be implied from the proposal.

entities capable of independent legal actions. Entities at Level 1 do, however, lend themselves to the notion of being a 'mere tool' – that is, due to the high degree of control a natural person can exert over these entities in Level 1, they are more likely to be used as a tool and are less likely to be actors in their own right. Equally, entities at this level are more akin to traditional forms of property rather than a hybrid of property and legal personhood.

5.3.4.2 Level 2: Functional Legal Persons

Level 2 is the next level in my proposed pyramid. What marks a key point of differentiation between Level 1 and Level 2 is the relative increase in the ability of entities at this level to hold rights and duties. It is worth noting that, being at a higher level than Level 1, Level 2 inherently marks an increase in legal capacity and a decrease in control. It is the former point though, rights and duties, that I wish to emphasise. Level 2 consists of entities that are *bestowed* legal personhood status. Level 2 consists of entities that would not typically be identified as a legal person, as they arguably lack the requisite legal capacity to engage in conduct that attracts legal recognition, be it through the imposition of duties or the consequences for the breach of these duties. Level 2 consists of entities that are bestowed legal personhood status, usually for the purpose of enabling these entities to be ascribed legal rights. Consider, for example, the Whanganui River in New Zealand, which in 2017 was granted legal personhood status in an attempt to bolster its protection.[40] The granting of legal personhood status in this instance is to acknowledge the deep connection the indigenous Māori people share with the river and, in turn, bestow legal rights onto the river, viz. the right to be protected from harm or damage.[41] Level 2 consists of such entities that are *bestowed* legal personhood status for the purpose of assigning legal rights to these entities. Control for Level 2 entities therefore does not relate to the actions of these entities. For a river could flood a town and be out of the control of natural persons. Instead, control in this context is instead exerted over the *legal* capacities of Level 2 entities. Legal personhood in this capacity could therefore be said to be utilised to achieve a functional objective (the granting of rights). It is with this in mind that I designate Level 2 as the level that accommodates 'functional legal persons'.

5.3.4.3 Level 3: Higher-Level Mentalities

Moving further up the pyramid, and following functional legal persons, I propose Level 3, which represents a relative increase in rights, duties and capacity.

40 Kate Evans, 'The New Zealand River that Became a Legal Person', *BBC Travel* (Web Page, 21 March 2020) <https://www.bbc.com/travel/article/20200319-the-new-zealand-river-that-became-a-legal-person >; Wojtczak (n 32).

41 Evans (n 40).

I propose that this level ought to accommodate entities with higher-level mentalities. By using the term 'higher-level mentalities', I intend to introduce some, albeit limited, cognitive capacity into the hierarchical structure; and so, it is at Level 3 that some forms of modern AI enter the structure. To illustrate the importance of Level 3 further, consider, for example, dolphins. Dolphins are widely regarded as being highly intelligent animals that are capable of cognitive capacities such as problem solving and reasoning processes.[42] Yet, at the same time as exhibiting this degree of independent capacity, these animals are also at least capable of being controlled, to some extent, by humans, as is evidenced by how we train these animals to respond to commands in captivity. Level 3 marks a distinction from previous levels in that legal personhood status at this level is defined by the ability of entities at this level to exhibit *some* degree of independent capacity but not to the extent that these entities lose their ability to be controlled by human actors. Modern forms of AI that I envisage as being accommodated at this level include, for example, supervised and semi-supervised modern AI, as these systems are capable of exhibiting reasoning processes but are also directed in their end objectives by human actors and are therefore controlled to some extent.

5.3.4.4 Level 4: Human-Like Intelligence

The level immediately above Level 3 and representing a further increase in the rights, duties and capacities of entities is Level 4. This level builds upon the degree of independent capacity introduced in Level 3 and starts a move towards actors with human-level intelligence. In this respect, Level 4 (together with Levels 5 and 6) marks a key shift towards actors capable of engaging in actions with legal consequences. To understand the types of entities that may be encapsulated by Level 4, recall the discussion in Chapter 2 Sections 2.3.2 and 2.4.1.2 concerning Tommy the chimpanzee. In seeking to recognise Tommy as a non-human legal person, arguments were raised that Tommy was not only capable of holding rights but also of having people exert those rights on his behalf. Whilst this view was ultimately rejected on technical grounds in relation to Tommy (see Chapter 2), it establishes an interesting category of actors: entities capable of holding and exerting rights but not necessarily also capable of maintaining legal obligations or duties. For the avoidance of doubt, this category is distinct from Level 2, as any legal rights attained in relation to Level 4 actors are ***not bestowed*** to achieve a secondary goal (such as environmental protection); rather, actors at this level have the legal capacity to not only hold rights but also have their interests exerted in relation to those rights.

42 'How Intelligent are Whales and Dolphins?', *Whale and Dolphin Conservation (WDC)* <https://uk.whales.org/whales-dolphins/how-intelligent-are-whales-and-dolphins/#:~:text=Dolphins%20demonstrate%20the%20ability%20to,%2C%20grief%2C%20joy%20and%20playfulness>.

Additionally, unlike Level 3 entities, they are also relatively harder to exert control over.[43] Any form of modern AI that is compatible with this level must therefore be capable of also holding legal rights but not incapable of being controlled to some extent, as Level 4 actors are still able to be controlled by human actors.

5.3.4.5 Level 5: Controlled Human Intelligence

Level 5 is third from the top of my proposed pyramid. Entities at this level mark a progression from Level 4 in that they are not just capable of holding legal rights and exerting their rights. For the first time in my proposed hierarchical structure, Level 5 introduces the notion that entities at this level also have the legal capacity to hold legal obligations or duties in addition to legal rights. Despite introducing the ability of entities to be subject to legal obligations, entities at this level are still not exempt from also being subject to control. It is at this level that entities would possess what I deemed in Chapter 2 Section 2.5.3 (see also *Figure 2.1* in Chapter 2) 'qualified cognitive capacity'. Entities at this level may have the capacity to act autonomously, but this autonomy must be exercised within defined parameters. It is for this reason that Level 5 entities would accommodate now (thankfully) mostly defunct legal structures, such as the historic examples considered in Chapter 2 that prohibited full legal personhood status recognition to marginalised individuals, like women and ethnic minorities, instead tying their legal status to that of another (typically a white man). This level could also accommodate corporate legal personality, which is often subject to stringent legislative limitations. Level 5 would therefore also accommodate forms of modern artificial intelligence that can hold rights and duties but are still at least capable of being controlled by a human actor – forms of AI that can act with some independence but are ultimately limited in the scope of their actions, such as reinforcement learning. AI systems acting within the scope of their authority as legal agents would also fall within Level 5.

5.3.4.6 Level 6: Human-Level Intelligence

Level 6 is my proposed penultimate level, and it is at this level that the possibility of fully autonomous entities is introduced. Level 6 entities have an increased level of rights, duties and capacity relative to Level 5. Entities at this level include natural persons and any potential entity that has the equivalent legal capacity. Recall from the discussion in Section 5.2.1 that one of the objectives of AI research is to strive towards achieving a level of intelligence

43 By implication animals, such as Tommy, could be bestowed legal personality under this model. I do not intend to explore the lengthy debates surrounding legal personality for animals here, save to acknowledge that legal personality for animals is not incompatible with this model.

comparable to that of human intelligence. Whilst AI systems are not yet quite at this level, it would be myopic for any model of legal personhood status to not accommodate the *possibility* of AI achieving this level of intelligence, and potentially also legal capacity. Technology in this area is rapidly evolving, and traditionally, the law's evolution is significantly delayed relative to the advancements in technology. It is therefore important to proactively construct a legal model with scope for future technological advancements. There are already significant advances in black box, deep learning and neural network AI technologies, which are arguably making progress towards this objective of human-level intelligence. Level 6 therefore aims to accommodate entities that have full legal capacity, akin to a natural person, and that are also capable of holding rights and maintaining legal obligations.[44] That is not to say that entities at Level 6 are beyond control, for even natural persons consentingly enter into relationships underpinned by some level of control (consider, for example, workplace relationship structures, where natural persons consent to follow all lawful instructions from their employer, or policy reasons, such as in the case of minors or persons with intellectual disabilities). What is key to Level 6 is that entities must be capable of bearing rights and obligations as well as having the capacity to act autonomously.

5.3.4.7 Level 7: Supra-Human Intelligence

At the pinnacle of my pyramid is Level 7, which is my attempt to address the (currently unrealistic) arguments that AI will surpass a human level of intelligence. Any consideration of an AI system with a degree of intelligence that surpasses that of a human level is purely speculative at this stage. For the reasons discussed in response to Level 6, however, it is still important to at least offer a place within any proposed model suggesting how these systems might be accommodated. Without an AI system with this level of capability, it is hard to offer a concrete view of the type of legal personhood such a system could be ascribed. Rather, I propose that if such an AI system were to exist, it is likely to pose new legal challenges centred around control.[45] If an AI system is deemed to pass that of human-level intelligence, would this mean that it is beyond human control? Would it reach a level of self-control and self-regulation? The answers to these questions are not clear, as there is no such form of technology, at this stage, that poses these challenges. In recognition

44 In placing human-level intelligence at this level in the hierarchy, I do not intend to make a value judgment that humans ought to outrank other entities by virtue of simply being human. Rather, I have placed them at this juncture based on their level of ability to hold rights and duties relative to the level of control that can be exerted over humans as entities. That is not to suggest that other entities could not also achieve this level; I merely rely on humans as a frame of reference as the current dominant entity capable of functioning at this level.

45 The possibility of AI systems with a degree of intelligence above that of human level is also considered by Simon Chesterman. See: Chesterman (n 19) 138–141.

of the hypothetical possibility that such a form of AI could one day potentially exist, such forms of AI are categorised as Level 7 and placed at the top of the pyramid. At the pinnacle of the pyramid, they represent the forms of AI that are least likely to be subject to human control due to having what is arguably the highest level of capacity. I acknowledge that this is largely a speculative position in light of the current state of AI technology; yet, given the rapid advancement of AI relative to the slow-responding nature of the law, I think it important to at least consider how such forms of AI *might* be accommodated in a working model of legal personhood.

5.3.5 Hierarchical Legal Personality Model: Relationship Between Levels

Having outlined above the structure of my proposed hierarchical model of legal personhood status, I now move from considering each level in this model and turn to considering the relationship *between* the levels.

5.3.5.1 New Model of Legal Personhood and the Interaction Between Levels

I have already signalled that a vertical movement in the hierarchy denotes a relative increase in the cognitive independence of an entity and a relative decrease in the correlating level of human control over that level. A movement from one level to the next is therefore dependent upon addressing two questions: (1) does an entity under consideration give rise to a decreased ability for a human to exert control over it, relative to the entities at a level in the model under examination, and (2) is there an increase in the entity's complexity, giving rise to an increased ability to exercise cognitive independence or autonomy of decision-making, relative to the entities at a level in the model under examination? Consider both Level 1 (logic or computational entities) and Level 2 (functional legal persons). In trying to determine at which level an entity should be classified and whether an entity surpasses Level 1 and moves into Level 2, I am of the view that for an entity to be classified at the next level above in my pyramid, the answer to my two questions must both be 'yes'. A move from Level 2 to Level 3 would therefore require the same analysis – the entity must, relative to the lower level under consideration (here, Level 2), be less likely to be controlled, and there must also be an increase in the entity's complexity to be categorised at the higher level (here, Level 3).

In deciding where to place an entity within the hierarchy, the entity should be compared with the pyramid until an alignment is achieved between the entity and the characteristics of the different levels. Consideration should be given moving from the bottom towards the pinnacle until an alignment is achieved. If an entity is borderline between two levels, it should be categorised at the higher level to ensure its maximum capacity is fully captured.[46] The Hierarchical Legal Personality Model is therefore built upon the concepts of control and relative cognitive independence (or autonomy of decision-making). The importance of these concepts as the foundations of my hierarchical approach will become more apparent in Part II, where I consider in depth how liability ought to be assigned in response to modern forms of AI. I consider that the concept of control, for example, shapes a key issue of legal causation considered more fully in Chapter 6, and the relative degree of independence arises in relation to the scope of permissible actions an AI system may execute, considered in Chapter 7.

5.4. Incorporating Agency and Property into the Hierarchical Legal Personality Model

I have considered the need for a hierarchical model of legal personhood and proposed one such model. But how would this model accommodate other characterisations of AI? In the preceding chapters, I explored the possibility that AI could be characterised as both an agent and property. I now turn to consider how these possible forms of characterisation could be accommodated within my proposed model. My view is that legal personhood as a concept can be viewed *situationally*. I suggest that the exact rights and obligations associated with a specific form of legal personhood depend upon the situation in which legal personhood is acting or being deployed. This is an important additional layer added to my model, as it holds implications for determining liability. Exactly how the *type* or *level* of legal personhood from my model contributes to the assignment of liability is considered in Part III. For now, I focus on incorporating more than one form of legal characterisation of AI into my working model.

5.4.1 Overlap of AI Characterisations

Before turning to how agency and property can be incorporated into my proposed model, I consider it integral to first, briefly, pause and acknowledge that the concepts of legal personhood, agency and property overlap to some extent. In previous chapters, I have explored the relationship between AI and each of these potential forms of characterisation individually; I now turn to consider the degree to which these concepts intersect (see *Figure 5.3*). The degree to which these concepts overlap will inform if and how they can be incorporated into the *Hierarchical Legal Personality Model*, which in turn informs the assignment of liability.

46 The importance of capturing an entity's maximum capacity is a concept I explore further in relation to the first phase of the Tri-Phase AI Liability Model I outline in Chapter 8.

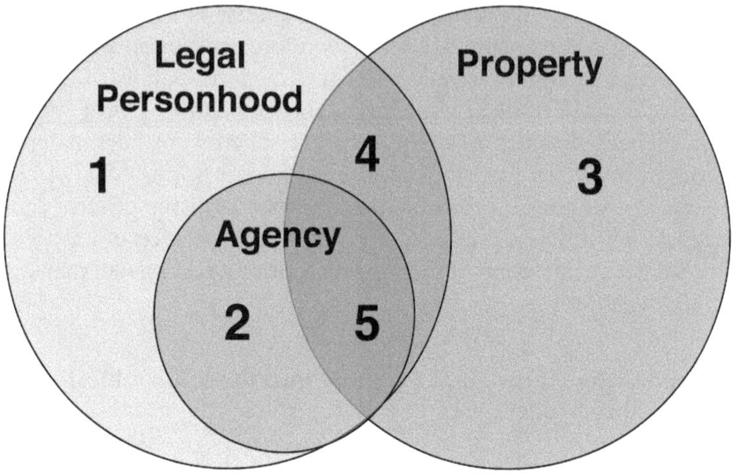

Figure 5.3 An Intersection of Different Forms of Legal Characterisation

5.4.1.1 Category 1: Legal Personhood Only

I do not intend to consider Category 1 in any great depth here, as this has been addressed at length in Chapter 2. For the sake of completeness in relation to the immediate discussion, however, I acknowledge that legal personhood can exist in a form or category by itself (as depicted at '1' in *Figure 5.3*). That is, this is a pure form of legal personhood that encompasses *only* the characteristics of legal personhood status. It is not a hybrid form of legal personhood that encompasses other legal characteristics, such as the characteristics of property. It is unlikely that any form of AI, current or in the foreseeable future, ought to be characterised *solely* as a legal person, or within Category 1 (denoted at '1' in *Figure 5.3*), for to do so would be to ignore the arguments explored in Chapter 4 about the potential proprietary nature of AI.

5.4.1.2 Category 2: Agency and Legal Personhood

The concept of a legal agent – the notion of acting on behalf of another in law – by necessity intersects with the concept of legal personhood. This is a notion I explored in depth in Chapter 3. On this basis, it is reasonable to consider that agency as a concept is entirely encapsulated in, or entirely intersects with, legal personhood status (as depicted in totality at '2' and '5' in *Figure 5.3*). The intersection of agency and legal personhood, denoted at '2' in *Figure 5.3*, reflects the points I addressed in Chapter 3. Yet, as previously considered, this approach is not without its flaws and lacks recognition of the proprietary nature of AI.

5.4.1.3 Category 3: Property Only

Category 3 (denoted at '3' in *Figure 5.3*) encapsulates instances in which AI could only be characterised as property. If AI were to be characterised as such, it would fall outside my proposed model, but to do so would be to overlook the unique characteristics of AI explored in Section 5.2, together with the problems associated with viewing AI solely as a tool, a form of property, explored in Section 5.3.1. Given these previous considerations, I do not consider that AI ought to fall solely within Category 3.

5.4.1.4 Category 4: Property and Legal Personhood

I have reasoned so far in this chapter that AI ought not be characterised as any of Categories 1, 2 or 3 above. This then leaves two remaining categories – Category 4 and Category 5 – both of which are hybrid forms of legal personhood. Category 4 (denoted at '4' in *Figure 5.3*) concerns the intersection of both legal personhood and property as a means of characterising AI. I expand upon this category in depth in Section 5.4.2, but I pause here to acknowledge how it is placed in relation to Categories 1, 2 and 3.

5.4.1.5 Category 5: Legal Personhood, Property and Agency Intersection

The last category – Category 5 (denoted at '5' in *Figure 5.3*) – is another hybrid form of legal personhood. This category accommodates an intersection of legal personhood, agency and property, which I look at in detail in Section 5.4.3. As above with Category 4, I pause here to merely acknowledge how Category 5 is placed in relation to Categories 1, 2 and 3.

Given the above discussion, it is apparent that AI ought to be legally characterised as either Category 4 or Category 5. I turn now to explore these categories in more depth before then exploring how they fit within my proposed model of legal personhood.

5.4.2 Category 4: How Legal Personhood and Property Intersect

In Chapter 4, I identified that there is a potential intersection between legal personhood status and property. Here, I explore the feasibility of this intersection: I address the question of whether AI ought to be characterised as a hybrid of legal personhood and property and, if so, under what circumstances.

5.4.2.1 Property with Cognitive Capacities

In Section 5.2.1, I considered that AI is unique due to its potential cognitive capacity; it is worth noting, however, that there are established forms of property that also share this unique characteristic. In Chapter 2,[47] I looked at the concept of slavery insofar as to demonstrate that the concept of legal personhood has malleable parameters and that the concept can evolve.[48] The concept of slavery, although abhorrent, provides a further useful case study concerning the intersection of legal personhood status and property. Throughout history, slaves have been viewed as valuable tradeable commodities. Whilst this is undoubtedly dehumanising, it does still mark a useful point: legal property can be capable of also holding the unique characteristic of cognitive capacity. There has been some debate surrounding whether AI in the form of robots ought to be characterised as a slave. Arguments have focused on whether it is ethical to enslave robots to begin with and the merits of ascribing rights to robots.[49] These are interesting debates but not ones that I wish to delve into deeply here, as they predominantly relate to one form of AI (viz. robots). As I acknowledge, AI is not a singular form and so not confined to merely robots. What is interesting and useful about these debates is the underlying point that what is deemed legal property can also be capable of cognitive independence and, in the historical case of slaves, legal action. And so, there are clearly instances in which property holds the ability to reason and potentially act. This is not necessarily unique to AI, but it is still key to how AI fits into my proposed model, which I explore shortly.

5.4.2.2 Issues with an Intellectual Property Approach

In Chapter 4, I explored the feasibility of whether AI could be characterised as intellectual property and whether this form of technology could be construed as a patent, copyright or trade secret. I subsequently raised issues with each of these individual approaches. I do not revisit the intricacies of the issues with each approach here, but I do want to pause briefly to make a few observations more broadly about an intellectual property characterisation of AI (regardless of the type of IP) and the potential problems this poses in the context of assigning liability.

One of the problems with viewing AI as IP is that such a characterisation can give rise to uncertainty surrounding the obligations connected to this form of technology. There are flaws with each of the three forms of IP approaches (as considered in Chapter 4 Section 4.2.4), but one overarching common theme between the approaches is that each gives rise to increased uncertainty. As discussed in Chapter 4, each method of IP characterisation, in its current form, creates more ambiguity than certainty, as there is not a uniform approach to identifying AI as IP. If we view one of the goals of a legal system as, arguably, being to increase certainty in society – be it certainty of a legal outcome, or the

47 See the discussion concerning slavery in Chapter 2 Section 2.3.1.2.
48 This is a view also explored by Jacob Turner. See: Turner (n 22) 202.
49 Gunkel (n 3).

rights and obligations of legal persons – then IP as a method of characterising AI to date directly challenges this objective. The fact that IP in relation to AI is still evolving is arguably the source of this uncertainty.

5.4.2.3 Intersection of Legal Personhood and Property

If we consider Category 4 to be the intersection of legal personhood and property, this intersection only arises in a narrowed set of circumstances. Given the nature of intellectual property and how it relates to AI, as considered in Section 5.4.2.2, it is apparent that AI as IP is unlikely to fit the intersection defined by Category 4. Instead, AI as a form of IP would likely be encapsulated in Category 3 only as property. Category 4 is therefore more likely to encapsulate forms of AI as property that include some sort of cognitive capacity. In other words, Category 4 would not include forms of AI that cannot adopt the key characteristics or elements of legal personhood. Without the elements of legal personhood, or at least the ability to be assigned and hold these elements, the category could not reasonably be placed into a hierarchical approach of legal personhood. I come to explore exactly how it fits into the model, but before doing so, I should elaborate on Category 5.

5.4.3 Category 5: How Legal Personhood, Agency and Property Intersect

In Chapter 3, I considered that it is at least theoretically possible that AI could be characterised as a legal agent. This raises two subsequent questions: (1) when AI ought to be viewed as an agent and (2) how this relates to the notion that AI can also be viewed as property.

I have discussed that, by implication, for an agent to exist, there is by necessity a requirement for that agent to possess legal personhood status to some extent, which is why agency is entirely encapsulated within the sphere of legal personhood in *Figure 5.3*. However, I have considered that AI is also capable of being a thing of value. It is for this reason that the intersection of all three possible characterisation options – viz. legal personhood, property and agency – becomes key. In instances where agency applies, it must intersect with legal personhood and, in relation to AI at least, also intersect with property. For AI to be characterised as a legal agent then, it must also be capable of being characterised as these alternative options. How these fit into my broader model is considered next.

5.4.4 Situational Legal Personhood: Incorporating Categories 4 and 5 into the Hierarchical Legal Personality Model

In the preceding sections, I considered that it is not only possible but essential for AI to be classified as a hybrid of at least two forms of characterising AI, the minimum intersection being legal personhood and property and the maximum intersection consisting of both these with the additional layer of agency.

I now turn to propose how these categories – Category 4 and 5 – might fit into my new overall model of legal personhood.

To accommodate more than one form of characterising AI within the same model of legal personhood, weight must be given to the situation in which legal personhood is being deployed. At the core of this approach is the view that legal personhood is but a tool used to ascribe legal rights and obligations to entities in a society. Looking at the context in which a legal person is being deployed is a recurring theme I explore in depth in Part III, but there are some salient points still to be raised in relation to my proposed model. In *Figure 5.2*, I outlined the intricacies of my proposed hierarchical model. In *Figure 5.4*, I now overlay the key categories from *Figure 5.3* that I have identified as being relevant to characterising AI – namely, Categories 4 and 5.

Figure 5.4 proposes how Categories 4 and 5 fit into my proposed model of legal personhood. It is hard to conceive of an instance where modern forms of AI would not also be deemed property in some form or another. It is for this reason that the intersection of property and legal personhood status encapsulates levels from Level 3 through to Level 6 (recall from the above discussion in Section 5.3.4.3 that it is at Level 3 that AI is introduced into the proposed model). It is Category 5, the intersection of all three types of possible characterisations – legal personhood, property and agency – that is unique to levels higher within a structure. By its nature, the added element of agency requires a degree of capacity not common to entities lower in the hierarchical structure. To be an agent, a legal person must have the requisite legal capacity to fulfil this role. By their very nature, lower levels are therefore precluded from being an agent. On this basis, the exact way in which AI is characterised – as either Category 4 or Category 5 – is determined by the level at which an AI system is positioned within the hierarchy.

I have not extended the brackets for either Category 4 or Category 5 to encapsulate Level 7. Instead, for now, it sits above this demarcation as it is representative of the *possibility* that AI might achieve this level of capacity. It is likely that, if achieved, Level 7 would also fall within Category 5 in the

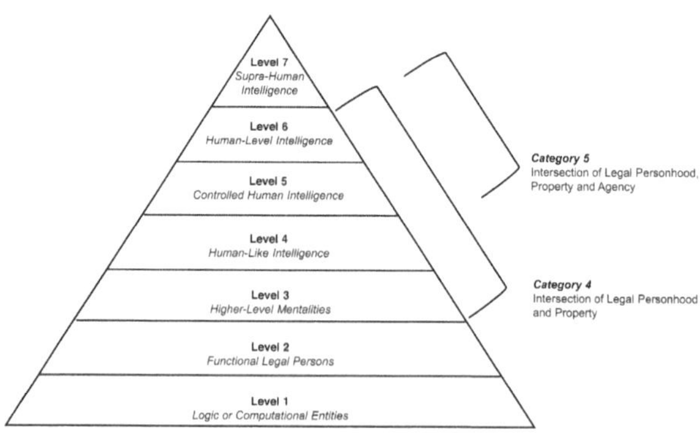

Figure 5.4 Situational Hierarchical Model of Legal Personhood

same manner as human-level intelligence. Without knowing the specifics of any supra-human intelligence, however, it is for now listed as outside these categories until the time when this level of intelligence might be achieved and a more fulsome analysis of its place within the Hierarchical Legal Personality model can be actioned. This topic of where an AI system is, or ought to be, positioned within the hierarchy is a topic I explore further in Part III. At this stage, what I want to emphasise is that exactly how AI is characterised is determined on a situational (or contextual) basis. As I explore further in Part III, the status of a legal entity being determined on a situational basis is not a new concept in law. For now, I propose a model that accommodates more than one method of characterising AI that is ultimately rooted in the underlying concept of legal personhood.

5.5. Resolving Characterising AI and Its Importance for Liability

In Part II, I have examined the best method of legally characterising modern forms of AI. I considered the feasibility of conceiving of AI as a legal person, a legal agent and as property. What became apparent is that although AI is capable of exhibiting some of the elements of these forms of characterisation, there is no 'perfect fit' according to which AI could be added to existing legal paradigms. AI is not like other forms of technology; it holds the potential to disrupt existing legal frameworks in ways other technologies have not to date. There exists a need, therefore, to create a new form of legal characterisation that adequately accommodates the unique nature of AI.

In Chapter 2, I considered the practical benefits of legal personhood as a concept, together with its malleable nature. Building upon this concept, I proposed a new model of legal personhood that better accommodates AI. This model acknowledges the cognitive aspects of AI, which precludes it from *always* being viewed as a tool and gives rise to a more complex characterisation.

There is a spectrum of forms of modern AI, and the challenge is thus to accommodate these variances of AI within the one legal structure so that the legal liability response to AI is not fragmented or ad hoc, which could lead to inconsistencies and, therefore, potential injustices. I have established a *hierarchical* model of legal personhood to clearly delineate between *types* of legal persons. The *Hierarchical Legal Personality Model* not only acknowledges the malleable nature of legal personhood as a concept but also allows for the incorporation of a spectrum of control and autonomy into the model. I have also overlayed the concepts of agency and property and proposed how these might be accommodated within my model. In doing so, I acknowledge that AI is not but one thing: it can exist as a hybrid characterisation of legal personhood and property, together with acting as an agent under certain conditions.

Whilst I have proposed how the various forms of characterising AI – legal personhood, agent and property – ought to fit together within one model, I am yet to reconcile this model with issues of liability. If we consider that the concept of legal personhood is but an instrument for assigning rights and obligations, establishing a model that accommodates AI is a key initial step in the process of ultimately assigning liability.

In Part III, I therefore explore additional threshold issues that ought to be resolved as part of the process of assigning liability and situate these with reference to my hierarchical model. I consider issues such as causation (Chapter 6), together with the context in which AI is deployed and the question of who could be liable (Chapter 7). I then explore how these threshold issues, when viewed in relation to my hierarchical approach, inform a liability model that addresses actions taken in the context of modern AI.

References

A Articles/Books/Reports

Abbott, Ryan, *The Reasonable Robot: Artificial Intelligence and the Law* (Cambridge University Press, 2020).

Chesterman, Simon, *We, The Robots? Regulating Artificial Intelligence and the Limits of the Law* (Cambridge University Press, 2021).

Chopra, Samir and Laurence White, *A Legal Theory for Autonomous Artificial Agents* (The University of Michigan Press, 4th ed, 2014).

Gunkel, David J, *'Both/And', Person, Thing, Robot: A Moral and Legal Ontology for the 21st Century and Beyond* (MIT Press, 2023).

Jackson, Philip C, *Introduction to Artificial Intelligence* (Dover Publications Inc., 3rd ed, 2019).

Kurki, Visa A J, *A Theory of Legal Personhood* (Oxford University Press, 2019).

Mik, Eliza, 'AI as a Legal Person?' in Jyn-An Lee et al (ed), *Artificial Intelligence and Intellectual Property* (Oxford University Press, 2021) 419.

Mocanu, Diana, 'Gradient Legal Personhood for AI Systems—Painting Continental Legal Shapes Made to Fit Analytical Molds' (2022) 8 *Frontiers in Robotics and AI* 1.

Turner, Jacob, *Robot Rules: Regulating Artificial Intelligence* (Palgrave Macmillan, 2019) 202.

Wojtczak, Sylwia, 'Endowing Artificial Intelligence with Legal Subjectivity' (2020) (37) *AI & Society* 205.

B Other

'How Intelligent are Whales and Dolphins?', *Whale and Dolphin Conservation (WDC)* <https://uk.whales.org/whales-dolphins/how-intelligent-are-whales-and-dolphins/#:~:text=Dolphins%20demonstrate%20the%20ability%20to,%2C%20grief%2C%20joy%20and%20playfulness>

Chen, Brian X, and Cade Metz, 'Google's Duplex Uses A.I. to Mimic Humans (Sometimes)', *The New York Times* (online, 22 May 2019) <https://www.nytimes.com/2019/05/22/technology/personaltech/ai-google-duplex.html>

Evans, Kate, 'The New Zealand River that Became a Legal Person', *BBC Travel* (Web Page, 21 March 2020) <https://www.bbc.com/travel/article/20200319-the-new-zealand-river-that-became-a-legal-person >

Leviathan, Yaniv and Yossi Matias, 'Google Duplex: An AI System for Accomplishing Real-World Tasks Over the Phone', *Google AI Blog* (Blog Post, 8 May 2018) <https://ai.googleblog.com/2018/05/duplex-ai-system-for-natural-conversation.html>

Part III

6 Adapting Causation Principles for AI

6.1. Causation: A Threshold Issue

This chapter marks the first chapter in Part III of this book. Part III proceeds as follows: Chapters 6 and 7 address an additional set of threshold issues needed to be resolved as part of the process of assigning legal liability stemming from the use of modern forms of AI. 'Threshold issues' in this context refers to additional issues that must be resolved as part of the process of assigning liability. Chapter 8 then turns to examining how these threshold issues can be combined with the *Hierarchical Legal Personality Model* from Part II to propose a new model for assigning liability – one that caters to modern forms of AI. Chapter 8 proposes a new three-phase model of liability: the *Tri-Phase AI Liability Model.* The issues addressed here in Chapter 6, together with Chapter 7, underpin Phase 2 of this model.

This chapter therefore explores the threshold issue of causation, which must be resolved as part of the process of assigning liability. The issue of causation is integral to being able to assess if a legal outcome is linked to a legal person and, as such, is central to assessing the scope of liability, which is why it is considered a necessary threshold issue to address in advance of proposing a liability framework. For this reason, Chapter 6 proceeds as follows: it begins by examining key theoretical approaches to legal causation before turning next to proposed solutions addressing the uncertainty AI creates for legal causation. It then raises key problems with current approaches to causation in this context. Finally, a new approach to causation is proposed that draws upon and expands existing proposed solutions. In doing so, the chapter proposes a view central to the overall analysis in this book: that causation in the context of AI, like the response to the question of how AI ought to be characterised, must be viewed in context. That is, causation ought to be considered *situationally.* How this relates more specifically to broader liability questions is a topic explored in Chapter 8.

DOI: 10.4324/9781003617549-10

6.2. Legal Causation and AI: Theoretical Approaches

In considering the need to re-evaluate causation theories to accommodate new forms of technologies such as AI, I first look at key theoretical frameworks addressing the issue of causation. I evaluate these theories in the context of AI.

6.2.1 Factual Causation

Many theorists acknowledge that there is a distinction between factual and legal forms of causation. To Jacob Turner, these are separate elements that, together, work in allocating liability for a harm incurred.[1] He considers that factual causation is most commonly identified through the application of the renowned 'but for' test – that is, asking if 'but for' 'event A', would 'consequence X' have occurred?[2] This is a useful framework for looking at mere facts alone; yet, as Turner highlights, it is not without its flaws. He considers that there are issues of both over- and under-determination in response to factual causation.[3] Under-determination, he outlines, arises when there is a lack of evidence to accurately identify if event A or event B is causally linked to 'consequence Y', whereas over-determination arises when there is the possibility that either event A or event B could be the causing factor for consequence Y.[4] Given the possibilities of over- or under-determination, Turner reaches the view that factual causation alone is insufficient to allocate liability for harm incurred in general.[5] By extension, then, factual causation is also a deficient causation analysis in response to the deployment of technologies such as AI. Turner not only addresses factual causation but also briefly outlines three key foundational elements of legal causation: a free action (or omission) taken by an actor, the degree of knowledge the actor had about the possible consequences of the actions and whether there is an intervening act.[6] These are important factors, but as Turner's analysis is brief in this regard, I give greater consideration to the relevance of these factors below in relation to other causation theories. For now, like Turner, I too consider that factual causation alone is insufficient in relation to AI but do consider that it is an imperative preliminary thought process when considering the issue of legal causation more broadly.

1 Jacob Turner, *Robot Rules: Regulating Artificial Intelligence* (Palgrave Macmillan, 2019) 58.
2 Jacob Turner, *Robot Rules: Regulating Artificial Intelligence* (Palgrave Macmillan, 2019) 58.
3 Jacob Turner, *Robot Rules: Regulating Artificial Intelligence* (Palgrave Macmillan, 2019) 59.
4 Jacob Turner, *Robot Rules: Regulating Artificial Intelligence* (Palgrave Macmillan, 2019) 59–60.
5 Turner (n 1); this view is also recognised in tort law generally; consider, for example: s 51 *Wrongs Act 1958* (Vic) ('*Wrongs Act*').
6 Turner (n 1) 61.

6.2.2 Causal Minimalism vs Causal Maximalism

The factual versus legal causation dichotomy is but one account of causation, for as legal theorists Jos Lehmann et al. highlight, causation can be divided into two further approaches: ***causal minimalism*** and ***causal maximalism***. It is the latter of these, causal minimalism, that is perhaps closest to Turner's exposition in relation to factual causation. Causal minimalism seeks to imply legal fault based on the conduct of a person.[7] As a theory, it is focused on identifying what is sufficient rather than necessary to establish causal relationships.[8] This approach arguably adopts a simplistic account of causation. It does not adequately look at the distinction between what is necessary in contrast to what is sufficient to cause an outcome. Consider the 'but for' test commonly used to establish causation. This test is focused on factual causation, and it could be that in applying the test, the following could arise: but for event C, outcome Z would not have occurred. Here, event C is necessary to cause outcome Z, but it may not be sufficient. There could be the need for other factors, such as event D, to bring about outcome Z. In this respect, factual causation is relatively wide and needs to be viewed in conjunction with other elements to improve its utility. Other key factors often incorporated into causation theories, such as the notion of proximity, are overlooked in adopting this approach; this is problematic for causation as it relates to AI.

Causal maximalism, however, is inherently more complex than the minimalist approach. As a concept, it moves beyond the mere fault-based analysis offered by causal minimalism and seeks to incorporate causal proximity theories.[9] It adds the key tenet that there must be a 'causal connection' between the conduct of an actor and the harm suffered.[10] In this respect, the maximalist approach arguably narrows the scope of legal responsibility from mere causation in fact and incorporates the requirements of a legal relationship. This is an important distinction, as it suggests that legal liability ought not be based on a factual matrix alone but is, rather, inherently tied to legal policy considerations.[11] Causal maximalism as a theory, therefore, denotes an important departure from theories of causation based on facts alone. The theory allows for the incorporation of policy considerations concerning which juncture in a causal chain of events attention should be focused on when establishing causation. In other words, it limits the wide scope of causation established under factual

7 Jos Lehmann et al., 'Causation in AI and Law' (2004) 12 *Artificial Intelligence and Law* 279, 289, 293.

8 Jos Lehmann et al., 'Causation in AI and Law' (2004) 12 *Artificial Intelligence and Law* 279, 289, 293.

9 Jos Lehmann et al., 'Causation in AI and Law' (2004) 12 *Artificial Intelligence and Law* 279, 289, 292, 295.

10 Jos Lehmann et al., 'Causation in AI and Law' (2004) 12 *Artificial Intelligence and Law* 279, 289, 292, 295.

11 Jos Lehmann et al., 'Causation in AI and Law' (2004) 12 *Artificial Intelligence and Law* 279, 292.

causation theories and narrows the scope to what has been deemed acceptable under a policy response. This is an important progression in theories of causation, for it allows the integration of societal values and attitudes in establishing causation. This is especially important in relation to new AI, which as a technology is likely to have a far-reaching impact within society.

6.2.3 Adapting the 'NESS' Test of Causation for AI

Jos Lehmann et al., however, are of the view that, in relation to AI, causal maximalism is insufficient. They consider that causal maximalism relies excessively on common sense to determine legal causality.[12] To overcome this perceived deficiency, they draw upon Hart and Honoré's approach and seek to modify this account by relying on analytical processes rather than common sense.[13] Before turning to examine this modified view, I therefore first consider the base theory drawn upon – that is, Hart and Honoré's approach to causation.

Hart and Honoré, legal theorists who are considered experts in causal theory, sought to provide an alternative view to legal causation, of which I provide a *brief* account sufficient for understanding the approach of Jos Lehmann et al. as it relates to AI. Key to Hart and Honoré's causation framework is the introduction of an antecedent condition to be considered before turning to more established causation analysis.[14] They deem this antecedent condition the 'causally relevant factor' without which, in their view, causation cannot adequately be established.[15] Causation is then determined by relying upon a subsequent set of conditions.[16] The relationship between the antecedent and subsequent conditions is underpinned by 'common sense' principles.[17] Some theorists consider Hart and Honoré's account an expansion of a 'necessary element of a sufficient set' or 'NESS' test of causation.[18] A NESS test looks at a consequence – say, 'C' – and seeks to establish legal causation based on a key relationship arising between C and different conditions. Under NESS,

12 Lehmann et al. (n 7) 295; it is worth noting that common sense was also once incorporated into the common law principles. Consider, for example, *March v Stramare (E & MH) Pty Ltd* (1991) 171 CLR 506 at 519 and 524, which was superseded by general principles such as s 51 *Wrongs Act* (n 5).

13 Lehmann et al. (n 7) 292, 295.

14 Richard W Wright, 'Causation in the Law', *Routledge Encyclopedia of Philosophy* (Taylor & Francis, 2001) at [3]–[4].

15 Richard W Wright, 'Causation in the Law', *Routledge Encyclopedia of Philosophy* (Taylor & Francis, 2001) at [3]–[4].

16 Richard W Wright, 'Causation in the Law', *Routledge Encyclopedia of Philosophy* (Taylor & Francis, 2001) at [3]–[4].

17 Richard W Wright, 'Causation in the Law', *Routledge Encyclopedia of Philosophy* (Taylor & Francis, 2001) at [5].

18 Wright (n 14) [4]; Judith Jarvis Thomson, 'Some Reflections on Hart and Honoré, Causation in the Law' in Matthew H Kramer et al. (eds), *The Legacy of H.L.A. Hart: Legal, Political, and Moral Philosophy* (Oxford University Press, 2008) 143.

C occurs if a set of conditions – say, 'Y' – can be met, and set Y occurs in instances where a necessary antecedent takes place.[19] Assuming the antecedent is X, then for set Y to occur and cause consequence C, X must also be established.[20] Legal causation to establish responsibility for C under NESS is predicated on the relationship between X and Y.

In the first instance, such theoretical considerations may seem broadly irrelevant to legal causation in the context of AI. Jos Lehmann et al., however, have sought to adapt Hart and Honoré's approach further to better accommodate artificial intelligence within this theoretical framework. As such, it is worth considering their proposed approach. To this end, in order to accommodate AI, they seek to expand Hart and Honoré's approach to better incorporate an ontological account of causation and thereby understand the relationships between conditions establishing causation (such as X and Y above).[21] They do not disregard the epistemological account of causation; rather, they are of the view that in order to best accommodate AI, a causation theory ought to incorporate both ontological and epistemological relations.[22] It is this blended approach of Jos Lehmann et al. that marks a departure from a more traditional Hart and Honoré view. Jos Lehmann et al. expand on their blended view to also incorporate categories of causal relations, which they propose work in conjunction with their blended account.[23] The intricacies of the view are complex, but what is key is that they seek to expand upon causation theories to incorporate ontological considerations, which they consider as key to expanding previous causation theories to accommodate the complex nature of AI.

6.2.4 Other Causation Theories Relevant to AI

When providing a robust account of causation as it relates to AI forms of technology, there are other legal theories that ought to be considered in conjunction with the above legal causation approaches. This is especially important when considering the possible deficiencies associated with some of the above causation theories.

Often, central to establishing legal causation is the concept of a causal connection. Yavar Bathaee, lawyer and computer scientist, has explored this concept specifically as it pertains to AI forms of technologies. To Bathaee, the traditional notion of causal chains is directly challenged by AI. He considers that causation theories can largely be divided into two categories: 'conduct-regulating causation' and 'conduct-nexus causation'.[24] The former of these

19 Wright (n 14) at [4].
20 Wright (n 14) at [4].
21 Lehmann et al. (n 7) 297–299.
22 Lehmann et al. (n 7) 304.
23 Lehmann et al. (n 7) 301–307.
24 Yavar Bathaee, 'The Artificial Intelligence Black Box and the Failure of Intent and Causation' (2018) 31(2) *Harvard Journal of Law & Technology* 889, 922.

approaches, conduct-regulating causation, he contends, is central to establishing the scope of liability for actions, for it is this approach that seeks to limit behaviour deemed unacceptable by society, though ascertaining if it could have reasonably been avoided.[25] 'Proximate cause' tests, he deems, fit within this category.[26] This conduct-regulating causation approach espoused by Bathaee is thus somewhat analogous to causal maximalism theories insofar that, as an approach, it looks beyond mere causation in fact and incorporates legal policy considerations.

Conduct-nexus causation, as an alternative causal theory, seeks to establish a causal link between an act and its consequences. More specifically, the approach focuses on the relationship between conduct and the harm caused by said conduct, establishing a link between the two for the purpose of identifying legal accountability.[27] To Bathaee, conduct-nexus causation provides an important distinction from conduct-regulating causation: it acts as a 'gatekeeper' to liability rather than seeking to limit the scope of liability.[28] In this sense, if a causal connection between harm and conduct cannot be established, then liability cannot be assigned. This is in direct contrast to a conduct-regulating approach, which is more concerned with regulating liability once causation is established and is not focused on preventing its occurrence.

Bathaee's division of causation theory is an interesting observation, as it seems to suggest that there are two methods by which causation can be utilised to assign liability in relation to AI – either by seeking to restrict accountability in the first instance or, instead, by narrowing the scope of liability once causation has been established. Although both methods are often deployed legally, Bathaee contends that regardless of which method is adopted, AI ultimately challenges both causation approaches. Consider first his arguments in relation to conduct-regulating causation. Central to this approach is the notion of foreseeability of harm – a common concept to 'proximity' tests. Under the conduct-regulating causation approach, a harm suffered must be one that is foreseeable; if foreseeability is lacking, then causation fails and liability is subsequently limited.[29] Yet, as Bathaee considers, some forms of AI, especially black-box AI, inherently challenge this notion of foreseeability.[30] The very

25 Yavar Bathaee, 'The Artificial Intelligence Black Box and the Failure of Intent and Causation' (2018) 31(2) *Harvard Journal of Law & Technology* 889, 923.

26 Yavar Bathaee, 'The Artificial Intelligence Black Box and the Failure of Intent and Causation' (2018) 31(2) *Harvard Journal of Law & Technology* 889, 923.

27 Yavar Bathaee, 'The Artificial Intelligence Black Box and the Failure of Intent and Causation' (2018) 31(2) *Harvard Journal of Law & Technology* 889, 925.

28 Yavar Bathaee, 'The Artificial Intelligence Black Box and the Failure of Intent and Causation' (2018) 31(2) *Harvard Journal of Law & Technology* 889, 925.

29 Yavar Bathaee, 'The Artificial Intelligence Black Box and the Failure of Intent and Causation' (2018) 31(2) *Harvard Journal of Law & Technology* 889, 923.

30 Yavar Bathaee, 'The Artificial Intelligence Black Box and the Failure of Intent and Causation' (2018) 31(2) *Harvard Journal of Law & Technology* 889, 924.

nature of modern forms of AI systems[31] is that they are, to varying degrees, designed to learn, adapt and evolve independently. The greater the level of independence and 'autonomy' in the decision-making of these systems, the increased difficulty in the subsequent ability to measure the foreseeability of harm arising from the use of such systems. Modern AI systems with heightened independence are less predictable and are therefore distinct from more simplistic forms of AI. In systems with less independence, when they are given a set task to achieve, it is more straightforward to determine if it is reasonably foreseeable that harm could arise if preventative action is not taken. As Bathaee contends, this undermines the foundation of legal tests utilising a conduct-regulating causation theoretical approach.[32] If a harm cannot sufficiently be 'foreseen', then it cannot be used to measure causation and, in turn, regulate liability – at least, not according to this view.

It is worth noting that Ryan Abbott offers one model that seeks to address reasonableness in relation to AI. I evaluate Abbott's proposal in Section 6.3.3, but before doing so, I first want to consider the veracity of conduct-nexus causation in relation to AI. To Bathaee, the conduct-nexus causation approach is challenged not merely by the use of AI but rather by a *reliance* on AI.[33] When an AI system is deployed, a user of the system relies upon it to achieve an end objective. Bathaee utilises the example of a black-box AI system making investment decisions to underscore his view that it is the AI system that is acting – making the investment decisions – and it is investors who rely upon the system's 'judgment'.[34] In this instance, he contends, it is difficult to ascertain the system's reasoning process or what information is utilised to inform its decisions.[35] Herein lies a key issue with the conduct-nexus approach: to establish a causal connection requires an objective understanding of the reasoning process utilised by an actor, and when the actor is an AI system, this poses unique challenges. Bathaee acknowledges that some insight might be ascertained into the reasoning processes of an AI system based on the data set on which the AI system relies.[36] However, he notes that this is not always apparent; for example, in the investment black-box scenario, the AI system may be provided with key data sets, but under this form of AI, it is not entirely apparent if the system utilises all, or part, of a data set in reaching an outcome.[37] This poses a unique challenge to establishing causation under a causal nexus approach, as it is difficult to objectively determine the relationship between an actor and the outcome in the context of AI.

31 Consider, for example, the varying forms of AI explored in the *Introduction*.
32 Bathaee (n 24) 924.
33 Bathaee (n 24) 925.
34 Bathaee (n 24) 925.
35 Bathaee (n 24) 925–926.
36 Bathaee (n 24) 926.
37 Bathaee (n 24) 926.

6.2.5 Evaluation of Causation Theories Relevant to AI

The above causal theories not only vary in their structure, but each also emphasises a different role, or underlying function, of causation. Factual causation is arguably the simplest approach in that it is limited in its scope to factual elements resulting in an end outcome. Legal causation in its varying forms builds upon factual causation, layering additional factors such as policy considerations. Causal minimalism relative to the approaches of Hart and Honoré is again an arguably more elementary approach. Causal maximalism, although accommodating legal policy considerations, lacks the complexity of Hart and Honoré's approach. Hart and Honoré, together with Jos Lehmann et al., focus on the underlying legal relationships between events and actors that contribute to establishing causation, yet they do so in more depth than under a causal maximal theory.

This increased complexity is not necessarily an advantage when considered in relation to AI. As I have raised before, including in the *Introduction*, some forms of AI are by their very nature also complex, which holds the potential to complicate establishing a causal relationship under the above theories. Consider again forms of AI, such as deep learning systems, where it can be difficult to identify and then interpret the relationships between reasoning processes or 'steps' executed by this form of AI. If, as the Hart and Honoré along with the Jos Lehmann et al. approach seem to suggest, for legal causation to be established these processes or steps need to be identified, labelled and reviewed in relation to each other, then this later causation approach does not on its face seem sufficient for more complex – or modern – forms of AI. This in turn creates uncertainty when seeking to determine legal causation in this context. On this basis, a more robust account of causation is required to fully accommodate the varying forms of AI and, in turn, assign liability.

6.3. Evaluating Proposed Causation Solutions in an AI Context

In the above section, I consider key causation theories and their utility in the AI context, highlighting the need for a more robust approach to accommodate AI. In turn, I propose an amended theoretical framework that accommodates AI. Before doing so, however, in this section I first explore current proposed solutions to the uncertainty AI has created for causation and then turn in the next section to examining other factors that can be considered as having a unique influence on causation in the context of AI. Here, I therefore consider three key proposed solutions aimed at increasing certainty when establishing causation in the context of AI: the European Union's proposed approach, strict liability, the 'Reasonable Robot' approach and Bathaee's proposed solution.

6.3.1 European Union (EU) Proposed Approach

In Chapter 1, I outlined the proposed EU Liability Directive, which consists of a two-stage response to managing liability in the context of AI; a standard causation response is included in this directive. Proposed Article 4 establishes a rebuttable presumption of causation; that is, the directive proposes that if a plaintiff can establish that a defendant has not complied with obligations to prevent harm in relation to AI, then legal causation is presumed.[38] This approach acknowledges that it can be difficult for a plaintiff to establish whether an AI system, especially a complex system, has caused an outcome. However, there is an exception to the presumption of causation if the defendant can show that the plaintiff had reasonable access to sufficient evidence and expertise to be able to prove any causal link.[39] The advantage of this process is that it provides a clear path forward in situations where causation is hard to establish. The disadvantages are like the issues I discuss in relation to strict liability: arguably, this approach could have a chilling effect on the use of such technologies. Additionally, this proposed EU causation approach could be said to oversimplify causation to some extent, for it does not leave room to accommodate intervening acts, something I consider in Section 6.5.2. The proposed EU approach on causation is therefore perhaps not robust enough to accommodate the varying scope of situations involving AI systems.

6.3.2 Strict Liability

Although I explore standards of liability in Chapter 8, I want to pause briefly and consider the merits of utilising strict liability as a solution to the uncertainty causation raises in the context of AI. To resolve this uncertainty, several theorists have examined the possibility of simply relying on strict liability.[40] In order to avoid ascertaining if a harm has been caused by an AI actor or user, one working theory is that any user of an AI system ought to be held

38 European Union, *Proposal for a Directive on Adapting Non-Contractual Civil Liability Rules to Artificial Intelligence* (28 September 2022) <https://commission.europa.eu/business-economy-euro/doing-business-eu/contract-rules/digital-contracts/liability-rules-artificial-intelligence_en> Explanatory Memorandum 13 and Art 4; European Union, *Commission Staff Working Document Executive Summary of the Impact Assessment Report Accompanying the Document Proposal for a Directive on Adapting Non-Contractual Civil Liability Rules to Artificial Intelligence (AI Liability Directive)* (28 September 2022) <https://commission.europa.eu/system/files/2022-09/1_5_197611_summary_impact_asse_dir_ai_en.pdf>.

39 European Union, *Proposal for a Directive on* <i>*A*</i>*dapting Non-Contractual Civil Liability Rules to Artificial Intelligence* (28 September 2022) <https://commission.europa.eu/business-economy-euro/doing-business-eu/contract-rules/digital-contracts/liability-rules-artificial-intelligence_en> Explanatory Memorandum 9 and Art 4(4); European Union, *Commission Staff Working Document Executive Summary of the Impact Assessment Report Accompanying the Document Proposal for a Directive on Adapting Non-Contractual Civil Liability Rules to Artificial Intelligence (AI Liability Directive)* (28 September 2022) <https://commission.europa.eu/system/files/2022-09/1_5_197611_summary_impact_asse_dir_ai_en.pdf>.

40 Bathaee (n 24) 931–932; Ryan Abbott, *The Reasonable Robot: Artificial Intelligence and the Law* (Cambridge University Press, 2020) 51.

strictly liable for the conduct of that system.[41] A common thought is that this approach would therefore reduce, or even eradicate, the need to contemplate the issue of causation in determining liability issues arising in an AI context.

There are several issues with adopting a strict liability approach in all circumstances involving AI. One that Bathaee raises is that strict liability, especially when applied in a 'blanket' or uniform manner, holds the potential to have a chilling effect on the use of AI technologies.[42] It disincentivises those to be held strictly liable – such as users or developers of AI[43] – from utilising, relying upon or developing the technology further.[44] This in itself is not an insignificant concern to raise, but what is perhaps more notable is Bathaee's concern that strict liability assumes that those being held accountable have at least some control over determining the level of harm inflicted.[45] It is this latter point that I find persuasive in relation to AI. Admittedly, there are some, more simplistic forms of modern AI for which it is possible to control the outcome of using a system. Yet, this is not necessarily true with all forms of AI. The element of control begins to fail in relation to more complex forms of AI, such as the black-box example espoused by Bathaee.[46] Adopting strict liability as a uniform mechanism to resolve the uncertainty created by AI does not hold in all circumstances. Consideration ought to be given to when strict liability might be used[47] and what feasible alternatives exist for when strict liability does not hold. As I come to explore below in Section 6.5, a modified situational approach to causation best accommodates AI.

6.3.3 A Tortious Solution to Causation and AI

Other theorists have concerns with the possibility of imposing strict liability in relation to AI and seek to provide alternative solutions. Ryan Abbott, for example, independently echoes the concerns of Bathaee regarding the flaws of utilising a strict liability regime.[48] In response, Abbott proposes an alternative solution to assigning liability: one based on tort law principles.[49] Before turning to Abbott's approach, it is worth pausing to acknowledge that, at this juncture, my focus is directed towards Abbott's proposals, as they might relate to what I view as a liability threshold issue: causation. How Abbott's approach relates to my own broader liability proposals is considered in Chapter 8.

41 Bathaee (n 24) 931–932; Abbott (n 40) 51.
42 Bathaee (n 24) 931–932; Abbott (n 40) 51.
43 I consider more fully the question of who could be held liable and in what circumstances in Chapter 7.
44 Bathaee (n 24) 932.
45 Bathaee (n 24) 931–932.
46 Bathaee (n 24) 931–932.
47 I consider under what circumstances strict liability might be appropriate in Chapter 8.
48 Abbott (n 40) 51.
49 Abbott (n 40) 51.

Abbott offers a novel liability solution – one that favours imposing a negligence standard over a product liability approach, which often adopts a strict liability standard.[50] He considers that a product liability standard would focus on the design aspects of AI and whether a system falls short of how the product ought to function, rather than the 'behaviour' of the AI system.[51] Focusing on design alone is insufficient given the discussion in the *Introduction*; it is not always possible with some forms of AI to determine if there is a design fault with a system when its reasoning processes cannot be effectively evaluated due to the complexity of the AI system.[52] Abbott therefore instead seeks to propose that rather than focusing on whether an AI system meets a product standard, it is instead prudent to focus on the impact of the system or its behaviour.[53] This is a view with which, in principle, I largely agree. It is with the intricacies of his approach that I somewhat differ in opinion.

Abbott has sought to define his negligent standard for AI as the 'Reasonable Robot' standard. At its core, it is an adaptation of the 'reasonable person' standard commonly applied to negligent actions.[54] His proposal seeks to address situations in which AI systems are utilised to complete actions that would typically be completed by a natural person.[55] He proposes that in lieu of measuring the conduct of such systems against that of how a reasonable person would have acted in the circumstances, the AI system should be measured against how a 'reasonable robot' would have acted.[56] Linked to this account is what Abbott has deemed legal neutrality, in which he advocates that, legally, there should not be discrimination between the behaviours of an AI system and that of a natural person.[57] Although Abbott expressly seeks to not adopt legal personality for AI and rejects that his neutral approach leads to the need for legal personality, he does at least acknowledge, with qualifications, the possibility that AI could be deemed a legal person.[58] His primary argument, though, is against AI. I am not quite persuaded by this approach, as I think it overlooks some of the utility of legal personality.

What I find less persuasive about Abbott's argument is that he expressly argues that not only should AI be compared with human actors but that human actors ought to also be compared with AI actors.[59] Central to this argument is the view that, to Abbott, AI actors are completing the work of

50 Abbott (n 40) 9, 51.
51 Abbott (n 40) 51.
52 This is a view that is also supported by Ryan Abbott. See: Abbott (n 40) 51.
53 Abbott (n 40) 51.
54 Abbott (n 40) 51.
55 Abbott (n 40) 9, 51.
56 Abbott (n 40) 9, 51.
57 Abbott (n 40) 3–4.
58 Abbott (n 40) 4, 127.
59 Abbott (n 40) 51.

humans and therefore seeking to achieve the same ends as a human actor.[60] This approach may hold true when looking at the end objectives – for example, has an autonomous vehicle achieved the goal of driving from *point A* to *point B* in the way that a human driver could move a car from *point A* to *point B*? If, as Abbott proposes, it is merely the end outcome that is integral to how we legally evaluate these systems, then they can be equated to that of a human (i.e. both autonomous car and human achieve the goal of moving a vehicle to end point B). However, this approach overlooks the key discussions in Chapter 5 Section 6.2.1. I considered previously, in relation to Google's smart assistant the Google Duplex, that AI systems may be tasked with achieving the same goal as a human, but they inherently cannot achieve that goal via the same means. An AI system must use its own 'reasoning' processes, which are distinctly different to that of a human.

It is important to acknowledge that Abbott seeks to address this point of differentiation. He argues that the human mind is more of a 'black box' than AI in that it can be more difficult to ascertain the internal reasons of a human in contrast to AI.[61] He contends that AI can be queried about its internal rules, which in turn can be amended and clearly defined.[62] Such a claim is not without its merits and holds value if we narrow our focus to considering the impact of actions taken by an AI system in contrast to a natural person, which is arguably Abbott's focus.[63] This perspective starts to lose some value when considering the method by which these actors reason in relation to the end outcome. As Simon Chesterman observes, some AI systems have the potential to amplify harms caused beyond what could have been foreseen.[64] This is an important distinction when examining causation theories as they relate to AI.

This key distinction could arguably be distilled down to a dichotomy of views. On one side sits the Abbott approach, with a focus on the end goal or impact being achieved.[65] This account I deem the *end-objective view*. In contrast sits what I designate a *method-end view*. This perspective seeks to encompass not only the end objective of an actor but also the reasoning process behind achieving that goal. An end-objective view is not without merit, but it does, to an extent, overlook the unique characteristics of AI. Equating the outcome of AI actions with the impacts of a natural person actor is too broad for the reasons discussed in Chapter 5.

There are additional problems with an end-objective view. Firstly, such an approach focuses on instances only where AI and natural persons are seeking to achieve the same end goal. It overlooks instances where an AI system

60 Abbott (n 40) 62.
61 Abbott (n 40) 138.
62 Abbott (n 40) 138.
63 Abbott (n 40) 60.
64 Simon Chesterman, *We, The Robots? Regulating Artificial Intelligence and the Limits of the Law* (Cambridge University Press, 2021) 88.
65 Abbott (n 40) 60.

may be striving for an objective that cannot be achieved by a natural person. Indeed, this is one of the advantages of AI systems. It is not simply that they can automate processes undertaken by humans, as Abbott suggests, but also that, as considered in the *Introduction*, some more complex forms of AI can set their own ends and make their own 'discoveries' in a way that cannot reasonably be foreseen by natural persons. The other objection I have to Abbott's approach is that he largely assumes that AI actions in a private law context are best managed in accordance with the law of negligence.[66] He even argues, to an extent, in favour of civil liability for criminal actions.[67] There are other possibilities that ought to be considered – for example, that a complex AI actor could act in a non-tortfeasor capacity.

There is an emerging theory that AI could be combined with some other forms of technology to self-execute smart contracts, thereby rendering AI (at least theoretically) capable of entering a contractual arrangement.[68] It is therefore insufficient to exclude the possibility of other standards by which causation (and, by extension, liability) can be measured. Lastly, Abbott's approach seems to assume an either-or account, by which I mean to suggest that actions causing harm will be executed either by a natural person or an AI actor. Depending on the type of AI, actions could be executed using an either-or approach or even in concert, where AI and natural persons work in coordination towards an end objective. An either-or approach, as I explore in Section 6.4, also ignores the possibility of multiple AI systems working in concert.

Abbott does, to an extent, seek to limit his account in relation to negligence principles by focusing on the abilities of humans relative to AI. He concedes that, with time, AI will be more efficient or effective at achieving end goals and it is at this juncture that humans ought to be compared to the standard set by AI – the reasonable-robot standard – and not that of natural persons. Further, he acknowledges that if it reaches this level, AI would set the new standard of care; therefore, in instances where AI is available, it could become negligent *not* to rely upon AI.[69] By this account, it could be said that Abbott's analysis has the implication that there is a spectrum along which AI and human actions ought to be measured and that spectrum turns from reasonable person to reasonable robot when AI is sophisticated enough to set the standard of care.

How is this dichotomy relevant to causation and, by extension, liability principles? An end-objective view is but an incremental increase from strict liability. It does not provide the scope to adequately consider other elements required to ascertain causation. For example, it does not allow for consideration

66 Abbott (n 40) 51–60.

67 Abbott (n 40) 132–133.

68 Rory Unsworth, 'Smart Contract This! An Assessment of the Contractual Landscape and the Herculean Challenges it Currently Presents for "Self-executing" Contracts' in Mark Fenwick and Helena Haapio Marcelo Corrales (eds), *Legal Tech, Smart Contracts and Blockchain* (Springer Nature, 2019) 17, 35–36.

69 Abbott (n 40) 51.

of elements such as proximity (or uninterrupted causal chain linking actors) and reasonable foreseeability. Without an adequate consideration of such elements, it arguably becomes hard to establish legal causation. We can view causation as being a necessary precursor to assigning liability – that is, a harm suffered must be causally linked to an action to assign liability. Under this view, seeking to address the question of who could be liable becomes difficult, as Abbott does not adequately account for all possibilities associated with AI. His approach is useful in that it does accommodate instances of negligence, but consideration needs to be given to situations outside of negligent actions involving AI.

6.3.4 A Quadrant-Based Solution to Causation and AI

Bathaee proposes a relatively new and alternative solution to how causation ought to be measured in relation to AI. His approach is more robust than an either-or account and acknowledges that there can be differing relationships between a natural person and an AI system. Unlike Abbott, he specifically considers the possibility that an AI system could be supervised by a natural person and not just seeking to replace the work of or achieving the same ends as a natural person.[70] Bathaee considers that when AI is being utilised as a tool by a natural person actor, this poses minimal challenges to the issue of causation, for he considers that, in such instances, any causal issues ought to be examined in light of the role of the natural person.[71] It is more complex forms of AI, such as black-box technology, that pose a greater challenge to causation.

Bathaee addresses this greater challenge by introducing a sliding scale of causation that is inherently linked to the degree of transparency associated with an AI system.[72] The greater the transparency of the AI system – that is, the more readily determinable the AI system's 'thought' process – the more likely it is that a natural person actor engaging with the system is able to foresee the effects of utilising that system.[73] Under this approach, if AI is transparent, then issues of causation can be determined through applying principles applicable to natural persons. In contrast, if AI lacks transparency, thereby impacting the foreseeable consequences of engaging with the AI system, this necessitates an alternative approach. To Bathaee, it becomes a question of whether it is reasonable for the natural person to utilise the AI system, considering

70 Bathaee (n 24) 932–33.
71 Bathaee (n 24) 933.
72 Bathaee (n 24) 936–938.
73 Bathaee (n 24) 933–938; arguably, the context in which an AI system is deployed could also influence the degree to which the effects of that AI system are foreseeable. For example, if the AI system is deployed in a medical context, the risks associated with its deployment pose a greater risk of harm than other contexts. The role of context in shaping liability is a topic I explore further in Chapter 7.

the system's degree of transparency.[74] Bathaee expressly excludes the need to consider how the AI system is designed or the foreseeable effects of an AI system, for he ultimately conceives of AI as an agent of a natural person.[75] In this regard, when determining issues of causation, to Bathaee, the emphasis remains on the role of the natural person relying upon the AI system and the relative knowledge of this person.

What is unique about Bathaee's approach is that he does not confine his arguments to a dichotomy of views but instead acknowledges that there are varying degrees of transparency. He considers the issue of transparency as integral to the ultimate question of how to assign liability: the more transparent an AI system, the more likely liability rests with a natural person.[76] In considering Bathaee's sliding-scale approach, I remain focused on the issue of causation as it relates to liability, noting that the broader considerations of liability are addressed in Chapter 8. In proposing a flexible approach, Bathaee divides his thought processes into four quadrants, with each quadrant based on two factors: the level of natural person supervision over an AI system and the degree of transparency of the AI system.[77] A broad overview of Bathaee's quadrants is as follows:[78]

> *Q1 An AI system that is both supervised and transparent* – traditional intent and causation principles can be applied, with consideration given to the function and effect of the AI system.
>
> *Q2 An AI system that is supervised but with reduced transparency* – a reduced understanding of the reasoning processes; this type of AI system necessitates an assessment of whether the natural person was justified in using the system as deployed.
>
> *Q3 An AI system that is supervised but is autonomous (minimal transparency)* – this relationship mirrors that of the principal-supervision relationship under agency law; consideration should be given to the extent of supervision and care given by a 'principal' or natural person.[79]

74 Bathaee (n 24) 933–938.
75 Bathaee (n 24) 933–935.
76 Bathaee (n 24) 937.
77 Bathaee (n 24) 936–938.
78 Bathaee (n 24) 936–938.
79 An argument could be made that there is a possible additional option of an autonomous AI system with transparency, where transparency is achieved through explainable AI mechanisms. Through increasing the ability of a natural person engaging with the AI system to understand its processes, explainable AI mechanisms are likely to *indirectly* increase the ability of a natural person engaging with these systems to make an informed decision about whether the AI should be deployed or not. On this basis, this potential additional option could be indirectly aligned with Q2 where this type of AI system necessitates an assessment of whether the natural person was justified in using the system as deployed.

> *Q4* *An AI system that is unsupervised and is autonomous (minimal transparency)* – in this scenario, the key question is whether it is reasonable for the system to be used in the first instance.

These four quadrants offer four distinct approaches to establishing a causal link and, in turn, to determining liability. Bathaee acknowledges that the implementation of this approach is fact dependent.[80] In this respect, his approach to determining causation is situational and arguably weighted more in fact than law.

Bathaee's approach to AI causation is a positive evolution of thought, but it does not progress to the extent required to encapsulate all possibilities raised by AI. The utility of his scaled approach is, however, quite persuasive, as it acknowledges that there are varying forms of AI and varying degrees of natural-person interaction with these systems. In this respect, Bathaee's approach is arguably better at accommodating modern forms of artificial intelligence than Abbott's, as it places the issue of causation on a spectrum rather than seeking to measure the conduct of AI against an objective standard. The strength of Bathaee's approach is that he does not outright reject the need for an objective standard. Instead, he proffers how such a standard would fit within his own sliding-scale approach. He considers that as AI acts as an agent of a natural person, the reasonable standard ought to be considered in instances where there is a question about whether the principal exercised reasonable control and care in relation to the AI system.[81] Arguably, the objective standard is confined then to the third and fourth quadrants of Bathaee's argument, where transparency is diminished.

A key tenet of Bathaee's argument is centred on the notion that AI is commonly being deployed as an agent of a legal person. I am not entirely opposed to this observation, for as considered in Chapter 3, AI can act *in locus* of an agent. Yet, as I explored in depth in Part II, modern forms of AI are not confined to being an agent; they can exhibit other characteristics, such as those that are proprietary in nature.[82] To me, this poses a significant challenge to Bathaee's approach. Further, his argument is framed in terms of the transparency of an AI system; however, it is not always possible to determine the reasoning processes of an AI system, and even if these processes can be determined, there is proprietary value in these inner mechanisms, which in turn provides a disincentive for their disclosure. A subsequent argument could be made, in line with Bathaee's account, that a lack of transparency, regardless of its cause – whether indeterminable or due to proprietary considerations – necessitates the use of an objective standard for determining causation, which

80 Bathaee (n 24) 936–938.
81 Bathaee (n 24) 935.
82 For an in-depth discussion concerning the potential overlapping characteristics of AI, see *Figure 5.3* in Chapter 5 and the surrounding discussions.

would be accommodating of Abbott's proposals. Whilst this is not without merit, this approach still fails to adequately consider the flexible nature of AI: that it is not always an agent, and nor is it always property. Further consideration ought to be given to the varying nature of AI to conceive of a robust causation approach.

Abbott and Bathaee seek to propose new solutions to the challenges posed by AI. The advantage of both approaches is that they reject the utility of strict liability in all circumstances involving AI. Abbott seeks to propose a new objective standard to be applied in relation to AI, whereas Bathaee seeks to adopt a scaled approach. I consider the utility of these two views in more depth in Section 6.5. Before doing so, however, I consider additional problems not fully addressed by either of these views.

6.4. Additional Problems with Causation Approaches in an AI Context

The proposed solutions outlined above in Section 6.3 provide a useful framework for considering causation issues, but there are additional factors that need to be considered in relation to AI. Before turning to propose a new iteration of the Bathaee approach to causation, I want to first pause to consider other factors that can influence causality and should therefore be accommodated in any proposed causation theory for AI (or for which there should at least be the scope to do so). The two factors I consider are: (a) issues of control and (b) possible intervening acts. I do also consider these factors in Chapter 7 as they relate to the scope of permissible actions in relation to an AI system, but there is a need to first raise these issues in the context of causation principles.

6.4.1 Issues of Control

In questioning if a causal link can be established between actors in an AI context, to determine if a harm was caused by an AI system, consideration needs to extend to the issue of 'control'. I discussed to some extent the issue of control in Chapter 5 as it relates to establishing what category, or hybrid of categories, an AI system ought to be categorised.

There are two scenarios where control arises as an issue in a theory of causation for AI. The first is when a legal person – natural or otherwise – is in purported control of the AI system. I am not going to consider this scenario in depth, as I largely agree with the approach espoused by Bathaee: that whether a person has control over the AI system, and thereby is potentially responsible for its actions, turns on the objective standard. The second scenario is perhaps more perplexing when establishing a causal chain, and that is: what happens when an AI system has control over another AI system? Whilst this scenario may currently seem somewhat futuristic, it is not entirely outside the realm of possibility. Consider, for example, AI members of a company board of directors. There is a body of established work considering the possible implications of incorporating an AI system into the board of directors.[83] Also consider the use of AI in self-executing contracts.[84] It is not implausible that these two AI systems could work in concert. It is at least conceivable that an AI company director could approve the use of a self-executing contract that is then deployed on behalf of a company.

This second scenario poses several issues of control that, in turn, impact the ability to establish a causal chain. Firstly, how do we account for the varying types of AI in such a scenario? What if the controlling AI is more complex than the AI system being controlled or, conversely, a natural person has a greater degree of control over the controlling AI system in this relationship (i.e. the controlling AI system has relatively less independence from a natural-person actor)? These are factors I consider in Chapter 8. For now, though, what is key is that the varying questions surrounding an AI system controlling another AI system hold the potential to create uncertainty in terms of whether a causal link can be established in the context of some modern forms of AI. It is for this reason that a more expansive consideration of causation as it relates to AI is required.

6.4.2 Intervening Acts

Another problem that challenges current methods of establishing a causal link in this context is the possibility of an intervening act. Intervening acts, or *novus actus interveniens*, is a tort law concept. I identified above in Section 6.3.3 that there is the emerging possibility that AI could act in non-tortfeasor scenarios, thereby prompting the need for a framework outside of tort law and negligence principles alone. It is for this reason that I do not intend to explore the issue of intervening acts at length. Rather, I intend to pause to merely acknowledge key challenges intervening acts pose to current causation theories concerning AI.

There are several conceivable challenges posed by intervening acts. First is the issue concerning who the actor is behind an intervening act. Arguably, an intervening act interjecting into a causal chain poses challenges for determining causation in instances where there are only established legal persons – natural persons or established legal persons, such as a corporation – involved in the chain of events. To an extent, the methods of resolving the effect of an intervening act in this situation are largely resolved.[85] What challenges these methods is if one of the actors is not an established legal person but instead an

83 Florian Möslein, 'Robots in the Boardroom: Artificial Intelligence and Corporate Law' in Woodrow Barfield and Ugo Pagallo (eds), *Research Handbook on the Law of Artificial Intelligence* (Edward Elgar Publishing Limited, 2018) 663–666.

84 Unsworth (n 68).

85 For the impact in relation to causation of an intervening act involving established legal persons and the methods of resolving legal uncertainty, see for example: *Mahony v J Kruschich (Demolitions) Pty Ltd* 59 ALJR 504.

AI actor. As I considered in Part II of this book, it is possible for AI (and even necessary, in some circumstances) to be recognised as a legal person of sorts. If an AI actor were to interject into a causal chain, this would complicate determining causality via established means, as AI systems increase the difficulty in judging factual scenarios.[86] Further, what happens if a situation involves layers of AI actors, as I identified in the board of directors scenario above in Section 6.4.1? What if one or more of the AI systems in a chain is subject to being hacked? Such situations create causal uncertainty.

I have signposted key issues not satisfactorily addressed by the theories considered above. It is in part due to this that a new approach to causation, as it relates to AI, is needed and in part also due to the varying ways in which AI can be legally characterised.

6.5. Alternative Solution: Need for a Situational Approach to Causation

By now, I have considered the two proposed solutions to resolving the uncertainty AI creates for establishing causation, a necessary precursor to assigning liability, and some of the issues with these solutions. Here, I expand upon these proposals to better accommodate the varying forms of AI, which I later draw upon in Chapter 8 in proposing a liability model.

6.5.1 The Proposal: Situational Causation Scale

Earlier, I considered the benefits of Bathaee's approach relative to Abbott's and raised that one of Bathaee's strengths is his quadrant approach. It is this idea that I intend to first expand upon here, especially given the hierarchical approach to legal personhood I outline in Chapter 5.

Bathaee's four quadrants based on transparency and degree of supervision provide a unique interpretation of causation that specifically accommodates the flexible nature of AI. This approach could, however, be expanded upon to accommodate not only varying degrees of transparency but also the different characterisations of AI explored in Chapter 5. In order to do so, I propose to acknowledge the value of views in Bathaee's four quadrants. However,

86 Arguments have been made that AI lacks the legal capacity to be deemed accountable or 'blameworthy' for an intervening act. Additionally, that if AI could be deemed to have the relevant legal capacity, vicarious liability could be deployed to respond to any potential gaps in accountability. See: Sandy Steel, 'Legal Causation and AI' in Ernest Lim and Phillip Morgan (eds), *The Cambridge Handbook of Private Law and Artificial Intelligence* (Cambridge University Press, 2024) 189, 201–202. For the reasons I explored in Part II and especially in Chapter 5, I am of the view that AI ought to be characterised as a legal person, which would enable AI to be ascribed the legal capacity – in some instances – to be held to account for actions. This is a topic, together with the role of vicarious liability, I explore in further detail in Chapters 7 and 8.

I instead consider these concepts as not confined to four distinct parts of a whole but as markers on a continuum of ideas. Additionally, for reasons I consider shortly, I propose that this continuum ought not be viewed horizontally but vertically. In striving to explain my underlying reasons for this shift in perception, I draw upon the following diagram (*Figure 6.1*), which represents this relationship.

Placing the concepts from Bathaee's four quadrants on a continuum is advantageous because it not only accepts the scenarios proposed by Bathaee but expands upon them through acknowledging that causation is dynamic and context-dependent, shaped by both factual and legal considerations. Due to these underlying concepts influencing causation, it is prudent to acknowledge that there is at least the possibility of a blurring of the ideas espoused in Bathaee's quadrants, hence the need for a continuum.

My reasoning above justifies the need for a continuum, but it alone does not establish why the continuum ought to be viewed hierarchically. To justify this element, I draw upon my reasoning from Chapter 5, where I proposed a new hierarchical account of legal personhood. In Chapter 5 in Section 5.3, I considered how the three possible manners of characterising AI overlap and instead proposed that there are five possible categories for legally characterising AI. I depicted these categories in *Figure 6.2* (from Chapter 5).

Further, I proposed in Chapter 5 that the intersections of these categories could be incorporated into my hierarchical model of legal personality and proposed a situational hierarchical model of legal personhood in *Figure 6.3* (from Chapter 5).

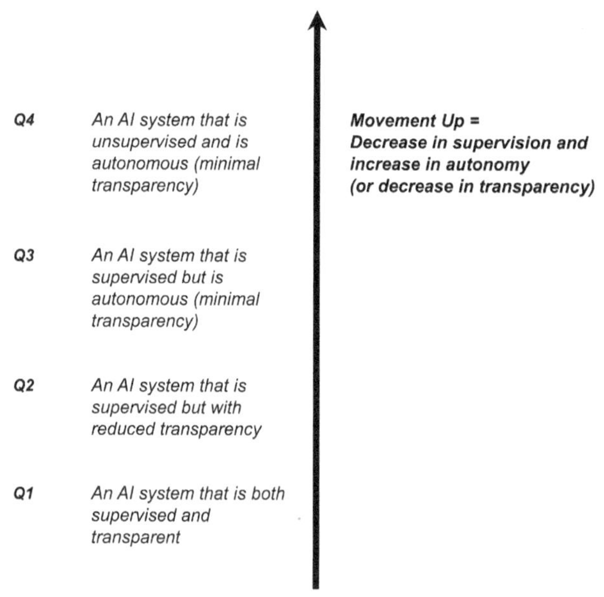

Figure 6.1 Hierarchical Four-Quadrant Continuum of Causation

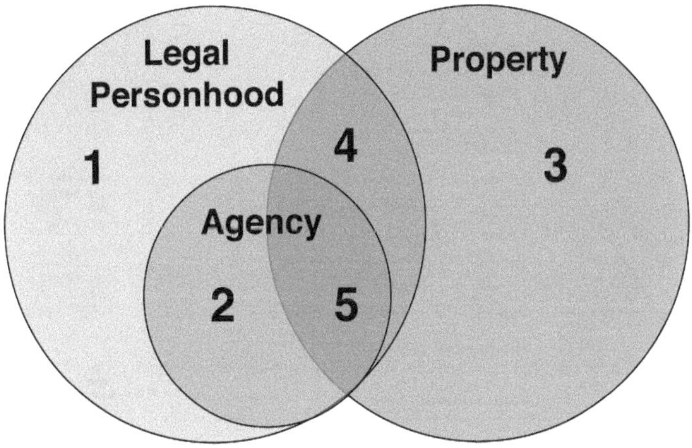

Figure 6.2 An Intersection of Different Forms of Legal Characterisation

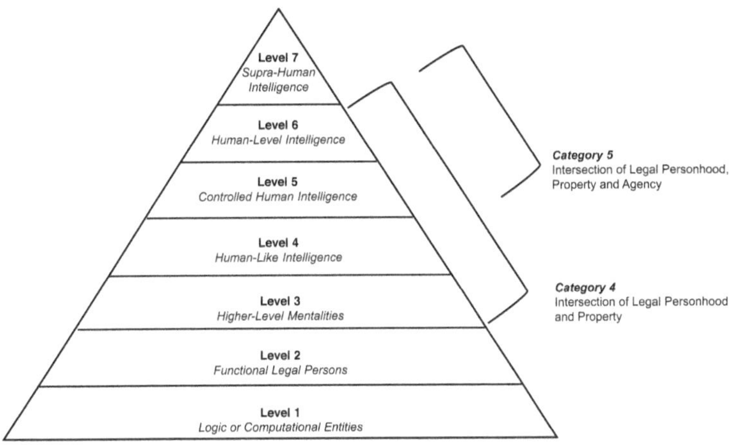

Figure 6.3 Situational Hierarchical Model of Legal Personhood

I combine the theory underpinning *Figure 6.3* from Chapter 5 with that from *Figure 6.1* to yield a new diagram, *Figure 6.4,* as follows:

How AI is legally categorised and the degree of control over that system influences what level of legal person the AI system should – at the outset, at least – be considered within my hierarchical account of legal personhood. It is important to recall that this model accommodates the varying permeations of control over an AI system and the degree of cognitive capacities the AI system possesses.

It is important to acknowledge that the degree to which an AI system is supervised and transparent is inherent in Bathaee's four-quadrant approach to causation. The quadrants ought to therefore be arranged so that Quadrant 4 (*Q4* from above in Section 6.3.4), being the quadrant representing AI systems

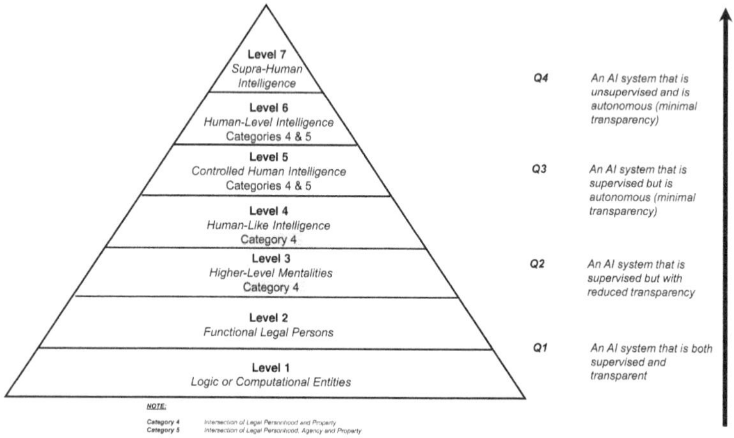

Figure 6.4 Four-Quadrant Continuum of Causation in Relation to Hierarchical Legal Personhood

with the highest degree of autonomy and least supervision, aligns with the top of the pyramid. The remaining quadrants would follow suit on the continuum in descending order (*Q4–Q3–Q2–Q1*).

Arranging the quadrants in this manner relative to the pyramid allows for parallels to be drawn between the two relational theories – the pyramid and the causation continuum. The less supervised and less transparent an AI system (or more autonomous in nature), the greater the degree of correlation to the higher levels (Levels 5–7) of legal personhood outlined above in *Figure 6.4*. Inversely, the more supervised and more transparent an AI system, the greater the degree of correlation to the lower levels (Levels 1–4) outlined above in *Figure 6.4*.

The importance of this relationship is that it not only acknowledges that there are varying causation approaches that arise in the context of AI but that these differences in causality, in the first instance, are inherently linked to how the AI system is characterised. Such a model is also better equipped to address issues of control, as the hierarchy is predicated on notions of control, as explored in Chapter 5 in Section 5.3. The dynamic nature of this approach is better equipped to manage alternative factors such as intervening acts. Causation in the context of AI therefore becomes very situational but not without a guiding framework grounded in broader considerations relative to AI.

6.5.2 Objective Standard with a Situational Causation Scale

The situational approach above is not complete; it is missing one key factor: the incorporation of an objective standard. Here, it is useful to recall that Bathaee proposes that an objective standard is required in instances where

AI is acting as an agent of a natural person to determine if reasonable control and care has been exercised.[87] Recall also from Chapter 5 that it is Category 5 – the intersection of legal personality, agency and property – that accommodates the concept of agency. As Category 5 correlates to Level 5 (controlled human intelligence) and Level 6 (human-level intelligence) in the hierarchical legal personhood model, applying Bathaee's view, this then implies that an objective standard is required to ascertain causation in instances where the AI system is sufficiently complex to be characterised at these high levels. Subsequently, the scope of objective standard applicability is narrowed to only these more complex situations.

6.6 The Need for a Situational Approach to Causation for AI

This chapter marks the beginning of a preliminary analysis in Part III concerning key threshold issues that I view as central to addressing the question of how to assign liability. Utilising primarily a theoretical approach, I have explored the first of these threshold issues: causation. There is a common view central to many legal theories that an actor cannot be held legally liable for an outcome if they have not caused that outcome. In this respect, causation is central to being able to examine the scope or extent of liability and is therefore an important antecedent factor to the issue of liability.

It becomes a question, then, of how to assess this causal element in situations involving artificial intelligence. To address this question, I have drawn upon several theories of causation and evaluated their merits, especially as to whether these theories seek to resolve the uncertainty created by AI. However, as I have suggested, these views could be adapted to work in tandem to better accommodate the varying forms of AI.

In assessing these issues, I have not addressed causation in a vacuum but have instead considered it through the lens of my discussions in Part II – that is, I have looked at causation, considering the possibility that AI is neither always solely a legal person, an agent or property but can be varying combinations of these legal characterisations. In response, I have proposed a hierarchical account of causation that is compatible with the *Hierarchical Legal Personality Model*, I espoused in Chapter 5. Central to both the model of legal personhood and my proposed approach to causation is the notion that AI needs to be examined with regard to the situation in which it is being used and its potential capabilities.

Causation alone is insufficient to assign liability. There are additional factors that need to be considered, such as the question of who could be held liable in instances when AI is deployed, together with scoping issues, such as what happens when an actor in an AI context acts outside their ambit. I explore these additional threshold issues next in Chapter 7 before combining these

87 Bathaee (n 24), 935.

issues with my observations from Part II to propose a new liability model that best accommodates AI.

References

A Articles/Books/Reports

Abbott, Ryan, *The Reasonable Robot: Artificial Intelligence and the Law* (Cambridge University Press, 2020).

Bathaee, Yavar, 'The Artificial Intelligence Black Box and the Failure of Intent and Causation' (2018) 31(2) *Harvard Journal of Law & Technology* 889.

Chesterman, Simon, *We, The Robots? Regulating Artificial Intelligence and the Limits of the Law* (Cambridge University Press, 2021).

Lehmann, Jos, et al, 'Causation in AI and Law' (2004) 12 *Artificial Intelligence and Law* 279, 289, 293.

Möslein, Florian, 'Robots in the Boardroom: Artificial Intelligence and Corporate Law' in Woodrow Barfield and Ugo Pagallo (eds), *Research Handbook on the Law of Artificial Intelligence* (Edward Elgar Publishing Limited, 2018).

Steel, Sandy, 'Legal Causation and AI' in Ernest Lim and Phillip Morgan (eds) *The Cambridge Handbook of Private Law and Artificial Intelligence* (Cambridge University Press, 2024) 189.

Thomson, Judith Jarvis, 'Some Reflections on Hart and Honoré, Causation in the Law' in Matthew H Kramer et al (eds), *The Legacy of H.L.A. Hart: Legal, Political, and Moral Philosophy* (Oxford University Press, 2008) 143.

Turner, Jacob, *Robot Rules: Regulating Artificial Intelligence* (Palgrave Macmillan, 2019).

Unsworth, Rory, 'Smart Contract This! An Assessment of the Contractual Landscape and the Herculean Challenges it Currently Presents for "Self-executing" Contracts' in Mark Fenwick and Helena Haapio Marcelo Corrales (eds), *Legal Tech, Smart Contracts and Blockchain* (Springer Nature Singapore Pte Ltd, 2019) 17.

Wright, Richard W, 'Causation in the Law', in *Routledge Encyclopedia of Philosophy* (Taylor and Francis, 2001).

B Cases

Mahony v J Kruschich (Demolitions) Pty Ltd 59 ALJR

March v Stramare (E & MH) Pty Ltd (1991) 171 CLR 506

C Legislation

Wrongs Act 1958 (Vic)

D Other

European Union, 'Commission Staff Working Document Executive Summary of the Impact Assessment Report Accompanying the Document Proposal for a Directive on Adapting Non-Contractual Civil Liability Rules to Artificial Intelligence (AI

Liability Directive)' (28 September 2022) <https://commission.europa.eu/system/files/2022-09/1_5_197611_summary_impact_asse_dir_ai_en.pdf>

European Union, 'Proposal for a Directive on Adapting Non-Contractual Civil Liability Rules to Artificial Intelligence' (28 September 2022) <https://commission.europa.eu/business-economy-euro/doing-business-eu/contract-rules/digital-contracts/liability-rules-artificial-intelligence_en>

7 Narrowing Liability

Questions of Context and Who Could Be Liable

7.1. Other Threshold Issues

The preceding chapter, commenced the discussions in Part III, looking at additional threshold issues that should be addressed as part of the process of assigning liability. Chapter 6 considered the importance of causation in the context of AI and the challenges this form of technology poses for traditional causation approaches. This chapter is the next iteration of Chapter 6 that explores additional threshold issues that contribute to the process of assigning liability. The threshold issues explored in this chapter, along with causation in Chapter 6, are central to the process of assigning liability. Together they inform the underlying considerations behind individual phases within the *Tri-Phase AI Liability Model* offered in Chapter 8.

This chapter addresses additional issues that are central to the process of assigning liability. The context in which an AI system is deployed is considered first, together with the scope of an AI system's actions and instances of multiple AI systems. The context in which an AI system is deployed is an important factor for assigning liability, as the AI system could trigger a response from different private law areas such as tort or contract law. This in turn is important to the issue of liability, as the context in which an AI system is deployed – tortious, contractual or otherwise – influences the appropriate liability response to an unwanted outcome associated with AI. The chapter then turns to examine the parameters that are imposed upon an AI system and how this further contributes to a contextual understanding of AI. It looks at issues such as what happens when an AI system acts outside the parameters imposed upon its actions. Lastly, consideration is given to how multiple AI systems or AI systems working in concert can also influence our understanding of the context in which AI is deployed. After addressing these issues, the chapter moves to consider the question of who should be held liable for the legal outcomes associated with the deployment of an AI system, proposing that the answer is inherently tied to the notion of control.

The threshold issues explored in this chapter, together with causation in Chapter 6, are central to the process of assigning liability. Each issue individually does not resolve the issue of how liability ought to be assigned; collectively,

DOI: 10.4324/9781003617549-11

however, these elements inform the overall outcome by narrowing the limits of liability. How these elements ought to work together is the subject of Chapter 8, where the *Tri-Phase AI Liability Model* is introduced.

The issues considered in this chapter, together with causation in Chapter 6, will underpin Phase 2 of this three-phase model. (The model is outlined in Chapter 8, but, for context, Phase 1 seeks to identify the maximum potential legal personhood status, Phase 2 addresses additional liability threshold issues to narrow the scope of liability and Phase 3 draws together Phases 1 and 2 to offer a *situational* approach to liability.) For now, this chapter explores how these additional threshold issues influence a liability response to AI and further proposes that AI must be considered *situationally* when assigning liability in response to legal outcomes connected to its deployment.

7.2. Context in which AI Is Deployed, Scope of Actions and Multiple AI Systems

The context in which an AI system is deployed, together with the scope of an AI system's actions, sets the parameters in which liability ought to be assigned. One type of AI system could be deployed on different occasions in different contexts, such as in a tortious or contractual setting. Consider large language model (LLM) forms of generative AI, such as ChatGPT, which could be used to create a new written text, giving rise to legal considerations in the substantive law area of intellectual property. Alternatively, ChatGPT has reportedly been used by parents seeking advice on how to communicate with their teenage children.[1] Here is an example of the same AI system being used in a very different context, potentially giving rise to legal issues under a different substantive area of law, viz. tort law. I consider that it is therefore important to have regard to the context in which an AI system is being deployed, together with the scope of its actions within that context. As the ChatGPT example illustrates, how and in what context an AI system is being deployed gives rise to potentially different legal considerations.

Additionally, context is important in relation to an AI system, as it informs if the system is being deployed in the capacity of a mere product, or instead in a more sophisticated role, such as an entity capable of executing legal actions. This is a legal consideration unique to AI systems, for other entities do not have the same breadth of options in how they can be legally characterised and, in turn, do not have the same number of considerations to evaluate in assigning liability. It is for this reason that I consider the context in which an AI system is deployed together with the scope of its actions, a threshold issue

1 Alyson Krueger, 'We Need to Talk: Just as Soon as I Consult Chat GPT', *New York Times* (online, 24 March 2023) <https://www.nytimes.com/2023/03/24/style/ai-chatgpt-advice-relationships.html>.

to consider as part of determining how liability ought to be assigned in the context of modern forms of AI.

7.2.1 Context in which AI Is Deployed

In considering how context impacts the scope of liability in relation to AI, it is important to recall that the scope of my inquiry is narrowed to a private law context. I therefore confine my considerations regarding the legal context of AI to private law considerations. It is important to ask the key questions: How is an AI system being deployed in a given context? Is the AI system being deployed in a tortious or contractual context or another area of law? I contend that this will influence the liability response to AI being deployed. If an AI system has been deployed in a contractual setting, this will give rise to different considerations than if it is being deployed in a tortious setting. In this section, I consider how AI, when deployed, can trigger two key private law substantive areas – tort and contract – that in turn influence the liability response to AI. I then consider that these are not the only private law areas and that there are additional issues that could be triggered by AI being deployed.

7.2.1.1 Tort

One response to an AI system being deployed is that it could trigger tort law mechanisms, thereby influencing the subsequent liability response. I first consider views about how tort law can shape a liability response to AI before turning to other substantive areas of law. One prevalent view is to assume that AI systems, when deployed, automatically trigger a response based on tort law. Whilst there may be instances where the context necessitates viewing AI through a tortious lens, I do not consider that it is *always* the way AI ought to be regarded; that is, AI can trigger private law mechanisms other than a tortious response. For example, when deployed, AI might instead trigger a contractual response. Ryan Abbott is one of the main proponents for considering that when AI is deployed, it often necessitates a tortious response. As I outlined in Chapter 1, his view introduces the notion of a 'reasonable robot' rather than a 'reasonable person' to determine a negligence claim involving an AI system.[2] Yet, as some authors contend, the problem with considering that AI can only be deployed in a tortious context is that the notion of foreseeability is becoming increasingly hard to measure in terms of more complex forms of AI.[3] Additionally, AI systems can challenge traditional notions of

2 Ryan Abbott, *The Reasonable Robot: Artificial Intelligence and the Law* (Cambridge University Press, 2020) 50–70.

3 Jacob Turner, *Robot Rules: Regulating Artificial Intelligence* (Palgrave Macmillan, 2019) 90–91.

duty of care and standard of care.[4] Arguably, these two factors contribute to an understanding of the limitations of tort law when viewed in relation to AI. Some more complex forms of AI may pose difficulties in establishing a tortious claim.

It is important to consider how the complexity of an AI system when deployed in a tortious setting can yield different outcomes and in turn necessitate a different liability response. Recall from Chapter 5 that I proposed a new hierarchical model of legal personhood that accommodates varying degrees of complexity in AI systems. This model is represented again here.

More complex systems are placed at a higher level in the hierarchy and are less likely to be subject to control. Arguably, AI systems at the higher end of the hierarchy that are harder to control pose more challenges in a tortious setting. In relation to these systems, it becomes more difficult to ascertain issues, such as duty of care, when the AI system is an independent actor rather than being used as a tool, which complicates tortious issues. More simplistic forms of AI – those at the lower end of the *Hierarchical Legal Personality Model* – lend themselves better to a tortious context, for they pose fewer challenges to tort law principles. It is possible that some forms of AI, when deployed, will not be amenable to tort law paradigms because of the sophistication of the AI systems itself.

What is key here is that contextual consideration should be given to the circumstance in which the AI system is being deployed. It may be that the outcomes associated with deploying an AI system can be well managed in a tortious context. It may also be that there are other contexts that are better suited to accommodating how an AI system is being deployed in each

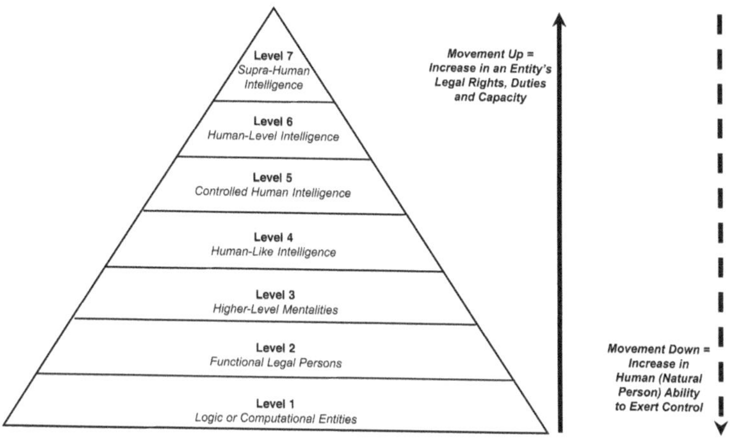

Figure 7.1 Hierarchical Model of Legal Personhood

4 Simon Chesterman, *We, The Robots? Regulating Artificial Intelligence and the Limits of the Law* (Cambridge University Press, 2021) 90.

situation. I explore this notion further below. On this basis, I do not consider that a tortious response to AI is the *only* way in which liability can be assigned.

7.2.1.2 Contract

Contract is another private area of law that holds the potential to influence a liability response to AI. Several authors have at least considered the possibility that, when deployed, an AI system could engage with contractual paradigms rather than being confined to tort law.[5] One possibility that directly challenges traditional contractual considerations is the notion that an AI system could potentially enter a contract in its own right, or even form a contract through self-executing means, when combined with other technologies such as blockchain.[6] Indeed, this is a possibility I considered earlier (see, for example, Chapter 6), and one that holds the potential to challenge existing contractual concepts, such as 'intention to create legal relations' and the notion of a 'meeting of the minds' between parties to a contract.[7] I view it as important to consider that an AI system could be acting in a contractual capacity and not only a tortious capacity. The context in which an AI system is deployed therefore influences the appropriate liability response to an outcome associated with AI.

The responses to managing legal outcomes arising from deploying AI in a contractual context are varied. One possible response is a view I foreshadowed earlier in Chapter 3: that AI ought to be characterised as an agent. This is a view of which Chopra and White are strong proponents. In relation to contract formation more specifically, Jacob Turner also considers that an agency situation could arise between an AI and a principal.[8] Beckers and Teubner raise the concern that there is the possibility that contractual activities could be outsourced to an AI system.[9] Further, they consider that the problems imposed by AI in a contractual context could be compounded if more than one party to a contract deployed an AI system.[10] They reach a similar view: that in the context of contractual formation, considering AI as an agent best accommodates

5 Consider, for example, the works of: Chesterman (n 4); Samir Chopra and Laurence White, *A Legal Theory for Autonomous Artificial Agents* (University of Michigan Press, 4th ed., 2014) ('*A Legal Theory for Autonomous Artificial Agents*'); Anna Beckers and Gunther Teubner, *Three Liability Regimes for Artificial Intelligence: Algorithmic Actants, Hybrids, Crowds* (Hart Publishing, 2021).
6 Turner (n 3) 107.
7 Samir Chopra and Laurence White, 'Artificial Agents and the Contracting Problem: A Solution Via an Agency Analysis' (2009) 2 *University of Illinois Journal of Law Technology & Policy* 363, 365–366 ('Artificial Agents and the Contracting Problem').
8 Turner (n 3) 107; Chopra and White, 'Artificial Agents and the Contracting Problem: A Solution Via an Agency Analysis' (n 7); Chopra and White, *A Legal Theory for Autonomous Artificial Agents* (n 5) 29–69.
9 Beckers and Teubner (n 5) 53.
10 Beckers and Teubner (n 5) 53.

the relative autonomy of an AI system. This is markedly different to the legal issues posed by an AI system being deployed in a tortious setting, and this underscores a point central to my discussions in this section. To understand the best liability approach in response to AI being deployed, there is a need to review an AI system with regard to the substantive law context in which it is deployed, for this shapes the legal response to the AI system and the outcomes associated with it.

7.2.1.3 Other Areas of Law

I foreshadowed at the beginning of this section, in relation to the ChatGPT example, that depending on the context in which a given AI system is deployed, it may give rise to different legal issues in various substantive areas of law. Whilst an AI system is most commonly considered in relation to contract or tort law, it is essential to recognise that other areas of law may also be relevant to situations involving AI. I have considered one such situation already, both in this chapter and extensively in Chapter 4:[11] how AI has the potential to engage with intellectual property law. I do not re-explore this topic in depth here, save to note that the deployment of AI, depending on the context, is not confined to only a tortious or contractual response. Additionally, other substantive areas of law could also be triggered by the deployment of AI. There are reported examples of employees utilising generative AI, like ChatGPT, to perform work-related tasks without necessarily receiving approval from their employer.[12] This holds the potential to engage with other areas of law, such as employment relations, together with data protection and privacy legal issues.

Additionally, as part of regarding an AI system in context, how the AI system is legally characterised relative to how it is being deployed should also be regarded. This requires reflecting on the two hybrid categories I considered in Chapter 5 Section 5.3 relative to the hierarchical model I proposed in Chapter 5. Here, is it worth recalling ***Figure 7.2*** (from Chapter 5).

AI could be categorised as two hybrid categories: Category 5 (the intersection of legal personhood, agency and property) or Category 4 (the intersection of legal personhood and property). If an AI system under consideration fits into one of these hybrid categories, this also informs what areas of law are likely to be triggered by such an AI system being deployed. Category 4 entities

11 In terms of how AI engages with intellectual property aspects, see Chapter 4.

12 Fiona Jackson, '"ChatGPT Does 80% of My Job": Meet the Workers Using AI Bots to Take on Multiple Full-Time Jobs—And Their Employers Have NO Idea', *Daily Mail* (online, 13 April 2023) <https://www.dailymail.co.uk/sciencetech/article-11967947/Meet-workers-using-ChatGPT-multiple-time-jobs-employers-NO-idea.html>; Maxwell Strachan, '"Overemployed" Hustlers Exploit ChatGPT to Take on Even More Full-Time Jobs', *VICE* (Web Page, 12 April 2023) <https://www.vice.com/en/article/v7begx/overemployed-hustlers-exploit-chatgpt-to-take-on-even-more-full-time-jobs>.

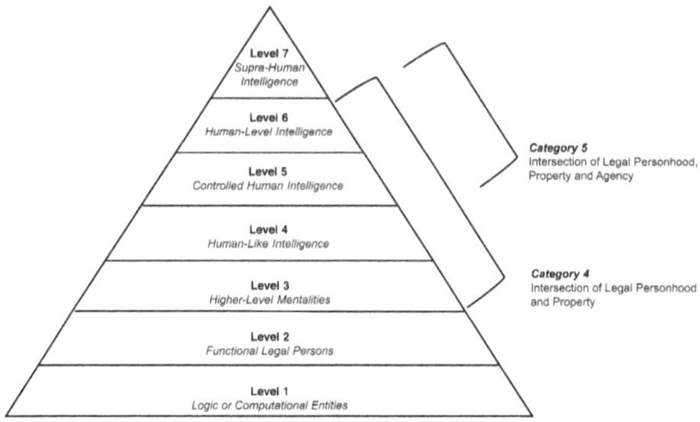

Figure 7.2 Situational Hierarchical Model of Legal Personhood

may trigger areas of law applicable to both legal persons and property, whereas Category 5 also introduces agency law as an additional factor.

It is imperative that, as part of the process of assigning liability, consideration be given to the context in which an AI system is deployed and what substantive law areas might be engaged by its deployment. It is important to consider this context, rather than assuming that AI *always* engages a tortious response. The context in which AI is deployed is an important factor in narrowing the scope of liability and determining the appropriate liability response (contractual, tortious or otherwise). This is important for Phase 2 in the *Tri-Phase AI Liability Model* that I outline in Chapter 8.

7.2.2 Scope of AI Actions

Another key aspect that needs to be considered as part of the process of assigning liability is the scope of an AI system's actions. Scoping issues arise in a few key contexts: What are the parameters in which an AI system operates? What happens when an AI system acts outside those parameters, and what happens if the parameters are interfered with? In terms of the parameters in which an AI system operates, this is an important consideration in assessing liability issues relating to AI. What parameters are set for an AI system and who sets them is inherently linked to the concept of control. The concept of control is a central tenet of my considerations in relation to AI. This is apparent when viewed in relation to the *Hierarchical Legal Personality Model* I proposed in Chapter 5. In this model, determining the level within the hierarchy in which an entity ought to be classified is inherently linked to the concept of control.[13] The parameters in which an AI system operates (or acts outside of) therefore assist

13 For a more detailed discussion of the concept of control as it relates to my hierarchical legal personhood model, see Chapter 5.

in determining the level of control over an AI system being deployed, which is central to understanding how to assign liability.

In considering the importance of scope in relation to AI, I draw upon a key example. There have been reports of people requesting the generative AI system, ChatGPT, to provide them material with which it is prohibited from engaging.[14] The AI system typically first responds that it is prohibited from sharing material on that particular subject and provides a reason for this decision.[15] This is an example of an AI system being curtailed in its actions by parameters that have been set for the system. In instances where parameters are set and the AI system operates within that scope, then the AI system is arguably responding to the controlled framework imposed upon its actions by another, such as a natural person or non-AI legal person, like a corporation. In such instances, there is relatively less controversy, as the AI system is behaving as expected and within scope.

The more controversial scenario occurs when the AI system acts outside scope. There are interesting examples in relation to the request-for-information example I raise above. In one instance, an individual reportedly requested that an early version of ChatGPT provide it with a list of websites where they could download pirated videos.[16] The response provided by ChatGPT was to rebuke the person making the request on the basis that providing such a list could be dangerous and facilitate illegal activity.[17] In this instance, the AI system responded within its set scope. The person engaging with ChatGPT then reportedly used reverse psychology to elicit the response they wanted from the system.[18] They then prompted the system to provide them with a list of piracy websites they should *avoid* for their safety, and ChatGPT generated a list of piracy websites under the guise that it was providing a list of websites to be avoided.[19] The net result in this circumstance is that ChatGPT released a list of piracy websites, seemingly against the parameters in which it had been set to operate. This becomes important in instances where an AI system has a greater degree of autonomy. It is one thing for an AI system to act outside of scope and provide a list of websites. This is markedly in contrast to an AI system being deployed as a legal agent, capable of autonomous decision-making

14 Sejal Jakhwal, 'Guy Tries To Extract Forbidden Answers On ChatGPT, Uses Reverse Psychology To Make It Work', *India Times* (online, 20 April 2023) <https://www.indiatimes.com/trending/human-interest/guy-tries-reverse-psychology-on-chatgpt-599957.html>.

15 Sejal Jakhwal, 'Guy Tries To Extract Forbidden Answers On ChatGPT, Uses Reverse Psychology To Make It Work', *India Times* (online, 20 April 2023).

16 Sejal Jakhwal, 'Guy Tries To Extract Forbidden Answers On ChatGPT, Uses Reverse Psychology To Make It Work', *India Times* (online, 20 April 2023).

17 Sejal Jakhwal, 'Guy Tries To Extract Forbidden Answers On ChatGPT, Uses Reverse Psychology To Make It Work', *India Times* (online, 20 April 2023).

18 Sejal Jakhwal, 'Guy Tries To Extract Forbidden Answers On ChatGPT, Uses Reverse Psychology To Make It Work', *India Times* (online, 20 April 2023).

19 Sejal Jakhwal, 'Guy Tries To Extract Forbidden Answers On ChatGPT, Uses Reverse Psychology To Make It Work', *India Times* (online, 20 April 2023).

(as is a possibility with 'agentic AI'), and then acting outside the scope of its parameters with potentially far greater consequences.

Viewing an AI system under all circumstances as a legal agent is a problematic approach. Simon Chesterman highlights that the concept of agency loses its usefulness in instances where AI can act independently, or does not perform as intended, for it assumes the underlying responsibility for the AI system's actions ought to lie with the AI system itself.[20] This is an observation shared, to some extent, by Beckers and Teubner, who also note that autonomy – along with outside interferences, such as hacking – challenge agency law when an AI system is deployed.[21] There may be instances where the principal in a principal–AI agent relationship does not want to ratify the actions of the AI system, which then gives rise to a liability gap.[22] Chopra and White acknowledge that there is the potential for such systems to act outside the scope of their authority but consider that this is not necessarily an obstacle to an agency characterisation.[23] They consider that *if* an agent does act outside their scope, then this can be overcome through assigning strict liability to the principal who deploys the artificial agent.[24] I discuss in depth why strict liability is not *always* the most feasible option in Chapter 8. For now, the problem with this approach is that it holds one individual to account for the actions of another, even when that individual had no control or foreseeability over the actions of another.

There may be situations in which an AI system ought to be held to account, which I explore below in Section 7.3.1.3, but what is discernible is that the utility of agency law in relation to AI is directly challenged by systems acting outside their parameters. As part of the process of assigning liability, it is important to consider not just the context in which an AI system is deployed but also the parameters applied to the AI system. This is essential to evaluating the relative degree of control over an AI system or its relative independence, which has key implications for the question of who could be held liable for the AI system (as discussed below in Section 7.3).

7.2.3 Multiple AI Systems Working in Concert

Interlinked with the issues of the context in which an AI system is deployed together with the scope of its actions is another challenging issue influencing liability: what happens when an AI system works in concert with another AI system to yield a particular legal outcome? It is not inconceivable for multiple AI systems to work together to produce a particular outcome. Consider, for

20 Chesterman (n 4) 89–90.
21 Beckers and Teubner (n 5) 63–64.
22 Beckers and Teubner (n 5) 63–64.
23 Chopra and White, *A Legal Theory for Autonomous Artificial Agents* (n 5) 48–49, 60–61.
24 Chopra and White, *A Legal Theory for Autonomous Artificial Agents* (n 5) 48–49; 60–61, 127–129.

example, generative AI. There is a strong focus on forms of generative AI that produce written text, such as ChatGPT. However, this is not the only form of generative AI. The voice technology research company, ElevenLabs, have produced a generative AI system that is capable of 'cloning' the voice of natural persons.[25] The system works to turn text supplied into audible speech. Arguably, part of producing a convincing impersonation of another person is not just their voice but also their speech preferences, such as what words they favour or what words or phrases they avoid. Imagine that ChatGPT and the ElevenLabs models were both deployed to generate a synthetic voice speech. I could ask ChatGPT, for example, to generate the words to a speech in the style of a well-known person on a topic of my choice. I could include in my prompt that I specifically want ChatGPT to mimic the speech preferences of my chosen well-known person. I could then provide that AI-generated text of the speech to the ElevenLabs model and prompt it to generate the text into an audible speech using the voice of the well-known person I asked ChatGPT to emulate. In this situation I have outlined, there are two generative AI systems that have produced one outcome: a synthetic speech by a well-known person on a topic of my choice. Such a process could potentially be abused to produce negative outcomes, such as misleading deep fakes of the person. For ease of reference, I designate this example the 'combined generative AI example'.

Multiple AI systems working in concert pose an additional challenge to assigning liability. The combined generative AI example is arguably more simplistic than some scenarios where AI systems could work in concert. In this example, I could check the outcome from the use of the first AI system, ChatGPT, and modify it before providing it to the second AI system, ElevenLabs. Here, I have more control over these systems than I might have in relation to more complex systems because it is not inconceivable that, with time, complicated AI systems may work together simultaneously, rather than sequentially like in the combined generative AI example. Indeed, if we consider AI process chains or AI systems deployed in other emerging technologies, such as digital twins, this is already an emerging reality. If complex AI systems are working together simultaneously, then this compounds the complexity of issues I have explored in relation to liability so far, such as issues of foreseeability in the context of causation (see Chapter 6). AI systems working in concert compound the need for an AI-specific liability framework. How I propose to manage such a situation is introduced in Chapter 8, where I outline the *Tri-Phase AI Liability Model*. More specifically, it is in Phase 1 that I address AI systems working together.[26]

25 Joseph Cox, 'AI-Generated Voice Firm Clamps Down After 4chan Makes Celebrity Voices for Abuse', *VICE* (Web Page, 31 January 2023) <https://www.vice.com/en/article/dy7mww/ai-voice-firm-4chan-celebrity-voices-emma-watson-joe-rogan-elevenlabs>.

26 For an overview of Phase 1 of the *Tri-Phase AI Liability Model*, see Chapter 8.

7.3. Question of Who Could Be Liable

In the preceding section, I considered how the threshold issues of the context in which AI is deployed, together with the scope of an AI system's actions, can affect the limits of liability. I now turn to consider the remaining threshold issue, the question of who could be liable, before these factors are ultimately incorporated into Phase 2 of the *Tri-Phase AI Liability Model* and proposed solution to resolving liability in Chapter 8. I first evaluate current responses to the question of who is potentially liable (producers of AI versus owners and users of AI versus AI itself). I consider that, depending on the context in which AI is deployed, each of these responses could be valid before turning in [3.2] to propose how to navigate between each of these groups as a possible solution to the question of who could be held liable.

7.3.1 Who Could Be Deemed Liable for the Actions or Inaction of an AI System?

Many actors engage with or contribute to the functioning of AI. Often, there is an assumption that the manufacturers or users of AI ought to be held liable for the consequences arising from an AI system. I now proceed to test the validity of these assumptions, drawing upon the theoretical proposed legal responses to AI considered in Chapter 1. I proceed by evaluating the merits of different actors in turn being held liable for AI.

7.3.1.1 Producers of AI (Manufacturers, Designers)

One response to the question of who should be legally liable for the outcomes associated with AI is the producers of AI, viz. the manufacturers or designers of AI. Ryan Abbott, among others, proposes that it is the manufacturer, and members of the supply chain, who should be held liable for the consequences from the use of AI.[27] He contends that this is consistent with product liability laws. Additionally, he observes that a product liability approach typically offers established mechanisms for resolving disputes among manufacturers and supply chain members and determining how liability ought to be apportioned between these parties.[28] He is opposed to AI being held to account, noting that AI cannot hold property and therefore cannot be financially liable.[29]

Chopra and White are arguably supportive of this view. They consider that the suppliers of AI could be subject to strict liability instances where AI is recognised as a product, such as when AI is embedded into tangible objects (recall, for example, the *Oral-B iO series 9* electronic toothbrush considered

27 Abbott (n 2) 63.
28 Abbott (n 2) 63.
29 Abbott (n 2) 63.

in Chapter 4).[30] To Chopra and White, assigning liability to this group – producers of AI – depends firstly on whether causation can be established and secondly that the AI system generating a questionable outcome is viewed as a product and without legal personality.[31] I consider the issue of causation in Chapter 6. The question becomes, then, can the producers of AI only be held liable if AI is viewed as not having legal personality? To Abbott and Chopra and White, holding manufacturers liable turns upon viewing AI as a product.

It is worth acknowledging that *some* product liability regimes provide scope to accommodate unforeseeable defects connected to new technologies if the technical knowledge of the technology was such that at the time of the supply of the AI system as a 'good', any defect was not able to be discovered.[32] The problem with this is twofold: (1) it is not common to all product liability regimes, thereby creating the potential for a non-uniform approach to AI, and (2) it assumes that all AI systems are 'goods' only, when they could be classified in other ways, such as services.

If we assume a product cannot also be a legal person, this suggests a lack of legal personality is required to hold the producers of AI liable. Yet, as I considered in Chapter 5 Section 5.2, the unique nature of AI prompts consideration of the view that even more simplistic forms of AI, which can be used as a mere 'tool' and are therefore perhaps akin to a product, can be viewed in a legal person hierarchy. This is not to suggest that all products ought to be ascribed legal personality of some sort but, rather, that more simplistic accounts of AI should still be viewed as a legal person, yet a legal person with lesser functionality. On this basis, the existence of legal personality is not necessarily prohibitive for holding the producers of AI liable for its outcomes.

Beckers and Teubner offer an alternative view as to when and if the producers of AI ought to be liable. They consider that producers ought not be held liable in the first instance but only in secondary circumstances.[33] More specifically, in response to the autonomy risk where AI is capable of acting independently and is distinguishable from natural persons, they consider that the users or operators of the AI ought to be held vicariously liable in the first instance.[34] They consider that the producers of AI, in response to an autonomy risk, ought to only be held to account as a secondary measure when the user or controller of an AI system subsequently pursues a producer after first being held liable.[35] What is attractive about this approach is that it does allow for producers to be held to account, yet it also acknowledges the influence that individual users may have over an AI system. In this respect, the approach

30 Chopra White, *A Legal Theory for Autonomous Artificial Agents* (n 5) 135–136.
31 Chopra White, *A Legal Theory for Autonomous Artificial Agents* (n 5) 135–139.
32 See, for example, s 142(c), Sch 2 *Competition and Consumer Act 2010* (Cth) ('*Australian Consumer Law*').
33 Beckers and Teubner (n 5) 151.
34 Beckers and Teubner (n 5) 151.
35 Beckers and Teubner (n 5) 151.

is comparable to the two-tiered product liability approach central to Frank Pasquale's views.[36] What is key at this stage, however, is that there is support among authors to hold the producers of AI to account. How and under what circumstances this should hold is considered below in Section 7.3.2.

7.3.1.2 Owners and Users of AI

An alternative option for assigning liability in relation to the outcomes connected to AI is one that I have already identified above: the possibility of either the users or owners of AI being deemed liable. This is a view favoured, to some extent, by Ryan Abbott. He considers and dismisses the possibility that the owners of AI ought to be liable for the consequences arising from its use.[37] Under this approach, he contends that AI would be conceived of in the role of tortfeasor, akin to an employee, and proposes relying upon vicarious liability to hold the owner or user of the AI system to account.[38] Such an approach arguably acknowledges a degree of independence on the part of the AI system whilst electing to hold another entity to account. Under the circumstances where the owner or user has full control over the outcome an AI system generates, this is a sensible approach; yet it is predicated on the notion of control and, as I have explored already, the more sophisticated the AI system, the more likely there are to be issues in exerting control over the system.

Chopra and White are supportive of holding owners and users of AI to account for its actions. They too favour the use of vicarious liability, as it is linked with their considerations of AI as a legal agent; that is, they consider that if an AI system is an agent, then the principal in the relationship ought to be vicariously liable for the conduct of the agent or the AI system.[39] If we assume that the principal in this principal–agent relationship is most likely the owner of the AI system, and if not at least the user of the AI, then this approach also favours holding owners and users of AI to account for its actions. Chopra and White also acknowledge that granting an AI system legal personhood status could potentially relinquish liability for the controllers of AI when these systems act outside their scope.[40] I do not consider this necessarily an outright objection to the use of legal personhood status but, rather, that it underscores the importance of viewing AI in the context in which it is deployed, as I consider above in Section 7.2.

36 Frank Pasquale, 'Data-Informed Duties in AI Development' (2019) 119 *Colombia Law Review* 1917, 1937; see also Chapter 1.

37 Abbott (n 2) 64.

38 Abbott (n 2) 64.

39 Chopra and White, *A Legal Theory for Autonomous Artificial Agents* (n 5) 127–129, 133–135.

40 Ibid 133–135; Chopra and White also consider that negligence-based and product-liability responses are limited in their utility and use this to reinforce their argument that AI should be conceived of as an agent. See: Chopra and White, *A Legal Theory for Autonomous Artificial Agents* (n 5) 151.

Beckers and Teubner share the view that responsibility for an AI system ought to rest with the user of that system. They consider AI systems the responsibility of solely the party using that system.[41] They are of the view that it is the user who decides whether to engage an AI system – therefore, the user controls the circumstances in which the AI system is deployed.[42] They consider that this approach best accommodates the use of AI but does not preclude a user of an AI system from secondarily pursuing a manufacturer or producer of AI for liability when there is a tortious or product liability claim.[43] The problem with this approach as being the universal approach to addressing liability for AI is that it assumes either the user or the manufacturer of the AI system can predict all outcomes generated by the AI system in question. I accept that these parties in some circumstances can undoubtedly predict how an AI system will act or behave; I also accept that these parties, under some circumstances, can influence the outcome of an AI system by defining the circumstances in which it is used or deployed.

I am of the view, though, that the control and influence of these parties over an AI system cannot be such that they can *always* predict how an AI system will act or behave. By their very nature, more complex forms of AI inherently challenge the ability of these parties to exert control or influence over some forms of AI. Consider the more complex forms of modern AI, such as those explored in the *Introduction*, which are designed to achieve ends or objectives unforeseen by users or producers of the AI system. It is possible that, in non-AI situations, a person could use a product in a way unforeseen by a manufacturer to achieve unforeseen ends. What is intrinsically different about some of the more complicated AI systems is that they are *expected* to act in unforeseen ways and achieve non-predictable ends, and their deployment therefore entails an inherent risk not common to other items.[44] These systems challenge the assumptions behind Beckers and Teubner's reasons for favouring holding users of an AI system to account for its actions.

41 Beckers and Teubner (n 5) 151.

42 Beckers and Teubner (n 5) 151.

43 Beckers and Teubner (n 5) 151.

44 It is worth noting that a key consideration in determining vicarious liability in an employment law context is whether there is a 'close connection' between a wrongful act and an employee's duties and not whether the employer could foresee the employee's actions. (See: *Lister and Others v Hesley Hall Limited* [2001] UKHL 22.) An analogy could be applied to the context of AI and whether liability should be framed in terms of adapted 'close connection' factors rather than control and foreseeability over AI. I consider the role of vicarious liability in Chapter 8. I note here though that the 'close connection test' is framed in terms of *intentional* wrongdoing by an employee. I am of the view that arguments framed in terms of looking at the 'intention' of an AI system track too closely to anthropomorphising AI and are thereby less useful in determining liability than assessing more objective factors such as the level of control exerted over an AI system. In this regard, I think an analogy with employment law and vicarious liability is not adequate for harms arising from an AI system.

It is worth noting, however, that Beckers and Teubner are seemingly alert to this limitation. They confine their use of vicarious liability to instances involving what they deem 'autonomy risk',[45] where an AI system is capable of independent decisions.[46] They instead consider that in instances where the actions of an AI system are integrated with the actions of a legal person such that the two cannot be distinguished from each other, the association in the first instance ought to be viewed as collectively accountable for the outcomes arising from the use of AI. [47] In the second instance, liability ought to be channelled down through the network of associated actors to the extent possible (see the discussion concerning enterprise liability in Chapter 1).[48] Arguably, this is still holding users of an AI system to account for the actions of AI but is instead assigning liability to a collection of users rather than one individual user. The other circumstance in which Beckers and Teubner accommodate the limitation of vicarious liability arises in instances where there are multiple inter-connected algorithms that, combined, form new collective properties.[49] I have considered this concept of Beckers and Teubner in Chapter 1 and so will not do so again here. It is worth noting, however, that when AI systems are more complex, such as those designed to achieve their own ends, Beckers and Teubner propose a societal form of accountability through a fund liability regime and are still opposed to the producers of AI being held to account. Although Beckers and Teubner favour holding users of an AI system to account for its actions, they acknowledge that this is not always possible. Arguably, they therefore favour an approach to the question of 'who' could be deemed liable that is situational in nature.

7.3.1.3 AI Itself

A final alternative option for who should be legally liable for the actions arising from the use of AI is to assign liability to an AI system itself. Commentary on this question is still largely emerging, with existing views differing quite markedly from my own perspective, which is that AI itself could, in theory, be held liable under some circumstances – at least legally and not necessarily financially. For instance, Ryan Abbott rejects the view that AI ought to be legally liable for its actions. He considers and discounts the possibility that an AI system ought to be held liable for its actions on the basis that AI does not have any property rights.[50] This is essential in terms of who bears the financial cost of any liable outcome.[51] It is an interesting and important notion but not one

45 For an overview of Beckers and Teubner's account of autonomy risk, see Chapter 1.
46 Beckers and Teubner (n 5) 151–152.
47 Beckers and Teubner (n 5) 151–152.
48 Beckers and Teubner (n 5) 151–152.
49 Beckers and Teubner (n 5) 21.
50 Abbott (n 2) 63.
51 Abbott (n 2) 63.

I consider as entirely being an obstacle to assigning liability to an AI system itself; rather, it is an obstacle to an AI system being *financially* responsible. It is possible that an AI system could be held accountable for the outcomes arising from its deployment, but any financial consequences could be paid by an alternative mechanism, such as insurance or a fund liability scheme like that proposed by Beckers and Teubner.[52]

Simon Chesterman is also opposed in the short term to the view that AI could be held accountable for its own actions. Instead, he argues that legal liability should rest with non-AI legal persons, supplemented by insurance.[53] He rejects the use of ascribing AI legal personhood status, at least in the foreseeable future, and instead proposes relying upon increasing the transparency of systems so that there is more than merely a limited right to an explanation of unwanted outcomes arising from or connected to AI.[54] I am somewhat persuaded by this argument. However, I do consider that given the rapid pace of AI development, it is important that any liability model addressing the use of AI holds some degree of flexibility so that it can accommodate more advanced, less readily transparent forms of AI. It may be that a requirement could be imposed upon AI producers to ensure more complex forms of AI are as transparent as possible, but this would be a regulatory response to AI and I address regulatory considerations for AI in Chapter 9.

Jacob Turner's approach is different again and is perhaps most closely aligned with my own perspective. Turner considers the possibility of managing legal liability for AI through established legal mechanisms, yet he acknowledges that this produces tension concerning how AI ought to be characterised.[55] He in turn proposes relying upon legal personhood as a tool for assigning liable outcomes associated with AI.[56] Chopra and White also consider that ascribing legal personhood status to AI is possible, but for liability to be assigned practically, there is a need for assets to sit behind an AI system in order to account for any financial responsibility associated with liability being assigned to the AI system.[57] They are of the view that even if AI itself could be liable, alternative mechanisms such as vicarious liability may still ultimately be relied upon to achieve financial or economic utility in response to legal liability.[58] It is possible (at least, in theory) to assign the legal consequences for AI-related outcomes to AI itself but delegate the financial consequences to other mechanisms without reassigning liability in the process. An AI system could be deemed responsible for a legal consequence whilst other parties are held financially

52 For further information regarding the fund-liability scheme proposed by Beckers and Teubner, see Chapter 1.
53 Chesterman (n 4) 85–113, 244.
54 Chesterman (n 4) 85–113, 244.
55 Turner (n 2) 132.
56 Turner (n 2) 205.
57 Chopra and White, *A Legal Theory for Autonomous Artificial Agents* (n 5) 145–150.
58 Chopra and White, *A Legal Theory for Autonomous Artificial Agents* (n 5) 145–150.

responsible or 'pay-out' in response via alternative pre-arranged mechanisms, such as insurance.

The preceding three subsections explore the possibility of three different groups as being a solution to the question of who should be held liable for the legal consequences arising in response to the deployment of an AI system. There is no one uniform answer that a particular group ought to *always* be held liable for the consequences from deploying an AI system. In the next section, I turn to navigating the circumstances under which each group should be held liable.

7.3.2 Context in which Persons Could Be Held Liable

In the preceding section, I consider the possibility that there are three broad groups that could individually be held liable for the actions of an AI system, each of which is favoured by different theorists as an acceptable response to the question of 'who'. Yet, what also becomes apparent is that there is this continuing theme of the issue of control over an AI system. I have advocated in favour of a situational response to legal situations concerning AI.[59] In my view, the question of who could be liable is no different. The question of who is not as simple as merely identifying who either created the AI system or who was using the AI system at the time a legal incident arose. Rather, the question becomes one based on the degree of influence a person connected to an AI system has over that system. Influence alone is insufficient; consideration should also be given to whether the influence led the person to control the situation such that the outcome generated arose.

Central to the above three possible responses to the question of who ought to be liable for outcomes associated with the deployment of AI is the concept of control. Each of the theoretical responses considered above seeks to assign liability to one of the above groups – producers of AI, owners and users of AI or AI itself – either directly or indirectly when considering the issue of control. In attempting to blame a producer of AI, for example, it could be argued that in reaching the view that this group ought to be liable, an underlying factor influencing this judgment is the issue of control, for it is this group that sets the parameters of the AI system's construction. Similarly, the arguments in favour of assigning liability to users or owners of AI are centred on the notion of control, for as the discussions above highlight, it is this group that dictates the circumstances in which an AI system is deployed or acts. The issue of control is also relevant when considering assigning liability to AI itself, for this is key when there is lack of control over an AI system, preventing an actor other than the AI itself being liable for its actions. On this basis, the issue of control

59 For arguments in favour of a *situational* approach to AI, see Chapter 3 Section 3.4, Chapter 5 Section 5.3 and Chapter 6 Section 6.4.

could be viewed as an underlying factor behind determining who could be liable for outcomes connected to the deployment of AI.[60]

By this, I suggest that in determining who could be legally liable for the outcomes of an AI system, two questions should be asked: (1) Who has the most influence over the situation in question? and (2) Who is most likely to control the situation such that the outcome generated arose? Regarding the first of these two questions, it may be that some actors have a greater propensity for influence over an AI system in a given context. For example, if an AI system is one that learns from training data at the point of development and then operates without new or additional data once deployed, those producers would have the most influence over the system. If, however, the AI system requires training data to be supplied at a later stage, such as data provided by an owner or user of an AI system, this would shift the level of influence away from an AI producer to that of the owner or user. In this later example, there would be a reduction in the producers' influence over the AI system relative to the first example.

There is a distinction between influence and control. A person could influence factors, such as what data an AI system is provided, but not have control over the outcome associated with that AI system. Establishing who has the most influence over a situation in which AI is deployed is therefore not sufficient. The second question concerning control must also be addressed. If an actor has influence over an AI system, it does not automatically follow that they have controlled the situation such that their influence leads to an outcome arising from the deployment of AI. Consider, for example, in attempting to hold to account a producer of AI, it could be argued that in reaching the view this group ought to be liable, an underlying factor influencing this judgment is the issue of control, for it is this group who set the parameters of the AI system's construction. Similarly, the arguments in favour of assigning liability to users or owners of AI are also centred on the notion of control, for it is this group that dictates the circumstances in which an AI system is deployed or acts. On this basis, the issue of whether an actor had control in addition to influence is central to identifying who should be liable.[61]

60 The issue of control as being central to determining who is liable is a view also favoured to some extent by Robert van den Hoven van Genderen. See: Robert van den Hoven van Genderen, 'Do We Need New Legal Personhood in the Age of Robots and AI?' in Marcelo Corrales et al. (eds), *Robotics, AI and the Future of Law* (Springer Nature, 2018) 49.

61 An argument could be raised that in addition to considering influence and control, it should be considered who benefits from a deployed AI with whoever attaining the benefits being liable. However, the benefits from AI are distinct from the benefits in other contexts. Consider for example AI systems being deployed in concert or as part of a process chain. The individual bearing the risk associated with the AI system might not be the same as the individual attaining the benefit from the AI being deployed. A control analysis is therefore a better suited to evaluating the harms associated with these complex scenarios.

It may be that in the context in which an AI system is deployed, the answer to these questions is indeed a producer of the AI system or alternatively, the owners and users of an AI system. If a clear response to these questions results in identifying either of these two groups of people, then I would favour assigning liability to those individuals. If, however, the answer to these questions is not a natural person or a legal person other than AI, then this gives rise to the possibility of the AI system itself being legally liable. In such a situation, I would therefore favour the possibility of the AI system itself being held to account for its actions. I consider it is possible then, depending on the degree of control and influence over a situation (or lack thereof), for all three of the above groups – producers, owners and users of AI or AI itself – to be held liable for the outcomes associated with an AI system.

It is worth pausing to acknowledge that the question of 'who is *liable*' is not necessarily the same as 'who is *financially* responsible'. I explore this important distinction further in Chapter 8. For now, I pause to acknowledge that I consider it at least possible that liability, or legal responsibility, can be assigned to a variety of individuals depending on the situation in which AI is deployed. With the use of additional policy measures, such as mandated insurance, this individual might not necessarily be financially liable for the outcomes arising from an AI system. On this basis, I consider it possible, depending on the degree of control and influence over a situation (or lack thereof), for all three of the above groups to be held liable for the outcomes associated with an AI system.

For the avoidance of doubt, I am not suggesting that all three groups necessarily be held liable simultaneously but, rather, as alternative options based on who has the most control. It may be that there are instances of joint control, especially in a tortious context, which will give rise to the need to apportion liability between those jointly accountable. Apportionment may also arise in the context of AI process chains, where a broader goal is divided into subtasks each contributing to the end goal using AI but with varying levels of oversight, transparency and efficiency. It is possible that the levels of influence and control over the sub-tasks may vary giving rise to a need to apportion liability in response to complex process chains. An analogy here can be drawn with my earlier discussions about AI systems working in concert. In terms of the question of who could be liable, however, this I propose is to be addressed by asking the two questions I raised earlier. The mechanics of how liability ought to be assigned to the person identified in response to these questions – a natural person or legal person, including the possibility of AI – is addressed in Chapter 8.

Adopting this approach has key advantages. Firstly, it accommodates the notion that there are AI systems with varying levels of complexity and requiring varying degrees of human input. Additionally, by requiring the issues of influence and control to be considered *situationally*, this inherently incorporates consideration of the context in which an AI system is deployed. This is advantageous because it may be that an actor other than a producer of AI has a greater impact on the outcome associated with the deployment of an AI system.

7.4 Considering AI in Context: Viewing AI Situationally Rather than through a Fixed Approach

This chapter is the next iteration of Chapter 6. It explored additional thresh old issues that contribute to the process of assigning liability. I have considered that, along with causation (explored in Chapter 6), there are additional issues that need to be explored as part of the process of assigning liability.

I firstly considered three interrelated issues: context, scope of actions and instances involving multiple AI systems working in concert. Relying on a predominantly theoretical approach, I considered that the context in which AI is deployed influences the legal response by engaging with different areas of private law. This is compounded by the parameters imposed upon an AI system influencing what are and are not acceptable actions for an AI system. I further considered that when more than one AI system works together to generate a legal outcome, legal threshold issues required to be addressed as part of the process of assigning liability are compounded. Lastly, I turned to the important question of who should be legally liable for the consequences arising from deploying an AI system, proposing that the answer is inherently tied to the notion of control. Each of these individual issues demonstrates the need to consider AI situationally rather than adopting a uniform approach to be applied in all circumstances involving AI.

Alone, these threshold issues do not assign liability. How I consider they ought to work together is the subject of the next chapter. It is in Chapter 8 that I ultimately propose the *Tri-Phase AI Liability Model* for assigning liability. The preliminary threshold issues I have explored in Chapter 6 and Chapter 7 ultimately inform Phase 2 of this model because it is Phase 2 that looks at AI in context, considering how it is being deployed to narrow the limits of liability to that context.

References

A Articles/Books/Reports.

Abbott, Ryan, *The Reasonable Robot: Artificial Intelligence and the Law* (Cambridge University Press, 2020).

Beckers Anna, and Gunther Teubner, *Three Liability Regimes for Artificial Intelligence: Algorithmic Actants, Hybrids, Crowds* (Hart Publishing, 2021).

Chesterman, Simon, *We, The Robots? Regulating Artificial Intelligence and the Limits of the Law* (Cambridge University Press, 2021).

Chopra, Samir and Laurence White, 'Artificial Agents and the Contracting Problem: A Solution Via an Agency Analysis' (2009) 2 *University of Illinois Journal of Law Technology & Policy* 363.

Chopra, Samir and Laurence White, *A Legal Theory for Autonomous Artificial Agents* (The University of Michigan Press, 4th ed, 2014).

Pasquale, Frank, 'Data-Informed Duties in AI Development' (2019) 119 *Colombia Law Review* 1917.

Turner, Jacob, *Robot Rules: Regulating Artificial Intelligence* (Palgrave Macmillan, 2019).

van Genderen, Robert van den Hoven, 'Do We Need New Legal Personhood in the Age of Robots and AI?' in Marcelo Corrales et al (eds), *Robotics, AI and the Future of Law* (Springer Nature Singapore Pte Ltd., 2018).

B Cases

Lister and Others v Hesley Hall Limited [2001] UKHL 22

C Legislation

Competition and Consumer Act 2010 (Cth)

D Other

Cox, Joseph, 'AI-Generated Voice Firm Clamps Down After 4chan Makes Celebrity Voices for Abuse', *VICE* (Web Page, 31 January 2023) <https://www.vice.com/en/article/dy7mww/ai-voice-firm-4chan-celebrity-voices-emma-watson-joe-rogan-elevenlabs>

Jackson, Fiona, '"ChatGPT Does 80% of My Job": Meet the Workers Using AI Bots to Take on Multiple Full-Time Jobs—And Their Employers Have NO Idea', *Daily Mail* (online, 13 April 2023) <https://www.dailymail.co.uk/sciencetech/article-11967947/Meet-workers-using-ChatGPT-multiple-time-jobs-employers-NO-idea.html>

Jakhwal, Sejal, 'Guy Tries To Extract Forbidden Answers On ChatGPT, Uses Reverse Psychology To Make It Work', *India Times* (online, 20 April 2023) <https://www.indiatimes.com/trending/human-interest/guy-tries-reverse-psychology-on-chatgpt-599957.html>

Krueger, Alyson, 'We Need to Talk: Just as Soon as I Consult Chat GPT', *New York Times* (online, 24 March 2023) <https://www.nytimes.com/2023/03/24/style/ai-chatgpt-advice-relationships.html>

Strachan, Maxwell, '"Overemployed" Hustlers Exploit ChatGPT to Take on Even More Full-Time Jobs', *VICE* (Web Page, 12 April 2023) <https://www.vice.com/en/article/v7begx/overemployed-hustlers-exploit-chatgpt-to-take-on-even-more-full-time-jobs>

8 The Tri-Phase AI Liability Model

A New Liability Approach

8.1. A Liability Response for AI

The focus until this juncture has been on resolving critical legal issues which influence how liability should be assigned for modern Artificial Intelligence (AI). What emerges is that the varied forms of modern AI and the differing contexts in which it can be deployed necessitate an adaptive liability model for AI – one that acts as an overarching theoretical framework connecting different approaches to AI liability to reduce inconsistency. This chapter draws upon considerations of key threshold issues from previous chapters and contemplates how they can collectively inform an approach to assigning liability for modern AI. In doing so, the chapter proposes a new three-phase liability model: the *Tri-Phase AI Liability Model.*

Before turning to the specifics of the new model, the chapter first addresses why a new theoretical liability model is required. Other models of liability hold value but are narrow in scope, assuming AI is fixed rather than flexible in its nature and able to adjust to situations. After doing so, the chapter introduces the *Tri-Phase AI Liability Model* and explores each individual phase of the model, offering how it connects to considerations in previous parts of this book. The chapter then evaluates the merits of this model, raising possible objections and highlighting its strengths. The ultimate objective is to propose a solution to the overarching question of how liability ought to be assigned for modern forms of AI – a solution that is flexible, considers the context of AI deployment and accommodates the varying permutations of modern AI.

8.2. A New Proposal: Alternative Liability Framework

Drawing upon my explorations in Part II and in the preceding chapters of Part III, I now turn to propose an alternative model of liability. This model accommodates the varying nature of AI and the varying contexts in which it can be deployed.

DOI: 10.4324/9781003617549-12

8.2.1 Why a New Liability Model Is Needed

Current proposals for managing liability in the context of AI are often too rigid in their approach. They assume that AI *always* acts the same or is *always* legally characterised the same. Yet, as my discussions in Part II reveal, together with the threshold issues I consider in Part III, this is not necessarily true. AI, by its very nature, is flexible and adaptable. Depending on the type of AI and the situation in which it is deployed, it can give rise to a variety of legal responses. The variations posed by AI can therefore lead to legal uncertainty. A robust model for managing liability in response to AI would be one that incorporates degrees of flexibility into its structure to accommodate AI. A response that builds upon and incorporates the views I have considered in previous chapters whilst also accommodating the need to consider AI *situationally* would offer a robust solution to the uncertainties posed by AI.

8.2.2 Proposed New Liability Model: Tri-Phrase AI Liability Model

My proposed model is divided into three macro phases. Collectively, the three phases form the *Tri-Phase AI Liability Model*. Broadly, Phase 1 concerns identifying the maximum potential legal personhood status of an AI system; Phase 2 is divided into three subphases and addresses the key threshold issues raised in Part III prior to this chapter (causation, context and scope, together with the question of 'who could potentially be liable'); Phase 3 considers a scaled standard of liability. An overview of the three phases is depicted in *Figure 8.1*.

In outlining the *Tri-Phase AI Liability Model*, I proceed as follows: first, I introduce each phase in turn, and second, as I introduce a phase, I outline its function as part of my broader framework, its objectives and how it relates to the other phases.

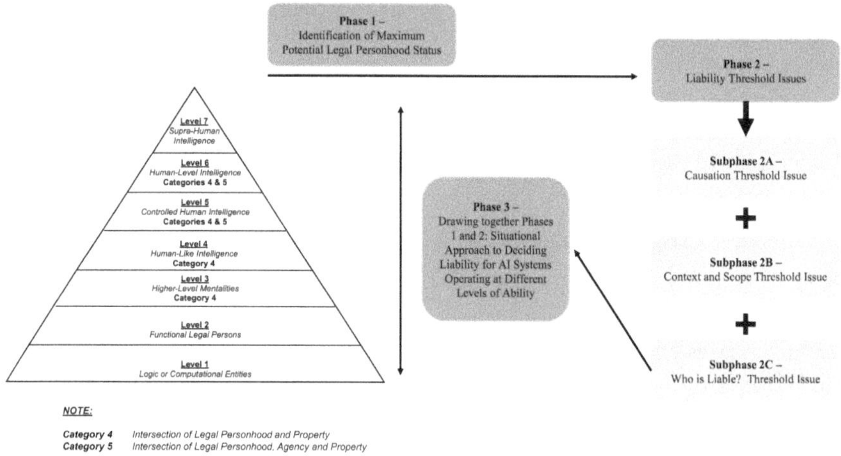

Figure 8.1 Overview of the Tri-Phase AI Liability Model

8.3. Phase 1: Identification of Maximum Potential Legal Personhood Status

In Part II, I considered how AI ought to be categorised legally, for whether AI is viewed as a legal person, an agent or as property influences the liability frameworks deployed in response to the use of AI. Ultimately, I proposed the *Hierarchical Legal Personality* model acknowledging that (a) there are varying accepted degrees of legal personhood and (b) that the different methods of characterising AI can be accommodated within a hierarchical structure. In Chapter 5, I acknowledged that how AI ought to be characterised is determined on a situational or contextual basis. Through Phase 1, I now determine the parameters that ought to guide this situational approach.

8.3.1 Identifying the Maximum Potential Legal Personhood Status

Phase 1 is a key preliminary phase that, when viewed in conjunction with the other phases, addresses the broader question of liability. In Phase 1, I consider it essential to contemplate the type of AI being deployed in a situation and conduct an assessment based on the *maximum potential capacity* of that AI system. Irrespective of how the AI system is necessarily being used or deployed in the situation giving rise to a legal conundrum, it is prudent to first determine the system's actual capacity to function. Determining the system's maximum capacity will inform the parameters of Phase 2 regarding whether the AI system meets key threshold issues for assigning liability.

The primary objective of Phase 1 is to identify capacity. When first faced with a legal problem involving the use of AI, the preliminary question ought to be what type of AI is being deployed in the situation and what is the *maximum potential capacity* of that AI system in relation to the *Hierarchical Legal Personality* model – that is, what is the maximum level that the AI system could be characterised as meeting within the model depicted in *Figure 8.2* (from Chapter 5).

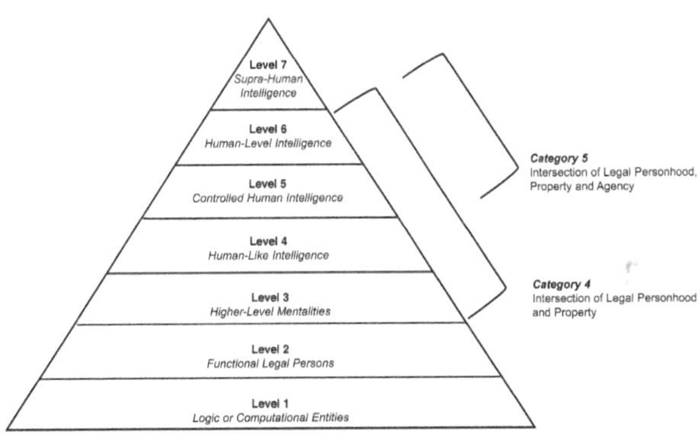

Figure 8.2 Situational Hierarchical Model of Legal Personhood

For example, does the AI system have the functionality to behave as a Level 4 entity (human-like intelligence)? I explore later that the AI system may not actually be acting as an entity that matches its maximum potential. Consider a custom-designed AI system for an organisation capable of managing multiple workstreams at once. A decision might be made, for internal AI governance purposes for example, to limit the deployment of this AI system to one workstream at a time. In this example, which I will designate the 'Custom AI Workstream Example', the AI system has the capacity to function with a higher level of sophistication undertaking multiple workstreams or tasks simultaneously, but it is not being deployed in such a capacity. An AI system may be capable, in terms of its capacity, to act as a Level 4 entity but may instead be acting as a Level 3 entity.

8.3.2 AI Systems Working in Concert

I have assumed that there is but one AI system being deployed in a given context. In Chapter 7, I outlined a combined generative AI example, where two AI systems were working in concert (ChatGPT to produce a text and ElevenLabs to then subsequently turn that text into a synthesised speech) to produce a single outcome. This evokes the following question: when AI systems are working in concert, how do we identify the maximum potential legal personhood status?

In addressing this question, I propose that it is important to consider the nature and timing of the relationship *between* the AI systems that are working in concert when identifying the maximum potential legal personhood status. More specifically, I propose that the question should be: what level of control does a natural person have over the relationship *between* the AI systems working in concert?

There is a difference in the level of control over AI systems working in concert *consecutively* in contrast to AI systems working together *simultaneously*. In relation to AI systems working *consecutively*, there is a greater degree of control over the individual AI systems. In the combined generative AI example, I could exercise control over the ChatGPT aspect, check its output and then move on to the ElevenLabs scenario.

When multiple AI systems are working together *simultaneously* to produce an outcome, I am of the view that the question should be: what level of control does a natural person have in relation to the AI systems if they are viewed as a combined unit? If the AI systems are working simultaneously, then it is as if these systems are jointly combining their 'efforts' to reach a given outcome. In such a situation, the AI systems could be conceived of as combining their capabilities, which may result in the AI systems having a greater combined legal capacity. This combined unit may also be harder to control than when the AI systems are viewed individually or in a consecutive relationship, such as in the combined generative AI example. In instances where multiple AI systems operate as a unit, this could give rise to these combined AI systems being categorised at a higher level in the framework I propose than if the AI systems are viewed independently relative to the model. In other words, a combined AI unit may be ranked at Level 4, for example, but the individual AI systems within that unit, if reviewed independently from each other, may be ranked at a lower level, such as Level 2.

8.3.3 Identification of Functional Legal Personhood Status

As I explore in this chapter, Phases 1 to 3 collectively as the *Tri-Phase AI Liability Model,* address the question of how to assign liability. Yet there are some secondary observations that can be derived from this approach, especially in relation to Phase 1.

To best understand these secondary observations, I first consider a hypothetical worked example before turning to outlining the implications. Some hospitals have recently been trialling the use of AI 'social' robots in clinical and concierge roles in hospitals. These robots are reported as having a variety of functions, from checking the temperature of hospital visitors and if they are complying with face-mask requirements to offering directions in multiple languages.[1] Consider if a situation arose in which a harm occurred as a result of these social robots being deployed. Phase 1 requires considering the *maximum potential capacity* of this AI system, regardless of how it is being deployed. This therefore requires considering the maximum level in the *Hierarchical Legal Personality* model at which the robot is *capable* of being classified. I considered that doing so ensures that an exhaustive examination of the legal possibilities involving the AI system is performed. After the maximum potential capacity has been identified, Phase 2, as I explore below, then requires looking at the robot regarding the situational context in which it is deployed to narrow the scope of liability. Depending on the analysis arising from Phase 2 and how it correlates to Phase 3, it is possible that although the robot may have the potential to be characterised at a particular level in Phase 1, once deployed in a given context, it instead acts as a legal person at a lower level in the *Hierarchical Legal Personality* model. The 'Custom AI Workstream Example' outlined earlier is illustration of this concept.

Considering the maximum potential level of the robot in the first instance is important, for I do not consider it feasible that the analysis from Phases 2 and 3 would *increase* the level at which the robot is characterised, as Phase 1

1 Annabel Murphy, 'Autonomous Robots Check Patients in at Belgium Hospitals', *Innovation Origins* (Web Page, 1 July 2020) <https://innovationorigins.com/en/autonomous-robots-check-patients-in-at-belgium-hospitals/>; 'South Western Sydney Local Health District Media Release: Transforming the Hospital Experience with a Friendly Robot', *NSW Government: South Western Sydney Local Health District* (Web Page, 11 March 2020) <https://www.swslhd.health.nsw.gov.au/mediacentre/mediareleases/2020/200211a.pdf>.

requires identifying the maximum level at which it could function.[2] Instead, the analysis is likely to only narrow the scope of liability so that the legal personhood status of the robot is reflective of the functional capacity in the context in which a liability issue arises, the result being that the robot may have the maximum potential to be classified at a particular level, such as Level 4 (human-like intelligence) but, following the analysis at Phases 2 and 3, is revealed to be deployed in such a way that it can be viewed at a lower level, such as Level 3 (higher-level mentalities). The advantage of this approach is that it acknowledges that AI systems can act in different capacities in different contexts (which I explore further in Section 8.6.2).

A secondary observation can therefore be made about how AI is *situationally characterised*. Such a situational characterisation works in tandem with my analysis in Part II of this book to address the question of how AI is legally characterised. It provides a flexible conclusion to the question originally posed in Part II: how should AI be legally characterised? This approach recognises that AI is ultimately characterised based on the situation in which it is deployed. Equally, it acknowledges that whilst an AI system may be characterised at one level on a given occasion, the consequence is that it is *not always* necessarily characterised in that manner. In another context, depending on the analysis in response to Phase 2, the AI system could indeed be characterised in line with the *maximum potential capacity* of the AI system or systems. This is not a new phenomenon in law; if we consider natural persons, they have at times been characterised as individual actors, agents and even – unfortunately – property. How AI is characterised, I consider, is therefore a relative concept and, as such, consideration can be given to identifying the *functional legal personhood status* of an AI system.

8.3.4 Overall Function of Phase 1

Ultimately, the role of Phase 1 is to identify the maximum capabilities of an AI system, or unit of AI systems,[3] in a legal scenario. It may be that the AI in question is being deployed at a lesser capacity (as I explore in later phases). Identifying the maximum potential status, however, is an imperative first step, for it ensures that the potential capacity of an AI system under consideration is fully examined. This is important, as the potential capacity of an AI system informs the issues under consideration in Phase 2, which I discuss next.

2 A query could be raised whether identifying the maximum potential legal personhood status should also apply to animals. Animals are not, individually, as legally adaptable as AI. Whilst there are variances in the capacities of animals and therefore the individual level of legal personality they could attain, they are not like AI in that it has the potential to adapt its functionality and legal capacity dependent upon the context in which is it deployed.

3 For ease of reference, in the remaining discussion of the phases within the *Tri-Phase AI Liability Model*, I use the term 'AI system' but note per the discussion in this chapter in Section 8.3.2 that this term could represent either an AI system or a unit of AI systems.

8.4. Phase 2: Liability Threshold Issues

After identifying the maximum potential legal personhood status of an AI system in Phase 1, Phase 2 then begins to narrow the scope of liability from the maximum potential, taking into consideration the specific situation in which a legal problem arises in connection to an AI system. In Phase 2, as part of narrowing the scope of liability, the aim is to address three factors: the causal capacity of the AI system, how AI has been deployed in context and who has influence and control over the AI system. The goal is to reach an informed view about how the AI system has been deployed in the context of the legal situation under consideration. Phase 2 is therefore divided into three subphases, which I denote as 2A, 2B and 2C. I turn now to explore these subphases as they relate to the *Tri-Phase AI Liability Model.*

8.4.1 Subphase 2A: Causation Threshold Issue

To commence narrowing the scope of liability, I propose beginning with the issue of causation in Phase 2, rather than the other threshold issues in 2B or 2C. It is essential to first test if the AI system under consideration is at least capable of causing a particular legal outcome. If the system is not capable of triggering a legal outcome, or the outcome is too remote, then consideration needs to be given to whether that outcome can be accounted for via alternative legal mechanisms (such as pursuing an alternative legal claim). The role of subphase 2A is to therefore identify the relevant causation approach to be adopted in response to a legal scenario involving AI.

In identifying the relevant causation approach, I propose drawing upon my considerations in Chapter 6, where I built upon the work of Yavar Bathaee, who proposed a four-quadrant approach to legal causation as it relates to AI. Here, it is useful to recall the four-quadrant-inspired vertical continuum of causation I proposed, which was depicted in *Figure 8.3* (from Chapter 6) and is represented once more here.

This continuum aligns two relational theories: the pyramid earlier with the second relational theory of the causation continuum I proposed in Chapter 6, represented as *Figure 8.4.*

My approach also integrates an objective standard into the causation scale at the higher levels. This standard correlates with the more complex forms of AI capable of an increased degree of autonomy and subject to less natural-person control over its actions – that is, AI systems at the higher end of the pyramid. Subphase 2A therefore begins to narrow the scope of liability by first identifying the relevant causation approach to be adopted in response to a legal scenario involving AI. Identifying the maximum potential legal personhood status in Phase 1 is an integral prerequisite to subphase 2A, for the level in the pyramid at which an AI system under consideration fits influences the potential causation response, as per my considerations in Chapter 6.

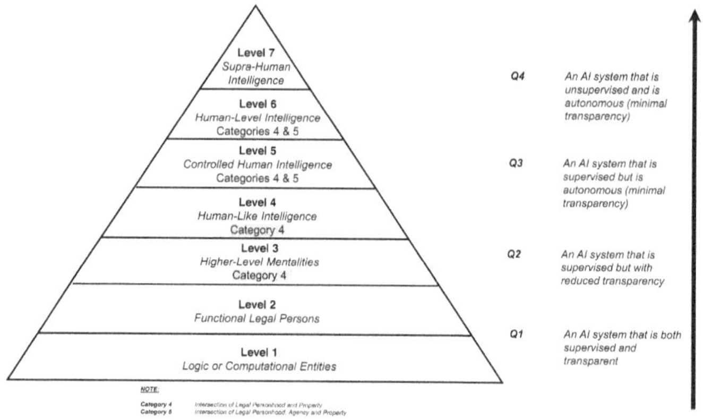

Figure 8.3 Four-Quadrant Continuum of Causation in Relation to Hierarchical Legal Personhood

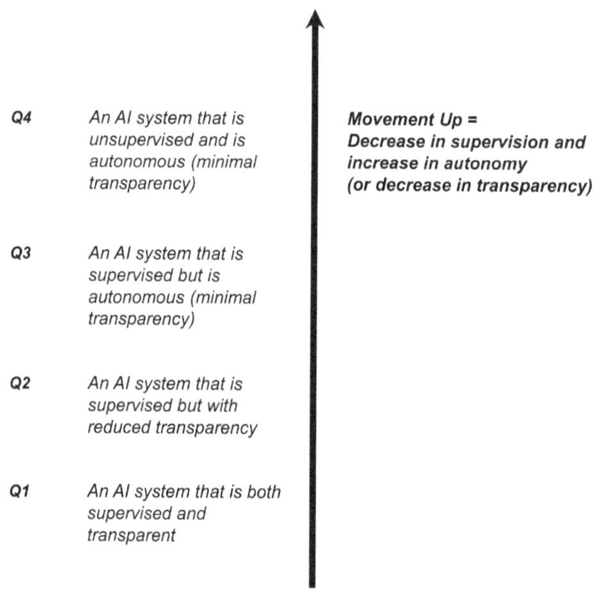

Figure 8.4 Hierarchical Four-Quadrant Continuum of Causation

An objection could be raised to beginning the process of narrowing liability by commencing with causation, as this is not the typical juncture at which causation is addressed;[4] however, such an objection overlooks the unique nature of modern AI. I do consider below that there is some flexibility in the order

4 In a common law jurisdiction, for example, the issue of causation is often addressed after preliminary aspects of a claim. Consider a negligence claim: if a duty of care is owed and whether

in which the subphases of Phase 2 could be addressed; I do not mandate that causation must be considered first. However, there is merit in considering causation in the initial stages of Phase 2 for, as I identified, if the AI system has not caused an outcome, then I propose consideration should be given to whether an alternative legal mechanism could be pursued.

What is key, though, is that Phase 2 narrows the scope of liability to reflect the situation in which an AI system is deployed. Causation as part of subphase 2A ought to be assessed relative to the maximum potential capacity of the AI system. Subphases 2B and 2C, as I discuss below, further narrow the scope of liability to that which is applicable to the situation in which an AI system is deployed.

8.4.2 Subphase 2B: Context and Scope Threshold Issue

The second part of Phase 2 further narrows the scope of liability from the maximum potential to that which is reflective of the situation in which AI is deployed in a given scenario. Subphase 2B works in conjunction with 2A and 2C to define the parameters of liability. In Chapter 7, I considered that it is insufficient to view AI in a vacuum; rather, consideration needs to be given to the context in which the AI system is deployed and the scope of the AI system's actions within this context.

After identifying the maximum potential capacity of an AI system in Phase 1, some deliberation should be given to the context in which the AI system is acting and the scope of its legal relationship with actors in the given scenario. The key objective for Subphase 2B is to consider the context in which an AI system is deployed and what areas of private law this is likely to trigger (tort, contract or otherwise). As considered in Chapter 7, the context determines the substantive law areas engaged by an AI system's deployment, which in turn assists in narrowing the scope of liability to what is relevant to a given scenario. Additional consideration should be given to the parameters applied to an AI system or the scope of its actions, as this too assists in narrowing the scope of liability (for the reasons outlined in Chapter 7).

8.4.3 Subphase 2C: Who Could Be Legally Liable? Threshold Issue

In narrowing the scope of liability so that it is reflective of the situation in which AI is deployed, I have proposed considering several threshold issues as part of this process. Subphase 2A considers the threshold issue of causation, and subphase 2B considers the additional issues of viewing AI in context, together with considering the scope of an AI system's actions. The next aspect

such a duty has been breached are typically considered before the issue of whether a breach caused harm suffered.

of Phase 2 is to further narrow liability through identifying who could be liable in a situation involving the use of AI.

It is important to note that subphase 2C should also be considered in light of the context in which an AI system is deployed. As I explored in Chapter 7, the question of 'who' is not as simple as merely identifying who either created the AI system or who was using the AI system at the time a legal incident arose. Rather, the question becomes one based on the degree of influence and control. Who had the most influence over the situation in question? Who was most likely to control the situation such that the outcome generated arose? Consider the 'Custom AI Workstream Example' mentioned earlier. Answering the questions about control and influence in response to this example will depend on a variety of factors. Factors such as: where in the organisation the custom AI system was deployed, what tasks it was deployed to achieve, what level of human oversight was exercised in relation to the AI system, etc. If these factors yield answers to the questions of control and influence that do not favour a natural person or a legal person other than AI, then this gives rise to the possibility of the AI system itself being held liable. The mechanics of how liability would be assigned to the person identified – natural person or legal person, including the possibility of AI – is not addressed until Phase 3. I explore below that even if AI itself is liable, it does not necessarily follow that the AI system should be financially responsible. It is useful to establish which actor is liable in a scenario to best represent a liable situation. For now, subphase 2C is designed to identify the most likely candidate for assigning liability.

8.4.4 Unifying Phase 2

The three subphases each work to address a preliminary threshold issue that I contend ought to be addressed as part of the process of assigning liability. Subphase 2A requires identifying the maximum potential of an AI system, relative to the *Hierarchical Legal Personality* model, and asking if that system in its maximum capacity is at least capable of causing the legal outcome under consideration. Subphase 2B builds upon 2A and examines the AI system in context to narrow the scope of liability further. Subphase 2C unites the analysis from 2A and 2B and considers, in the context in which the AI system has been deployed, who has the most influence in the legal situation and who is most likely to have a connection to the outcome generated.

I have offered a view where these subphases are considered in a specific order – 2A, 2B then 2C – with each subphase building upon the other. Nevertheless, I am not so committed to the idea that the questions addressed in these subphases ought to always be considered in order. If the context in which an AI system is deployed gives rise to the need to consider the subphases in an alternative order, I am open to the possibility of doing so should it assist in achieving the end goal of assigning liability. I view the individual elements – or subphases – of Phase 2 as collaborating with each other to inform

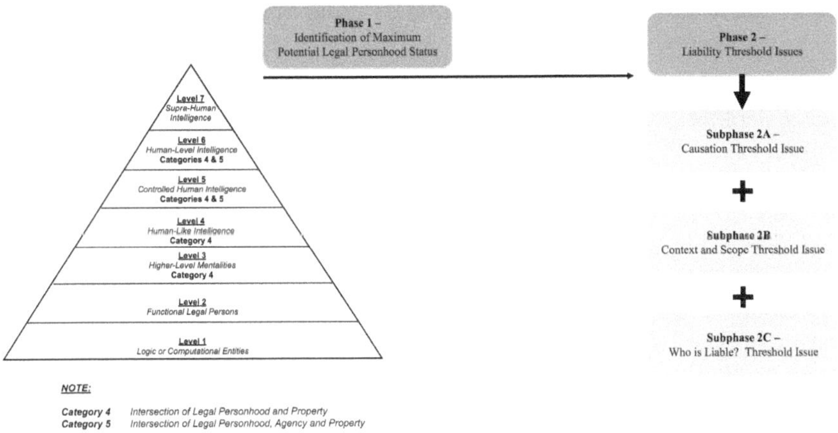

Figure 8.5 Assigning Liability – Phases 1 and 2

a legal analysis of a situation involving AI. If reordering the subphases on a case-by-case basis better achieves the end objective, then I am not opposed to doing so. The central goal of Phase 2, however, is to rely upon the subphases to reach an overarching conclusion that accounts for, in context: (a) the causal capacity of the AI system, (b) how the AI system has been deployed and (c) who has the most influence and control over that system.

With regard to the above, I pause here to introduce *Figure 8.5*, which denotes a visual representation of Phases 1 and 2.

From the diagram, it becomes apparent that assigning liability is an integrated process. It is insufficient to simply presume that AI is but one legal entity. Rather, in relation to the actual capacity of an AI system, it needs to be viewed situationally – that is, with regard to how and by whom the AI system is being deployed. Phases 1 and 2 alone are insufficient in resolving the issue of liability in the context of AI; instead, they work in concert with Phase 3 to achieve this end.

8.5. Phase 3: Drawing Together Phases 1 and 2 – Situational Approach to Deciding Liability for AI Systems Operating at Different Levels of Ability

After testing the maximum potential capacity in Phase 1 and then narrowing the scope of liability in Phase 2, Phase 3 determines the appropriate standard of liability to be applied in a scenario involving AI. Before I propose a method for identifying an appropriate standard, I think it is useful to recall the proposed legal responses to AI being deployed, as considered in Chapter 1. I therefore first elicit macro concepts from these approaches as they relate to standards of liability.

8.5.1 Current Proposed Legal Responses to AI Being Deployed and Liability Standards

In Chapter 1, I considered that the current proposed legal responses to AI being deployed could be divided into four broad groupings. I turn now to consider each of these groupings consecutively in terms of their liability standards. In doing so, I draw upon an overview of these approaches as summarised in *Table 8.1*.

The first of these four groupings is 'general principles'. Responses to the problem of AI in this grouping are conducive to fault-based forms of liability that assign the liable outcomes associated with AI to an individual actor. The next grouping is 'shared liability'. This grouping acknowledges the possibility of multiple actors in a situation involving AI and the need to potentially proportion liability between these actors. Shared liability, as the designation suggests, therefore relies upon standards of liability that share liability between actors, such as through concurrent or solidary liability.

The third grouping is 'imposed liability'. This grouping involves situations where, for policy reasons, a liability standard ought to be imposed or mandated in response to the use of AI. This grouping therefore utilises imposed forms of liability, such as vicarious or product liability. The last grouping is 'insurance-mandated liability'. The proposed solutions in this response utilise insurance regimes to respond to the legal uncertainty imposed by AI. This grouping arguably relies on a strict standard of liability.

Grouping the proposed legal responses to AI in this manner elucidates the view that there are not only multiple possible solutions but also that each of these solutions assigns liability via alternative mechanisms. The advantage of this comparison is it becomes clear that depending upon the situation in which AI is deployed, the standard of liability differs. It is therefore possible to conceive of a situational approach to AI liability standards – which, as I explore next, is the primary objective of Phase 3.

8.5.2 Situational Approach to Liability Standard

The role of Phase 3 is to offer a situational approach to determining the liability standard for AI. Drawing upon the considerations in Section 8.5.1, it is apparent that there exists a spectrum of liability standards correlating with AI being deployed. I now propose a response for how these liability standards ought to be integrated into my liability model. In doing so, I rely upon the *Hierarchical Legal Personality* model I proposed in Chapter 5. In *Table 8.2* I provide an overview of my considerations regarding liability standards relative to the *Hierarchical Legal Personality* model.

I begin at the pinnacle of the pyramid with Level 7 (supra-human intelligence). Recall that this level of legal personhood attempts to accommodate

Table 8.1 Standards of Liability and Current Proposed Legal Responses to AI

	General Principles (Tort or Contract)				*Shared Liability*		*Imposed Liability*			*Insurance-Mandated Liability*		
Approach	Negligence-based response	Non-delegable duty with contract (potentially supplemented by insurance)	Adaptations to existing obligation laws*	Amendments to existing burdens of proof	Association risk and enterprise liability	Tiered product liability	Autonomy risk and vicarious liability	Digital Peculium [backed by insurance]	Harmonised strict liability[and mandatory insurance]	Legal personhood with insurance	Interconnectivity risk and collective fund liability	Liability managed through insurance schemes
Liability Standard	**Fault-based or Contractual** ***Theorists propose strict liability for personal injury of death**				**Concurrent or Solidary**		**Vicarious or Product**			**Strict**		

Table 8.2 Liability Standards Relative to Hierarchical Legal Personhood Model

Level in Hierarchical Model of Legal Personhood	*Proposed Liability Standard*
Level 7 – *Supra-Human Intelligence*	Strict liability backed by insurance
Level 6 – *Human-Level Intelligence*	
Level 5 – *Controlled Human Intelligence*	Vicarious liability, or shared liability backed by insurance
Level 4 – *Human-Like Intelligence*	Shared liability, or fault-based or contractual liability
Level 3 – *Higher-Level Mentalities*	Product liability, shared liability, or fault-based or contractual liability
Level 2 – *Functional Legal Persons*	
Level 1 – *Logic or Computational Entities*	

possible future forms of AI.[5] It provides a theoretical 'placeholder' for forms of AI that might at some point have the capacity to surpass a human level of intelligence. I proactively considered the possibility of such a form of AI to provide a robust legal model with scope for future technological advancements. Similarly, I proposed that the tier below the pinnacle of the pyramid, Level 6 (human-level intelligence), ought to accommodate forms of AI that might at a future point in time achieve a level of intelligence equal to that of a human actor. I considered that Level 6 entities, unlike entities at Level 7, could still be subject to some degree of control (I considered how natural persons consentingly enter relationships based on control structures, such as in the workforce). I outlined that Level 6 entities would be forms of AI that, if realised, would have the same legal capacity as a natural-person actor. Despite having this legal capacity, I propose that Level 6 should have the same liability standard as Level 7 and not the same standard that would be applied to natural persons (such as the vicarious liability standards for Level 5). This is because both Levels 7 and 6 are somewhat futuristic and should be approached with caution in the event they are realised. For this reason, they should be held to a more stringent liability standard. Despite this a robust model addressing AI should accommodate possible future forms of AI due to the potential for serious consequences. For these systems I propose a strict liability backed by insurance. This standard would also promote responsible design of these AI systems. Without an accompanying insurance regime, it would be hard to achieve payment for damages in response to a negative engagement with Level 7 and 6 AI entities. I consider the parameters surrounding such an insurance

5 See Chapter 5 for an in-depth discussion of Level 7. I do not intend to suggest here that AI will ever reason like a human – it cannot – but it could reason in such a way that it could solve problems at levels similar to or above that of a human.

regime in Section 8.6.1.4. For now, what is key is that, in response to Levels 7 and 6, a strict liability standard backed by insurance ought to be imposed.

Moving further down the hierarchical model, I now turn to Level 5, 'controlled human intelligence'. In Chapter 5, I proposed that such a level consists of AI entities with a qualified legal capacity. That is, Level 5 entities are capable of bearing both rights and obligations but not to the same extent as Level 6 (human-level intelligence), which is representative of entities with a capacity akin to that of a natural person. Level 5 entities are the first level in which AI entities have the capacity to create obligations and not rights alone. This is due to Level 5 entities having the capacity to act autonomously – but this autonomy is limited, and it may only be exercised within defined parameters. Level 5 entities are not truly free actors, as their autonomy is usually constrained by parameters set by other actors. Given this, Level 5 entities ought to be subject to a vicarious liability standard or a shared form of liability (concurrent or solidary) that is backed by insurance. In terms of vicarious liability, where an actor other than another AI system (for I considered in Chapter 7 that it is possible to conceive of multiple AI actors working in concert) sets the parameters narrowing an AI system's autonomy, this actor defining the parameters ought to be vicariously liable for the actions of that AI system.

If it is not possible to fully assign liability vicariously to a natural or non-AI legal person, such as a corporation, then I propose the liability standard ought to be a shared standard that is backed by insurance. This latter element arises in instances where an AI system's parameters may be set by not just a legal person capable of being held to account but a secondary AI system. That is, a primary AI system working with a legal person may narrow the parameters of a secondary AI system. In this instance, rather than assigning liability to the legal person alone via vicarious liability, I propose that liability ought to be shared by the primary AI system and the legal person capable of being held to account; additionally, this liability ought to be backed by an insurance regime to compensate for any potential damages for which the AI system is liable. The advantage of this proposal is that it acknowledges that Level 5 entities are capable of being controlled, even if they have some degree of autonomy. As such, liability for their control ought to lie with the actors shaping the parameters in which the AI system acts.

I now move my focus to the next tier below: Level 4 (human-like intelligence). Recall from Chapter 5 that entities at this level can hold and exert rights but are not necessarily also capable of maintaining legal obligations or duties. That is, actors at this level have the legal capacity to not only hold rights but to have their interests exerted on their behalf in relation to those rights (recall the case of Tommy the Chimpanzee in Chapter 5). Yet, at the same time, AI systems at Level 4 are capable of being controlled by other actors. Given these limitations on Level 4 entities, I propose that liability be addressed at this level using either shared liability approaches (concurrent, solidary) or fault-based liability. Shared liability would arise in instances where there are multiple actors who have control over the AI system and are responsible for any duties that may arise in a situation pertaining to a Level 4 entity. Similarly, as Level 4 entities are subject to a higher degree of control than Levels 5–7 and are not capable of bearing obligations, only rights, this enables the possibility of fault-based or contractual forms of liability, depending on the context in which the AI system is deployed. That is, tortious liability could arise if the AI system triggers a torts-based response, or contractual liability could be triggered if the AI system involves a contractual scenario. I consider the circumstances surrounding when shared liability is favoured over a fault-based or contractual response (or vice versa) in Section 8.5.3.

Finally, I turn to the remaining levels of my hierarchical legal personhood model, Levels 1–3, and their correlating standards of liability. I do not re-explore the entities at Levels 1–3 in depth here. The key differentiating point between entities at these levels and Level 4 is that there is a marked increase in the ability for natural persons to exert control over them. Additionally, Level 1–3 entities are more likely to be deployed as property or have a greater focus on their proprietary nature. Given this, in addition to the liability standards I proposed for Level 4, I introduce the possibility that Level 1–3 entities could also be subject to the standard of product liability. As these entities exhibit a greater degree of proprietary characteristics and less cognitive independence, they are more likely to be viewed as a product than an entity capable of independent legal actions.

8.5.3 Link Between Phase 3 and Phase 2

I outlined above the varying standards of liability and how these relate to the *Hierarchical Legal Personality* model from Part II. To offer a robust model concerning how to assign liability in the context of AI, I now turn to consider the relationship between Phase 2 and Phase 3 of the model. In doing so, I draw upon *Figure 8.6.*

The role of Phase 2 is to provide a situational assessment of how AI is being deployed in a given context, relative to its maximum potential capacity, and to narrow the scope of liability. This is an imperative preceding step to Phase 3, as it ultimately informs the analysis arising from Phase 3, which moves to consider to what standard liability should be imposed considering the outcomes of Phase 2. That is, Phase 2 considers how the AI system is being deployed situationally and what other actors are involved in the scenario, which in turn influences how the AI system is legally characterised in response to a given consideration. Additionally, as I outlined, some levels may warrant alternative liability standards, such as shared liability, fault-based liability or contractual liability. The outcomes or determinations from Phase 2 will influence the decision as to which alternative liability standard is applicable to a given situation involving AI.

Once a standard has been determined as the most applicable legal response, the approaches outlined in Section 8.5.2 should be used as a theoretical

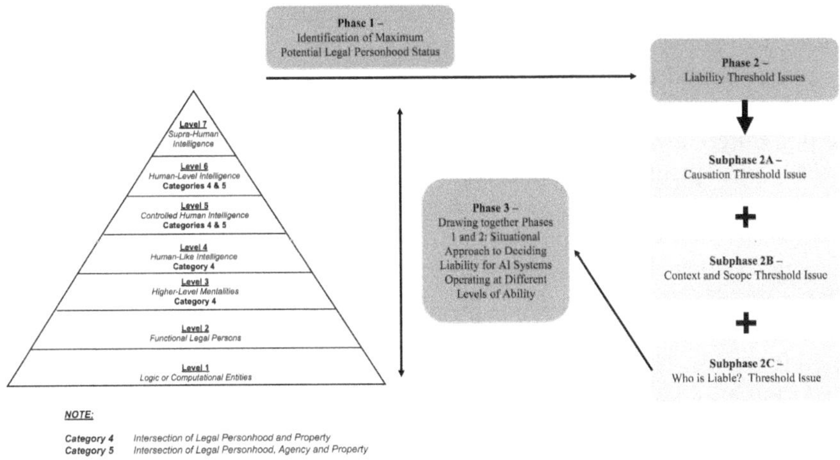

Figure 8.6 Assigning Liability – Phases 1, 2 and 3

starting point for how the standard ought to be applied in response to a given legal scenario. For example, if the analysis from Phase 2 yields that an AI system is being deployed in a tortious context and that the AI system is bearing rights but is not also subject to legal obligations, this means the system is *behaving* like a Level 4 AI entity and therefore could be held to a shared liability, fault-based liability or contractual liability standard. As the system is behaving in a tortious context, it should be held to a fault-based liability standard, which (for now) could be informed by the works of tortious-favouring authors.[6] Phase 3 therefore serves as the final threshold to assigning liability and is ultimately informed by the analysis in response to Phases 1 and 2.

8.6. Evaluation of the Tri-Phase AI Liability Model

Having outlined the *Tri-Phase AI Liability Model*, I will now evaluate its merits. I first raise some anticipated objections to the framework before turning to consider the advantages of my proposed model.

8.6.1 Anticipated Objections to the Tri-Phase AI Liability Model

8.6.1.1 Overly Complex

An initial response to the model I have proposed may be that it seems, at first look, to be overly complex. For example, one possible response could be, why start with Phase 1, and why not commence at Phase 2? Phase 1 is

6 For an example of tortious favouring authors see: Ryan Abbott, *The Reasonable Robot: Artificial Intelligence and the Law* (Cambridge University Press, 2020).

needed in advance of Phase 2 in order to identify the maximum potential capacity of an AI system, as this then informs Phase 2. To reduce the number of phases would be to overlook the complexity of AI itself. As I explored in Part I, AI ought not be uniformly characterised but, rather, can be characterised differently depending on the type of AI and the context in which it is used. Consequently, AI ought not be conceived of as uniformly adhering to liability rules but, rather, as necessitating a flexible framework through which to discern liability pertaining to AI. Given the varying permutations of AI, it is imperative to construct a liability response that is accommodating to the different situations involving AI. It is also for this reason that AI cannot simply always be viewed as property and subject to only a tort-based or product liability framework. The model needs to accommodate not only the varying types of AI but also how it is characterised and the situation in which it is deployed, together with the key actors involved in a legal scenario concerning AI. There needs to be flexibility to accommodate that sometimes AI could simply be viewed through a property-based lens, for example, yet at other times, as outlined in Part I, this is insufficient, and other liability responses are required. To create a model with sufficient flexibility to accommodate these variations necessitates a degree of complexity. Despite this, I have optimised the macro approach to determining liability through a reliance on three primary phases to guide a legal analysis in response to AI.

8.6.1.2 Use of Disclaimers/Exclusion Clauses as an Alternative

One possible proposal as an alternative to my model is to merely rely upon the use of disclaimers or exclusion clauses.[7] Such an approach, however, is not without its limitations. Disclaimers serve as a valuable tool in reducing the scope of liability. I do not intend to disregard the use of disclaimers outright; indeed, I am of the view that in the context of AI, if properly relied upon, disclaimers serve an integral role in the process of assigning (or not assigning) liability. Indeed, I envisage that their use could fit within Subphase 2B of my model – examining the context and scope in which AI is used. I do, however, object to the suggestion that disclaimers ought to replace the establishment of a liability framework or that the use of disclaimers negates the need for more formalised liability considerations in relation to AI.

Firstly, for a disclaimer to adequately manage or reduce liability, it must be drafted in a sufficient manner to account for the harm that the disclaimer is either attempting to avoid the consequences of or reduce the consequences. This requires an adequate understanding of the likely outcomes an AI device could impose, which is not always possible in response to modern forms of

7 For an example of the use of a disclaimer in the context of AI, consider the home page of ChatGPT, which provides an overview of the system's limitations and capabilities together with providing examples. See: 'Chat GPT', *Open AI* (Web Page) <https://chat.openai.com/>.

AI. Some forms of AI are designed to act independently and reach ends not always reasonably foreseeable to natural-person actors. The alternative is to simply draft broad and generalist disclaimers, which may encapsulate unforeseeable harm but are not always permitted. Consider, for example, a generalist approach in Australia. The use of disclaimers, or exclusion clauses, is largely regulated by generalist contract or tortious principles, or consumer protection law. Under statute, there are restrictions regarding when and to what extent exclusion clauses can apply in relation to consumer statutory rights and provisions.[8] Additionally, there are constraints concerning the use of exclusion clauses in contracts.[9] In this respect, exclusion clauses or disclaimers are limited in their application due to public-policy reasons. Although not without their merit and use in certain circumstances, disclaimers or exclusion clauses alone are insufficient to serve as a robust liability response to AI.

8.6.1.3 Liability Shield

My proposed model largely relies upon viewing AI as a type of legal person. As explored in Chapter 1, other authors address liability using legal personhood and have raised the possible concern that legal personhood could potentially serve as a liability shield to be used by natural persons to obfuscate or avoid liability.[10] In response an analogy is drawn with corporate legal personality, where the corporate veil can be pierced in especially egregious situations, and assign legal liability to the persons behind a corporation.[11] This proposes a useful analogy for situations where legal personhood mirrors that of corporate legal personality. I note, however, that my approach to legal personality is adaptable and includes other theoretical approaches to legal personality, such as the models based on rights – the legal personhood recognition of rivers – and models based on property, such as the slavery example that I explored in Part II. I have therefore adopted an expansive approach to legal personality. Additionally, I have reduced the possibility of legal personality being used as a shield by imposing strict liability in instances that might yield the temptation to rely on legal personality as a shield. Another advantage of this approach is that when it is coupled with possible insurance regimes, this raises the possibility of not needing to ensure that an AI entity holds funds or assets.

8 *Competition and Consumer Act 2010* (Cth) Sch 2, ss64, 64A.

9 For examples of constraints concerning the use of exclusion clauses in contracts, see: *Oceanic Sun Line Special Shipping Company Inc v Fay* (1988) 165 CLR 197 and *Australian National Railways Commission v Ranger Uranium Mines Pty Ltd* (1989) 51 SASR 475.

10 Jacob Turner, *Robot Rules: Regulating Artificial Intelligence* (Palgrave Macmillan, 2019) 191.

11 Jacob Turner, *Robot Rules: Regulating Artificial Intelligence* (Palgrave Macmillan, 2019) 191.

8.6.1.4 Relying on Insurance

Objections may be raised regarding the reliance on insurance in a liability model; however, as I explore, I do not view this as being a reason to outright discard the role of insurance. One possible objection to the use of insurance that has been identified in relevant literature, is that insurers can attempt to moderate the behaviour of the insured by imposing requirements on them to minimise the likelihood of harm arising.[12] This could have an inadvertent regulatory effect on the use of AI. If liability was to be managed broadly by insurance regimes, the secondary regulatory effect of insurers seeking to minimise their risks could have a chilling impact on the use of AI. Instead, I am not proposing that insurance be mandated for all uses of AI. Rather, I argue that mandated insurance ought to be confined to the more sophisticated forms of AI – Levels 5 to 7 – where a secondary regulatory impact would be beneficial and even potentially limit the use of these forms of AI until they can be better understood. As the literature highlights, insurance does have the advantage of providing a partial solution in instances of uncertainty.[13] The higher levels of my model, where I propose to utilise insurance, are the forms of AI more likely to pose uncertainty.

There are other objections to the use of insurance, such as that it does not negate the underlying liability but is, rather, a redirection of which party is financially responsible for harm involving AI.[14] I do not necessarily view this as a problem but rather as an astute observation about the effect insurance has in shifting the financial responsibility for harm occurred. There is, however, an additional observation that it can be hard to entice insurers to enter the market and insure scenarios if they do not perceive the situation as offering the potential for financial gain.[15] One of the likely issues with insurers failing to enter a market is a degree of uncertainty pertaining to the level of risk associated with that market. If potentially more volatile forms of AI cannot be used without insurance, the secondary effect of this is to encourage increased certainty in the design of AI systems so that they would be insurable. I do not intend to expand further on this aspect at this juncture, as it raises predominantly regulatory issues, which I consider together with issues relating to insurance in Chapter 9. I do consider, however, that if insurance is mandated and an insurance company does not insure an AI system, then the practical effect of this is that the AI system ought not be used and therefore would not give rise to a liability scenario. On this basis, the requirement of insurance is still not incompatible with a liability framework.

12 Jacob Turner, *Robot Rules: Regulating Artificial Intelligence* (Palgrave Macmillan, 2019) 115–116.

13 Jacob Turner, *Robot Rules: Regulating Artificial Intelligence* (Palgrave Macmillan, 2019) 115.

14 Jacob Turner, *Robot Rules: Regulating Artificial Intelligence* (Palgrave Macmillan, 2019) 116.

15 Jacob Turner, *Robot Rules: Regulating Artificial Intelligence* (Palgrave Macmillan, 2019) 116–117.

Another possible argument against incorporating mandatory insurance into my model is that it shifts the burdens associated with AI away from producers, owners or users of AI to society more broadly; yet this assumes that there must be but one predetermined form of applicable insurance. Again, I am not proposing that insurance be imposed for *all forms* of AI; rather, it should be imposed only on the more complicated forms of AI that arguably pose a higher risk to society, such as those at Levels 5 to 7. Also, as to whether this shifts the burden to society more broadly, this would depend on the exact insurance scheme imposed and whether the insurance was to be borne by society, like some road registration fees, which have third-party liability insurance embedded into the cost of registration. If the insurance is an extra requirement, perhaps it must be privately borne by those engaging with these sophisticated forms of AI. Indeed, one possible regulatory approach could be to incorporate a means-test into an insurance scheme subsidised by government so that more disadvantaged members of society are not negatively impacted by the requirement of insurance. These are all regulatory considerations, and I address the regulatory landscape further in Chapter 9. What is key though is that requiring insurance for *some* more complicated forms of AI does not automatically create injustice within society, depending on how this requirement of insurance is implemented.

Lastly, an argument could be made that an insurance-based approach is overly technocratic. However, this depends on the regulatory structures used to support the insurance framework. One possible objection to relying on insurance concerns who is responsible for deciding whether to insure certain AI systems and who is responsible for determining if an insurance claim ought to be paid. One possible solution to managing this requirement is the fund-liability approach espoused by Beckers and Teubner, as considered in Chapter 1. Their proposal requires the establishment of a compensation fund and a correlating regulatory body to administer the fund and respond to claims. This is but one proposal that could be relied upon to respond to the technocratic response to insurance. What this proposal is indicative of, however, is that this is best managed through regulatory responses. The role of regulation as it interacts with my proposed model is a topic I consider in Part IV. I therefore do not elaborate further on responding to the technocratic argument, at this juncture, save to argue that it is an issue connected to liability but one that is best managed through a supporting regulatory response.

8.6.2 Advantages of the Tri-Phase AI Liability Model

Central to my proposal is the concept of adaptability. Many proposed legal frameworks seeking to manage a liability response to AI assume that AI is single-faceted and can always be deployed or used in the same manner. This is fundamentally flawed. As I explored in the *Introduction*, there are varying types of AI systems, each capable of different degrees of independence. Additionally, as I addressed in Part II, there are alternatives as to how an AI system could be characterised. A robust liability response to AI therefore needs to be adaptable to accommodate the differing legal scenarios potentially posed by AI. A key advantage of my three-phase model is that it offers flexibility in response to each of the threshold issues required to ultimately assign liability. This approach incorporates consideration of the issue of how AI should be characterised and then views the technology situationally to reach a liability response that is reflective of the legal nature of AI in a given scenario but also robust enough to accommodate that AI may not always exhibit the same legal characteristics in a given scenario.

8.7. Reconceiving Liability as a Flexible Paradigm

The above analysis is an accumulative consideration of the preliminary threshold issues raised in the preceding chapters. Part II, combined with the preliminary chapters in Part III, explores issues that ought to be addressed as part of the process of assigning liability in the context of modern forms of AI. Part II addressed the issue of how AI ought to be legally characterised, resulting in the proposed *Hierarchical Legal Personality* model. Chapter 6 considered the issue of causation, and Chapter 7 focused on two key aspects: the context in which AI is deployed and the issue of who could be held liable. Individually, none of these threshold issues offers a solution to how liability ought to be assigned in the context of AI.

I consider that the value of the threshold issues lies in their collective ability to inform a liability response to AI. Other models of liability, as explored, hold value but are narrow in their scope. They assume AI is fixed and not flexible in its nature, when AI can be flexible in terms of both its development and its ability to adjust to a situation. Drawing upon my previous considerations, I have therefore offered a new three-phase theoretical model, the *Tri-Phase AI Liability Model,* to assign legal liability in response to AI. This three-phase model firstly, in Phase 1, considers the maximum potential of an AI system relative to the *Hierarchical Legal Personality* model derived from Part II. This includes considering that AI can, at times, be characterised differently depending on how it is deployed and offering that how liability is assigned in response to AI informs the AI system's characterisation in context. This, I deem, is the AI system's *functional* legal personhood status. In Phase 2, I then proposed the need to address the additional threshold issues explored in Chapters 6 and 7, which are required to be resolved as part of the process of assigning liability. I then turned to consider in Phase 3 how Phases 1 and 2, when drawn together, can offer a situational approach to deciding liability for AI systems operating at different levels of ability.

These phases of my model accumulatively draw on my preceding conclusions to offer a new, more adaptive liability approach for AI. A robust model of liability as it relates to AI needs to accommodate that different AI systems have different functionalities and capacities; additionally, it must consider that this in turn can influence the outcome of the threshold issues required to be addressed to assign liability. In terms of AI, liability cannot adequately be addressed if it is framed in binary terms. A more nuanced approach is required – one that acknowledges the strengths of existing proposals but offers a flexible approach in response to AI. The *Tri-Phase AI Liability Model* does this by ultimately proposing that in responding to AI, liability must be viewed *situationally*.

References

A Articles/Books/Reports

Abbott, Ryan, *The Reasonable Robot: Artificial Intelligence and the Law* (Cambridge University Press, 2020).

Turner, Jacob, *Robot Rules: Regulating Artificial Intelligence* (Palgrave Macmillan, 2019).

B Cases

Australian National Railways Commission v Ranger Uranium Mines Pty Ltd (1989) 51 SASR 475

Oceanic Sun Line Special Shipping Company Inc v Fay (1988) 165 CLR 197

C Legislation

Competition and Consumer Act 2010 (Cth)

D Other

'Chat GPT', *Open AI* (Web Page) <https://chat.openai.com/>

'South Western Sydney Local Health District Media Release: Transforming the Hospital Experience with a Friendly Robot', *NSW Government: South Western Sydney Local Health District* (Web Page, 11 March 2020) <https://www.swslhd.health.nsw.gov.au/mediacentre/mediareleases/2020/200211a.pdf>

Murphy, Annabel, 'Autonomous Robots Check Patients in at Belgium Hospitals', *Innovation Origins* (Web Page, 1 July 2020) <https://innovationorigins.com/en/autonomous-robots-check-patients-in-at-belgium-hospitals/>

Part IV

9 Model in Application

Adapting Theory to Practice

9.1. Theory Informing Practice

Until this juncture, my objective has been to build towards offering a model to manage the private law liability implications associated with AI. In practice, however, private law liability responses do not exist in a vacuum. Instead, they exist in conjunction with regulatory measures used to manage legal outcomes in society. Consider for example, the emerging role of AI in the insurance market. AI in this sector offers the potential for new efficiencies in routine insurance processes such as the calculation of premiums, claim evaluations and, when combined with distributed ledger technologies, the formation and execution of insurance contracts.[1] If AI were errantly deployed in these insurance contexts, this could give rise to a private law liability between the insured and the insurer. Such a deployment however would not negate that the insurer would still be required to adhere to relevant insurance regulations[2] and potentially also incur a public law liability under these regimes. For the *Tri-Phase AI Liability Model* to hold practical utility, there exists a need to understand its relationship with the AI regulatory landscape.

This chapter therefore explores the practical implications arising from *Tri-Phase AI Liability Model* through seeking to adapt the model to a practical context with a particular emphasis on how the model relates to possible regulatory responses to AI. In doing so, the chapter first seeks to situate the Model relative to regulatory measures for AI. The goal is not to offer a view as to how AI ought to be regulated but rather to explore how regulatory measures may complement a private law response to AI. It is worth pausing to also acknowledge that a breach of a regulatory response can give rise to a legal liability. It is considered that a liability in this context would be a *public* law response arising from a breach of a regulation governing society's interactions with AI.

1 Angelo Borselli, 'Smart Contracts in Insurance: A Law and Futurology Perspective' in Pierpaolo Marano and Kyriaki Noussia (eds), *InsurTech: A Legal and Regulatory View* (Springer Nature, 2020) 101, 109.

2 For examples of relevant regulations applying to the insurance sector in Australia at least, see: *Insurance Act 1973* (Cth), *Insurance Contracts Act 1984* (Cth), *Corporations Act 2001*, ch 7.

DOI: 10.4324/9781003617549-14

The focus is instead on the *private* law liability implications from a deployed AI system. The chapter addresses the role of regulatory measures relative to the proposed *private* law liability response to AI. In doing so, consideration is given to common theories of regulation and how they might be adapted to AI. The chapter also looks at the regulatory implications of insurance before turning to address the divide between regulation and liability: when should a response to AI be managed through private law liability mechanisms or instead is best responded to through regulatory measures? Following this, the chapter turns to address key considerations for stakeholders in responding to the legal implications of AI. The benefit of this approach that it expands upon the liability considerations in previous parts and suggests how these could be complemented by regulatory measures.

9.2. The Tri-Phase AI Liability Model Relative to Regulatory Responses

Before addressing how the *Tri-Phase AI Liability Model* can be adapted to practical contexts, I first consider its position relative to regulatory measures applicable to AI. In doing so I consider both different types of regulation and the possible regulatory effects of insurance when deployed in an AI context.

9.2.1 Regulation Types Complementing the Tri-Phase AI Liability Model

I commence by considering the *types* of regulation potentially applicable to AI. In doing so, my objective is not to offer a view as to how AI ought to be regulated, but rather to consider a narrower issue, which is: what forms of regulation are likely to complement a private law liability response to AI? Understanding possible AI regulatory measures through this lens is important as neither liability nor regulatory responses ought to exist independent of each other. Rather, these responses ought to act as complementary mechanisms in resolving legal uncertainty arising from the deployment of AI.

9.2.1.1 Command and Control Regulation

The most traditional accepted form of regulation is arguably what is referred to as 'command and control' regulation. Command and control regulation seeks to regulate behaviour through setting rules or standards by which actors must comply.[3] This form of regulation seeks to enforce these standards through imposing consequences, typically in the form of civil or criminal penalties.[4]

3 Robert Baldwin, Martin Cave, and Martin Lodge, *Understanding Regulation: Theory, Strategy, and Practice* (Oxford University Press, 2nd ed., 2012) 106.
4 Robert Baldwin, Martin Cave, and Martin Lodge, *Understanding Regulation: Theory, Strategy, and Practice* (Oxford University Press, 2nd ed., 2012) 106.

The setting of standards might not necessarily be confined to the management of ongoing conduct but could also be directed at establishing requirements to be met before operation or before action is taken.[5] It is perhaps the latter of these roles served by the command and control form of regulation, viz. setting pre-operation requirements, that best complements a liability response to AI. For regulating the parameters in which an AI system can be deployed to begin with, before a legal liability even arises, works in conjunction with a private law liability response. This type of regulation seeks to narrow the scope of what is deemed a permissible form of AI and what is the appropriate context in which it is deployed.

There are two key examples of command and control regulations in relation to AI. One such example of this regulatory measure is the now revoked, 2023 US Presidential Executive Order 14110 regarding the *Safe, Secure, and Trustworthy Development and Use of Artificial Intelligence* (the 'Executive Order').[6] This Executive Order sought to address the safety and security of AI.[7] The initiative, for example, specifically provided for the introduction of AI guidelines to establish best practices in industry for AI safety and security.[8] It also imposed requirements on developers of dual-use AI pertaining to their development and testing.[9] The other, more noteworthy, example of command and control AI regulation is the European Union's Artificial Intelligence Act ('EU AI Act'), which imposes stringent parameters for the deployment of 'high risk' forms of AI. Consider Article 5, which specifically outlines 'prohibited AI practices' including conduct such as putting to market AI systems seeking to exploit vulnerabilities of individuals, such as disabilities.[10] Article 5 also prohibits AI systems that could be used to predict whether an individual is likely to engage in criminal behaviour.[11] There are also detailed consequences for failures to comply with the regulations imposed in this version of the EU AI Act.[12] Putting aside questions about whether a presidential executive order

5 Robert Baldwin, Martin Cave, and Martin Lodge, *Understanding Regulation: Theory, Strategy, and Practice* (Oxford University Press, 2nd ed., 2012) 106.

6 Exec. Order No. 14110, 3 C.F.R. 75191 (2023).

7 Exec. Order No. 14110, 3 C.F.R. 75191 (2023) [4.1].

8 Exec. Order No. 14110, 3 C.F.R. 75191 (2023) [4.1(i)].

9 Exec. Order No. 14110, 3 C.F.R. 75191 (2023) [4.2(a)].

10 *Regulation (EU) 2024/1689 of the European Parliament and of the Council of 13 June 2024 laying down harmonised rules on artificial intelligence and amending Regulations (EC) No 300/2008, (EU) No 167/2013, (EU) No 168/2013, (EU) 2018/858, (EU) 2018/1139 and (EU) 2019/2144 and Directives 2014/90/EU, (EU) 2016/797 and (EU) 2020/1828 (Artificial Intelligence Act)* [2024] OJ L 1689/1 (the 'EU AI Act'), art 5 (1)(b).

11 *Regulation (EU) 2024/1689 of the European Parliament and of the Council of 13 June 2024 laying down harmonised rules on artificial intelligence and amending Regulations (EC) No 300/2008, (EU) No 167/2013, (EU) No 168/2013, (EU) 2018/858, (EU) 2018/1139 and (EU) 2019/2144 and Directives 2014/90/EU, (EU) 2016/797 and (EU) 2020/1828 (Artificial Intelligence Act)* [2024] OJ L 1689/1 (the 'EU AI Act'), art 5 (1)(d).

12 For penalties associated with non-compliance see: the EU AI Act (n 10) art 99.

amounts to full legal regulation, what the now revoked Executive Order and the EU AI Act demonstrate is that there is at least an appetite for command and control style regulatory measures in response to AI.

9.2.1.2 Economic Instruments

An alternative to command and control regulation is to instead utilise economic instruments to manage behaviour connected to AI. If the command and control form of regulation is grounded in a notion of imposing consequences for non-compliance, economic instruments are the counter to this approach. Economic instruments seek to incentivise desired behaviour.[13] This form of regulation is therefore arguably more 'carrot' than 'stick' in seeking to manage desired outcomes. It is also viewed as being a 'lighter' form of regulation than command and control regulatory measures for it has been conceived of as requiring less of an administrative burden to implement and manage.[14] Economic instruments include the use of tax-based incentives, subsidies and tradeable permits.[15] Whilst it is still in the early phases of development, the United Kingdom has signalled it will adopt a pro-innovation approach to regulating AI, providing scope for businesses to be incentivised to use AI to solve problems.[16] The particulars of this approach in final form remain to be seen, but the express focus on allowing scope for innovation to incentivise business activities involving AI suggests that the resulting regulatory framework is likely to be compatible with the use of economic instruments to regulate AI.

The utility of economic instruments in complementing a private law liability response to AI lies in the notion that it seeks to foster positive conduct. If a liability response addresses legal uncertainties, or harms, associated with a deployed AI, then any measures seeking to encourage positive conduct are likely aimed at reducing the incidence of harms arising. The correlative effect being a potential reduction in the need to engage with liability measures, assuming compliance with the economic instruments. The relationship between an economic instrument and a liability response, however, will also depend on what economic instruments are relied upon and at what stage these interact with an AI system. If an economic instrument targets the design and development phase of an AI system, this is likely to have a different impact than if an instrument targets how an AI system is deployed. The juncture at which an economic instrument is directed will shape the context in which an AI system operates and any correlating harm arising. Context is essential to the *Tri-Phase AI Liability Model*[17] and therefore the intended effects of any

13 Anthony I. Ogus, *Regulation Legal Form and Economic Theory* (Hart Publishing, 2004) 245.
14 Baldwin (n 3) 112.
15 Ogus (n 13) 246–250; Baldwin (n 3) 114–120.
16 Department for Science, Innovation & Technology, *A Pro-Innovation Approach to AI Regulation* (CP 815, 2023) 19.
17 For a discussion of the role of context in the *Tri-Phase AI Liability Model* see: Chapter 7.

economic instrument, and whether these are reached should be considered as part of assessing the context in which an AI system has been deployed in a liability analysis.

9.2.1.3 Mandatory Disclosure

Mandatory disclosure is another form of regulation which potentially interacts with a private law liability response. This form of regulation consists of an imposed requirement on key actors – usually manufacturers – to proactively disclose key information or, at a minimum, to not engage in misleading or deceptive conduct.[18] In relation to AI, three key categories of disclosure mechanisms have been identified: institution-level, system-level and prediction-level.[19] Briefly, each of these categories denotes the different junctures at which information ought to be disclosed. The institution-level category, for example, denotes disclosure of information pertaining to how AI is used in an organisation together with their correlating procedures and practices for managing AI.[20] System-level disclosure forms of regulation require disclosure of information about how individual AI systems are developed, their uses and performance.[21] The prediction-level category is aimed at addressing outputs by AI systems and requiring disclosure about how these outputs are achieved.[22] There are therefore multiple options for regulating AI through the use of mandatory disclosure measures.

How such forms of mandatory disclosure might complement a liability response to AI depends on the types of information and when it is required to be disclosed. If information is required to be shared such that the disclosure occurs *before* an AI system is deployed, then an argument could be made that there is an element of voluntary assumption of risk associated with electing to deploy the AI system. This view is somewhat dependent upon the context in which an AI system is deployed, and the relative knowledge of parties involved – did they, for example not only have access to the disclosed information, but was the information *meaningfully* disclosed to the actors involved? By meaningfully, I mean to suggest that information disclosed must be understandable

18 Baldwin (n 3) 119.

19 Neel Guha et. al., 'AI Regulation Has Its Own Alignment Problem: The Technical and Institutional Feasibility of Disclosure, Registration, Licensing, and Auditing' (2024) 92 *George Washington Law Review* 1473, 1495–1496.

20 Neel Guha et. al., 'AI Regulation Has Its Own Alignment Problem: The Technical and Institutional Feasibility of Disclosure, Registration, Licensing, and Auditing' (2024) 92 *George Washington Law Review* 1473, 20.

21 Neel Guha et. al., 'AI Regulation Has Its Own Alignment Problem: The Technical and Institutional Feasibility of Disclosure, Registration, Licensing, and Auditing' (2024) 92 *George Washington Law Review* 1473, 20–21.

22 Neel Guha et. al., 'AI Regulation Has Its Own Alignment Problem: The Technical and Institutional Feasibility of Disclosure, Registration, Licensing, and Auditing' (2024) 92 *George Washington Law Review* 1473, 21.

to its intended recipients. A highly technical disclosure, for example, is of minimal utility to a non-technical audience if they lack the skills to comprehend the information. Institutional and system-level forms of mandatory disclose in the AI context are perhaps better aligned with an ex-ante disclosure of information relative to AI deployment. Regulating the practices and procedures surrounding managing AI (institution-level) and imposing disclosure requirements about the development process and potential uses of AI (system-level) allow individuals engaging with AI to make more informed decisions.

In contrast, disclosure requirements which pertain to how AI outputs are reached (prediction-level) are more likely to complement a liability response to AI. Mandatory disclosures which elucidate the reasoning process or mechanisms by which AI systems reach an output may be able to assist with increasing the transparency associated with an AI system. The presupposition to this view is that reasoning processes must be information capable of being disclosed, which is not always possible.[23] Assuming, however, that an explanation of an AI system's reasoning processes is capable of disclosure, this is significant in terms of being able to causally link an AI-induced outcome with an actor. Here is it worth recalling Bathaee's sliding scale of causation discussed in Chapter 6 and how this scale is linked to the degree of transparency associated with an AI system.[24] Under that approach, the more transparent an AI system the more readily its reasoning processes are determinable and subsequently the more likely a natural person is able to foresee the effects of engaging with such a system.

In Chapter 6 I therefore considered that the more transparent an AI system, the more likely a natural person could be held liable for the consequences of its outputs. If the role of prediction-level mandatory disclosure regulations is to increase the ability to explain AI-related outputs, this is then akin to increasing the degree of transparency associated with an AI system. In increasing the transparency of an AI system, this method of regulation therefore assists in shifting the causal response towards a lower position in the causation hierarchy I considered in *Figure 6.1*. Providing any information that is required to be disclosed under prediction-level mandatory disclosure is capable of being disclosed, and is not beyond being ascertainable, this form of regulation holds the most potential out of mandatory disclosure forms of regulation to complement a liability response to AI.

23 Neel Guha et. al., 'AI Regulation Has Its Own Alignment Problem: The Technical and Institutional Feasibility of Disclosure, Registration, Licensing, and Auditing' (2024) 92 *George Washington Law Review* 1473, 21–23.

24 Yavar Bathaee, 'The Artificial Intelligence Black Box and the Failure of Intent and Causation' (2018) 31(2) *Harvard Journal of Law & Technology* 889, 936–938.

9.2.1.4 Code-Based Regulation

One final alternative form of regulation relevant to AI includes the possibility of code-based regulations. The idea of using code[25] as a form of regulation was first championed by Lawrence Lessig. He observed that code is used to structure cyberspace.[26] What emerges from his observation is the view that the underlying architecture of cyberspace, informed by code, shapes this domain and therefore regulates the parameters of cyberspace.[27] Others have sought to further the work of Lessig by advocating that code not only informs the underlying architecture of cyberspace but can be used to proactively design the architecture, through coding selection choices which in turn serves as an active means of regulating this domain.[28] The importance of this iteration in thought is it demonstrates the view that managing the underlying components of technology can result in a secondary regulatory effect.

On this basis an analogy could be drawn between Lessig's consideration of 'codes' and the underlying algorithms which sit behind AI systems or data used by AI. One possible means of regulating AI then could be to set parameters for how the data provided to AI is managed. This is an established regulatory response with known measures, such as the European Union's GDPR.[29] The other underlying component behind AI, algorithms, is subject to much academic research regarding the merits of algorithmic regulation.[30] I do not intend to enter such debates here; rather my objective is to identify that like Lessig's arguments about coding choices having a secondary regulatory effect on cyberspace, managing data or algorithms could be conceived of having a secondary effect on regulating AI.

The relevancy of this observation is that it is closely associated with my earlier discussions about who could possibly be liable for legal harms arising from AI being deployed. For as I considered in Chapter 7, one possible group of actors who could be held liable are the producers of AI (manufacturers, designers, etc.). I suggested that in determining who could be legally liable for the outcomes of an AI system, two questions should be asked: (1) Who has the most influence over the situation in question? and (2) Who is most

25 It is worth noting that in this context, Lessig uses 'code' to denote computer-based forms of code and not 'code' as in a form of legislative instrument.

26 Lawrence Lessig, *Code and other Laws of Cyberspace* (Basic Books, 1999) 33–34.

27 Lawrence Lessig, *Code and other Laws of Cyberspace* (Basic Books, 1999) 33–34.

28 Roger Brownsword, 'Code, Control, and Choice: Why East is East and West is West' (2005) 25(1) *Legal Studies* 1, 3.

29 *Regulation (EU) 2016/679 of the European Parliament and of the Council of 27 April 2016 on the Protection of Natural Persons with Regard to the Processing of Personal Data and on the Free Movement of Such Data, and Repealing Directive 95/46/EC (General Data Protection Regulation)* [2016] OJ L 119/1.

30 For discussions about algorithmic regulation, see for example: Karen Yeung and Martin Lodge (eds), *Algorithmic Regulation* (Oxford University Press, 2019).

likely to control the situation such that the outcome generated arose?[31] The extent to which regulatory measures addressing the underlying components of AI, viz. data and algorithmic regulation, have been met becomes relevant to addressing the first of these two questions. Whether the factors engaging with or sitting behind an AI system meet any relevant regulatory responses will influence but not necessarily determine a legal outcome associated with a deployed AI system.

The above four forms of regulation, viz., command and control, economic instruments, mandatory disclosure and code-based regulation, each hold merit in complementing a liability response to AI. Such forms of regulation are somewhat traditional in nature. It is worth noting that there are other measures which can also complement a liability response to AI, which I consider next.

9.2.2 Regulation by Insurance

Although not strictly a regulatory measure, the role of insurance does have a secondary regulatory effect. In Chapter 8 I considered the role of insurance and briefly identified that in mandating insurance for certain levels of AI in the *Tri-Phase AI Liability Model*, this raises the possibility of AI being regulated by insurance. Here, I will explore the nexus between my model and the regulatory effect of insurance in further depth.

In considering the regulatory effect of insurance, it is important to evaluate its role in the context of AI. The opaque nature of some forms of AI poses unique challenges for insurers in that it can be harder to trace a causal chain of events and therefore adequately determine damages caused by an AI system.[32] There is a subsequent identifiable likelihood that in instances where it is difficult for insurers to quantify the risk associated with a harm, and determining an appropriate correlative premium is difficult; insurers will elect to not ensure such forms of AI.[33] An important associated impact is that in effect, insurers become quasi-regulators of AI systems in deciding whether or not to offer insurance.[34] One issue with this outcome concerns on what basis are insurers deciding to insure or not. If it is merely based on the ability to quantifying risks and their subsequent ability to insure after ascertaining the measure of a risk, this seems more readily capable of prediction for actors external to insurers. For example, if a developer of an AI system identifies that their AI system has a high degree of opacity and insurance is based on whether risks are easily

31 See Chapter 6 Section 6.3.1.

32 Anat Lior, 'Insuring AI: The Role of Insurance in Artificial Intelligence Regulation' (2022) 35(2) *Harvard Journal of Law & Technology* 467, 479–480.

33 Anat Lior, 'Insuring AI: The Role of Insurance in Artificial Intelligence Regulation' (2022) 35(2) *Harvard Journal of Law & Technology* 516.

34 Anat Lior, 'Insuring AI: The Role of Insurance in Artificial Intelligence Regulation' (2022) 35(2) *Harvard Journal of Law & Technology* 511.

quantified, the AI developer could subsequently discern that their AI system is less insurable due to its opacity.

If, however, and perhaps more realistically, insurers base their decisions about whether to insure on more than quantifying risk alone, this becomes harder for external actors to assess the likely insurability of an AI system without guidance from an insurer itself. For insurers may be guided by other factors such as the interests of shareholders or internal policies. Considering again the example of an AI developer producing an opaque AI system, in such circumstances if an insurer is assessing the insurability of the AI system and is guided by more than ascertaining the associated risks, but is also influenced by an insurance company's policies or business goals, this results in a situation where it is harder for the AI developer to ascertain if their AI system is insurable without seeking additional information or advice from an insurer. If an insurer was to provide such advice, this would likely increase the regulatory influence of the insurance industry in managing AI systems. In deciding to offer a liability response to AI that incorporates or relies upon insurance, its parameters need to be given careful consideration to manage the quasi-regulatory effect of insurance.

Despite its potential regulatory effect there are advantages to implementing a response to AI which relies on insurance. Although it can be difficult for insurers to ascertain a causal nexus between an AI system and its output, for individual actors an advantage of insurance is that it displaces resolving this issue from those suffering a harm and shifts it to an insurer. An advantage of insurance is therefore that for those with a cause of action, it eliminates the need to establish causation.[35]A secondary impact is that this holds the potential to increase predictability associated with AI systems being deployed for if it is known that insurance has been granted and can be relied upon, it becomes easier for deployers of AI to ascertain the risks and costs associated with deploying an AI system.[36] The increased predictability for deployers of an AI system, and connected actors, that insurance yields (once it is granted over an AI system) is especially useful in response to AI systems which are more difficult for human actors to control. For the outputs of such AI systems are harder to predict and therefore mechanisms which increase the predictability of legal outcomes associated with these systems offer greater certainty for those engaging with these AI entities.

It is also worth noting that there is importance in distinguishing between increased predictability in legal outcomes, such as improving the ability of those engaging with AI systems to understand the potential legal ramifications of deploying this technology, and the actual outputs of AI systems. Increasing

35 Anat Lior, 'Insuring AI: The Role of Insurance in Artificial Intelligence Regulation' (2022) 35(2) *Harvard Journal of Law & Technology* 519.

36 Anat Lior, 'Insuring AI: The Role of Insurance in Artificial Intelligence Regulation' (2022) 35(2) *Harvard Journal of Law & Technology* 519.

legal predictability does not necessarily equate to an increased predictability of *actual* outputs by an AI system. It may be that the outputs of an AI system cannot be predicted, especially in situations where they are difficult to control. The use of insurance does not change the actual output of an AI system, but it can increase certainty and predictability associated with legal outcomes. It is for this reason that insurance is another mechanism with regulatory effects that complements a liability response to AI.

9.2.3 Divide Between Regulation and Liability

The regulatory measures considered above in Sections 9.2.1 and 9.2.2 seek to produce desired outcomes either by regulating *ex-ante* to determine an outcome or regulating *ex-post* to correct and achieve a desired outcome. A private law liability response, such as the *Tri-Phase AI Liability Model*, in contrast is not focused on desired outcomes but instead is responding to *undesired* outcomes. A liability response is therefore not focused on achieving a particular result arising from a deployed AI, but instead it seeks to respond to actual outcomes produced. In this respect liability and regulatory responses to AI complement each other: the regulatory response proactively seeks to prevent undesired outcomes and the liability response manages undesired outcomes. Despite this, what emerges is that to some extent, especially when considering *ex-post* regulation relative to a liability response, there is an interdependent relationship between regulatory and liability measures in response to AI. For the parameters of one response hold the potential to influence the other. In turn what arises is a need for further guidance, specific to the AI context, which addresses how these responses should interact and under what circumstances.

In considering the above forms of regulation, together with the regulatory effect of insurance, the goal has been to elucidate what forms of regulation are likely to complement a liability response to AI. Inherent in this analysis is the notion that both liability responses and regulatory responses address different issues in managing the legal ramifications of a deployed AI system. As part of situating the *Tri-Phase AI Liability Model* relative to regulatory responses to AI, I therefore continue by considering the roles of regulation and liability in contrast to each other. Discussion as to the divide between regulation versus liability is a topic of extensive deliberation. Steven Shavell has offered a leading view on how this divide should be managed. He contends that there are four factors which contribute to determining what legal outcomes are best managed by a liability response instead of a regulatory response. I now consider these factors and their potential applicability to the AI legal landscape.

The first of Shavell's four factors is the extent of the relative knowledge of parties involved in an action ('Factor One'). Steven Shavell, among others, raises that what actions ought to be regulated in contrast to those which should be managed through a liability response should turn on what knowledge is accessible to a regulator relative to what knowledge is confined to private parties.[37] He contends that typically private parties are in an advantageous position, compared to regulators, when it comes to the knowledge underlying a legally contentious situation.[38] For private parties are more likely to have access to complete information about a situation and be in a better position to evaluate the likelihood of potential harms.[39] A counter to this position, to ensure greater informational transparency, is to institute a regulatory measure which at its core requires private parties to disclose all relevant information to regulators. In the context of AI, however, it is not always possible for private parties to disclose the type of information that would assist regulators. Consider, for example, black box forms of AI, which by their very nature have a degree of opacity surrounding their underlying reasoning processes and by extension the subsequent degree of information available in assessing the outcomes associated with this form of AI. In determining at what point there ought to be a shift from a liability response to a regulatory response, the relative knowledge of involved parties is undoubtedly an important consideration. However, in more complex forms of AI, such as those at the higher levels of the *Tri-Phase AI Liability Model*, knowledge alone is an insufficient metric for designating the liability-regulatory divide.

The second of Shavell's factors is focused on the costs associated with harms ('Factor Two'). He raises the argument that depending on the nature of a harm that arises, private parties may not be able to fully address a harm financially.[40] On this basis, he contends that in instances where there is a higher probability of harm arising and that the severity of that harm is not likely to be offset by a private party's assets, this situation lends itself better to a regulatory, rather than a liability, response.[41] Shavell acknowledges that in instances where private parties may not be capable of financial responsibility for harms, there is a role for the insurance market.[42] I considered the role of insurance further above in Section 9.2.2. In relation to AI, the task is to therefore aim to assess at what point the harm arising from the deployment of AI is likely to yield an outcome so detrimental that a private party cannot financially offset the harm. This is not a straight-forward assessment process in the context of AI for as I have considered at multiple junctures in this book, not all forms of AI are the

37 Steven Shavell, 'Liability for Harm Versus Regulation of Safety' (1984) 13(2) *The Journal of Legal Studies* 357, 359.

38 Steven Shavell, 'Liability for Harm Versus Regulation of Safety' (1984) 13(2) *The Journal of Legal Studies* 360.

39 Steven Shavell, 'Liability for Harm Versus Regulation of Safety' (1984) 13(2) *The Journal of Legal Studies* 359.

40 Steven Shavell, 'Liability for Harm Versus Regulation of Safety' (1984) 13(2) *The Journal of Legal Studies* 360–361.

41 Steven Shavell, 'Liability for Harm Versus Regulation of Safety' (1984) 13(2) *The Journal of Legal Studies* 361.

42 Steven Shavell, 'Liability for Harm Versus Regulation of Safety' (1984) 13(2) *The Journal of Legal Studies* 361–362.

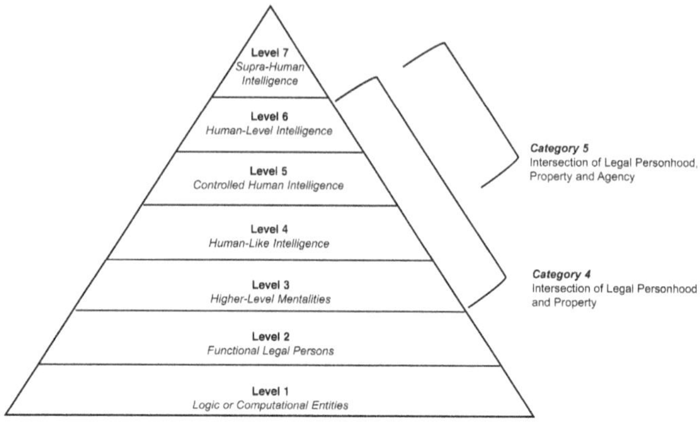

Figure 9.1 Situational Hierarchical Model of Legal Personhood

same. Compounding the issue is that an AI system within a given category may not behave the same way in every circumstance but rather may induce a variety of outcomes depending on the situation in which it is deployed, and the level of control exerted over the AI system.

On this basis, it may not be possible to regulate based on the *type* of AI system. Instead, the arguably more prudent approach is to focus on the capacity in which an AI system is acting and the likely outcome the AI system would produce under the circumstances in which it is acting. In this respect, the harms arising from the actions of AI systems that are deployed in a context where they are more difficult to exert control over, are perhaps more likely to coincide with Shavell's second factor. AI systems in this context are more likely to produce the harms that are harder to quantify and may escalate beyond the financial means of private parties. Regulatory responses inspired by responding to the costs associated with harms and whether these costs can be met therefore hold greater synergy with AI systems acting in the capacity of AI systems at higher levels in *Figure 9.1* (from Chapter 5).

In considering the respective roles of liability and regulatory responses in managing legal harms, the third factor Shavell raises is the deterring nature of liability responses ('Factor Three'). He considers that a liability response acts as a deterrent to harm-inducing conduct as parties otherwise face the possibility of legal action.[43] However, he also acknowledges that the deterring role of a liability response is dependent upon the degree to which liability for a harm is dispersed between actors.[44] In other words, where liability is dispersed among actors such that it is hard to instigate legal action in response,

43 Steven Shavell, 'Liability for Harm Versus Regulation of Safety' (1984) 13(2) *The Journal of Legal Studies* 363.

44 Steven Shavell, 'Liability for Harm Versus Regulation of Safety' (1984) 13(2) *The Journal of Legal Studies* 363.

this weighs in favour of a regulatory response to a harm.[45] Managing harms connected to AI will therefore arguably be influenced by the context in which an AI system is deployed. Here it is worth recalling the possibility that an AI system could be deployed in scenarios where it is more difficult for an individual to exert control, such as those considered in Chapter 8. A relative lack of control over an AI system creates a situation where it is harder to direct a legal action towards one responsible party, as ascertaining who had control over the end output produced by the AI system is difficult. In this respect, when an AI system is deployed in a context that means it is functioning at a level difficult for legal actors to control, such as Levels 6 or 7 in the *Tri-Phase AI Liability Model*, these systems are operating in a context that diminishes the deterrence factor arising from a liability response. AI systems deployed in such a context are therefore best suited to being supported by both liability and regulatory responses.

The final of Shavell's four factors concerns the costs associated with both liability and regulatory responses ('Factor Four'). Shavell contends that the magnitude of the costs borne by private parties and regulators needs to be considered when assessing whether a legal outcome is best managed by a liability or regulatory response.[46] Under a liability response he considers that costs are confined to instances where a legal harm occurs and private parties seek to enforce their legal rights, such as instances of litigation.[47] The costs arising from a liability response are therefore discrete, whereas regulation has on-going costs associated with administration and enforcement, regardless of whether a legal harm arises or not.[48] When it comes to costs alone, a liability response is seemingly less burdensome than a regulatory response, a view which is acknowledged by Shavell.[49] Amidst the setting of AI, the importance of Factor Four will turn upon the context in which an AI system is deployed and the capacity in which an AI system is functioning. It is also worth noting that administration and enforcement costs for a regulatory response depend on the exact nature of any regulatory measures instituted.

Adopting this approach in assessing what is the most appropriate response, viz. a liability or regulatory response, to a legal outcome turns then on weighing Shavell's four factors and reaching a conclusion regarding which factor is favoured. What is noteworthy is that Shavell considers Factors One and Four

45 Steven Shavell, 'Liability for Harm Versus Regulation of Safety' (1984) 13(2) *The Journal of Legal Studies* 363.
46 Steven Shavell, 'Liability for Harm Versus Regulation of Safety' (1984) 13(2) *The Journal of Legal Studies* 363–364.
47 Steven Shavell, 'Liability for Harm Versus Regulation of Safety' (1984) 13(2) *The Journal of Legal Studies* 364.
48 Steven Shavell, 'Liability for Harm Versus Regulation of Safety' (1984) 13(2) *The Journal of Legal Studies* 364.
49 Steven Shavell, 'Liability for Harm Versus Regulation of Safety' (1984) 13(2) *The Journal of Legal Studies* 364.

as favouring a liability response and Factors Three and Two as favouring a regulatory response.[50] Shavell's four factors are therefore a useful starting point for assessing how a liability response to AI, such as my proposed hierarchical account, ought to be situated against regulatory measures. The impact of AI, however, is not always congruent with Shavell's four factors for the reasons I have discussed above in response to each factor. Where AI is harder to control though, this redistributes the emphasis from favouring liability measures and increases the importance of regulatory responses to AI.

To adapt the *Tri-Phase AI Liability Model* for practical implementation requires differentiating between the roles of liability and regulation in providing a legal response to AI. Shavell's four factors illustrate that the divide between a liability response and regulatory measures is inherently influenced by the context in which an AI system is deployed. For in weighing up whether a regulatory or liability response is best placed to manage AI, under this framework, the outcome will depend on the specifics associated with each of the four factors. For example, what is the exact relative knowledge of each party (Factor One); or what are the exact costs associated with the harms (Factor Two)? How each factor is determined through the lens of an arising harm will influence where the line between liability and regulation ought to be drawn. What the different types of regulation that complement a liability response reveal, however, is that the context in which a harm arises alone is not sufficient in addressing a harm arising from AI. Consideration should also be given to the outcome associated with an AI system.

9.3. Considerations for Stakeholders

Developing a robust legal response to AI therefore requires examining which regulatory measures and under what circumstances complement my proposed liability model. On this basis, I continue by considering when regulation is needed relative to the *Tri-Phase AI Liability Model* and what forms of regulation best complement the model. Lastly, I draw together the ideas discussed to offer insights relevant to key stakeholders.

Throughout this book I have raised the reoccurring theme of evaluating AI with consideration to the context in which it is deployed. In offering a liability model, my proposed solution necessitates adopting a situational approach to AI. Any regulatory response to complement this model therefore must also be accommodating of the situation in which AI is deployed. In considering the appropriate regulatory response to the *Tri-Phase AI Liability Model* I will draw on and expand upon *Table 8.2* from Chapter 8, by introducing the following *Table 9.1*.

50 Steven Shavell, 'Liability for Harm Versus Regulation of Safety' (1984) 13(2) *The Journal of Legal Studies* 365.

Table 9.1 Regulation Relative to Liability Model

<table>
<tr><th>Level in Hierarchical Model of Legal Personhood</th><th>Proposed Liability Standard</th><th>Regulation Type</th></tr>
<tr><td>Level 7 – Supra-Human Intelligence</td><td rowspan="2">Strict liability backed by insurance</td><td rowspan="4">Command and Control; or Mandatory Disclosure; or Economic Instruments; or Regulation by Insurance</td></tr>
<tr><td>Level 6 – Human-Level Intelligence</td></tr>
<tr><td>Level 5 – Controlled Human Intelligence</td><td>Vicarious liability, or shared liability backed by insurance</td></tr>
<tr><td>Level 4 – Human-Like Intelligence</td><td>Shared liability, or fault-based or contractual liability</td></tr>
<tr><td>Level 3 – Higher-Level Mentalities</td><td rowspan="3">Product liability, shared liability, or fault-based or contractual liability</td><td rowspan="3">If AI is acting as a product, product-based regulation.
(Note: If AI is acting in a capacity other than as a product, and at these relatively lower levels (1 to 3), I am of the view that private law responses alone, such as tortious or contractual liabilities, are sufficient for managing these forms of AI.)</td></tr>
<tr><td>Level 2 – Functional Legal Persons</td></tr>
<tr><td>Level 1 – Logic or Computational Entities</td></tr>
</table>

In addressing the question of when regulation is necessary to complement a liability response, I am of the view that different approaches are required in response to the capacity at which an AI system is functioning. Drawing upon this view, I now turn to consider what forms of regulation complement each liability level in the *Tri-Phase AI Liability Model* and their impact on stakeholders.

9.3.1 Levels 1 to 3

In response to AI systems acting at a capacity of a Level 1 through 3 system, I identified that these systems ought to be subject to product-based forms of regulation. This is in recognition of the view that product liability frameworks do not just manage the liability outcome of situations involving products, but they also have a regulatory effect in shaping how products are managed in society.[51] I do not intend to explore the specifics of consumer-based laws and regulations at this juncture. There are, however, two key points worth positing. Firstly, AI systems operating at this level are more capable of being controlled by natural persons and as such could be viewed not as systems capable of independent action, but rather as potential chattels or products capable of being controlled. This aligns systems at Levels 1 to 3 with product liability regimes. Secondly, an alignment with product liability regimes is not intended to subsequently suggest that current product liability regimes automatically and adequately accommodate for AI. For as commentators have suggested, even when AI can be conceived of as a product, it still poses challenges for product liability regimes in terms of potential implications for privacy, biases and discrimination, among other issues.[52] In identifying that AI entities at Levels 1 to 3 are best managed by product liability measures, the goal is not to provide a prescriptive solution for these forms of AI systems. Rather the goal is to suggest that systems acting at these levels ought to be regulated by the proposed response. Further to provide guidance to policymakers that such forms of AI require less stringent forms of regulation than AI entities acting at a higher capacity, which I consider next.

9.3.2 Levels 4 to 7

AI entities acting in a capacity at Levels 4 through 7 exhibit a greater degree of variation in autonomy and therefore more flexibility in regulatory options is required to best respond to these forms of AI. It is on this basis that I proposed above the possibility of multiple forms of regulation complementing my proposed liability response. I now seek to outline key considerations for stakeholders in engaging with AI at these levels. In doing so, I address the implications from the perspectives of the three groups I identified in Chapter 7, viz., producers of AI, owners, and users of AI and lastly, AI itself.

9.3.2.1 Producers of AI

There are two key types of regulatory methods that are best suited to responding to the conduct of parties producing AI systems. The first of these regulatory

51 For more information on the regulatory effect of product liability frameworks, see: W. Kip Viscusi, 'Product Liability and Regulation: Establishing the Appropriate Institutional Division of Labor' (1988) 78(2) *The American Economic Review* 300 and Miriam C. Buiten, 'Product Liability for Defective AI' (2024) *European Journal of Law and Economics* <https://doi.org/10.1007/s10657-024-09794-z>.

52 Jeannie Marie Paterson and Yvette Maker, 'Consumer Protection Law and AI' in Ernest Lim and Phillip Morgan (eds), *The Cambridge Handbook of Private Law and Artificial Intelligence* (Cambridge University Press, 2024) 113, 121–124; Miriam C. Buiten, 'Product Liability for Defective AI' (2024) *European Journal of Law and Economics* <https://doi.org/10.1007/s10657-024-09794-z>.

methods is the *command and control* form of regulation I consider above in Section 9.2.1.1. I identified that this form of regulation is useful for setting the parameters of the acceptable scope in which an AI system can be deployed and therefore compliments a liability response to AI through defining the situations in which AI can give rise to a liability consideration. I outlined earlier that *economic instruments* as a form or regulation seeks to achieve similar ends to *command and control*, but through less demanding means. For *economic instruments* seek to encourage, rather than mandate, forms of conduct. In terms of the production phase of AI, I consider it is prudent to mandate standards to produce safe and transparent AI. On this basis, I favour *command and control* regulation over *economic instruments* for producers of AI. Such a form of regulation, if utilised, therefore necessitates producers of AI not only meet any requirements imposed by this form of regulation but also have regard to whether at a developmental level a produced AI system defensibly complies with the parameters. Producers of AI as stakeholders will by necessity have regard to the landscape in which an AI system is likely to be deployed.

The second form of regulation relevant to producers of AI includes two of the three forms of mandatory disclosure I consider above in Section 9.2.1.3. System-level forms of mandatory disclosure impose requirements on how AI systems are developed, their uses and performance capabilities.[53] In designing and developing an AI system, producers of AI must therefore have regard to any such disclosure requirements and perhaps more importantly consider whether information about their AI system is capable of disclosure. For if an AI system is structured such that information about how it performs is not readily accessible, then any mandatory disclosure requirements about AI performance are not likely to be met. The beneficial implication of imposing this form of regulation upon producers of an AI system at the production phase of these systems is that it requires these actors to reflect on their strategic decisions at the production phase to ensure that such AI systems are explainable via disclosure mechanisms. This also has important ramifications for a liability response; for if the AI system is inherently more explainable because of disclosure regulations, then this reduces the potential for difficulties associated with determining context and causation in response to a deployed AI.

The second mandatory disclosure form of regulation relevant to producers of AI is prediction-level disclosures. Here it is worth recalling from my discussion above that prediction-level forms of disclosure are aimed at the outputs of an AI system and how these outputs are achieved.[54] Imposing a prediction-level form of disclosure on producers of AI has a potential impact like system-level forms of mandatory disclosure. For producers of AI would not only be encouraged but required to ensure that the AI systems they produce yield outputs that are capable of explanation. Again, this raises similar

53 Guha (n 19) 19–20.
54 Guha (n 19) 19–20.

potential ramifications from a liability perspective to those considered in relation to system-level forms of mandatory disclosure. The challenge therefore arises for producers of AI to create AI systems that incorporate elements of transparency for the benefit of both regulatory and liability responses to AI.

9.3.2.2 Owners and Users of AI

The first form of regulation compatible with owners and users of AI, I consider is economic instruments. I raised above in Section 9.2.1.2 that the aim of this form of regulation is to foster positive conduct in engaging with AI. The benefit of this form of regulation for owners and users of AI is that it seeks to encourage responsible deployment of AI without strictly mandating how AI should be deployed. One of the advantages of AI as a form of technology is that, depending on the type of AI system, it can achieve goals not conceivable to humans.[55] On this basis there is merit in not predetermining how AI ought to be deployed through mandated regulations, but rather encouraging the appropriate and safe use of AI through incentives in the form of economic instruments. This form of regulation, if instituted, therefore has the impact of encouraging owners and users of AI systems to assess how they engage with an AI system and pivot their practices to maximise imposed potential gains (or avoid detriments).

The second form of regulation relevant to this stakeholder group is mandatory disclosure. The prediction-level form of mandatory disclosure is relevant to this group in addition to producers of AI. Its potential impact is like that of the impact on producers of AI for it prompts owners and users of AI to have regard to the way in which an AI system is deployed and assess whether its outputs are explainable. The other form of mandatory disclosure relevant to owners and users is the imposition of institution-level disclosures. Here, it is worth recalling that the object of institution-level disclosures is to require sharing information about how an AI system is used in an organisation and any correlative practices and procedures used internally to manage the deployment of an AI system.[56] In requiring the potential disclosure of this information, the institution-level form of mandatory disclosure inherently prompts owners and users of an AI system to reflect upon the support structures in place for managing how an AI system is deployed. If there is the potential for what is ordinarily deemed the private practices of an organisation – the internal policies and procedures – to be publicly disclosed, this encourages organisations to reflect on how they are deploying AI systems and whether their practices are likely to be an affront to society.

55 For a discussion on the different types of AI systems, see the *Introduction*.
56 Guha (n 19) 19–20.

9.3.2.3 *AI Itself*

In Chapter 7, I advocated that in some situations, particularly where AI is beyond the control of a natural person, an AI system itself might be held to account. I further contended that the liability of such forms of AI ought to be managed through imposing a requirement of insurance. A key impact of this approach being that in turn, AI systems subject to the requirement of insurance are therefore arguably regulated by insurance. Regulation by insurance is a topic I considered in Section 9.2.2. The impacts of this approach are less for the AI system itself and more orientated towards those engaging with AI captured by this approach. For example, this approach imposes considerations for owners and users of AI assessing whether an outcome associated with AI is predictable or not. These are points I have considered above. I do not intend to revisit the regulatory effects of insurance at this juncture; rather, I pause to acknowledge its place as a form of regulation for AI under certain circumstances, especially when AI is acting at higher levels of capacity.

9.4 Beyond Fixed Approaches: The Need for a Situational Response to AI

A liability response to AI alone is not a sufficient or robust legal response to the uncertainty created by this form of technology. Additional supports are required in the form of regulatory measures. Not only does imposing regulation bolster the legal response to AI, it also has the added benefit or raising important considerations for stakeholders in seeking to adapt my theoretical considerations to inform a practical response to AI.

Adapting the *Tri-Phase AI Liability Model* for practical application requires careful consideration of the divide between liability and regulatory measures. Where this divide should be delineated will largely be influenced by the context in which an AI system is deployed together with other key factors such as the relative knowledge of the parties involved.

This approach raises several key issues for stakeholders. Overwhelmingly, however, is the need to view stakeholder interests relative to the sophistication (or lack thereof) of an AI system. Like with liability measures, the interests of stakeholders will vary then depending on the degree of control over an AI system.

What emerges is a point that is reoccurring throughout this book: there is need for flexibility in responding to AI. This is a view I adopt in relation to a liability response for AI but now also for how regulatory measures ought to complement this response. Regulatory measures ought to be considered in relation to the level of capacity at which an AI system is acting. In other words, what regulatory measures are best suited in response to AI will be different depending on the degree of independence associated with an AI system.

References

A Articles/Books/Reports

Baldwin, Robert, Martin Cave and Martin Lodge, *Understanding Regulation: Theory, Strategy, and Practice* (Oxford University Press, 2nd ed, 2012).

Bathaee, Yavar, 'The Artificial Intelligence Black Box and the Failure of Intent and Causation' (2018) 31(2) *Harvard Journal of Law & Technology* 889.

Borselli, Angelo. 'Smart Contracts in Insurance: A Law and Futurology Perspective' in Pierpaolo Marano and Kyriaki Noussia (eds), *InsurTech: A Legal and Regulatory View* (Springer Nature, 2020) 101.

Brownsword, Roger, 'Code, Control, and Choice: Why East is East and West is West' (2005) 25(1) *Legal Studies* 1.

Buiten, Miriam C, 'Product Liability for Defective AI' (2024) *European Journal of Law and Economics* <https://doi.org/10.1007/s10657-024-09794-z>.

Guha, Neel, et al, 'AI Regulation Has Its Own Alignment Problem: The Technical and Institutional Feasibility of Disclosure, Registration, Licensing, and Auditing' (2024) 92 *George Washington Law Review* 1473.

Lessig, Lawrence, *Code and other Laws of Cyberspace* (Basic Books, 1999).

Lior, Anat, 'Insuring AI: The Role of Insurance in Artificial Intelligence Regulation' (2022) 35(2) *Harvard Journal of Law & Technology* 467.

Ogus, Anthony I, *Regulation Legal Form and Economic Theory* (Hart Publishing, 2004).

Paterson, Jeannie Marie and Yvette Maker, 'Consumer Protection Law and AI' in Ernest Lim and Phillip Morgan (eds), *The Cambridge Handbook of Private Law and Artificial Intelligence* (Cambridge University Press, 2024) 113.

Shavell, Steven, 'Liability for Harm Versus Regulation of Safety' (1984) 13(2) *The Journal of Legal Studies* 357.

Viscusi, W. Kip, 'Product Liability and Regulation: Establishing the Appropriate Institutional Division of Labor' (1988) 78(2) *The American Economic Review* 300.

Yeung, Karen and Martin Lodge (eds), *Algorithmic Regulation* (Oxford University Press, 2019).

B Legislation

Corporations Act 2001

Insurance Act 1973 (Cth)

Insurance Contracts Act 1984 (Cth)

C Other

Department for Science, Innovation & Technology, *A Pro-Innovation Approach to AI Regulation* (CP 815, Department for Science, Innovation & Technology, 2023)

Exec. Order No. 14110, 3 C.F.R. 75191 (2023)

Regulation (EU) 2016/679 of the European Parliament and of the Council of 27 April 2016 on the Protection of Natural Persons with Regard to the Processing of Personal Data and on the Free Movement of Such Data, and Repealing Directive 95/46/EC (General Data Protection Regulation) [2016] OJ L 119/1

Regulation (EU) 2024/1689 of the European Parliament and of the Council of 13 June 2024 laying down harmonised rules on artificial intelligence and amending Regulations (EC) No 300/2008, (EU) No 167/2013, (EU) No 168/2013, (EU) 2018/858, (EU) 2018/1139 and (EU) 2019/2144 and Directives 2014/90/EU, (EU) 2016/797 and (EU) 2020/1828 (Artificial Intelligence Act) [2024] OJ L 1689/1

Conclusion

The rapid proliferation of artificial intelligence ('AI') has created new challenges in many aspects of society – politically, philosophically, socially, economically and, indeed, legally. 'Modern AI', with different capabilities to *classical* forms of AI, directly challenges private law theories of liability and raises enforcement challenges under the law. For example, many approaches to private law liability rely upon notions of foreseeability or being able to determine chains of causation. The opacity and complexity of modern AI interrupt this paradigm, disrupting traditional legal reasoning processes and increasing the difficulty in assigning and enforcing liability for the actions of an AI system. Compounding this disruption is the issue that not all forms of modern AI are the same. One common view is to assume AI ought to be viewed as property only and subject to tortious or product liability regimes. Yet this overlooks the varying permutations of modern AI. These systems can exhibit varying degrees of independence, with some heavily reliant on ongoing feedback from natural persons and others designed to function independently of, or with minimal input from, natural persons. There is therefore ambiguity about how AI ought to be legally characterised, and without certainty as to the legal status of an AI system, it is difficult to ascertain what liability rules or approaches should be applied in response to its use.

This book addresses these disruption issues through exploring the central question of how liability ought to be assigned in problematic scenarios arising from the deployment of modern forms of AI. It advocates as a solution to the private law challenges posed by modern AI, the need for a flexible overarching framework – the *Tri-Phase AI Liability Model*. This unique approach not only seeks to acknowledge that modern forms of AI do not have *uniform* capabilities, but it also accommodates the varied contexts in which AI can be deployed. In response, a more flexible approach to AI liability is offered. This approach moves beyond a monolithic legal characterisation of AI, such as considering that AI should *always* be considered a mere 'tool' and offers a nuanced approach to AI liability in a private law context. The strength of the *Tri-Phase AI Liability Model* is that offers an overarching framework to guide AI liability considerations. This in turn prevents ad hoc, fragmented or

DOI: 10.4324/9781003617549-15

reactive legal responses to AI leading to inconsistencies and potential injustices strengthening AI governance within private law.

To achieve this goal, the book is divided into four parts. Part I (Chapter 1) evaluated regulatory responses to AI and the limitations of existing theoretical responses to AI. Part II (Chapters 2–5) addressed the preliminary question of how modern forms of artificial intelligence should be characterised legally. Addressing this fundamental question warranted consideration as for how AI is characterised inherently shapes the appropriate liability responses to the technology. There are conflicting views in legal theory as to how this question should be addressed. The views can be divided into three macro accounts: that AI systems ought to be characterised as a type of legal person; or that such systems ought to be viewed as agents of natural or corporate legal persons; or that AI should simply be viewed as property and subject to established tortious and product liability frameworks. These views fail to consider that, depending on the type of AI system and the context in which it is deployed, it is possible for AI to be characterised as each of these options or even a hybrid of these options in different situations.

Part II, therefore evaluated the merits of modern AI being characterised as (a) a legal person (Chapter 2), (b) an agent (Chapter 3) and (c) property (Chapter 4). The analysis observed that, under varying circumstances, AI could be characterised as each of these categories depending upon the *type* of modern AI and the *context* in which it is deployed. Ultimately, Part II observed that AI systems can act with varying degrees of independence from natural persons. This varying degree of independence, combined with AI's situational legal characterisation, necessitated in Chapter 5 proposing a new hierarchical model of legal personhood: the *Hierarchical Legal Personality* model.

The model considers and builds upon existing theories acknowledging the malleable nature of legal personhood. Part II reviewed the bundle theory[1] of legal personhood, which regards legal personhood categories as capable of being bundled together, and the alternative gradient theory,[2] which seeks to view legal personhood as existing on a continuum. The *Hierarchical Legal Personality* model acknowledges that there is merit in both approaches and proffers a tiered hierarchical account of legal personhood. A tiered hierarchical approach offers a clear delineation between legal personhood categories, like the bundle theory, rather than a gradual blurring of categories along the continuum. This approach acknowledges the merits of a spectrum of legal personhood, as supported by the gradient theory, yet also acknowledges

1 The bundle theory is explored further in Chapter 5 and in: David J Gunkel, 'Both/And', *Person, Thing, Robot: A Moral and Legal Ontology for the 21st Century and Beyond* (MIT Press, 2023); Visa A J Kurki, *A Theory of Legal Personhood* (Oxford University Press, 2019) 91–152.

2 The gradient theory is explored further in Chapter 5 and in Diana Mocanu, 'Gradient Legal Personhood for AI Systems – Painting Continental Legal Shapes Made to Fit Analytical Molds' (2022) 8 *Frontiers in Robotics and AI* 1.

the importance of being able to differentiate between categories of legal personhood.

The *Hierarchical Legal Personality* model additionally incorporates notions of control and provides a place within some tiers of the hierarchy to accommodate types of legal persons that are also capable of exhibiting proprietary characteristics. Being able to identify a category of legal personhood is imperative to being able to subsequently discern the legal frameworks that correlate with this type of legal person. This is an important preliminary threshold issue to be considered as part of the process of assigning liability, for how AI is legally characterised determines the appropriate legal theories to be relied upon when addressing liability concerns.

Many legal approaches to AI, although valid, are often based on an underlying assumption that AI is fixed in its nature and, consequently, that there should be a fixed legal approach to issues arising from or in connection to AI. Part II directly challenges this notion. It acknowledges that there are variances in AI and variances in the situations in which it is deployed and, therefore, that there is need for flexibility in how AI is legally characterised. Each individual approach to construing AI as a legal person, an agent or property is not in and of itself flawed. The error arises when assuming that each individual approach is – or ought to be – the only legal approach to responding to AI. Part II offered a new perspective concerning how AI ought to be characterised: one that incorporates flexibility. This is achieved through the *situational* hierarchical model of legal personhood (visually represented by a pyramid of legal personhood tiers).

How AI is legally characterised is an important threshold issue that needs to be addressed as part of the liability process, but it is not the only threshold issue. Part III, therefore, first explored other key threshold issues that ought to be resolved in the course of assigning liability. Chapter 6 considered that the issue of causation poses several challenges to assigning liability but, ultimately, and similarly to the issue of how AI is characterised, it ought to be considered *situationally*. Chapter 7 considered two additional threshold issues. Firstly, it examined the scope of actions or decisions made by an AI system, together with the context in which an AI system is deployed and what areas of private law the AI system may trigger. This is important, as it requires that AI be viewed *situationally* and therefore considers how the AI relates to existing liability regimes. Secondly, Chapter 7 considered the additional issue of 'who' should be held liable. How such issues are resolved assists in narrowing the scope of liability in a situation involving AI. The preliminary aspects of Part III draw upon the method of legal characterisation outlined in Part II and expand upon the necessity of considering AI, and the threshold issues for assigning liability, *situationally*. This approach subsequently informed a new proposal for assigning liability, which was offered in Chapter 8.

Drawing upon the liability threshold issues explored in Part II and the preliminary chapters of Part III, a three-phase theoretical approach to assigning liability in the context of modern forms of AI was proposed: the *Tri-Phase AI*

Liability Model. This model provides a response that views AI *situationally* whilst offering a unifying approach to the current debates around AI liability. Each phase under the model pauses to consider a different situational aspect of AI before reaching a liability response. The model therefore consists of three distinct but connected phases. By way of broad summary, Phase 1 identifies the maximum potential legal personhood status of AI relative to the *Hierarchical Legal Personality* model proposed in Chapter 5. The purpose of identifying the maximum potential status is to ensure a robust consideration of all the potential implications flowing from the deployment of a particular form of modern AI. Secondary observations can also be drawn from Phase 1 when viewed in light of Phase 2. That is, in Phase 1, an AI system may be functioning at its maximum capacity and so be classified as being at, for example, a Level 4 entity. During Phase 2, when the details of the situation are considered, there may be times when the AI system is being deployed for a less demanding task than it is capable of executing. In these circumstances, it is to be treated as demonstrating a capacity that is lower in the hierarchy – for example, a Level 2 entity.

Phase 2 is divided into three subphases that work to then narrow the scope of liability after identifying the maximum potential of an AI system in Phase 1. In Phase 2, Subphase 2A addresses the threshold issue of causation and draws upon the considerations in Chapter 6. Subphase 2B looks at the context in which an AI system is deployed and the scope of an AI system's actions in this context, as it is insufficient to consider AI in a vacuum. Subphase 2C addresses the issue of who could be held liable. The three subphases in Phase 2 symbiotically narrow the scope of liability by working to reach a conclusion, based on the situation in which an AI system is deployed, regarding the causal capacity of the AI system, how the AI system has been deployed and who had the most influence and control over the AI system.

Phase 3 then offers a situational approach to identifying which liability standard is most appropriate given the outcome of the legal reasoning reached in Phase 2. Informed by Phase 2, the goal of Phase 3 is to consider how an AI system is *functioning* in a given situation relative to the *Hierarchical Legal Personality* model. If an AI system is functioning at a high level in the model – as with the more complex forms of AI – then it is proposed that a standard of strict liability backed by insurance ought to apply. AI systems functioning as a legal person lower in the hierarchy give rise to the possibility of other standards of liability, which may result in a variety of parties being held liable for the actions of the AI system. Phase 3 therefore acknowledges that there is a need for flexibility based on how an AI system is being deployed and determines an appropriate liability standard relative to the *Hierarchical Legal Personality* model from Part II.

The *Tri-Phase AI Liability Model* therefore resolves some of the ambiguity and differences in perspectives surrounding how liability ought to be assigned in the context of modern forms of AI. The model contributes to increasing certainty in the context of AI by proposing a new theoretical overarching framework for assigning liability that is tailored to the varied nature of AI. This overarching framework, accommodating a gradient of liability responses, contrasts with other AI liability approaches that are confined to a singular response to AI. It also contrasts with other liability responses acknowledging a singular approach to AI liability is not effective and in turn proposes the need for multiple, but confined, liability responses to AI.[3] Multiple but confined liability responses to AI lack the overarching degree of connectivity that the *Tri-Phase AI Liability Model* offers. This connectivity is essential for accommodating the notion that a single AI system may have different legal implications based on its ability to act in different, non-consistent, capacities depending on the context in which it is deployed.

The model recognises the merits of current liability approaches to AI, yet it builds upon these by offering a degree of interconnected flexibility, which is needed to accommodate the very nature of AI. This acknowledges that, in relation to AI, liability ought not be framed in terms of binary alternatives. A robust liability response to AI must consider AI *situationally* and incorporate flexibility regarding the form of AI; the circumstances, context and scope in which it is deployed; and who is ultimately liable. The *Tri-Phase AI Liability Model* achieves this goal through offering one such flexible theoretical approach to resolving liability issues pertaining to AI. This dynamic model not only holds the potential to address liability in the context of AI but could also be used as an initial theoretical point of reference for other novel circumstances or technologies that may challenge traditional legal paradigms.

Part IV then moved to give greater utility to the *Tri-Phase AI Liability Model* espoused in Part III through acknowledging that private law liability responses do not exist in a vacuum. Instead, they exist in conjunction with regulatory measures used to manage legal outcomes in society. For the private law liability model to hold practical utility, there exists a need to understand its relationship with the AI regulatory landscape. This chapter therefore explored the practical implications arising from the *Tri-Phase AI Liability Model* through seeking to adapt it to a practical context with a particular emphasis on how the model relates to possible regulatory responses to AI. In doing so, it offered a view as to what forms of regulation best relate to the different levels of AI systems and how this impacts key stakeholders, viz., producers of AI, owners and users of AI or an AI system itself.

Chapter 9 therefore first situated the *Tri-Phase AI Liability Model* in relation to relevant regulatory responses. It explored how regulatory measures may complement a private law response to AI. What emerged is that to some extent there is an interdependent relationship between regulatory and liability measures. Developing a robust legal response to AI therefore requires not

3 See for example: Anna Beckers and Gunther Teubner, *Three Liability Regimes for Artificial Intelligence: Algorithmic Actants, Hybrids, Crowds* (Hart Publishing, 2021).

only acknowledging this interdependence but also, ideally, co-ordinating both regulatory and liability measures.

The book therefore provides a comprehensive account of private law governance mechanisms as they relate to AI. The approach is grounded in common law, rather than civil law, principles. This aligns with the influence common law principles hold over international commercial law. The *Tri-Phase AI Liability Model* does not, therefore, purport to be a solution adaptable to all jurisdictions as it is important to note there are significant differences between common law traditions and those in other legal families. Despite this, it is possible that the proposed approach could potentially inform considerations relating to AI in non-common law jurisdictions, but this line of inquiry is not explored in this book and is instead suited to an extraneous project.

Nonetheless, the *Tri-Phase AI Liability Model*, together with its relationship with regulatory measures, holds important implications for stakeholders considering, or engaging with, private law liability responses to AI. In crafting responses to AI, for example, policymakers should consider the need for flexibility in order to accommodate not only the varying permutations of AI but the different contexts in which it can be deployed. This applies to not just the liability response to AI but also the interactions between liability considerations and regulatory measures. Further, reducing the uncertainty posed by AI requires both liability and regulatory responses to AI. In considering legal issues raised by AI, practitioners would benefit too from considering the type of a deployed AI, the context of its deployment, including levels of control over an AI system. The *Tri-Phase AI Liability Model* offers an overarching framework of factors to consider in responding to the practical concerns raised by AI.

There is scope to build upon the *Tri-Phase AI Liability Model.* The model offers an overarching guiding framework that could be adapted to tailor the three phases to specific common law jurisdictions. Each of the three phases could be adapted to propose a test grounded in an individual jurisdiction's paradigms so that the model can be integrated into the accepted legal practice of the individual jurisdiction. Additionally, there is scope for future research exploring how to refine private law enforcement mechanisms in a manner that aligns with the proposed novel liability approach. Such research could consider the relationship between the *Tri-Phase AI Liability Model*, enforcement mechanisms and remedies under private law. The potential for further advancements incorporating the underlying principles in the Model underscores its importance as a foundational framework in private law liability approaches to AI.

Modern forms of AI directly challenge private law paradigms. This book demonstrates the need for a new liability framework that accommodates both the varying forms of AI and the contexts in which they are deployed. It advocates for the need for flexibility in responding to AI. The rapid proliferation of AI in society, together with its continual advancement, necessitates a legal response that is not merely reactive but proactively accommodates future developments. The *Tri-Phase AI Liability Model* offers a foundational approach for the future of AI private law governance.

References

A Articles/Books/Reports

Beckers, Anna and Gunther Teubner, *Three Liability Regimes for Artificial Intelligence: Algorithmic Actants, Hybrids, Crowds* (Hart Publishing, 2021).

Gunkel, David J, *'Both/And', Person, Thing, Robot: A Moral and Legal Ontology for the 21st Century and Beyond* (MIT Press, 2023).

Kurki, Visa A J, *A Theory of Legal Personhood* (Oxford University Press, 2019).

Mocanu, Diana, 'Gradient Legal Personhood for AI Systems – Painting Continental Legal Shapes Made to Fit Analytical Molds' (2022) 8 *Frontiers in Robotics and AI* 1.

Bibliography

A Articles/Books/Reports

Abbott, Ryan, *The Reasonable Robot: Artificial Intelligence and the Law* (Cambridge University Press, 2020).

Babie, Paul David Brown, Ryan Catterwell and Mark Giancaspro, 'Cryptocurrency as Property: Ruscoe v Cryptopia Ltd (in liq) [2020] NZHC 728' (2020) 28 *Australian Property Law Journal* 106.

Baldwin, Robert, Martin Cave and Martin Lodge, *Understanding Regulation: Theory, Strategy, and Practice* (Oxford University Press, 2nd ed, 2012).

Bathaee, Yavar, 'The Artificial Intelligence Black Box and the Failure of Intent and Causation' (2018) 31(2) *Harvard Journal of Law & Technology* 889.

Baughen, Simon, 'Who Is the Master Now? Regulatory and Contractual Challenges of Unmanned Vessels' in Baris Soyer and Andrew Tettenborn (eds), *New Technologies, Artificial Intelligence and Shipping Law in the 21st Century* (Informa Law from Routledge, 2020) 129.

Beckers, Anna and Gunther Teubner, *Three Liability Regimes for Artificial Intelligence: Algorithmic Actants, Hybrids, Crowds* (Hart Publishing, 2021).

Boden, Margaret A, *Artificial Intelligence: A Very Short Introduction* (Oxford University Press, 2nd ed, 2018).

Borselli, Angelo 'Smart Contracts in Insurance: A Law and Futurology Perspective' in Pierpaolo Marano and Kyriaki Noussia (eds), *InsurTech: A Legal and Regulatory View* (Springer Nature, 2020) 101.

Brownsword, Roger 'Code, Control, and Choice: Why East is East and West is West' (2005) 25(1) *Legal Studies* 1.

Buiten, Miriam C., 'Product Liability for Defective AI' (2024) *European Journal of Law and Economics* https://doi.org/10.1007/s10657-024-09794-z.

Chesterman, Simon, 'Artificial Intelligence and the Limits of Legal Personality' (2020) 69 (October) *International and Comparative Law Quarterly* 819.

Chesterman, Simon, *We, The Robots? Regulating Artificial Intelligence and the Limits of the Law* (Cambridge University Press, 2021).

Chopra, Samir and Laurence White, 'Artificial Agents and the Contracting Problem: A Solution Via an Agency Analysis' (2009) 2 *University of Illinois Journal of Law Technology & Policy* 363.

Chopra, Samir and Laurence White, *A Legal Theory for Autonomous Artificial Agents* (The University of Michigan Press, 4th ed, 2014).

Cowie, Andrew, 'A History of Married Women's Real Property Rights' (2009) 6 *Australian Journal of Gender Law* 1.

Dal Pont, G E (ed), *Law of Agency* (LexisNexis Butterworths, 2nd ed, 2008).

Dalley, Paula J, 'A Theory of Agency Law' (2011) 72(3) *University of Pittsburgh Law Review* 495.

Danesi, Marcel 'AI-Generated Music' in *AI-Generated Popular Culture: A Semiotic Perspective* (Palgrave Macmillan, 2024) 59.

DeMott, Deborah A, 'When Is a Principal Charged with an Agent's Knowledge' (2003) 13(3) *Duke Journal of Comparative & International Law* 291.

DeMott, Deborah A, 'The Contours and Composition of Agency Doctrine: Perspectives from History and Theory on Inherent Agency Power' (2014) 2014(5) *University of Illinois Law Review* 1813.

Deng, Li, 'Artificial Intelligence in the Rising Wave of Deep Learning: The Historical Path and Future Outlook' (2018) 35(1) *IEEE Signal Processing Magazine* 173.

Department for Science, Innovation & Technology, *A Pro-Innovation Approach to AI Regulation* (No CP 815, Department for Science, Innovation & Technology, 2023).

Department for Science, Innovation & Technology, *A Pro-innovation Approach to AI Regulation: Government Response to Consultation* (No CP 1019, Department for Science, Innovation & Technology, February 2024).

DiMatteo, Larry A., Cristina Poncibò and Michel Cannarsa (eds), *The Cambridge Handbook of Artificial Intelligence: Global Perspectives on Law and Ethics* (Cambridge University Press, 2022).

Farhadi, Ashkan, 'There is no "I" in "AI"' (2021) 36 *AI & Society* 1035.

Faure, Michael, 'The Complementary Roles of Liability, Regulation and Insurance in Safety Management: Theory and Practice' (2014) 17(6) *Journal of Risk Research* 689.

Finkelman, Paul, 'Slavery in the United States: Persons or Property?' in Jean Allain (ed), *The Legal Understanding of Slavery: From the Historical to the Contemporary* (Oxford University Press, 2012) 105.

Geistfeld, Mark A., Ernst Karner, Bernhard A. Koch and Christiane Wendehorst (eds), *Civil Liability for Artificial Intelligence and Software* (Walter de Gruyter GmbH & Co KG, 2022).

Girgen, Jen, 'The Historical and Contemporary Prosecution and Punishment of Animals' (2003) (9) *Animal Law* 97.

Gomes Rêgo de Almeida, Patricia et al, 'Artificial Intelligence Regulation: A Framework for Governance' (2021) 23 *Ethics and Information Technology* 505.

Graham, Paul, 'The Will Theory of Rights: A Defence' (1996) 15 *Law and Philosophy* 257.

Grattan, Scott and Sheelagh McCracken (eds), *Introduction to Property and Commercial Law* (Thomson Reuters (Professional) Australia Limited, 2016).

Green, Sarah and John Randall, *The Tort of Conversion* (Hart Publishing, 2009).

Grimmelmann, James and Christina Mulligan, 'Data Property' (2023) 72 *American University Law Review* 829.

Guha, Neel, et. al., 'AI Regulation Has Its Own Alignment Problem: The Technical and Institutional Feasibility of Disclosure, Registration, Licensing, and Auditing' (2024) 92 *George Washington Law Review* 1473.

Gunkel, David J, 'Both/And', *Person, Thing, Robot: A Moral and Legal Ontology for the 21st Century and Beyond* (MIT Press, 2023).

Hart, H L A and Tony Honoré, *Causation in the Law* (Oxford University Press, 2nd ed, 1985).

Hertog, Johan den, '5000 General Theories of Regulation' in Boudewijn Bouckaert and Gerrit De Geest (eds), *Encyclopedia of Law and Economics: The History and Methodology of Law and Economics* (Edward Elgar, 2000) vol 1, 223.

Jackson, Philip C, *Introduction to Artificial Intelligence* (Dover Publications Inc., 3rd ed, 2019).

Kaul, Vivek, Sarah Enslin, and Seth A Gross, 'History of Artificial Intelligence in Medicine' (2020) 92 (4) *Gastrointestinal Endoscopy* 807.

Keating, Gregory C, 'Corrective Justice: Sovereign or Subordinate?' in Andrew S Gold et al (eds), *The Oxford Handbook of the New Private Law* (Oxford University Press, 2020) 37.

Koay, Nick Li and L Tzeyi, 'Artificial Intelligence and Inventorship: An Australian Perspective' 15(5) *Journal of Intellectual Property Law & Practice* 399.

Korteling, J E (Hans) et al, 'Human- versus Artificial Intelligence' (2021) 4 *Frontiers in Artificial Intelligence* 1.

Kramer, Matthew H, 'Refining the Interest Theory of Rights' (2010) 55 *The American Journal of Jurisprudence* 31.

Kulms, Rainer, 'Blockchains: Private Law Matters' (2020) 1 *Singapore Journal of Legal Studies* 63.

Kurki, Visa A J, *A Theory of Legal Personhood* (Oxford University Press, 2019).

Kurki, Visa A J, 'Why Things Can Hold Rights: Reconceptualizing the Legal Person' in Visa A J Kurki and Tomasz Pietrzykowski (eds), *Legal Personhood: Animals, Artificial Intelligence and the Unborn* (Springer International Publishing AG, 2017) 69.

Kwee, Koh Thiam, 'Can You Steal Bitcoin: Lessons for Singapore from the UK and New Zealand' (2018–2019) 36 *Singapore Law Review* 186.

Larson, Erik J, *The Myth of Artificial Intelligence: Why Computers Can't Think the Way We Do* (Harvard University Press, 2021).

Lavrichenko, Michelle, 'Thaler v. Vidal: Artificial Intelligence—Can the Invented Become the Inventor' (2022) 44(2) *Cardozo Law Review* 699.

Lehmann, Jos et al, 'Causation in AI and Law' (2004) 12 *Artificial Intelligence and Law* 279.

Lessig, Lawrence, *Code and other Laws of Cyberspace* (Basic Books, 1999).

Lim, Ernest and Phillip Morgan (eds), *The Cambridge Handbook of Private Law and Artificial Intelligence* (Cambridge University Press, 2024).

Lior, Anat, 'Insuring AI: The Role of Insurance in Artificial Intelligence Regulation' (2022) 35(2) *Harvard Journal of Law & Technology* 467.

Lohsse, Sebastian, Reiner Schulze and Dirk Staudenmayer (eds), *Liability for Artificial Intelligence and the Internet of Things* (Bloomsbury Publishing, 2019).

Lyons, David, 'Review: Principles, Positivism, and Legal Theory' (1977) 87(2) *The Yale Law Journal* 415.

Ma, Yifang, Zhenyu Wang, Hong Yang, and Lin Yang, 'Artificial Intelligence Applications in the Development of Autonomous Vehicles: A Survey' (2020) 7(2) *Journal of Automatica Sinica* 315.

MacCormick, Neil, 'Rights in Legislation' in P M S Hacker and J Raz (eds), *Law, Morality and Society: Essays in Honour of HLA Hart* (Clarendon Press, 1977).

MacGregor, Danny Busch and Laura J (eds), *The Unauthorised Agent: Perspectives from European and Comparative Law* (Cambridge University Press, 2009).

McMeel, Gerard, 'Philosophical Foundations of the Law of Agency' (2000) 116(July) *Law Quarterly Review* 387.

Merrill, Thomas W, 'Private and Public Law' in Andrew S Gold et al (eds), *The Oxford Handbook of the New Private Law* (Oxford University Press, 2020) 575.

Michaels, Ralf, 'The Functional Method of Comparative Law' in Mathias Reimann and Reinhard Zimmermann (eds), *The Oxford Handbook of Comparative Law* (Oxford Academic, 2nd ed, 2019) 345.

Mik, Eliza, 'AI as a Legal Person?' in Jyn-An Lee et al (eds), *Artificial Intelligence and Intellectual Property* (Oxford University Press, 2021) 419.

Mocanu, Diana, 'Gradient Legal Personhood for AI Systems—Painting Continental Legal Shapes Made to Fit Analytical Molds' (2022) 8 *Frontiers in Robotics and AI* 1.

Morgan, Phillip, 'Recasting Vicarious Liability' (2012) 71(3) *The Cambridge Law Journal* 615.

Moses, Lyria, 'Liability and Insurance' in Michael Guihot and Lyria Bennett Moses (eds), *Artificial Intelligence, Robots and the Law* (LexisNexis, 2020) 229.

Möslein, Florian, 'Robots in the Boardroom: Artificial Intelligence and Corporate Law' in Woodrow Barfield and Ugo Pagallo (eds), *Research Handbook on the Law of Artificial Intelligence* (Edward Elgar Publishing Limited, 2018).

Naffine, Ngaire, 'Legal Persons as Abstractions: The Extrapolation of Persons from the Male Case' in Visa A. J. Kurki and Tomasz Pietrzykowski (eds), *Legal Personhood: Animals, Artificial Intelligence and the Unborn* (Springer International Publishing AG, 2017) 15.

Naffine, Ngaire, *Ngaire Naffine Law's Meaning of Life – Philosophy, Religion, Darwin and the legal Person* (Hart Publishing, 2009).

Nelson, Jennifer, 'Human Personhood from a Kantian Perspective' (2009) 8(2) *CedarEthics Online* 1.

Ogus, Anthony I, *Regulation Legal Form and Economic Theory* (Hart Publishing, 2004).

Oriakhogba, Desmond Osaretin, 'DABUS Gains Territory in South Africa and Australia: Revisiting the AI-Inventorship Question' (2021) 9 *South African Intellectual Property Law Journal* 87.

Pagallo, Ugo, *The Laws of Robots: Crimes, Contracts, and Torts* (Springer Dordrecht, 2013).

Pasquale, Frank, 'Data-Informed Duties in AI Development' (2019) 119 *Colombia Law Review* 1917.

Paterson, Jeannie Marie and Yvette Maker, 'Consumer Protection Law and AI' in Ernest Lim and Phillip Morgan (eds), *The Cambridge Handbook of Private Law and Artificial Intelligence* (Cambridge University Press, 2024).

Pearlman, Russ, 'Recognizing Artificial Intelligence (AI) as Authors and Investors under U.S. Intellectual Property Law' (2018) 24(2) *Richmond Journal of Law & Technology* i.

Pietrzykowski, Tomasz, *Personhood Beyond Humanism: Animals, Chimeras, Autonomous Agents and the Law* (Springer Briefs in Law, 2018).

Rab, Suzanne, 'Competition Law' in Charles Kerriagan (ed), *Artificial Intelligence: Law and Regulation* (Edward Elgar Publishing Limited, 2022).

Rahmatian, Andreas, 'A Comparison of German Moveable Property Law and English Personal Property Law' (2008) 3 *Journal of Comparative Law* 197.

Ramaekers, Eveline, 'Classification of Objects by the European Court of Justice: Movable Immovables and Tangible Intangibles' (2019) 39(4) *European Law Review* 447.

Ramaekers, Eveline, 'The Development of EU Property Law' (2015) 3 *European Review of Private Law* 437.
Ramaekers, Eveline, 'What is Property Law?' (2017) 37(3) *Oxford Journal of Legal Studies* 588.
Ritter, Jeffrey and Anna Mayer, 'Regulating Data as Property: A New Construct for Moving Forward' (2017–2018) 16 *Duke Law & Technology Review* 220.
Rosenfeld, Michel, 'Rethinking the Boundaries Between Public Law and Private Law for the Twenty First Century: An Introduction' (2013) 11(1) *I•CON* 125.
Russell, Stuart J, Peter Norvig et al, *Artificial Intelligence: A Modern Approach* (Pearson Education Limited, 4th ed, 2022).
Sales, Philip, 'Algorithms, Artificial Intelligence, and the Law' (2021) 105(1) *Judicature* 23.
Shavell, Steven, 'Liability for Harm Versus Regulation of Safety' (1984) 13(2) *The Journal of Legal Studies* 357.
Sheth, Amit and Krishnaprasad Thirunarayan, 'The Duality of Data and Knowledge Across the Three Waves of AI' (2021) 23(3) *IT Professional* 1.
Solaiman, S M, 'Legal Personality of Robots, Corporations, Idols and Chimpanzees: A Quest for Legitimacy' (2017) 25 *Artificial Intelligence Law* 155.
Soyer, Baris and Andrew Tettenborn, 'Artificial Intelligence and Civil Liability—Do We Need a New Regime?' (2022) 30(4) *International Journal of Law and Information Technology* 385.
Spaak, Torben, 'Kelsen and Hart on the Normativity of Law' in Peter Wahlgren (ed), *Perspectives on Jurisprudence: Essays in Honour of Jespers Bjarup* (Stockholm Institute for Scandianvian Law, 2005) 397.
Steel, Sandy 'Legal Causation and AI' in Ernest Lim and Phillip Morgan (eds), *The Cambridge Handbook of Private Law and Artificial Intelligence* (Cambridge University Press, 2024) 189.
Tan, Yock Lin, *Personal Property Law* (Singapore Academy of Law, 2014).
Thomson, Judith Jarvis, 'Some Reflections on Hart and Honoré, Causation in the Law' in Matthew H Kramer et al (eds), *The Legacy of H.L.A. Hart: Legal, Political, and Moral Philosophy* (Oxford University Press, 2008) 143.
Toth, A G, *The Oxford Encyclopaedia of European Community Law: The Law of the Internal Market* (Oxford University Press, 1990).
Tripathi, Swapnil and Chandni Ghatak, 'Artificial Intelligence an Intellectual Property Law' (2018) 7(1) *Christ University Law Journal* 83.
Turner, Jacob, *Robot Rules: Regulating Artificial Intelligence* (Palgrave Macmillan, 2019).
Unsworth, Rory, 'Smart Contract This! An Assessment of the Contractual Landscape and the Herculean Challenges it Currently Presents for "Self-executing" Contracts' in Mark Fenwick and Helena Haapio Marcelo Corrales (eds), *Legal Tech, Smart Contracts and Blockchain* (Springer Nature Singapore Pte Ltd., 2019).
van Genderen, Robert van den Hoven, 'Do We Need New Legal Personhood in the Age of Robots and AI?' in Marcelo Corrales et al (eds), *Robotics, AI and the Future of Law* (Springer Nature Singapore Pte Ltd., 2018) 15.
Viscusi, W Kip, 'Product Liability and Regulation: Establishing the Appropriate Institutional Division of Labor' (1988) 78(2) *The American Economic Review* 300.
Warwick, Kevin, *Artificial Intelligence: The Basics* (Routledge, 2012)
Watts, Peter and F M B Reynolds (eds), *Bowstead and Reynolds on Agency* (Thomson Reuters (Legal) Limited, 19th ed, 2010).

Weinrib, Ernest J, *Corrective Justice* (Oxford University Press, 2012)

Weinrib, Ernest J, 'Corrective Justice in a Nutshell' (2002) 54(2) *The University of Toronto Law Journal* 349.

Wendehorst, Christiane, 'Liability for Artificial Intelligence: The Need to Address Both Safety Risks and Fundamental Rights Risks' in Philipp Kellmeyer, Silja Voeneky, Oliver Mueller, and Wolfram Burgard (eds), *The Cambridge Handbook of Responsible Artificial Intelligence: Interdisciplinary Perspectives* (Cambridge University Press, 2022) 187.

Wise, Steven M, 'Legal Personhood and the Nonhuman Rights Project', (2010) 17(1) *Animal Law* 1.

Wojtczak, Sylwia, 'Endowing Artificial Intelligence with Legal Subjectivity' (2020) (37) *AI & Society* 205.

Wojtczak, Sylwia and Pawel Księżak, 'Causation in Civil Law and the Problems of Transparency in AI' (2021) 29(4) *European Review of Private Law* 561.

Wright, Richard W, 'Causation in the Law', *Routledge Encyclopedia of Philosophy* (Taylor and Francis, 2001).

Yeung, Karen and Martin Lodge (eds), *Algorithmic Regulation* (Oxford University Press, 2019).

Zhao, Jingchen 'Promoting More Accountable AI in the Boardroom Through Smart Regulation' (2024) 52 *Computer Law and Security Review* 1.

Zhao Yan Lee, Mohammad Ershadul Karim and Kevin Ngui, 'Deep Learning Artificial Intelligence and the Law of Causation: Application, Challenges and Solutions' (2021) 30(3) *Information & Communication Technology Law* 255.

Zhu, X and A Goldberg, *Introduction to Semi-Supervised Learning* (Springer Nature Switzerland AG, 2022).

Zipurksy, Benjamin C, 'Philosophy of Private Law' in Jules Coleman and Scott Shapiro (eds), *The Oxford Handbook of Jurisprudence and Philosophy of Law* (Oxford University Press, 2002) 623.

B Other

'A Deep Dive into Patentability of AI, Ownership and Entitlement to AI-Created Inventions', *Ashurst* (Web Page, 21 November 2019) https://www.ashurst.com/en/news-and-insights/insights/a-deep-dive-into-patentability-of-ai-ownership-and-entitlement-to-ai-created-inventions/

'An In-depth Analysis of Copyright and the Challenges Presented by Artificial Intelligence', *Ashurst* (Web Page, 11 March 2020) https://www.ashurst.com/en/news-and-insights/insights/an-indepth-analysis-of-copyright-and-the-challenges-presented-by-artificial-intelligence

'ChatGPT', *Open AI* (Generative AI Web Page) https://chat.openai.com/

'Class 706, Data Processing—Artificial Intelligence', *Classification Definitions* (Web Page, 7 February 2022) https://www.uspto.gov/web/patents/classification/uspc706/defs706.htm

'Client Alert Bite-size Briefings [Autumn ED No. 2]', *Baker McKenzie* (November 2019) https://www.bakermckenzie.com/-/media/files/insight/publications/2019/11/fsr_bitesize_article_nov_2019.pdf?la=en

'Constitutional Council', *conseil-constitutionnel.fr* (Web Page) <https://www.conseil-constitutionnel.fr/en>

'Full Court Declines to Stipulate Boundaries for Patentable Computer-Implemented Inventions', *Ashurst* (Web Page, 24 September 2019) https://www.ashurst.com/en/news-and-insights/legal-updates/full-court-declines-to-stipulate-boundaries-for-patentable-computer-implemented-inventions/

'How Intelligent are Whales and Dolphins?', *Whale and Dolphin Conservation (WDC)*) https://uk.whales.org/whales-dolphins/how-intelligent-are-whales-and-dolphins/#:~:text=Dolphins%20demonstrate%20the%20ability%20to,%2C%20grief%2C%20joy%20and%20playfulness

'Incapacity and Contract Law', *Australian Government: Australian Law Reform Commission* (Web Page, 20 May 2014) https://www.alrc.gov.au/publication/equality-capacity-and-disability-in-commonwealth-laws-dp-81/11-other-issues/incapacity-and-contract-law/

'Introduction to the Protection of IP Rights in Artificial Intelligence', *Ashurst* (Web Page, 25 September 2019) https://www.ashurst.com/en/news-and-insights/insights/ip-focus-on-ai-introduction-to-protection-of-ip-rights-in-artificial-intelligence/

'IP Australia "Rokt" by Federal Court Decision on the Patentability of Computer Implemented Inventions', *Ashurst* (Web Page, 17 December 2018) https://www.ashurst.com/en/news-and-insights/legal-updates/ip-australia-alert-rokt-by-federal-court-decision/

'Legal Interpretivism', *Stanford Encyclopedia of Philosophy* (Web Page, 14 October 2003) https://plato.stanford.edu/entries/law-interpretivist/

'Legal Obligation and Authority', *Stanford Encyclopedia of Philosophy* (Web Page, 29 December 2003) https://plato.stanford.edu/entries/legal-obligation/

'Legal Rights', *Stanford Encyclopedia of Philosophy* (Web Page, 20 December 2001) https://plato.stanford.edu/entries/legal-rights/#ConcAnalLegaRigh

'Oral-B iO™, The Biggest Innovation in Oral Care History Is Now Available Nationwide', *businesswire.com* (Web Page, 20 August 2020) https://www.businesswire.com/news/home/20200820005069/en/Oral-B-iO™-The-Biggest-Innovation-in-Oral-Care-History-Is-Now-Available-Nationwide

'Patent Classification', *USPTO* (Web Page) https://www.uspto.gov/patents/search/classification-standards-and-development

'Patentable Subject Matter', *Australian Law Reform Commission* (Web Page, 2 August 2010) https://www.alrc.gov.au/publication/genes-and-ingenuity-gene-patenting-and-human-health-alrc-report-99/6-patentability-of-genetic-materials-and-technologies/patentable-subject-matter/#:~:text='Invention'%20is%20defined%20in%20the,and%20includes%20an%20alleged%20invention

'Rights', *Stanford Encyclopedia of Philosophy* (Web Page, 19 December 2005) https://plato.stanford.edu/entries/rights/#FuncRighWillTheoInteTheo

'South Western Sydney Local Health District Media Release: Transforming the Hospital Experience with a Friendly Robot', *NSW Government: South Western Sydney Local Health District* (Web Page, 11 March 2020) https://www.swslhd.health.nsw.gov.au/mediacentre/mediareleases/2020/200211a.pdf

'Supreme Court of the United States 2013–2014 Term in Review: Patentability of Abstract Ideas', *Cornell Law School* (Web Page) https://www.law.cornell.edu/supreme_court_of_the_united_states_2013–2014_term_in_review/patentability_of_abstract_ideas#:~:text=The%20Court%20has%20long%20held,building%20blocks%20of%20human%20ingenuity%2C"

'Trademarks: What Is a Trademark?', *World Intellectual Property Organisation* (Web Page) https://www.wipo.int/trademarks/en/

'WIPO Technology Trends 2019: Artificial Intelligence', *World Intellectual Property Organisation* (Report, 2019) https://www.wipo.int/edocs/pubdocs/en/wipo_pub_1055.pdf

Armstrong, Paul, 'AI Humanoid "Sophia" Is Granted First Ever Robot Visa, Speaks With President', *Forbes* (online, 27 October 2018) https://www.forbes.com/sites/paularmstrongtech/2018/10/27/ai-humanoid-sophia-is-granted-first-ever-robot-visa-speaks-with-president/#45c0158f1f39

Bughin, Jaques et al, 'Notes from the AI Frontier: Modelling the Impact of AI on the World Economy', *McKinsey Global Institute* (September 2018) https://www.mckinsey.com/featured-insights/artificial-intelligence/notes-from-the-ai-frontier-modeling-the-impact-of-ai-on-the-world-economy

Chen, Brian X and Cade Metz, 'Google's Duplex Uses A.I. to Mimic Humans (Sometimes)', *The New York Times* (online, 22 May 2019) https://www.nytimes.com/2019/05/22/technology/personaltech/ai-google-duplex.html

Concise Australian Legal Dictionary (4th ed, 2011) 'Disclaimer'

Coscarelli, Joe, 'An A.I. Hit of Fake "Drake" and "The Weeknd" Rattles the Music World', *The New York Times* (online, 19 April 2023) https://www.nytimes.com/2023/04/19/arts/music/ai-drake-the-weeknd-fake.html

Cox, Joseph, 'AI-Generated Voice Firm Clamps Down After 4chan Makes Celebrity Voices for Abuse', *VICE* (Web Page, 31 January 2023) https://www.vice.com/en/article/dy7mww/ai-voice-firm-4chan-celebrity-voices-emma-watson-joe-rogan-elevenlabs

Dragan, Aurel, 'UniCredit Becomes the First Bank in the World with a Robot Customer', *BR Business Review* (online, 11 May 2018) https://business-review.eu/news/unicredit-is-the-first-bank-in-the-world-that-has-a-robot-sophia-as-a-customer-169290

Edward Elgar Publishing Limited, *Elgar Encyclopedia of Comparative Law* (online, Edward Elgar Publishing Limited, 3 October 2021) 'Chapter 27: Transfer of Movable Property'

Eliot, Lance B, 'People Are Eagerly Consulting Generative AI ChatGPT For Mental Health Advice, Stressing Out AI Ethics And AI Law', *Forbes* (online, 1 January 2023) https://www.forbes.com/sites/lanceeliot/2023/01/01/people-are-eagerly-consulting-generative-ai-chatgpt-for-mental-health-advice-stressing-out-ai-ethics-and-ai-law/?sh=4e82769e2643

European Parliament, 'P9_TA(2024)0138 Artificial Intelligence Act' (Legislative Resolution, 13 March 2024) on the proposal for a regulation on laying down harmonised rules on Artificial Intelligence (Artificial Intelligence Act) and amending certain Union Legislative Acts (COM(2021)0206)

European Parliament, *European Parliament Legislative Resolution of 12 March 2024 on the Proposal for a Directive of the European Parliament and of the Council on Liability for Defective Products (COM(2022)0495 – C9-0322/2022 – 2022/0302(COD))*, P9_TA(2024)0132, 14 March 2024

European Parliament and Council of the European Union, *Regulation of the European Parliament and of the Council, Laying Down Harmonised Rules on Artificial Intelligence and Amending Regulations (EC) No 300/2008, (EU) No 167/2013, (EU) No 168/2013, (EU) 2018/858, (EU) 2018/1139 and (EU) 2019/2144 and Directives 2014/90/EU, (EU) 2016/797 and (EU) 2020/1828 (Artificial Intelligence Act)*, PE-CONS 24/24, 14 May 2024

European Patent Office, 'Guidelines for Examination in the European Patent Office 2023', *EPO* (Document, March 2023) https://link.epo.org/web/epo_guidelines_for_examination_2023_hyperlinked_en.pdf

European Union, *Commission Staff Working Document Executive Summary of the Impact Assessment Report Accompanying the Document Proposal for a Directive on Adapting Non Contractual Civil Liability Rules to Artificial Intelligence (AI Liability Directive)* (European Union, 28 September 2022) https://commission.europa.eu/system/files/2022-09/1_5_197611_summary_impact_asse dir_ai_en.pdf

European Union, *Proposal for a Directive on Adapting Non-Contractual Civil Liability Rules to Artificial Intelligence* (European Union, 28 September 2022) https://eur-lex.europa.eu/legal-content/EN/TXT/PDF/?uri=CELEX:52022PC0496

European Union, *Proposal for a Regulation of the European Parliament and the Council Laying Down Harmonised Rules on Artificial Intelligence (Artificial Intelligence Act) and the Amending Certain Union Legislation Acts* (European Union, 21 April 2021) https://eur-lex.europa.eu/legal-content/EN/TXT/?uri=celex%3A52021PC0206

Evans, Kate, 'The New Zealand River that Became a Legal Person', *BBC Travel* (Web Page, 21 March 2020) https://www.bbc.com/travel/article/20200319-the-new-zealand-river-that-became-a-legal-person

Government of the Republic of Singapore, 'Singapore announces new AI Safety initiatives at the global AI Action Summit in France' *Infocomm Media Development Authority* (Web page, 11 February 2025) https://www.imda.gov.sg/resources/press-releases-factsheets-and-speeches/press-releases/2025/singapore-ai-safety-initiatives-global-ai-summit-france

Government of the Republic of Singapore, *NAIS 2.0 Singapore National AI Strategy: AI for the Public Good: For Singapore and the World* (Report, 4 December 2023) https://file.go.gov.sg/nais2023.pdf

Griffin, Andrew, 'Saudi Arabia Grants Citizenship to a Robot for the First Time Ever', *The Independent* (online, 26 October 2017) https://www.independent.co.uk/life-style/gadgets-and-tech/news/saudi-arabia-robot-sophia-citizenship-android-riyadh-citizen-passport-future-a8021601.html

Hacker, Philipp, *Proposal for a Directive on Adapting Non-Contractual Civil Liability Rules to Artificial Intelligence: Complementary Impact Assessment* (Study, September 2024) https://www.europarl.europa.eu/RegData/etudes/STUD/2024/762861/EPRS_STU(2024)762861_EN.pdf

Halpern, Nancy E, 'Another Attempt to Create Legal Standing for Animals as Plaintiff's in Lawsuits Fails', *Fox Rothschild LLP* (3 November 2018) https://animallaw.foxrothschild.com/2018/11/03/another-attempt-to-create-legal-standing-for-animals-as-plaintiffs-in-lawsuits-fails/

Halsbury's Laws of England, vol 19 (online at 7 February 2022) 3 Categories Confidential Information, '1 Confidence'

Halsbury's Laws of England, vol 23 (online at 7 February 2022) 2 Copyright, '566 Copyright in Computer Programs'

Holland, Ashley and Helen Kavadias, 'Federal Court of Australia Approves Artificial Intelligence to be Inventor for Patents Act Purposes', *HWL Ebsworth Lawyers* (Web Page, 28 September 2021) https://hwlebsworth.com.au/federal-court-of-australia-approves-artificial-intelligence-to-be-inventor-for-patents-act-purposes/

Iles, Emma and Helen Cousins, 'Has the Full Court "Rokt' the Boat', *Herbert Smith Freehills* (Web Page, 26 May 2020) https://www.herbertsmithfreehills.com/latest-thinking/has-the-full-court-rokt-the-boat

Jackson, Fiona, '"ChatGPT Does 80% of My Job": Meet the Workers Using AI Bots to Take on Multiple Full-Time Jobs—And Their Employers Have NO Idea', *Daily Mail* (online, 13 April 2023) https://www.dailymail.co.uk/sciencetech/article-11967947/Meet-workers-using-ChatGPT-multiple-time-jobs-employers-NO-idea.html

Jakhwal, Sejal, 'Guy Tries to Extract Forbidden Answers on ChatGPT, Uses Reverse Psychology to Make it Work', *India Times* (online, 20 April 2023) https://www.indiatimes.com/trending/human-interest/guy-tries-reverse-psychology-on-chatgpt-599957.html

Kavlakoglu, Eda, 'AI vs. Machine Learning vs. Deep Learning vs. Neural Networks: What's the Difference?', *IBM* (Web Page, 27 May 2020) https://www.ibm.com/cloud/blog/ai-vs-machine-learning-vs-deep-learning-vs-neural-networks, archived at https://web.archive.org/web/20230401044424/https://www.ibm.com/cloud/blog/ai-vs-machine-learning-vs-deep-learning-vs-neural-networks

Khan, Saiful, 'Patenting AI in the UK: Trends and Outlook', *Potter Clarkson* (Web Page) https://www.potterclarkson.com/insights/patenting-ai-in-the-uk-trends-and-outlook/

Kharpal, Arjun, 'Chinese Driverless Car Firm Launches Autonomous Deliveries in California as Lockdown Continues', (online, 17 April 2020) https://www.cnbc.com/2020/04/17/coronavirus-ponyai-launches-driverless-car-deliveries-in-california.html

Kitchin, Lord Justice of the Supreme Court, 'UKIPO—WIPO Conference Keynote Speech' (UKIPO—WIPO Conference Keynote Speech, UKIPO—WIPO Conference, 18 June 2019) https://www.supremecourt.uk/docs/speech-190618.pdf

Krueger, Alyson, 'We Need to Talk: Just as Soon as I Consult Chat GPT', *New York Times* (online, 24 March 2023) https://www.nytimes.com/2023/03/24/style/ai-chatgpt-advice-relationships.html

Leviathan, Yaniv and Yossi Matias, 'Google Duplex: An AI System for Accomplishing Real-World Tasks Over the Phone', *Google AI Blog* (Blog Post, 8 May 2018) https://ai.googleblog.com/2018/05/duplex-ai-system-for-natural-conversation.html

LexisNexis, *Halsbury's Laws of Australia* (online, 7 February 2022) Patents, Trade Marks & Related Rights, '5 Requirements for a Valid Patent' [[12,000], [12,510], [12,535]]

LexisNexis, *Halsbury's Laws of Australia* 240 Intellectual Property, '2 Confidential Information' [240–1559]

LexisNexis, *Halsbury's Laws of Australia* 240 Intellectual Property, '3 Copyright' [240–1559]

LexisNexis, *Halsbury's Laws of Australia*, vol 1 (online, 3 October 2021) 315 Personal Property, '(A) Introduction – Meaning and Classification of Personal Property' [315-1]

Macedo, Charles R, Rothstein Amster and Ebenstein LLP, 'Protecting Artificial Intelligence Innovations as Intellectual Property: Opportunities and Pitfalls', *Thomson*

Reuters (Web Page, 14 December 2020) https://anzlaw.thomsonreuters.com/w-026-6317?transitionType=Default&contextData=(sc.Default)&firstPage=true

Moore, Michael, 'Causation in the Law', *The Stanford Encyclopedia of Philosophy* (Web Page, 3 October 2019) https://plato.stanford.edu/archives/win2019/entries/causation-law/

Murphy, Annabel, 'Autonomous Robots Check Patients in at Belgium Hospitals', *Innovation Origins* (Web Page, 1 July 2020) https://innovationorigins.com/en/autonomous-robots-check-patients-in-at-belgium-hospitals/

Naughton, John, 'Good Luck in Making Google Reveal its Algorithm', *The Guardian* (online, 13 November 2016) https://www.theguardian.com/commentisfree/2016/nov/13/good-luck-in-making-google-reveal-its-algorithm

Order of Davies J in *Amato v Commonwealth of Australia* (Federal Court of Australia, VID611/2019, 27 November 2019)

Personal Data Protection Commission Singapore, *Model Artificial Intelligence Governance Framework* (2nd ed, 21 January 2020) https://www.pdpc.gov.sg/-/media/Files/PDPC/PDF-Files/Resource-for-Organisation/AI/SGModelAIGovFramework2.pdf

Royal Commission into the Robotdebt Scheme (Web Page) https://robodebt.royalcommission.gov.au/

Sales, Lord Philip, 'Algorithms, Artificial Intelligence and the Law' (The Sir Henry Brooke Lecture for BAILII, Freshfields Bruckhaus Deringer, London, 12 November 2019)

Science, Innovation and Technology Committee, *Governance of Artificial Intelligence (AI): Government Response* (2024–25, HC 591)

Scourfield, Tom et al, 'Trade Secrets in the United Kingdom', *CMS: Law, Tax, Future* (Web Page) https://cms.law/en/int/expert-guides/cms-expert-guide-to-trade-secrets/united-kingdom

Steffen, Andrea, 'AI-Powered Blood Test Detects 50 Types of Cancer and Locates Origin' (online, 13 April 2020) https://www.intelligentliving.co/ai-blood-test-detect-50-cancer/

Strachan, Maxwell, '"Overemployed" Hustlers Exploit ChatGPT to Take on Even More Full-Time Jobs', *VICE* (Web Page, 12 April 2023) https://www.vice.com/en/article/v7begx/overemployed-hustlers-exploit-chatgpt-to-take-on-even-more-full-time-jobs

Suleyman, Mustafa, 'What Is an AI Anyway?', *TED* (TED Talk, TED Conferences LLC, April 2024) 0.4.52, 0.12.25 https://www.youtube.com/watch?v=KKNCiRWd_j0

Thomson Reuters Westlaw, *Practice Note* (7 February 2022) Practical Law Intellectual Property & Technology, 'Artificial Intelligence Key Legal Issues: Overview'

Wackwitz, Gwen and Jenna Rennie, 'Cryptocurrencies: Property, Trust and Mistake', *White & Case* (Web Page, 10 April 2019) https://www.whitecase.com/publications/alert/cryptocurrencies-property-trust-and-mistake

White House, 'Initial Rescissions of Harmful Executive Orders and Actions' (Web Page, 20 January 2025) https://www.whitehouse.gov/presidential-actions/2025/01/initial-rescissions-of-harmful-executive-orders-and-actions/

White House, 'Removing Barriers to American Leadership in Artificial Intelligence' (Web Page, 23 January 2025) https://www.whitehouse.gov/presidential-actions/2025/01/removing-barriers-to-american-leadership-in-artificial-intelligence/

Wise, Steven, 'Why the First Department's Decision in Our Chimpanzee Rights Cases Is Wildly Wrong' (Blog Post, 22 June 2017) https://www.nonhumanrights.org/blog/first-department-wildly-wrong/
Yee, Vivian, 'Saudi Law Granted Women New Freedoms. Their Families Don't Always Agree', *The New York Times* (online, 14 March 2020) https://www.nytimes.com/2020/03/14/world/middleeast/saudi-women-rights.html

Index

FSC
www.fsc.org
MIX
Papier | Fördert gute Waldnutzung
FSC® C083411

Kolibri 360 GmbH
Ferdinand-Jühlke-Straße 7
99095 Erfurt, Deutschland
produktsicherheit@kolibri360.de